Wissenschaftliche Untersuchungen
zum Neuen Testament

Herausgeber / Editor
Jörg Frey (München)

Mitherausgeber / Associate Editors
Friedrich Avemarie (Marburg)
Judith Gundry-Volf (New Haven, CT)
Hans-Josef Klauck (Chicago, IL)

227

Identity Formation
in the New Testament

Edited by

Bengt Holmberg and Mikael Winninge

Mohr Siebeck

BENGT HOLMBERG is professor emeritus at Lund University, Sweden.

MIKAEL WINNINGE is associate professor at Umeå University, Sweden.

ISBN 978-3-16-149687-5
ISSN 0512-1604 (Wissenschaftliche Untersuchungen zum Neuen Testament)

Die Deutsche Nationalbibliothek lists this publication in the Deutsche National-
bibliographie; detailed bibliographic data is available in the Internet at *http://dnb.d-nb.de.*

The book was printed by Gulde-Druck in Tübingen on non-aging paper and bound by
Großbuchbinderei Spinner in Ottersweier.

Printed in Germany.

Preface

To a certain extent the present volume is a reflection of ideas expressed in lectures and seminar discussions during the Nordic New Testament Conference in August, 2007. However, as it now stands, it is a volume about different means of identity formation and identity negotiation in New Testament times as well as in the history of reception of the New Testament up to the present. In recent scholarship, New Testament ideology and its theoretical and practical use in church history is often analysed and deconstructed by applying gender perspectives and postcolonial theory.

The Nordic New Testament Conference 2007 took place at Sundsgårdens Folkhögskola (college of higher education), in the vicinity of Helsingborg in southern Sweden, August 18–22, 2007. The theme of the conference was *Strategies of Identification in the Hellenistic World: Ethnic, Social, and Ideological Perspectives*. A number of speakers were of course invited to give keynote lectures related to the overall topic. In addition, the conference hosted six seminar groups, where several papers were read and discussed. The themes were (1) *Personification in the New Testament Apocrypha*, (2) *Intertextual Means of Identity Formation*, (3) *Gender Identification*, (4) *The Role of Biblical Traditions in Identity Formation*, (5) *Various Strategies of Identification*, and (6) *Postcolonial Hermeneutics*. There was an open call for papers so that Nordic scholars interested in presenting their work were invited to submit proposals.

In the first seminar group, led by Jón Ma. Ásgeirsson (Iceland), the phenomenon of personification was studied and discussed. The making of a character is a category already in ancient rhetorical instruction. It has found a renewed interest in modern theories on the role of the reader(s) in contemporary literary studies. The focus of this seminar was on personification *in the New Testament Apocrypha*. One of the issues was how, and in what sense, *personae* are depicted, used or fabricated for instance in relation to characters in the New Testament or the wider cultural and literary environment of the early Christian era.

The second seminar group, led by Mikael Winninge (Sweden), focused on intertextuality. The concept of intertextuality is controversial, not least for methodological reasons. The word has been used with reference to different phenomena and various methods. Nevertheless, many scholars are convinced that certain texts influence the way in which other texts are composed and interpreted. Quotations are seldom a problem as such. However, the supposed amount of implicit influence is often a matter of dispute and the force of allusions can be difficult to evaluate. Not only is the Biblical material interesting here; various Greco-Roman texts have been adduced as relevant for the interpretation of New Testament texts. Phenomenological and methodological clarification of the concept of intertextuality is crucial, regardless of what texts are being discussed. And criteria are needed. One particular aspect that was considered is the way in which intertextuality functions within different frames of social identity. Special attention was paid to the use that some groups in the Hellenistic world could make of certain socially recognized texts as implements of identity formation. Moreover, rhetorical strategies in this process of social identity formation were investigated and discussed.

The third seminar group, led by Marianne Bjelland Kartzow (Norway), discussed identity formation in a gender perspective. For more than 25 years, scholars within the field of feminist studies have focused on women in the New Testament texts in order to question their role as silenced and marginalized. Reconstructions of early Christian history and readings by a hermeneutic of suspicion have been central tasks within this field. A growing awareness of the difficulties in using the category of 'woman' has made scholars ask whether the texts give any significant information about women as such, or if they primarily reflect male ideals and fantasies. The huge difference regarding legal rights, life condition and recourses between the upper class women and the slaves or prostitutes in the Hellenistic world make the use of the term 'woman' as a label for all female characters in Antiquity problematic. The tendency in New Testament scholarship to present history as a gender neutral concept has recently been challenged. The ancient world was gendered, and this influenced the rhetoric and ideology in the texts. In order not to show gender blindness, it is not enough to add a small section on 'women' at the end of a study. The field of male studies has focused for some years now on how New Testament texts operate within a culture where the question of whether a man performed the proper requirements of masculinity was crucial.

In the fourth seminar group, led by Jostein Ådna (Norway), the role of biblical traditions was the main issue. Among the forces forming the identity of early Christians, the Holy Scriptures of Israel were the most decisive. The early church shared with all strands in early Judaism the conviction that the true and only God had revealed himself to Israel, and that ever since the Holy Scriptures of this people contained the testimony of this revelation and the word of God. Hence, it is an interesting and rewarding enterprise to trace the influence of the Bible on the identity formation among various groups and communities within early Christianity. Both the transmission of individual biblical books and the development of biblical traditions in the Hellenistic period are complex phenomena. Papers that investigated certain details within the wide scope of this process as well as papers that addressed broader aspects, such as the influence of these texts and traditions on Christology, were discussed in the seminar.

The fifth seminar group, led by Sven-Olav Back (Finland), had planned to focus on liturgy as identity formation, because among other things liturgy functions as an expression and a celebration of the distinctive norms, values and ideals of the worshipping community. However, because of the diverse perspectives among those submitting paper proposals to the conference, the seminar group discussed various strategies of identification among early Christians and other contemporary groups.

The sixth seminar group, led by Lone Fatum (Denmark), focused on the hermeneutics of postcolonial theory. The term 'postcolonialism' was coined about 25 years ago. In general, it describes a paradigm of critical interpretation, analysing historical constructs of political domination by means of colonization and marginalization. It involves a number of different disciplines in order to deal with complex power relations, and to identify the relationship between the colonized, the collaborators and the colonizers is in itself an act of resistance. In Biblical studies in particular, postcolonial interpretation is defined and practiced as an oppositional reading strategy and, as such, it may be seen as a continuation of political and liberation theology and gender studies. It examines the role of the Gospel narratives and other New Testament texts in colonizing, decolonizing and new nation-building, and it works explicitly from the perspective of opposition to the centre and from the margins in order to identify the exclusive boundaries. The seminar discussed postcolonialism both as a theory, as a particular way of reading the New Testament in a modern-day borderland perspective, and as practice, exemplifying what it means to ask questions of the following kind: What characterizes the relations and administration of power in the symbolic world of Paul? How are centre and margins defined in the mission narratives of Acts? Whose world is constructed and who is excluded and by what means in the Pastoral letters? Who are the colonizers and how is 'the other' represented in the Gospel of John?

This book illustrates the paradoxical character of writing about early Christian identity on the basis of early Christian texts. On the one hand, the phenomenon of identity cannot be limited to the ideas and words that Christ-believers in these communities used to express their self-understanding, i.e. to ideas which can be more or less easily read off from the texts produced by that movement. Identity is a larger, more complex social reality with both cognitive, ritual, and moral dimensions, crystallized into social relations and institutions, and developing in both predictable and surprising directions over time. All this can be only partly expressed in texts.

On the other hand, texts are almost the only means available for grasping early Christian identity, just as for grasping most things which belong to that historical movement in its first century. Hardly any archaeological remains exist from the Christ-movement in the period during which the New Testament writings emerged. This is one reason why the essays in this volume naturally and inevitably are devoted to analysing New Testament texts in some attempts to show how they reveal the processes of identity formation. This is done in a variety of ways: through analysis of intertextuality and techniques of textual identity construction, through labelling and social cognition and through gender analysis coupled with the power-sensitive postcolonial reading of ancient Christian texts.

The first group of essays look closely at how New Testament texts compare with, or treat, older texts which stand in the same normative tradition, in other words with biblical and Jewish texts. This is the focus of Samuel Byrskog's analysis of the role of the first human beings (Adam/Eve) in Pauline Christology, possibly mediated through Jewish interpretation of the Eden narratives, as well as of Tobias Hägerland's exploration of possible points of contact between the excommunication rituals used in the Qumran community and those used in the Christian community in Corinth, and of Per Jarle Bekken's comparison of how Philo and John treat the question about the validity of self-testimony. Identity has dimensions both of continuity with a tradition, and of breaking new paths in relation to such a tradition.

The next group of essays deals with more explicitly literary techniques used in the service of constructing identity. Judith Lieu analyses how personification is achieved in Jewish and Christian texts, and what functions it can be given, while Lauri Thurén's close look at how antagonists are treated in New Testament writings leads to the conclusion that their existence is more of a rhetorical (or even theological) necessity than a historical reality. Thomas Kazen seeks to show how a collective or corporative understanding of the Son of Man figure helps us see the Christ-movement, and Raimo Hakola's analysis of the stereotyping of the Pharisees in Matthew is a variation of the same approach to understanding the relationship between a text and the history behind it, informed especially by social psychology. Finally, Rikard Roitto demonstrates the advantages of using theories of social cognition in order to determine the relationship between different kinds of social identity among the early Christ-believers.

In post-modern approaches, scholars often apply highly abstract and sophisticated theories and methods to biblical texts in order to elucidate realities that are anything but abstract, namely power relations. This is characteristic both of feminist or gender analysis, and of post-colonial exegesis. In the third group of essays, Halvor Moxnes begins by focusing on how the understanding of the male body is changed in some Christian texts, thus signalling a break with prevailing opinions that would affect Christian identity. Fredrik Ivarsson uses ancient protocols of masculine sexual behaviour, mainly dominance and self-restraint, to elucidate Paul's dominance techniques in 1 Corinthians, while Hanna Stenström brings perspectives of gender analysis to bear on the shaping of Jewish (in *Joseph and Aseneth*) and Christian (Rev) "virginal" identity, pointing both to similarities with and differences from the surrounding culture.

The last group of essays presents three ways of applying the insights of postcolonial theory. Hans Leander looks at Mark and the terminology of *parousia* as not only reflecting, but also forming, Christian identity in relation to imperial reality, while Christina Petterson compares how indigenous people are described as objects of Christian mission in Greenland and in Samaria and Asia Minor in a way that reflects "colonial" attitudes, as part of her discussion of how postcolonialism should and should not be applied in biblical exegesis. As is the case with several essays in this book, Anna Rebecca Solevåg's work on the martyrs Perpetua and Felicitas could be classified in more than one category. It uses both gender analysis and postcolonial insights to show how empire, family, and gender are reinterpreted in this narrative, in order to make suffering and persecution meaningful, thus continuing and elucidating some ways of thinking and acting that emerge already in the New Testament.

Hopefully, the application of so many different interpretative perspectives and approaches to the phenomenon of early Christian identity formation will help the reader to see how it emerges and appears in all its bewildering and intriguing complexity.

Table of Contents

Christology and Identity in an Intertextual Perspective: The Glory of Adam in the Narrative Substructure of Paul's Letter to the Romans

Samuel Byrskog

The Problem and the Task

Christology has to do with Christian identity. The books on New Testament Christology usually go through a number of labels and deeds attributed to Jesus. To the extent that we have given up the old distinction between "the person of Christ" and "the work of Christ," we find a broader spectrum of Christological thinking that relates, in theological terms, to soteriology and anthropology.[1] To understand Christ and what he has done is to understand ourselves. Some scholars use non-theological language to express a similar thinking about Christology, emphasizing the labeling processes and the importance of Jesus for the labeling group.[2] The early conviction that something crucial had happened in the person and work of Jesus Christ gave rise to a variety of interpretations of who Christ is and this meant that the early Christians nourished a sense of belonging to that decisive event – an identity.

In this new situation the concept of being the image of God lingers in the periphery of scholarly contributions. Yet this is a concept that unites an understanding of Christ with an understanding of human beings and what Christ is for them, and it epitomizes Christology as a part of identity formation. In New Testament scholarship it finds expression in the so-called Adam Christology. From early on in his career, James Dunn has stressed the occurrence of allusions and references to Adam in the Pauline letters. In Paul's letter to the Romans, which Dunn regards as the central guideline for Pauline theology, he finds such allusions in Rom 1:18–32; 3:23; 7:7–

---

[1] So Veli-Matti KÄRKKÄINEN, *Christology: A Global Introduction* (Grand Rapids: Baker, 2003), 11–12.

[2] For an early example of this trend, see Bruce J. MALINA and Jerome H. NEYREY, *Calling Jesus Names: The Social Value of Labels in Matthew* (F&F: Social Facets; Sonoma: Polebridge, 1988).

11; and 8:19–22.[3] The mention of Adam in Rom 5:12–21 is thus sur-
rounded by recurrent allusions to him elsewhere in the letter. Dunn's view
represents British scholarship, which goes back to Morna Hooker's influential article on Romans 1.[4] Others, however, deny the presence of such
motifs. Stanley Stowers argues strongly that Dunn's understanding of these
passages does not fit the pre-70 context of Paul.[5] The so-called Adam
Christology in Romans is a controversial point of debate and suggestive of
a plurality of scholarly approaches and opinions.

Scholars who agree to see several allusions to Adam in Romans are often content to say that while in 5:12–21 Adam is employed christologically, the other passages deal with the present situation of human beings.[6]
We rarely find attempts to co-ordinate the different allusions. *I wish to
bring the debate one step further by asking about the existence of a narrative substructure that holds together the allusions and the explicit reference to Adam in Romans and opens up avenues to a more dynamic thinking
about Christology and identity.* Paul discusses Adam in a prolific way also
in 1 Cor 15:21–49. His discussion in Romans depends partly on these reflections, which, in turn, might have been influenced by even broader
currencies. What is necessary in today's Christological debate, however, is
that we relate these grand theories of Pauline thinking to a clear conception
of the particular epistolary character of the sources. In Romans, if any-
where, Paul would be able to employ his earlier reflections in a mature and
consistent way.

Method: Modified Intertextuality

In order to investigate the narrative substructure of Romans, I will employ
a modified intertextual perspective. "Intertextuality" is one of those trendy
expressions that are being used in many different ways.[7] Sometimes it de-

---

[3] So in e.g. in James D. G. DUNN, *The Theology of Paul the Apostle* (Grand Rapids:
Eerdmans, 1998), 90–101.

[4] Morna D. HOOKER, "Adam in Romans 1," *NTS* 6 (1959–60), 297–306; "A Further
Note on Romans 1," *NTS* 13 (1966–67), 181–83. Cf. also A. J. M. WEDDERBURN, "Adam
in Paul's Letter to the Romans," in *Papers on Paul and Other New Testament Writers*
(ed. E. A. Livingstone; JSNTSup 3; Sheffield: Sheffield Academic Press, 1980), 413–30.

[5] Stanley STOWERS, *A Rereading of Romans: Justice, Jews, and Gentiles* (New Haven: Yale University Press, 1994), 86–89.

[6] So e.g. Christopher M. TUCKETT, *Christology and the New Testament: Jesus and
His Earliest Followers* (Edinburgh: Edinburgh University Press, 2001), 52.

[7] Ellen van WOLDE, "Trendy Intertextuality?," in *Intertextuality in Biblical Writings:
Essays in Honour of Bas van Iersel* (ed. Sipke Draisma; Kampen: Kok, 1989), 43–49.

scribes an author's way of borrowing and transforming a previous text; sometimes it indicates the dynamics of a reader's or hearer's referencing of one text in reading or hearing another. Richard Hays has been influential among New Testament scholars in introducing the term as a label for the study of Paul's use of Scripture. He has a seven-fold list of criteria for es-tablishing the presence of echoes and allusions: availability, volume, recur-rence or clustering, thematic coherence, historical plausibility, history of interpretation, and satisfaction.[8] It indicates an ambition to study Paul's use of Scripture historically and genetically, but not necessarily in terms of what Paul had intended the audience to understand. He also uses John Hol-lander's concept of rhetorical "transumption" or "metalepsis" (i.e. a tem-poral or diachronic figure of speech) in delineating the reading strategy of taking a literary text as an echo-chamber of earlier texts.[9]

Other scholars have warned against the naïve use of intertextuality as it is often used to refer to literary relations of conscious influence and inten-tional allusion to, citation of or quotation from previous texts in literary texts. The Canadian New Testament scholar Thomas Hatina argues for instance that it is inimical to historical criticism due to its poststructuralist ideological origin, its conception of text as infinite and inseparable from the reader, and its opposition to the notion of influence.[10] Graham Allen, an acknowledged expert on the theory of intertextuality, writes accord-ingly:

Intertextuality is one of the most commonly used and misused terms in contemporary critical vocabulary. [...] Intertextuality, one of the central ideas in contemporary literary theory, is not a transparent term and so, despite its confident utilization by many theorists and critics cannot be evoked in an uncomplicated manner.[11]

We will always run the risk of misusing theoretical concepts once they leave the hands of their originators and enter the open market of scholarly methodologies. My approach to intertextuality, while inherently historical, avoids some of the pitfalls mentioned above in that it is informed by theo-ries of social memory and orality.[12] In his monograph on Romans, Philip Esler criticizes Hays' intertextual approach for being too literary and too

---

[8] Richard B. HAYS, *Echoes of Scripture in the Letters of Paul* (New Haven: Yale Uni-versity Press, 1989), 29–33. See also Richard B. HAYS, *The Conversion of the Imagina-tion: Paul as Interpreter of Israel's Scripture* (Grand Rapids: Eerdmans, 2005), 34–45.

[9] Cf. John HOLLANDER, *The Figure of Echo: A Mode of Allusion in Milton and After* (Berkeley: University of California Press, 1981).

[10] Thomas HATINA, "Intertextuality and Historical Criticism: Is There a Relation-ship?," *BibInt* 7 (1999), 28–43.

[11] Graham ALLEN, *Intertextuality* (London: Routledge, 2000), 2.

[12] See e.g. Samuel BYRSKOG, "A New Quest for the *Sitz im Leben*: Social Memory, the Jesus Tradition and the Gospel of Matthew," *NTS* 52 (2006), 319–36.

focused on the reading of written texts.[13] What we need, according to Esler, "are ways of understanding the social (more than literary) processes
involved in Paul's reinterpretation of scripture [...] that make sense in a
context of oral and aural communication."[14] For Esler, the alternative approach includes collective memory, where prototypes from the past may be
used to negotiate social identity.[15] Although Esler might be correct to criticize Hays at this point, it should be noted that one of the basic insights of
Julia Kristeva and others was that the text is an intervention into a cultural
system of other texts that condition its meaning, the author of it being
more of its orchestrator than its originator. The text is dialogical and has
its origin, not in the intention of the author, but in the multiple discursive
contexts of the immediate culture of that text and that author.[16] *In theories
of the oral character of a text, the text is a web of meaning and meaning-
effects that depend on the cultural signs encoded in the text and that condition the experience of it during and after the performance. To the extent
that it contains traces of a cultural system of other written and oral texts, it
is a reservoir of collective memory and affects the hearers' negotiation of
how they remember the past socially and construe their social identity.*

From this perspective, the letter to the Romans can be seen as an epistolary echo-chamber of remembered inter-texts, resonating them, as it were,
and producing various meaning-effects to those who experience(d) its oral
performance. For the present purposes, I will explore possible conceptual
features in the sequential epistolary performance that may have aroused
echoes from stories about Adam.

Romans 1–3: The Loss of Glory

The Texts: Romans 1:23; 2:23; 3:23

In order fully to appreciate these sounds and echoes, it is necessary to outline the possible intertextual traces of Adam in Paul's depiction of the present human situation. According to Rom 1:23, men and women "exchanged the glory of the immortal God (ἤλλαξαν τὴν δόξαν τοῦ ἀφθάρτου

---

[13] For another important discussion of Hays' methodology, see Hans HÜBNER, "Intertextualität – die hermeneutische Strategie des Paulus," *TLZ* 116 (1991), 881–98.

[14] Philip F. ESLER, *Conflict and Identity in Romans: The Social Setting of Paul's Letter* (Minneapolis: Fortress, 2003), 177.

[15] Esler focuses on Abraham rather than Adam.

[16] See e.g. Julia KRISTEVA, *Desire in Language: A Semiotic Approach to Literature
and Art* (ed. Leon S. Roudiez; New York: Columbia University Press, 1980). I have used
ALLEN, *Intertextuality*, 30–47, as a brief introduction to Kristeva's thinking.

θεοῦ) for images resembling a mortal human being and birds and four-footed animals and reptiles." Stowers spends several pages of his book denying the presence of any allusions to Adam and the so-called fall story of Gen 1–3 in Rom 1:18–32 and argues for a generic similarity with Hellenistic decline of civilization narratives used for hortatory purposes.[17] He depends on John Levison's thesis that there existed no Adam speculation and no Adam myth before 70 CE,[18] concluding that Jewish literature before 70 CE shows little interest in the effects of Adams's transgression and that his fall cannot serve as an explanation for the human predicament.

Stowers misrepresents Levison. That Levison did not intend the conclusions that Stowers infers from his work becomes evident in a subsequent article where Levison sets out precisely to show that Rom 1:18–25 exhibits correspondences with the Greek *Life of Adam and Eve* to the extent that it is not "altogether implausible that Paul used some form of this narrative […] in the construction of his argument."[19] Levison's article can be developed further. What is particularly important in Rom 1:23 is the motif of exchanging God's glory. It theologizes the broad cultural pattern of honor and shame which Paul unfolds in chapters 2 and 3. Turning to the interlocutor in 2:17, Paul refers to the interlocutor's pride in the Law and his God and turns this pride against the interlocutor, accusing him in 2:23 of dishonoring God by transgressing the Law. Obedience to the Law is a matter of bringing glory to God. Furthermore, bringing the argument of the first three chapters to a close in 3:21–31, Paul forms an *inclusio* with 1:23 and explains the foundational statement that God's righteousness through Jesus' faithfulness is for all who believe, with the basic premise in 3:23 that all have sinned and fall short of God's glory.

The Inter-texts

a) LXX Psalm 105:20; Jeremiah 2:11; Deuteronomy 4:16–18

The motif of God's glory evokes a mosaic of echoes which mix voices that allude to Jews and to Adam. Stowers discusses the reference to LXX Ps 105:20 (MT 106:20) and, indirectly, LXX Jer 2:11. The texts say that the Israelites "exchanged their glory" (ἠλλάξαντο τὴν δόξαν αὐτῶν) (Ps 105:20) and that God's people "exchanged its glory" (ἠλλάξατο τὴν δόξαν αὐτοῦ) (Jer 2:11). Stowers denies that these texts echo in Romans, except for "some imagined brilliant reader," because the Israelites lost *their* glory,

---

[17] STOWERS, *A Rereading of Romans*, 86–100.

[18] John LEVISON, *Portraits of Adam in Early Judaism: From Sirach to 2 Baruch* (JSPSup 1; Sheffield: JSOT Press, 1988).

[19] John LEVISON, "Adam and Eve in Romans 1.18–25 and the Greek Life of Adam and Eve," *NTS* 50 (2004), 519–34 (523).

not God's, and they did not make idols of human beings and reptiles, as Rom 1:23 says.[20]

Both arguments fail to convince. The glory of the Israelites is their God. That is why the Psalmist goes on to say that they forgot God their Savior (LXX Ps 105:21); and that is why the prophet Jeremiah contrasts a nation which changes its false gods to God's people changing its glory (LXX Jer 2:11). When they exchange their glory, they exchange their God. Stowers's second argument fails to take the list in Deut 4:16–18 into account. The Deuteronomist tells how Moses commands obedience from the people by admonishing them not to make for themselves "a carved image, any idol, an image of male or female" (γλυπτὸν ὁμοίωμα, πᾶσαν εἰκόνα, ὁμοίωμα ἀρσενικοῦ ἢ θηλυκοῦ). The text goes on to prohibit images of any animal that is on the earth, of any winged bird that flies in the air, of any "reptile" (ἑρπετοῦ) that creeps on the ground, and of any fish that is in the water under the earth. The list includes mortal men as well as birds and four-footed animals and reptiles mentioned in Rom 1:23 and uses for them the terms "idol" (εἰκών) and "image" (ὁμοίωμα). Stowers is silent about this text. It did not take a very "brilliant reader" but only a hearer who knew the written Torah to hear an echo of it in the list enumerated by the per-former of Paul's text. And this hearer, to the extent that s/he also knew the Psalms and the Prophets, heard the passage in terms of how the Israelites lost their glory. The three inter-texts have sufficient terminological and conceptual similarities with Rom 1:23 to signal echoes that partly deter-mined how it was heard and experienced.

The reason why Stowers and others are reluctant to acknowledge these inter-texts is the ambition to regard the text in Romans as dealing with non-Jews only. Certainly Paul here uses traditional polemic against Gen-tiles, and he might indeed turn texts directed against the Israelites around and use them against Gentiles. Considering the letter as an echo-chamber of various inter-texts, it seems however appropriate to refrain from fixing the ethnic identity of men and women (ἄνθρωποι) referred to in 1:18 more than Paul does and to cope with a textual openness that allows the hearers to discern different paradigms for sinful mankind in the following verses.[21]

---

[20] STOWERS, *A Rereading of Romans*, 93. Stowers strangely admits that MT Ps 106:20 speaks of God's glory (p. 342 n. 39). NRSV also translates "they exchanged the glory of God." But the Hebrew reads "their glory" (*'et-kavodam*).

[21] Similarly Robert JEWETT, *Romans: A Commentary* (Hermeneia; Minneapolis: For-tress, 2007), 152: "[...] an encompassing description of what is wrong with the human race as a whole."

b) The Life of Adam and Eve 20:2; 21:6; 33:5; 35:2

The motif of exchanging, falling short of or being estranged from one's glory was also associated with Adam and traced back to the time before the people of Israel existed. The Greek *Life of Adam and Eve*, sometimes entitled the *Apocalypse of Moses*, articulates this view most clearly. On his death-bed Adam asks Eve to tell all the children how they transgressed. She does so at some length. According to some mss, Eve was the first one to be deprived of her glory. After eating the fruit which the devil had sprinkled with the evil poison of covetousness, she realized that she was naked, having lost the righteousness, and she cried out to the devil weeping: "Why have you done this, that I have been estranged from my glory" (ὅτι ἀπηλλοτριώθην ἐκ τῆς δόξης μου)? (20:2).[22] She tried to find leaves to cover her shame (αἰσχύνην) and began looking for Adam. After finding him, she spoke to him with the voice of the devil and persuaded him to eat of the fruit. He realized his nakedness and said to Eve: "O evil woman! Why have you wrought destruction among us? You have estranged me from the glory of God" (ἀπηλλοτρίωσάς με ἐκ τῆς δόξης τοῦ θεοῦ) (21:6).

We find here a similar ambiguity as in the LXX concerning whose glory is at stake. Eve speaks of her glory with which she was clothed; Adam speaks of God's glory. The reference to Eve's glory might be a secondary addition to the story. What is significant is that Adam sees his own nakedness in relation to his estrangement from God's glory. This does not mean that Adam is no more the image of God. As the story continues, Adam dies and Eve witnesses the return of God with his angels. The angels, worshipping God, pray for forgiveness for Adam on account of him being God's image: "Holy Jael, forgive, for he is your image (εἰκών σου) and the work of your holy hands" (33:5); "Forgive him, O Father of all, for he is your image" (εἰκών σου) (35:2). As God's image, Adam becomes estranged from God's glory and as God's image he suffers the consequences of his transgression.

It is difficult to date the *Life of Adam and Eve* with precision and the Latin version, which is probably a translation from the Greek, does not contain the sections referred to above. Due to the presence of Hebraisms in the Greek text, most scholars hold the archetypal Greek manuscript to be a translation from the Hebrew. We find no clear evidence of a post-70 situation. An interpolation into the Latin *Vita* 29:8 even refers to Herod's temple without mentioning its destruction. Johannes Tromp's recent text-critical investigation assumes that the first Greek version was composed

---

[22] The text is missing in several mss.

somewhere in the period between 100–300 CE.[23] If that is correct, it is not implausible that the Hebrew document(s) came into being already in the first century CE. M. D. Johnson argued in the introduction to his translation in *Old Testament Pseudepigrapha* that the span for the original composition is between 100 BCE and 200 CE and, building on the investigation of J. L. Sharpe, that it was composed in Pharisaic circles in Palestine.[24] It's non-allegorical and midrashic character might point in this direction.

c) Philo, De virtutibus 203–205; the Book of Wisdom 2:23–24; the Book of Jubilees 3:17–31

It is thus not unlikely that some ancient hearer/reader in the first century CE experienced Paul's statement in Rom 1:23 as an echo of what happened to Adam and that this hearer/reader captured some of the culturally imbedded signals in the text. The *Life of Adam and Eve* articulates in fact what is hinted at in earlier texts.

Philo, speaking in *De virtutibus* of the nobleness of "the first man who was created out of the earth" (203), suggests that Adam's deliberate decision to choose what was false and disgraceful and evil and to despise what was good and honorable and true meant that he defiled himself as God's image and was deprived of blessedness and happiness (205). The Book of Wisdom, which most scholars agree echoes in Rom 1:18–32, says that God made humankind (τὸν ἄνθρωπον) "an image of his own eternity" (εἰκόνα τῆς ἰδίας ἀιδιότητος) but through the devil's envy death entered into the world and those who are of his party experience it (2:23–24). Elsewhere in Wisdom Adam figures as the first-formed father of the world's transgression (10:1). The Book of Wisdom was probably written by an oppressed Egyptian Jew during the first or second century BCE. The unrighteous ones are the Gentiles and their evil is traced back to the time of Adam and connected with him being God's image. The *Book of Jubilees*, from the second century BCE, elaborates in 3:17–31 the story of Adam's disobedience and expulsion in a way that includes the Israelites. While all the beasts are expelled with Adam, to Adam alone it is granted to cover his shame, so that those who know the Law will cover their shame and not be like the Gentiles (3:30–31). Here Adam's failure and shame are related to

---

[23] Johannes TROMP, *The Life of Adam and Eve in Greek* (PVTG 6; Leiden: Brill, 2005), 28.

[24] M. D. JOHNSON, *OTP* II, 252. Sharpe's dissertation, *Prolegomena to the Establishment of the Critical Text of the Greek Apocalypse of Moses* (Duke University, 1969), was never published. For a recent review of it, see Tromp's summary in *The Life of Adam and Eve in Greek*, 5–8. Tromp also gives an updated discussion of research on the Greek text.

the Law of Israel. The idea is that Adam's covering of his shame finds its recurrent manifestation through the observance of the Law.

The Echoes in Romans 1:23; 2:23; 3:23

At closer scrutiny, the argument that Adam's fall cannot serve as explanation for the predicament of Jews and Gentiles according to the first chapter of Romans because it does not fit the pre-70 situation, fails to convince. The year 70 is no decisive turning-point for the speculations about Adam. My argument is not that Adam is alluded to in the entire section of Rom 1:18–32. Rather, I have focused on the motif of exchanging God's glory. Rom 1:23 seems to echo inter-texts that indicate an emerging trajectory which gradually explicates how Adam exchanged God's glory and comes to full expression in the first or second century CE writing entitled the *Life of Adam and Eve*. The rabbinic literature develops it further.[25] Since Adam was God's image, and remained so, his shame mentioned in some of these texts suggests in effect that he was estranged from God's glory.

The author of *Jubilees*, while not speaking explicitly of God's glory, articulates the idea that the Israelites were included in the shame of Adam and may cover it by observing the Law. In this way they avoid being like the Gentiles. By implication, transgression of the Law reveals the shame of Adam. It is therefore logical that Paul uses the language of shame and glory when he turns to his interlocutor and in the climactic statement of Rom 2:23 accuses the one who transgresses the Law for dishonoring God. Adam's shame becomes visible through the transgression; God's glory is exchanged and defiled. Paul turns the argument of the *Jubilees* around and likewise employs Isaiah's report about Israel's oppression by the Gentiles as a scriptural proof for the Jewish failure to honor God (Isa 52:5). The *Jubilees* defends the Israelites, like Isaiah, and distinguishes them from the sinful Gentiles. Similarly, without true observance of the Law, Paul's interlocutor shares in the Gentile predicament going back to Adam's shame and is included among those who exchange the glory of the immortal God for images of human beings and animals.

It is possible to maintain the hypothesis that beneath the surface of Paul's depiction of the human predicament lies a narrative substructure of Adam's failure to live up to being God's image and the resulting shame of defiling God's glory. In 3:23 Paul brings these intertextual echoes to a cli-

---

[25] See e.g. Jacob JERVELL, *Imago Dei: Gen 1,26f. im Spätjudentum, in der Gnosis und in den paulinischen Briefen* (FRLANT 58; Göttingen: Vandenhoeck & Ruprecht, 1960), 112–114. Jervell fails however, like most of his contemporaries, to distinguish the later rabbinic development from earlier tendencies and neglects the importance of the *Life of Adam and Eve*.

max with an emphatic "all," and indicates a way forward. The change from
the aorist "sinned" (ἥμαρτον) to the present tense "fall short" (ὑστεροῦν–
ται) shows that he looks at the current disgraceful situation from the perspective of a comprehensive sinful past of all men and women and, by implication, thinks of God's righteousness through Jesus Christ as the restoration of God's glory. This is in line with the expectation expressed in the
Life of Adam and Eve 39:2. Adam, as we saw, never lost his status as
God's image. At his burial, God promises that he will establish him in dominion on the throne of his seducer. In the rabbinic literature it is Adam's
glory that will be restored (*Gen R.* 12:6; *Num R.* 11:3). Already the Qumranites expressed their anticipation of glory as "all the glory of *adam/*
Adam" (1QS IV, 23; CD III, 20; 1QH XVII, 15). At 3:23 Paul hence forms
an *inclusio* with 1:23 and explains the important statement that God's
righteousness through Jesus' faithfulness is for all who believe with the
premise that all have sinned and fall short of God's glory, indicating that
his central Christology echoes a narrative substructure that not only tells of
Adam's failure but also looks forward to the restoration of God's glory.

Romans 5–8: The Way to Glory

Romans 5:2, 12–21

From this perspective it comes as no surprise that a few verses before ex-
pounding the relationship between Adam and Christ in 5:12–21, Paul ex-
horts the hearers/readers to boast in their hope of sharing God's glory
(5:2).[26] And this boasting, he explains a few verses later, means essentially
that they boast in God through their Lord Jesus Christ through whom they
now have received reconciliation (5:11). Paul has arrived at a point in his
argumentation where he begins to christologize the intertextual concept of
Adam's glory and indicates a hope for a glorious future.

It is significant that he continues these references in the first half of
chapter 5 with a long section where Adam explicitly comes to the surface
and is related to Christ. The emphatic "therefore" (διὰ τοῦτο) in 5:12 indicates a connection back to the previous section and shows that he wants to
explain the reason for the previous exhortations. Boasting in God through
the Lord Jesus Christ and in the hope of sharing God's glory is based on
what is expounded about Adam and Christ. The intertextual echoes in the
references to God's glory in 1:23; 2:23; 3:23 are thus explicitly confirmed

---

[26] For text-critical issues, see Samuel BYRSKOG, *Romarbrevet 1–8* (Kommentar till
Nya testamentet 6a; Stockholm: EFS-förlaget, 2006), 123.

to the hearers/readers, and christologically focused. The initial "therefore" signals a link which can be best explained if we assume that the hearers/readers had already heard the echoes of Adam's lost glory.

The point of 5:12–21 is that Christ did what Adam failed to do and that their actions had consequences for all men and women.[27] The long digression in 5:13–17 serves to assure the hearers/readers of the fact that there were differences between the two figures, but Paul's aim is still to compare them. Whereas Adam was disobedient, Christ was obedient; whereas Adam's disobedient trespass led to condemnation and sin, Christ's obedient act of righteousness leads to justification and life. The future life, which Paul mentions three times as the result of Christ's obedience (5:17, 18, 21), is equivalent to the future glory (cf. 6:4; 8:18, 21). As it seems, Paul articulates, through a mosaic of intertextual echoes, an Adam Christology which presupposes the failure of the first Adam and transfers the hope of restoration to Christ as the new, faithful Adam. Therefore, that is, because Christ did what Adam did not do when he exchanged God's glory, the believers are to boast in God through the Lord Jesus Christ and in the hope of sharing God's glory.

Romans 7:7–13

Paul's discussion of the Law in 7:7–13 reads like a commentary on the statement in 5:13–14 that sin was in the world before the Law, and that death exercised dominion from Adam to Moses. The much discussed question of possible allusions to Adam in Romans 7 rarely takes into account the fact that the hearers/readers encountered this chapter of Romans after experiencing the performance of chapter 5.[28] When Paul in 7:13 concludes that it was sin working death in "me" and that sin becomes sinful beyond measure through the commandment, he explicates what it meant that sin was in the world already before the Law and how it came about that death exercised dominion already at the time of Adam. To be sure, the shadows of the mythical Medea lurk in the background as Paul later on in the chapter explains the *akrasia* of the "I."[29] But to the extent that the one man

---

[27] See further BYRSKOG, *Romarbrevet 1–8*, 135–46.

[28] The most recent monograph on the topic is the one by Hermann LICHTENBERGER, *Das Ich Adams und das Ich der Menschheit: Studien zum Menschenbild in Römer 7* (WUNT 164; Tübingen: Mohr Siebeck, 2004). Lichtenberger gives a good survey of the previous discussion.

[29] See Samuel BYRSKOG, "Anthropologie als Heilsgeschichte. Römerbrief 7,14–20," in *Verantwortete Exegese: Hermeneutische Zugänge – Exegetische Studien – Systematische Reflexionen – Ökumenische Perspektiven – Praktische Konkretionen.* FS Franz Georg Untergassmair (ed. Gerhard Hotze and Egon Spiegel; Vechtaer Beiträge zur Theologie 13; Berlin: LIT-Verlag, 2006), 245–52.

through whom sin came into the world is Adam according to chapter 5, the "I" who experienced death according to chapter 7 also resembles Adam.

In order to bring home his argument about the Law before Sinai, Paul focuses on the commandment "you shall not covet." This is the commandment which came and revived sin and killed "me." The transgression of Adam, of which Paul speaks in 5:12–21, and which leads to death even over those whose sins were not like the transgression of Adam (5:15), is defined in chapter 7 as covetousness, ἐπιθυμία (7:7). Again Paul produces an intertextual echo of Adam that makes covetousness into a core element of sin and surfaces in the *Life of Adam and Eve.* In 19:3, a few lines before Adam is estranged from God's glory, Eve tells how the serpent sprinkled his evil poison on the fruit that she was to eat and explains that this poison is covetousness. "For covetousness," she continues, "is the κεφαλή of every sin." Other texts outside the Pauline corpus say similar things,[30] but this text is particularly significant in that it couples covetousness to the sinful act of Adam and Eve and expounds its consequences in terms of losing God's glory. The fact that Paul makes covetousness the central sinful act in spite of the fact that the verb ἐπιθυμεῖν does not appear in the Genesis story is not an argument against the presence of allusions to Adam – these allusions are probable on other grounds. On the contrary, it points decisively to echoes from textual worlds similar to the ones expressed in the *Life of Adam and Eve.* Read intertextually, Rom 7:7–13 resonates how it was that Adam lost God's glory and died.

Romans 8:18–30

When Paul brings the entire first half of Romans to a climax in chapter 8, he indicates links back to the discussion of the human predicament in 1:18–32 and counters it in 8:29–30 by connecting the idea of Christ as the image of God with the final glorification of the believers. The entire section of 8:18–30 deals with the future glory of the believers. It is therefore logical that the row of descriptions of what it means to be conformed to the Son's image, ἡ εἰκὼν τοῦ υἱοῦ αὐτοῦ,[31] according to God's purpose ends with the climactic reference to their glorification.

There is a similar apocalyptic perspective in 1:18–32 as in 8:18–30. The language of revelation heads both sections and indicates a comparable perspective of divine disclosure. Moreover, creation also plays an important

---

[30] E.g. Jas 1:15; *4 Macc.* 2:4; *Spec.* 4.84. *Apocalypse of Abraham* 23:8–14, perhaps originally a Hebrew document from ca 100 CE, also brings this idea back to Adam and Eve and tells how Azazel is permitted to have dominion over those who, like Adam and Eve, desire evil.

[31] I understand this expression to be epexegetic, "the image, which is his Son."

role in these passages. Just as creation may point towards the revealing of God's children in 8:19–22, so it points towards God's eternal power and divine nature in 1:20. And just as men and women were in bondage to corruption and decay and exchanged God's glory according to 1:23, the creation will be set free from decay and obtain the freedom of the glory of God's children according to 8:21. Paul turns the dark picture of 1:18–32 around and forms an *inclusio* to the entire first half of Romans by pointing to the glorious future of those who love God and are called according to his purpose.

At this point in the sequential argument of the letter, Paul uses his previous discussion and formulates a Christology that makes Christ into the image of God. Three interrelated observations add up to the conclusion that he employs an Adam Christology. First, from 1:23; 2:23; and 3:23 we may assume that the glorification of the believers was heard/read as the retaining of God's glory which mankind had exchanged and lost. The believers' glory is intrinsically bound up with God's glory. Secondly, the language of Christ as God's image carries connotations to Adam. In addition to the obvious uses of the concept of image for Adam in the Old Testament and Jewish texts, some of which have been noticed above, 1 Cor 15:45–49 contrasts the first and the second Adam and says that the believers have borne the image of the man of dust and will also bear the image of the man of heaven. Paul's interest is here in describing the resurrection body. In fact, in Rom 8:23 we find a similar use of "bodies" just before the reference to the image of God's son. However, the Greek term εἰκών was no natural equivalent to σῶμα and indicates therefore that it was Paul's mention of Adam that evoked ideas of being created as God's image. The somewhat redundant statement in Rom 8:29b that the Son, as God's image, will be the firstborn among many brothers also leads to ideas connected with Adam. In 5:18–21 Paul made the point that both Adam and Christ should be seen in relation to many that follow; and in 1 Cor 15:20, a few verses before, referring to Christ as the last Adam, he speaks of Christ's resurrection as the first fruits of those who have fallen asleep. Thirdly, we should notice that the notions of God's image and of glory are closely related for Paul, in spite of the fact that they are not associated in the creation accounts. According to 1 Cor 11:7 the man is the image and glory of God. Paul alludes to the creation accounts and adds the concept of glory to point out that man exists to God's honor. In 2 Cor 3:18; 4:4 the transformation of the believers from one degree of glory to another is first said to be into the same image as the Lord, whose glory they see as in a mirror, and then connected to the gospel of the glory of Christ, who is the image of God. The second verse makes it probable that the use of "image" in the former verse carries Christological connotations. The language of Christophany in 2 Cor 3:18; 4:4 indicates that Paul's idea of Christ as the image and glory of God has its roots in a fundamental visionary experience. Since the two concepts are not associated in the creation accounts, but, as we have seen, in the *Life of Adam and Eve*, it is likely that his experience was colored by intertextual echoes of Adam being the one who is and remains God's image and his expectation that the glory of Adam will be restored. In Rom 8:29–30 Paul would therefore use this fundamental Christology which was at the heart of his own experience of the Risen Lord and make the narrative substructure of Adam culminate in the conviction that the glorification of the believers means in effect that they will be conformed to the image of God's son.

Conclusions

The Narrative Substructure about Adam

The reading of Romans presented above has argued that we cannot do away with Adam as a substantial part of Paul's Christological argumentation. *In Romans we find an implicit narrative substructure that centers on Adam, the image of God, who with all mankind has lost God's glory and as the new Adam, Christ, will retain it and bring glory to all men and women. Paul does not present this Adam Christology paradigmatically but unfolds it progressively through allusions and with rhetorical finesse, until he explicitly combines the concepts of image and glory towards the end of chapter 8 and climactically concludes the entire first half of Romans with a reference to the future glorification of the believers.* As Levison has pointed out,[32] the *Life of Adam and Eve* should be upgraded as an important inter-text presenting a story which includes several of the elements of God's lost glory that echo in Romans. The hearer/reader acquainted with that story, or with a version of it, could hardly miss this significant narrative substructure of Paul's epistolary communication.

Some scholars, in addition to Dunn, would argue that Adam was a crucial if not *the* crucial center of Pauline Christology. N. T. Wright understands the Adam Christology to be an Israel Christology and makes this view fundamental for his understanding of Jesus as Messiah and Lord and of the people of God.[33] Against Wright we can observe that the Adam speculations were not so uniform as to provide a basis for his equation of

---

[32] LEVISON, "Adam and Eve," 519–34.

[33] N. T. WRIGHT, *The Climax of the Covenant: Christ and the Law in Pauline Theology* (Edinburgh: T & T Clark, 1991), 18–40 *et passim*.

Adam and Israel and that several of the passages in Paul's letters which Wright mentions hardly refer to Israel alone. Seyoon Kim, while critical of both Dunn and Wright, thinks that the Adam Christology was an important development of Paul's fundamental vision of Jesus Christ as the image of God on the Damascus road.[34] The strength of his hypothesis is the presence of terms and concepts related to the term "image" in visionary experiences recounted in other texts. Unfortunately, however, he relies uncritically on later rabbinic ideas concerning Adam in order to make his case. Although they arrive at different and debatable conclusions, Dunn, Wright and Kim agree that Adam was a core element in Paul's understanding of Christ, to the extent that we can speak of a center of Pauline Christology.

The present study, while not taking a stand on the different views of the development of Pauline Christology generally, adds to the observations of these scholars a focus on Adam's role in the sequential epistolary performance of Romans. Allusions and references to Adam were heard/read intertextually as part of a narrative substructure echoing his destiny.

Christology as Inclusive Story

This study leads to reflections concerning Christology and identity both from the perspective of the narrativization of history in the substructure of Romans and from a more pronounced theological perspective. Dunn, Wright, and Kim – to mention only these three – construct their conceptions by tracing tradition-historical connections and by combining a variety of Pauline passages into Christological schemes. Christology is propositional, it seems, and seen in terms of certain fundamental ideas and beliefs concerning Jesus Christ.

The focus on the sequential epistolary performance brought to attention in this study brings with it a different, narrative perspective on the role of Christology in identity formation. As one of the few New Testament scholars who has reflected hermeneutically on the Biblical concept of *Imago Dei*, Samuel Vollenweider, while skeptical as to its anthropological dimensions, points to its realization in the singular history of Jesus:

Allein schon diese Beobachtung rät davon ab, die Gottebenbildlichkeit als diese oder jene ontologische Gegebenheit zu identifizieren. Sie scheint sich vielmehr in einer *zeitlichen* Gestalt zu inkarnieren. In ihrer Gottebenbildlichkeit haben die Glaubenden teil an einer

---

[34] Seyoon KIM, *Paul and the New Perspective: Second Thoughts on the Origin of Paul's Gospel* (Grand Rapids: Eerdmans, 2002), 165–213.

bestimmten Geschichte, konkret an den Ereignissen von Kreuz und Auferstehung Christi.[35]

Vollenweider's observation, which assumes that history should be conceptualized in terms of events located temporally in the past, can be carried over to the way history is employed narratively in the Pauline Adam Christology. *Looking at the Adam Christology from the perspective of intertextuality and social memory rather than tradition history, it emerges as an unfolding story which interacts with other similar stories and mnemonically negotiates meaning and identity to the hearers/readers.* History is narrativized. Prototypes, whether we think of Abraham or Adam or other forms of ancestor worship, are part of narrative structures that make sense of history, not as an event merely located temporally in the past, but as the remembered, and thus narrativized past, which interacts with the search for identity in the present.

This is in line with how memory functions socially. The social memory usually learns to remember and narrate the past according to conventional plot structures and mnemonic patterns. It narrativizes history and gives social meaning by positioning past events in relation to each other. The socialization into a mnemonic community provides patterns that help each individual to mentally string such events together into coherent, culturally meaningful narratives. Identities are projects and practices, not properties, and emerge from the ways we are positioned by and position ourselves in the narratives of the past.[36]

To the extent that Adam functions as a prototype of both the fallen mankind and the resurrected Christ, Christology becomes much more dynamic and much less propositional in that it deals with the grand narrative of God's dealings with his creation and invites believers into the history and story of Christ. The approach to Christology proposed here is essentially one that seeks coherent narrative substructures and that may liberate us to recover Christology as the inclusive telling of a magnificent drama.

Adam Christology and the Plurality of Christologies

The presence of this kind of Adam Christology also challenges us to take seriously the presence of a plurality of Christologies in today's theological

---

[35] Samuel VOLLENWEIDER, "Der Menschgewordene als Ebenbild Gottes. Zum frühchristlichen Verständnis der *Imago Dei*," in Vollenweider, *Horizonte neutestamentlicher Christologie: Studien zu Paulus und zur frühchristlichen Theologie* (WUNT 144, Tübingen: Mohr Siebeck, 2002), 53–70 (65–66).

[36] See further BYRSKOG, "A New Quest for the *Sitz im Leben*," 325–26. Cf. also "A Century with the *Sitz im Leben*: From Form-Critical Setting to Gospel Community and Beyond," *ZNW* 98 (2007), 1–27 (26–27).

landscape. To the extent that we wish to relate New Testament Christology to the post-modern and post-secular situation of the 21st century, it is noteworthy that Adam rarely comes into focus in the present debate. The hermeneutical potentials of the fact that Paul used Adam in the narrative substructure of Romans 1–8 as a means to argue for the final glorification of all Jews and Gentiles who believe, are regularly neglected in the different attempts to formulate Christological reactions to the global pain of mankind as well as in the dialogues between various ethnic and religious groups.

The reason is perhaps the strong focus on Christ that emerges from conceptualizing him as the new Adam. It might be worthwhile to remind ourselves of the exceptional importance that Wolfhart Pannenberg attached to the Adam imagery in Paul's Christology. Being very aware of the challenge of secularism and the inter-religious dialogue of last century, he has in the second volume of his systematic theology, published for the first time in 1991, two long chapters on "Würde und Elend des Menschen" and "Antropologie und Christologie," respectively, and he places Paul's Adam Christology at the center of the discussion.[37] In Pannenberg's anthropology it is important to demonstrate that belief in God is not foreign to the human being. S/he is destined for fellowship with God, because s/he is created to be his image. Here he also finds the link from anthropology to Christology. Christology moves from below, Pannenberg insists. With the help of the concept of Jesus as the new Adam, he develops his understanding of Jesus' humanity as the fulfillment of human destiny. Jesus is the eschatological new human and the prototype of the new humanity, bringing to fulfillment the destiny of humanity as God's image. And this is a corporate reality, not only individual, according to Pannenberg. Human destiny, which is to enter into fellowship with God, can only be fulfilled in the community of God's images.

Pannenberg perceptively realizes that the Adam Christology presents a conceptual bridge between anthropology and Christology and a foundation for negotiating the salvific identity of God's community. He is provocatively emphatic on the public character of truth and the encompassing validity of Christ as the new Adam of all humanity. In a global situation, where truth is far from uniform and contextual, and where Christologies are linked with culture specific movements, we might wish to modify his theological proposals. The present debate about the force of Paul's Adam Christology must seek to hear the basic contours of the story once again, that is, listen to the universal story of honor and shame that unites all

---

[37] Wolfhart PANNENBERG, *Systematische Theologie* (3 vols.; Göttingen: Vandenhoeck & Ruprecht, 1988–1993), 2:203–364.

God's images and invites them into the restoration of true honor and glory. *The challenge of manifesting a Christology which unfolds and brings about the unity and restoration of mankind should not be limited to Western intellectuals alone, but brings us to regions beyond our philosophical and theological heritage and into the landscapes of the contextual and intercultural Christologies of those whose voices we have just begun to hear.* Instead of locking Christ into propositional categories of our own legacy of abstract thinking, and instead of giving up Christology entirely, we might turn back to the stories that unfold Christology as a dynamic divine drama. *The narrative substructure about Adam in Paul's letter to the Romans can be heard and remembered as a textualized drama that, in the midst of various kinds of performances, invites peoples of all nations into God's glorious future and tells of his manifold and mysterious provision to bring all into fellowship with him.*

The Controversy on Self-Testimony according to John 5:31–40; 8:12–20 and Philo, *Legum Allegoriae* III.205–208

Per Jarle Bekken

The Aim and Course of this Study

Philo of Alexandria is a representative of Diaspora Judaism and of Judaism in the late Second Temple period. His writings have also been used to illuminate the background and the wider context of the New Testament and the Early Church. Thus, many studies have investigated the way in which Philonic material might illuminate various aspects of the Gospel of John.[1] It is the aim of this essay to shed new light on the controversy on the self-testimony reflected in John 5:31–40 and 8:12–20 against the background of the Jewish forensic data that can be found in the discourse selected from Philo's treatise *Legum allegoriae* III.205–208.[2] I will argue that Philo of Alexandria provides a Jewish referential background for the controversy on self-testimony reflected in John 5:31–40 and 8:12–20.[3] Thus, the data

---

Some years ago I was invited to contribute to the Festschrift in honor of Professor Peder Borgen's 75th birthday, but due to personal circumstances I was not able to do so. Therefore, it is a privilege to dedicate the present study to Peder Borgen in honor of his 80th birthday.

[1] See Peder BORGEN, *Early Christianity and Hellenistic Judaism* (Edinburgh: T & T Clark, 1996), 105, for references.

[2] In this essay the Gospel of John = John. The author may also be referred to as 'the Evangelist'. The Biblical texts are quoted according to *The Holy Bible. Revised Standard Version* (2.ed. Grand Rapids, Mich.: Zondervan Bible Publishers, 1971). The Philonic texts are rendered according to *Philo. Works.* (LCL. Cambridge, Mass.: Harvard University Press; London: William Heinemann, 1926–1962).

[3] By "referential background" I mean the general setup of institutions, conventions, philosophies, ideas, etc., which, without necessarily being explicitly referred to in a text, nonetheless form a background of that to which the text refers, and this in such a way that one should know about this background in order to catch the full implication of the text. We can imagine cases in which such features and implications of a text are fully shared by the author and the reader, in such a way that the sender's and receiver's horizons coincide. Here I will assume the view that a receiver has a correct understanding of a text, when the sender and receiver fully share features of the background to which the

in *Leg*. 3.205–208, neglected among the interpreters of John, delivers documentation about the view that the controversy on self-testimony in John 5:31–40 and 8:12–20 is a specifically "Christian" version of a discussion, which has most probably also existed among Jews in Alexandria. This study will prove that aspects of the debate reported by John on this forensic topic can be located within a Jewish context exemplified by Philo. Specifically, the view represented by Philo, that only God was capable of giving a self-authenticating testimony, supplies a Jewish context for the point made by the Evangelist that Jesus could testify to himself because of his divine origin. By unfolding and supporting such a hypothesis by means of a comparison between Philo and John, I hope to suggest fresh answers to some of the questions raised among scholars concerning the Johannine texts.

The course of this study will be: First, an outline of the relevant texts in Philo and John. Then, the current state of research will be sketched. Finally, I will argue my hypothesis by the way of a comparison between Philo and John.

An Outline of Leg. 3.205–208 Within its Literary Context

Leg. 3.205–208 is located within the literary context of one of the two main groups of expository writings in the Philonic corpus, viz. the exegetical commentaries on Genesis.[4] This series covers the main part of Genesis 2–41. In general, they take the form of a verse–by–verse running commentary on the biblical texts. In *Legum Allegoriae* III, Philo comments on Genesis 3:8b–19. He uses the verses from Genesis as headings and starting points for expositions of other parts of the Pentateuch. Thus, the structure of the immediate literary context of *Leg*. 3.205–208, viz. *Leg*. 3.200–219, can be displayed in the following way:

---

message of the text refers. Cf. Per Jarle BEKKEN, *The Word is near You: A Study of Deuteronomy 30:12–14 in Paul's Letter to the Romans in a Jewish Context* (BZNW 144; Berlin/New York: Walter de Gruyter, 2007), 155–157.

[4] The exegetical commentaries on Genesis fall into two subordinate series: a) *Questions and Answers on Genesis and on Exodus*. b) *The Allegorical Commentary on Genesis* consists of *Allegorical Laws 1–3*; *On the Cherubim*; *On the Sacrifices of Abel and Cain*; *The Worse Attacks the Better*; *On the Posterity and Exile of Cain*; *On the Giants*; *On the Unchangeableness of God*; *On Husbandry*; *On Noah's Work as Planter*; *On Drunkenness*; *On Sobriety*; *On the Confusion of Tongues*; *On the Migration of Abraham*; *Who is the Heir of Divine Things?*; *On Mating with the Preliminary Studies*; *On Flight and Finding*; *On the Change of Names*; *On God*; *On Dreams*. The other main group of expository writings is *The Exposition of the Laws of Moses*, in which Philo to a great extent paraphrases and expands the biblical texts.

Leg. 3.200: Quotation of the main biblical text, Gen 3:16: "And to the woman He said, 'I will greatly multiply thy sorrows and thy groaning'".

Leg. 3.200–202: Direct paraphrasing exegesis of the word "sorrow" (λύπη) from Gen 3:16 as the lot of sense-perception in contrast to gladness, exemplified by the way in which both the slave and the athlete take a beating.

Leg. 3.203–210: Whereas God has appointed pains on the woman-sense, he has bestowed on the noble soul an abundance of 'blessings'. This topic is exemplified by a quotation of Gen 22:16 followed by an exegetical paraphrase of the words "By myself I have sworn" (203–208) and "for whose sake thou has done this thing" (209–210). References to other biblical texts, such as Num 12:7 (204) and Deut 6:13 (208) are given.

Leg. 3.211–219: Philo returns to the main text of Gen 3:16: Direct paraphrasing exegesis of the word "groaning" (στεναγμός). There are references to other biblical texts, such as Exod 2:23 (212; 214), Exod 20:24 (215), and Gen 17:15–16 (217–218), Gen 18:11 (218), and Gen 21:6 (219).

With regard to the content of *Leg*. 3.205–208, it consists of Philo's paraphrasing exegesis of the words "By myself I have sworn" from Gen 22:16. In § 204 Philo refers to some interlocutors, who object to the case of an oath taken by God: "Some have said, that it was inappropriate for him to swear". Then follows an immediate definition of an oath supplied by Philo:

For an oath is added to assist faith, and only God and one who is God's friend is faithful, even as Moses is said to have been found "faithful in all his house" (Num 12:7). Moreover, the very words of God are oaths and laws of God and most sacred ordinances; and a proof of His sure strength is that whatever He saith cometh to pass, and this is especially characteristic of an oath. It would seem to be a corollary from this that all God's words are oaths receiving confirmation by accomplishment in act.

In §§ 205–208, Philo returns to the objection of the other interpreters and his own subsequent answer. Thus, this text consists of a dialogue, in which a solution to the problem raised by the interpreters is offered in the form of "questions and answers". The text can be structured and rendered in this way:

The problem propounded by other interpreters:

(205) They say indeed that an oath is a calling God to witness to a point which is disputed; so if it is God that swears, He bears witness to Himself, which is absurd, for he that bears the witness must needs be a different person from him on whose behalf it is borne.

Question:

What then must we say?

Answer:

First that there is nothing amiss in God bearing witness to Himself.

For who else would be capable of bearing witness to Him?

Secondly, He Himself is to Himself all that is most precious, kinsman, intimate, friend, virtue, happiness, blessedness, knowledge, understanding, beginning, end, whole, everything, judge, decision, counsel, law, process, sovereignty.

(206) Besides if we once take "by Myself have I sworn" in the right way, we shall quit this excessive quibbling.

Philo's final answer to the objection and the solution of the problem:

Probably then the truth of the matter is something like this. Nothing that can give assurance can give positive assurance touching God, for to none has He shown His nature, but He has rendered it invisible to our whole race. Who can assert of the First cause either that It is without body or that It is a body, that It is of such a kind or that It is of no kind? In a word who can make any positive assertion concerning His essence or quality or state or movement? Nay He alone shall affirm anything regarding Himself since He alone has unerringly exact knowledge of His own nature.

Conclusion:

(207) God alone therefore is the strongest security first for Himself, and in the next place for His deeds also, so that He naturally swore by Himself when giving assurance as to Himself, a thing impossible for another than He.

Consequence:

It follows that men who say that they swear by God should be considered actually impious; for naturally no one swears by Him, seeing that he is unable to possess knowledge regarding his nature. No, we may be content if we are able to swear by His name (as we have seen) the interpreting word. For this must be God for us the imperfect folk, but as for the wise and perfect, the primal Being is their God.

(208) Moses too, let us observe, filled with wonder at the transcendency of the Uncreate, says, "and thou shalt swear by His name" [Deut. vi. 13], not "by Him," for it is enough for the created being that he should be accredited and have witness borne to him by the Divine word; but let God be His own most sure guarantee and evidence.

With regard to its content, it is clear that Philo here renders a discussion on the rule of self-testimony and the problem that arises when it is applied to God. Philo refers to some other interpreters, who deny that anyone can give witness in his own case. Accordingly, they also hold it to be absurd that God can bear witness to himself. Philo refutes such an objection by arguing in various ways that it is only God who is capable of giving witness to himself. I will await a further analysis of both the "form" and the content of this Philonic text and its probable setting, until I reach to the point of comparison with the Johannine texts. Next, I will give a brief sketch of these two texts.

An Outline of John 5:31–40 and 8:12–20 Within their Literary Contexts[5]

John 5:31–40

The context of John 5:31–40 is as follows: According to John 5:1–18, the accusations against Jesus are twofold: 1. He has broken the laws of the Sabbath since it was not lawful to carry a pallet; 2. In his justification of the healing on the Sabbath, Jesus claimed that he was doing the same work as God the Father. He made himself equal to God, and the Jews sought to kill him (John 5:18).

In the following section, John 5:19–30, the relationship between the Son and God, the Father is characterized. A conclusion is reached in v. 30: "I can do nothing on my own authority; as I hear, I judge; and my judgment is just, because I seek not my own will, but the will of him who sent me."

On what evidence do the claims of Jesus rest? In John 5:31–40 the Evangelist delivers the legitimation of Jesus in order to explain further the relationship between God, the Father and the Son.[6] Thus, the trial scene described in the remaining part of John 5 is characterized by a forensic debate between Jesus and his Jewish opponents, in which the Baptist, Jesus' own works, God the sender, and the Scriptures serve as witnesses to Jesus.[7] Here follows a kind outline of the text:

The claim of Jesus:

If I alone bear witness to myself, my testimony is not true; there is another who bears witness to me, and I know that the testimony which he bears to me is true.

First testimony:

You sent to John, and he has borne witness to the truth. Not that the testimony which I receive is from man; but I say this that you may be saved. He was a burning and shining lamp, and you were willing to rejoice for a while in his light.

Second testimony:

But the testimony which I have is greater than that of John; for the works which the Father has granted me to accomplish, these very works which I am doing, bear me witness that the Father has sent me.

---

[5] It is beyond the scope of this study to investigate John's use of oral or written gospel traditions in these texts.

[6] Cf. Hartwig THYEN, *Das Johannesevangelium* (HNT 6; Tübingen: Mohr Siebeck, 2005), 319.

[7] For a rhetorical analysis of John 5:31–47, see Harold W. ATTRIDGE, "Argumentation in John 5," in *Rhetorical Argumentation in Biblical Texts: Essays from the Lund 2000 Conference* (ed. by A. Eriksson, T. H. Olbricht, and W. Überlacker. Emory Studies in Early Christianity, vol. 8; Harrisburg, Penn.: Trinity Press International, 2002), 188–199, esp. 196–199.

Third testimony:

And the Father who sent me has himself borne witness to me. His voice you have never heard, his form you have never seen; and you do not have his word abiding in you, for you do not believe him whom he has sent.

Fourth testimony:

You search the scriptures, because you think that in them you have eternal life; and it is they that bear witness to me, yet you refuse to come to me that you may have life.

John 8:12–20

As regards the location of this text within its literary context, John 8 is seen by most scholars as a direct continuation of chapter 7, so that John 7:1–8:59 is a unit. Thus, John 8:12 is a saying of Jesus as the light of the world, comparable to John 7:37. This theme is used here to introduce the theme of testimonies to Jesus (John 8:13–20), which seems to be a further development of the discourse in John 5:31–40. In John 8:21–30, questions are raised about whence Jesus comes and whither he goes, about who the Father is and who Jesus is. The similar theme of his identity and his relationship to his Father is further developed in John 8:31–59, although in new terminology.

The affirmation that Jesus is the truth made known to men leads to the development of the theme in which Jesus and his adversaries are contrasted. The objections by the critics and Jesus' answer can be listed as follows:

The claim of Jesus:

Again Jesus spoke to them, saying, "I am the light of the world; he who follows me will not walk in darkness, but will have the light of life."

The objection of the Pharisees:

The Pharisees then said to him, "You are bearing witness to yourself; your testimony is not true."

The reply of Jesus to the objection by a threefold argument:
(First argument)

Jesus answered, "Even if I do bear witness to myself, my testimony is true, for I know whence I have come and whither I am going, but you do not know whence I have come and whither I am going.

(Second argument)

You judge according to the flesh; I judge no one. Yet even if I do judge, my judgment is true, for it is not I alone who judge, but I and he who sent me.

(Third argument)

In your law it is written that the testimony of two men is true; I bear witness to myself, and the Father who sent me bears witness to me."

Question:

They said to him therefore, "Where is your Father?"

Answer:

Jesus answered, "You know neither me nor my Father; If you knew me, you would know my Father also."

Editorial note:

These words he spoke in the treasury, as he taught in the temple; but no one arrested him, because his hour had not yet come.

Having presented the relevant texts briefly, I now turn to some of the main questions posed by scholars with regard to the Johannine discourses as a foil for the formulation of the thesis of the study.

A Brief Survey of Previous Research

Are there legal and forensic traditions in the Philonic corpus which may shed light on the legal features of the passages of John 5:31–40 and 8:12–20? A survey of the scholarly literature can substantiate the conclusion that the field is open for a comparative study of Philo and John on this issue.[8] Discussing John 5:31 and 8:13–14, J. Beutler presents the commonly accepted view that John here reflects a judicial principle attested in Jewish, Greek and Latin sources, viz. that a person cannot serve as his own witness.[9] Although Beutler has discussed the Philonic material about witness,

---

[8] Among scholars who have examined the forensic aspects in John the following have made helpful contributions: Théo PREISS, *Life in Christ* (StBth 13; London: SCM. Translation of *La Vie en Christ.* Neuchâtel–Paris, 1951); Nils A. DAHL, "The Johannine Church and History," in *Current issues in New Testament Interpretation: FS O. A. Piper* (ed. W. Klassen and G. F. Snyder. New York: Harper, 1962), 124–142; Josef BLANK, *Krisis: Untersuchungen zur johanneischen Christologie und Eschatologie.* (Freiburg: Lambertus Verlag, 1964); Severino PANCARO, *The Law in the Fourth Gospel: the Torah and the Gospel, Moses and Jesus, Judaism and Christianity according to John* (NovT Suppl 13; Leiden: Brill, 1975); Johannes BEUTLER, *Martyria: Traditionsgeschichtliche Untersuchungen zum Zeugnisthema bei Johannes* (Frankfurter Theologische Studien 10; Frankfurt am Main: Verlag Josef Knecht, 1972); Andrew T. LINCOLN, *Truth on trial: The lawsuit motif in John's Gospel* (Peabody, Ma.: Hendrickson Publishers, 2000). However, none of these scholars has drawn on Philo's writings to illuminate the judicial connotations of John 5:31–40 and 8:12–20.

[9] Cf. BEUTLER, *Martyria*, 256 n. 182, for references.

which he characterizes as non-forensic, he does not draw on this data in the course of his analysis of John 5:31–37 and 8:12–17.[10] Concerning John 8:13–14, Beutler represents a view commonly held among scholars: "Die Ausnahme von der genannten Rechtsregel ist in dem besonderen Fall Jesu begründet."[11] In a review of Beutler's book, Borgen commented on such a point of view:

> Thus, he [sic. Beutler] here overlooks that Philo, (who refers the view of others) in *Leg. All.* 3, 205, states an exception to the rule against self-witness in a way which corresponds to that of John. According to Philo, only God is capable of giving witness to himself. John correspondingly states that Jesus can witness to himself because of His divine origin. Thus, John presupposes Jewish debate on the forensic rule against self-witness and the problem that arises when it is applied to God. The Evangelist did not himself create the exception to the rule when it was applied to Jesus, as Beutler claims.[12]

Unfortunately, Borgen has not followed up this hypothesis in his later studies on John by an extensive analysis of this Philonic text in comparison with the two Johannine texts. Thus, the present study will be an effort to unfold the thesis at which Borgen has hinted by a detailed comparative analysis of the relevant texts.

If we presuppose that the Philonic data provides a Jewish context for understanding the controversy reflected in John 5:31 and 8:13–14, we can ask more specifically if there are any particular aspects of these Johannine texts that Philo also illuminates. As a background for our attempt to answer this question, it will be profitable to begin with some of the problems with regard to the Johannine texts that scholars have discussed.

Is there a contradiction between the statements in John 5:31 ("If I alone bear witness about myself, my testimony is not deemed true") and John 8:14 ("Jesus answered: 'Even if I do bear witness about myself, my testimony is true …'")? According to John 5:31–32, Jesus is seen as a human being, who is dependent on, and in need of, his Father's testimony. On the other hand, in John 8:14 Jesus' own witness is viewed as self-authenticating. C. K. Barrett comments on John 5:31:

> In this verse there is a formal contradiction with 8.14 […]. In each place the speech is *ad hominem* and the meaning is sufficiently plain; yet it may be questioned whether a writer

---

[10] BEUTLER, *Martyria*, 147–148.

[11] Cf. BEUTLER, *Martyria*, 268, for further references to scholars maintaining such a view.

[12] BORGEN, "Review of J. Beutler, *Martyria: Traditionsgeschichtliche Untersuchungen zum Zeugnisthema bei Johannes*. Frankfurter Theologische Studien 10; Frankfurt am Main: Verlag Josef Knecht, 1972," *Biblica* 55 (1974), 583.

who had fully revised his work would have left the two statements in their present form.[13]

Thyen thinks that the contradiction is "nur scheinbar" and objects to Barrett's understanding:

Da muss man Johannes nicht der Flüchtigkeit verdächtigen und wie Barrett fragen, „ob ein Schriftsteller, der sein Werk vollständig durchgesehen hat, die zwei Aussagen in ihrer vorliegenden Form hätte stehen lassen" (Komm. 279). Denn gerade in diesem gewiss nicht zufällig ,stehen gebliebenen', sondern absichtsvoll gesetzten Wiederspruch besteht ja das Paradox der Sendung Jesu als des fleischgewordenen Logos.[14]

Darum kann und muss der Sohn dem Satz, dass sein Zeugnis, wenn es denn ein Zeugnis in eigener Sache wäre, unglaubwürdig ist, in 8,14 den anderen Satz hinzufügen, dass aber sein Zeugnis gleichwohl glaubwürdig ist, weil es nämlich gar nicht das Seine ist.[15]

A. Lincoln states his understanding of John 5:31 and 8:14 as follows:

On the one hand, in 5:31, 32, Jesus as a human being is totally dependent on his Father and in need of the Father's validating testimony. On the other hand, here in 8:14, he is so at one with God that his witness is self-authenticating, for by definition God needs no one to validate God's testimony.[16]

As we shall observe in more detail below, Philo can provide a Jewish context, which testifies to Lincoln's reading of John 8:14, and which might explain Jesus' exceptional identity as the one who can testify to himself. The point is that only God is capable of giving testimony to himself, and therefore his witness is self-authenticating.

J. Blank has raised another question concerning John 8:14:

Wie kan Jesu Wissen um seinen Ursprung und sein Ziel, also um seinen Weg, Grund sein für die Wahrheit des Selbstzeugnisses?[17]

Blank suggests this answer:

Jesu Wissen um sein Woher und Wohin bezeichnet sein vollkommenes Um–sich selber– Wissen; Jesus weiss so um sich selbst, dass ihm sein Woher und Wohin bekannt ist. [...] Somit ist deutlich: Jesu Wissen um sein Woher und Wohin ist nichts anderes, als das Wissen um seinen Ausgang vom und seine Rückkehr zum Vater; sein Wissen um den Vater überhaupt als Ursprung und Ziel seiner selbst.[18]

As we shall see, John's way of reasoning about Jesus' self-authenticating testimony has an analogy in Philo.

---

[13] Charles Kingsley BARRETT, *The Gospel according to St John: An Introduction with Commentary and Notes on the Greek Text* (2. ed.; London: SPCK, 1978), 264.

[14] THYEN, *Das Johannesevangelium*, 319.

[15] THYEN, *Das Johannesevangelium*, 320.

[16] LINCOLN, *Truth*, 84–85.

[17] BLANK, *Krisis*, 217–218.

[18] BLANK, *Krisis*, 218.

How should we understand the various testimonies by John the Baptist, the Father, the works, and the Scriptures? What is their reference and do they have the same status as witnesses?

According to Barrett there is a discussion in John about which testimonies are of primary or secondary authority. Only the testimony by God himself is a satisfactory testimony to Jesus. The others – the testimony by the Baptist, the testimony by the works done by Jesus in the Father's name, and the testimony by the Old Testament – these are all derived testimonies, and therefore they have real but secondary authority.[19]

According to Lincoln, the various testimonies which are adduced to provide proof for Jesus 'do not constitute a straightforward list where each is distinct and has the same status as witness, as commentators frequently suggest'.[20] Lincoln holds the view that

> Jesus works, which are given him by the Father, and the Scriptures, which are the Father's word, can, then, both be seen as the visible aspects of the Father's testimony. This testimony is contrasted to that of the Baptist.[21]

Thyen, who shares a similar perspective, thinks, however, that John makes some sort of distinction between the witnesses of God to Jesus, viz. the "works" and the "Scriptures", explicitly mentioned in John 5:36 and 5:39 and the Father's witness referred to in John 5:37a.[22] This point of view, then, raises the question: Does the Evangelist, by the reference to the Father's direct witness in John 5:37a, think of a particular occasion or a particular kind of witness? Scholars have made several different suggestions. Most scholars take it to refer to the Father's witness through the "works" of Jesus and the "Scriptures".[23] Other interpreters have seen this as an allusion to the voice from heaven at the baptism.[24] Barrett has suggested that it refers to the testimony by God, granted to those who first believe in Jesus.[25] Schnackenburg has connected the idea of the testimony of the Father in John 5:37a with the verb σφραγίζω in John 6:27b, which, according to Liddell and Scott's Greek-English Lexicon means to "to accredit as an en-

---

[19] BARRETT, *The Gospel*, 258.

[20] LINCOLN, *Truth on trial*, 77.

[21] LINCOLN, *Truth on trial*, 77.

[22] Cf. THYEN, *Das Johannesevangelium*, 323.

[23] So, e.g. DAHL, "The Johannine Church", 109; PANCARO, *The Law*, 224; THYEN, *Das Johannesevangelium*, 323.

[24] Cf. for example, Ragnar ASTING, *Die Verkündigung des Wortes im Urchristentum, dargestellt an den Begriffen „Wort Gottes", „Evangelium" und „Zeugnis"* (Stuttgart: Kohlhammer, 1939), 679; Johannes SCHNEIDER, *Das Evangelium nach Johannes* (Theologischer Handkommentar zum Neuen Testament. Sonderbd.; Berlin: Evangelische Verlagsanstalt, 1976), 133.

[25] BARRETT, *The Gospel*, 267.

voy", with an equivalent in the Hebrew and Aramaic word חתם, "to seal", which is the technical term for sealing as a witness.[26] Thus, Schnackenburg's understanding suggests that the testimony of the Father in John 5:37a points to the way in which God has sealed the Son of Man and has borne witness to Him as his envoy.[27]

The questions about the meaning of these various testimonies and in particular that of the Father will be discussed more fully in the comparison between John and Philo.

Should John 5:37b be treated as a parenthesis or should it be put on the same footing as John 5:38a, i.e. as a reproach? The opinions of the scholars are divided on this point. If the words of v. 37b are a parenthesis, they are not meant as a reproach, but as a statement of a fact and/or of a recognized principle. Then the Evangelist rejects the notion that the "Jews" have ever heard the voice of God or seen his form. The principle is that there is no direct access to the Father: God is transcendent, and his form and voice are not immediately accessible and assessable. Fact and principle need not both be affirmed. Scholars such as Dahl, Borgen, and Pancaro hold the view that John 5:37b should be taken as a reproach and it alludes to the revelation on Mount Sinai.[28] There the Israelites heard the voice of God, and according to some Jewish texts and traditions they also saw his "form" – in spite of Deuteronomy 4:12.[29] Since John 6:46 declares that there is no vision of God apart from the Son, it is probable that God's "form," which appeared on Mount Sinai, is identified with the Son of God. Hence, in John's interpretation the "Jews", who refuse to believe in Jesus, prove that they did not see God's "form" and therefore they have no share in the preview of the Son, given to Israel at Mount Sinai.[30]

In the light of the evidence in Philo I suggest a Jewish referential background for the interpretation of John 5:37b, which also seems to fit in well with the preceding v. 37a.

---

[26] Cf. Henry George LIDDELL and Robert SCOTT, *A Greek–English Lexicon: A New Edition* (Oxford: Clarendon Press; Reprint, 1958), 1742; Marcus JASTROW, *A Dictionary of the Targumim, the Talmud Babli and Yerushalmi, and the Midrashic Literature* (New York: Judaica Press, 1996), 513–514.

[27] Rudolf SCHNACKENBURG, *The Gospel according to St John: Volume 2.* (Translated by C. Hastings, F. McDonagh, D. Smith, and R. Foley. London: Burns & Oates, 1980), 38. BORGEN (*Early Christianity*, 210–211) follows Schnackenburg in this interpretation of John 5:37 and John 6:27b.

[28] Cf. DAHL, "The Johannine Church", 109; BORGEN, *Bread*, 151; PANCARO, *The Law*, 218–226.

[29] DAHL ("The Johannine Church", 109) refers to Sir 17:6 and *Mekilta* (Exod 19:11).

[30] Cf. BORGEN, *Philo, John and Paul: New Perspectives on Judaism and Early Christianity* (BJS 131; Atlanta, Ga.: Scholars Press, 1987), 165.

I turn now to compare the texts of Philo and of John with emphasis on some neglected points of similarities.

A Jewish Controversy on Self-Testimony: A Comparison between John and Philo

As we shall see, there are points of similarities between John 5:31–39; 8:12–20 and *Leg.* 3.205–208.

The Controversy about the Issue of Self-Testimony

Both John and Philo refer to a controversy about the validity of self-testimony. In John, the controversy takes place between Jesus and his interlocutors, represented by the "Jews" (John 5:31–40) and the "Pharisees" (John 8:12–20). According to *Leg.* 3.205, the controversy is between Philo himself and probably some other group of interpreters.[31]

The Use of "Questions and Answers" in the Context of Learned Settings

The Johannine discourses are genetically quite diverse, with parallels to a wide range of literary patterns and generic "forms."[32] Dialogic discourses, with either friendly or hostile interlocutors, are common in John. According to R. Bauckham, the polemic dialogues and discourses in John, punctuated by questions and objections, meets the historiographical criterion of appropriateness to both the speaker and the situation.[33] Observations on John 8:12–20 in the light of Philonic evidence may support such a consideration.

---

[31] In *Sacr.* 91–93 Philo refers to the same conflict and most probably the same interlocutors: "But, when he tells us that God swore an oath, we must consider whether he lays down that such a thing can with truth be ascribed to God, since to thousands it seems unworthy of Him. For our conception of an oath is an appeal to God as a witness on some disputed matter (*Sacr.* 91)." To the issue of various groups of interpreters in Alexandria, cf. e.g. David HAY, "Philo's References to Other Allegorists," *Studia Philonica* 6 (1979–1980), 41–75; David HAY, *Both Literal and Allegorical: Studies in Philo of Alexandria's Questions and Answers on Genesis and Exodus* (BJS 232; Atlanta, Ga.: Scholars Press, 1991).

[32] See, e.g. BEUTLER, "Literarische Gattungen im Johannesevangelium: Ein Forschungsbericht 1919–1980", ANRW 2.25.3 (1985) 2506–2568; ATTRIDGE, "Genre Bending in the Fourth Gospel", *JBL* 121 (2002), 3–21.

[33] Richard BAUCKHAM, "Historiographical Characteristics of the Gospel of John", *NTS* 53 (2007), 17–36.

First, the controversy reflected in John (John 8:12–20) and Philo (*Leg.* 3.205–208) follows the structure of a dialogue, including the form of "questions and answers".[34] The dialogue in John 8:12–20 is introduced by the pronouncement of Jesus about himself (8:12) and followed by the objection of the Pharisees (8:13), which in turn leads to Jesus' refutation of their objection in the form of a threefold reply (8:14–18). This answer raises another question from the Pharisees followed by Jesus' final answer.

Philo may use complex forms of dialogues, including the devices of objections and replies. In Philo's writings, such objections are introduced by simple formulas, for example phrases such as "some said" (ἔφασαν δέ τι– νες) and "they say" (φασί), which can be found in *Leg.* 3.204–205. Such phrases are also used when Philo states explicitly that he records the views of others.[35] Philo's answer to the objection made by the interlocutors in *Leg.* 3.205 is introduced as a question: "What then must we say (τί οὖν λεκτέον)?" Likewise, the subsequent answers are quite organized: "First (πρῶτον) that there is nothing amiss in God bearing witness to Himself ... Secondly (ἔπειτα), He Himself is to Himself all that is most precious ..." Examples of similar forms used in questions and answers are found in *Leg.* 1.34–35; 1.60–61; 1.102–103; *Virt.* 171–174.[36]

Secondly, the passage in John 8:12–20 is bounded by an editorial note in v. 20, which comments on the setting of the dialogue: "These words he spoke in the treasury, as he taught (διδάσκων) in the temple ..." According to John, Jesus' public teaching, reported in the form of a dialogue with his interlocutors, often took place in the synagogue or the temple (cf. 6:59; 7:14, 28; 18:20).[37] Philo's writings in general make it clear that John's use of this form is appropriate when he reports a dialogue within a learned setting in Judaism, such as the synagogue or the temple.[38] Thus, Philo testifies to the use of questions and answers and problem-solving exegesis as part of the teaching activity of the synagogue, as suggested by his report on the expository activity among the Therapeutae:

... the President of the company ... discusses (ζητεῖ) some questions arising in the Holy Scriptures or solves (ἐπιλύεται) one that has been propounded by someone else, (*Contempl.* 75).

---

[34] Cf. BORGEN, "The Gospel of John and Philo of Alexandria", in *Light in a Spotless Mirror: Reflections on Wisdom Traditions in Judaism and Early Christianity* (ed. by J. H. Charlesworth and M. A. Daise; Harrisburg/London/New York: Trinity Press International. A Continuum imprint, 2003), 45–76.

[35] Cf. *QG* 1.8; 2.64; 3.13; *Opif.* 77.

[36] Cf. BORGEN, *Philo of Alexandria: An Exegete for His Time* (NovT Sup 86; Leiden: Brill, 1997) 129; 131; 135.

[37] See Judith LIEU, "Temple and Synagogue in John", *NTS* 45 (1999), 51–69, esp. 69.

[38] Cf. *Spec.* 1.214; *Leg.* 1.33; 1.48; 1.91; 2.103; *QG* 1.62.

The verb ζητέω and the composite verb ἐπιζητέω are also used elsewhere in Philo's writings whenever an exegetical question is raised, and answers and solutions are given.[39] Moreover, in *Contempl.* 79 the leader is said to have conversed with (διαλέγομαι ["hold converse with", "discuss"]) his audience, and since questions and answers were part of the discourse, the verb most probably means "to discuss" in this context.

However, a comparison of John with Philo shows obvious differences as well. Firstly, in contrast to Philo, the Johannine text is not part of an exegetical exchange, even when such a setting is apparent in the immediate context (John 5:1–18 and 6:28–59).[40] Secondly, although there is no direct reference to a particular learned setting in *Leg.* 3.205–208, which is the case in John 8:12–20, there are in general many observations which support the hypothesis that Philo's writings draw on the expository activity of the synagogues.[41] Here I only want to make the point that, against the background of the teaching activity in learned Jewish settings, learned authors, such as John and Philo, would probably draw on the form of "questions and answers" as a rhetorical or literary device in their own discourses.[42]

The Ruling about the Need for More Than One Witness

The forensic debate referred to by both John and Philo regards the validity of self-testimony. The Pharisees object to Jesus' assertion about himself by claiming that it cannot be true, since it is a self-testimony and therefore invalid according to the laws of testimony. In John 8:17, there is an explicit reference to the Old Testament and halachic ruling about the need for more than one witness, with reference to the laws of testimony, such as Deut 19:15. In a passage of the Mishnah that deals with marriage cases, it is stated: "None may be believed when he testifies of himself" (*m. Ketub.*

---

[39] See, BORGEN, *Philo of Alexandria*, 100–101.

[40] Cf. BORGEN, *Early Christianity*, 110–113; 211–223.

[41] Cf. Valentin NIKIPROWETZKY, *Le commentaire de l'Écriture chez Philon d'Alexandrie: son caractère et sa portée; observations philologiques* (ALGHJ 11; Leiden: Brill, 1977), 179–180.

[42] For the proposal that the Johannine language, genres, conflicts, use of Scripture, targumizing of the Jesus tradition, and so on, might presuppose a synagogue framework, cf. e.g. Birger OLSSON, "'All my teaching was done in synagogues ...' (John 18,20)", in *Theology and Christology in the Fourth Gospel: Essays by the Members of the SNTS Johannine Writings Seminar* (ed. G. Van Belle, J.G. Van der Watt, and P. Maritz; BETL 184; Leuven: Leuven University Press, 2003), 203–224.

2:9).[43] In John 5:31 we need to presuppose such a forensic referential background regarding the invalidity of self-testimony. Accordingly, in John 5:31 Jesus himself conceded to the need for more than one witness for a testimony to be valid, and he consequently appealed to the Father's testimony on his behalf as a second witness. Thus, it seems that the words of Jesus – "If I witness about myself, my testimony is not valid (ἀληθής = 'valid')" – should be understood in accordance with the general agreement on what constitutes a valid testimony.[44]

Also in *Leg.* 3.205, the biblical laws of testimony seem to be presupposed by the objection against self-testimony put forward by those to whom Philo refers: "... so if it is God that swears, He bears witness to Himself, which is absurd, for he that bears the witness must needs be a different person from him on whose behalf it is borne."[45] Moreover, Philo's reply to this objection in *Leg.* 3.205–208 that God is the only one who can witness in his own case, because God alone is the only valid witness to himself, indicates that, as in John, the issue which is discussed is that of the validity of a witness.[46]

The Concept of Self-Testimony applied to God

In both Philo and John, the concept of self-testimony is applied to God. Borgen's suggestion therefore seems to be accurate when he claims that "John presupposes Jewish debate on the forensic rule against self-witness and the problem that arises when it is applied to God."[47]

According to *Leg.* 3.205, the objection against self-testimony, even when applied to God, is stated by Philo's interlocutors, referred to as "they":

---

[43] The reference is taken from *The Mishnah. Translated from the Hebrew with Introduction and brief Explanatory Notes* (Translated by H. Danby. New York, NY: Oxford University Press, 1933), 247.

[44] Cf. THYEN, *Das Johannesevangelium*, 319: "Das es in diesem Rechtsstreit nicht um die Rekonstruktion oder ‚Aufdeckung' irgendeiner abstrakten ‚Wahrheit', sondern ganz konkret um die Glaubwürdigkeit des Zeugen geht, wird man das Predikat der Apodosis οὐκ ἔστιν ἀληθής am besten mit „*ist nicht glaubwürdig*" wiedergeben."

[45] Philo deals with the question of testimony in *Spec.* 4.55–78. In *Spec.* 4.53–54 he refers to various biblical texts prohibiting the evidence of a single witness such as Num 35:30, Deut 17:6 (on death sentences), and Deut 19:15 (on all offences).

[46] Cf. the conclusion reached in *Leg.* 3.208: " ... but let God be his own evidence (πίστις) and most sure witness (μαρτυρία βεβαιοτάτη)" [our translation].

[47] BORGEN, "Review", 9.

They say indeed that an oath is a calling God to witness to a point which is disputed; so if it is God that swears, He bears witness to Himself, which is absurd, for he that bears the witness must needs be a different person from him on whose behalf it is borne.[48]

Philo's reply to this objection is that there is an exception to the rule against self-testimony, viz. that only God is capable of giving witness to himself: "First that there is nothing amiss in God bearing witness to Himself. For who else would be capable of bearing witness to Him?" (*Leg.* 3.205). This issue is repeated several times throughout *Leg.* 3.206–208:

Nay He *alone* (μόνος) shall affirm anything regarding Himself since He *alone* (μόνος) has unerringly exact knowledge of His own nature (206).

God therefore is the strongest security first for Himself, and in the next place for His deeds also, so that He naturally swore by Himself when giving assurance as to Himself, a thing impossible for another than He (207).

[…] but let God be His own most sure guarantee and evidence (208).

Such statements make the point that God's witness is self-authenticating, because no one but God alone (μόνος) is able to testify to God. It is also interesting to note that, according to Philo, the main reason is that God has not revealed his true nature to the human race:

Nothing that can give assurance can give positive assurance touching God, for to none has He shown His nature, but He has rendered it invisible to our whole race. Who can assert of the First cause either that It is without body or that It is a body, that It is of such a kind or that It is of no kind? In a word who can make any positive assertion concerning His essence or quality or state or movement? Nay He alone shall affirm anything regarding Himself since He alone has unerringly exact knowledge of His own nature (*Leg.* 3.206).

… so that He naturally swore by Himself when giving assurance as to Himself, a thing impossible for another than He. It follows that men who say that they swear by God should be considered actually impious; for naturally no one swears by Him, seeing that he is unable to possess *knowledge* regarding his nature (*Leg.* 3.207).

It is my hypothesis that such a kind of self-authentic witness by God and the reasoning documented by Philo provides a referential background for the statement in John 5:37–38.

According to John 5:37a, Jesus said: "And the Father who sent me has himself (ἐκεῖνος) borne witness to me." As pointed out above, it is not clear to what the specific witness borne by the Father refers. Together with Thyen, I hold the view that there is a distinction between the other witnesses, viz. the "works" and the "Scriptures", explicitly mentioned in John

---

[48] Cf. similar "definitions" of an oath in *Decal.* 86; *Spec.* 2.10; *Sacr.* 91; *Plant.* 81.

5:36 and John 5:39, and God's own witness referred to in John 5:37.[49] If the Father's witness alludes to God's self-authenticating testimony, which corresponds to the kind found in Philo, an explanation might be given both for the emphasis on the demonstrative pronoun ἐκεῖνος in John 5:37a and for the statement that follows in John 5:37b–38: God's voice has not been heard, nor has his form been seen; and they [i.e. the "Jews"] do not have his word abiding in them. My proposal is that the words of John 5:37b are a statement of a fact and of the recognized principle about God's transcendence. The fact is the notion that the "Jews" have never heard the voice of God or seen his form.[50] The principle is that there is no direct access to the Father: God is transcendent, and his form and voice are not immediately accessible and assessable. Thus, the meaning of John 5:37–38 can be paraphrased as follows: Jesus said: The most adequate evidence of all is that the Father has himself borne witness to me. This is a self-authenticating testimony, because *only* my Father *himself* can testify to the divine relationship between himself and me. If you suggest any other ways in which God might have been expected to give witness, this must be denied. The reason is that there is no direct sighting or hearing of God, so you have never heard his voice and you have never seen his form; and because you refuse to believe in me, this shows that his word could not be abiding in you.[51]

Such an understanding of John 5:37–38 is also supported by Jesus' claim in John 5:34 that he does not accept witness from any human being. The meaning of this statement in the context is that a human witness, such as the Baptist's, would not have been adequate from Jesus' point of view. The matter which requires evidence is that of the relationship of Jesus to the Father, and this cannot rest on human assumptions, but only on God. Accordingly, only God can testify to divine relationships. Moreover, John 8:14 seems to follow the same argumentative pattern as John 5:37–38. In John 8:14, the validity of the self-authenticating testimony of Jesus, who

---

[49] Cf. THYEN, *Das Johannesevangelium*, 323. Cf. also Raimo HAKOLA, *Identity Matters: John, the Jews and Jewishness* (NovT Sup 118; Leiden/Boston: Brill, 2005), 150.

[50] Barnabas LINDARS, *The Gospel of John* (London: Oliphants, 1972), 229, commenting on John 5:37b, is probably right when he claims that the Jewish rabbis would certainly agree with Jesus about the issue of divine transcendence. The evidence in Philo, *Leg.* 3.205–208, substantiates such a point of view.

[51] It is plausible that John 5:37–38 implies a polemic directed against Jewish claims to participate in the Sinai theophany as visionaries. Elsewhere in John, we meet the denial that anyone has ever seen God (John 1:18; 6:46), which seems to be a polemic against the idea of Moses' ascent to heaven when he ascended the mountain and against similar claims of, or for, other human beings. See Philo, *Mos.* 1.158–159; cf. also Josephus, *A.J.* 3.96; 12.1; 4Q491 11 I, 12–19; *Mek.* (Exod 19:20); *Rab.* (Num 12:11); *Midr.* (Ps 24:4 and 106:2).

knows his own divine origin, is marked out in contrast to the the Pharisees' lack of knowledge: "... but you do not *know* whence I *come* and whither I am *going*".[52] Whereas John 5:37–38 suggest that the self-authenticating witness of God could not be validated by any other means, John 8:14 correspondingly points out that Jesus is one with God to such an extent that his testimony is self-authenticating. Again, the implicit presupposition in both texts is that by definition, God needs no one to validate God's self-testimony. In addition, in John 8:18 the line of thought is that Jesus' witness to himself and his Father's testimony amount to the same thing because of the unity between the Son and the Father. The observation that can be made is that Jesus, when speaking of himself, uses the expression – "I am the one who bears witness about myself" – to stress his identification with God as a self-authenticating witness. Thus, the theme of God's self-authenticating witness in John becomes christological: God testifies to himself through the words and works of Jesus.

The Epistemological Argument for Jesus' Testimony as Self-Authenticating

In John 8:14, Jesus takes upon himself the role of God. This is an exception from the rule that no one can witness in his own case:

Even if I do bear witness about myself, my testimony is true, for I *know* whence I *come* and whither I am *going*, but you do not *know* whence I *come* and whither I am *going*.

The reason is stated as an epistemological argument. Jesus knows from where he has come and where he is going. W. Meeks emphasizes the issue of Jesus' descent and ascent as the content of his esoteric knowledge, and as the key to understanding Jesus' identity throughout John's Gospel:

The pattern in John of descent and ascent becomes the cipher for Jesus' self–knowledge as well as for his foreignness to the men of this world. His testimony is true *because* he alone knows "where I come from and where I am going" (8:14). The evangelist has laid the groundwork for this statement. In 3:8 he introduced the motif, with the statement to Nicodemus that of both the Spirit and of the one born of the spirit (= "from above") "you do not know where he comes from and where he goes." The Jerusalemites at the feast of the Tabernacles think they know where Jesus is from: his Galilean origin precludes his

---

[52] Cf. THYEN, *Das Johannesevangelium*, 424, who reads John 8:14 in light of John 5:34: "Die ‚Wahrheit' auch seines Zeugnisses für sich *selbst* begründet Jesus also mit seinem *Wissen* um sein Woher und sein Wohin. Wie er als der einzige Sohn, „den Gott nicht dazu gesandt hat, dass er die Welt verurteile, sondern dazu, dass die Welt durch ihn gerettet werde" (3,17), um seinen Auftrag weiss und – wie er 5,34 bereits erklärt hatte – keines Menschen als seines Zeugen bedarf (ἐγὼ δὲ οὐ παρὰ ἀνθρώπου τὴν μαρ–τυρίαν λαμβάνω), ist es unvermeidlich, dass er für sich selbst zeugen muss." Unfortunately, Thyen has not applied a similar way of reasoning in his interpretation of John 5:37–38 as compared to the way he reads John 8:14.

being the Prophet or the Christ (7:37–52) [...] the dialogue itself tells the reader that the Jews do not really know where Jesus is from (7:28–9: he is from God), but in a later dialogue he has them admit that they do not know where he is from (9:29: "We know that God spoke to Moses, but this man—we do not know where he is from"). Pilate also asks Jesus, "Where are you from?" (19:9) and receives no answer. The descent and ascent of the Son of Man thus becomes not only the key to his identity and identification, but also the primary content of his esoteric knowledge which *distinguishes* him from men who belong to "this world."[53]

There is an important parallel to this epistemological argument in Philo. In a way that corresponds to John 8:14, Philo refers in *Leg.* 3.205–206 to the esoteric knowledge of God with regard to his essence, quality, state, and movement as the reason why God can testify to himself:

Secondly, He Himself is to Himself all that is most precious, kinsman, intimate, friend, virtue, happiness, blessedness, *knowledge*, *understanding*, beginning, end, whole, everything, judge, decision, counsel, law, process, sovereignty [...] In a word who can make any positive assertion concerning His essence or quality or state or *movement*? [...] (205).

Nay *He alone* shall affirm anything regarding Himself since *He alone* has unerringly exact *knowledge* of His own nature (206).

A presupposition of this way of arguing about God seems to be the wide currency of the principle "like is known by like" in antiquity.[54] Philo's emphasis that God's existence cannot be apprehended by any human co-operation is probably due to this principle of likeness.[55]

The Contrast Between the Divine and the Human Testimony

There seems to be a contrast between the validity of a divine and a human testimony in John. Bultmann made this point in his comment on John 5:34: Jesus cannot accept the witness of men, since that would mean "that there is a commensurable relationship between human and divine standards ..."[56] In both John 5:31 and 8:14 Jesus presupposes that if he, as merely a human being, had witnessed in his own case, his testimony would be invalid. However, because of another divine testimony, and because of his divine union with the Father, Jesus claims that he can witness in his own

---

[53] Wayne A. MEEKS, "The Man from Heaven in Johannine Sectarianism," *JBL* 91 (1972), 44–72, esp. p. 60.

[54] The principle is recorded according to the work *Against the Professors* 1.303 by Sextus Empiricus (2nd–3rd century AD).

[55] Cf. Karl Olav SANDNES, "Whence and Whither: A Narrative Perspective on Birth *Anōthen* (John 3,3–8)", *Biblica* 86 (2005), 153–173, esp. pp. 158–162, who compares Philo and John on this point.

[56] Rudolf BULTMANN, *The Gospel of John: A Commentary* (Translated by G. R. Beasley-Murray. Oxford: Basil Blackwell, 1971), 264.

case (John 8:14). This contrast between a human and a divine level is also presupposed by John in the following statements on Jesus' testimony:

Not that the testimony which I receive is from man ... (John 5:34)

But the testimony which I have is greater than that of John; for the works which the Father has granted me to accomplish ... bear me witness that the Father has sent me, (John 5:36).

The Baptist's witness obviously served a different purpose compared to the others. It was not evidence in the legal sense which was required, but a pointer, at a human level, to Jesus as the agent of salvation, so that men might turn to Jesus and be saved (John 5:33–36).

It is interesting that Philo provides a parallel to this distinction between a divine and a human testimony. In *Leg.* 3.208 Philo distinguishes between God, the strongest guarantee for himself and his deeds, and the human being, who is unable to possess knowledge about God's nature, and who thus cannot testify to God. On this basis Philo draws the conclusion:

... for it is enough for the created being that he should be accredited and have witness borne to him by the divine word: but let God be His own most sure evidence and witness (*Leg.* 3.208).

The "Works" as an Aspect of God's Testimony to Himself

John 5:36 says that Jesus' "works" bear witness to him that "the Father has sent me". In the Johannine context "signs," such as the healing of the paralytic (John 5:1–9) and the feeding of the 5000 (John 6:1–21), exemplify the witnessing function of Jesus' "works": They prove Jesus' relationship to the Father, because they are performed on God's authority with the aim of fulfilling his redemptive purpose. In John, there is an emphasis on Jesus' functional union with his Father for the purpose of avoiding any ditheistic accusations of Jesus.[57] In John 5:36 John solves this problem by emphasizing that Jesus was entirely dependent on God.[58] According to John 8:29, Jesus did nothing by himself, but only what he had been taught by his Father. Moreover, John 10:25, 32, 37 emphasize that the "works of

---

[57] On the problem of Johannine Christology and monotheism, see, e.g., Lars HART-MAN, "Johannine Jesus-Belief and Monotheism," in *Aspects on the Johannine Literature: Papers presented at a conference of Scandinavian New Testament exegetes at Uppsala, June 16–19, 1986* (ed. L. Hartman and B. Olsson. CBNT 18; Uppsala: Almqvist & Wiksell International, 1987), 85–99.

[58] Correspondingly, when Philo in *Det.* 160–161 solves the problem of ditheism with regard to Moses, he makes it clear that God himself is active, while Moses was passive when he appeared as a god. This is seen from Philo's statement of the biblical expression that God *gave him* as "god to Pharaoh" (Exod 7:1). Cf. BORGEN, "The Gospel", 68.

the Father" are the "works" of Jesus. Thus, again, the idea that God can testify to himself and also to his own works seems to be presupposed when the Christological claim is made in John 5:36 and 10:25 that "the works of the Father" testifies to Jesus and to the divine origin of his mission.[59]

In *Leg.* 3.207, such an idea of God's self-authenticating witness is also expressed: "God alone therefore is the strongest security first for Himself, and in the next place for His *deeds* also ..."[60]

The Interpreting Word of God Testifies to the Human Being.

John 5:39 mentions the witness of the Scriptures: "You search the Scriptures (ἐρευνᾶτε τὰς γραφάς), because you think that in them you have eternal life; and it is they that bear witness to me." In the literary context of John, chapters 5–6, John 5:39 functions as a hermeneutical principle with a parallel formulated in John 5:46: "If you believed Moses, you would believe me, for he wrote of me." The phrase ἐρευνᾶτε in John 5:39 is a Greek equivalent for the technical term for performing midrashic exegesis (דרשׁ). The Scripture quoted in John 6:31 and its midrashic exposition in the subsequent vv. 31–58 can be seen to serve as an illustration of the searching of the Scriptures and their witness to Jesus mentioned in John 5:39.[61] Thus, on the basis of the hermeneutical key formulated in John 5:39 for example, the pronouncement in John 6:35a, "I am *the bread* of life", renders the precise meaning of the central term in the Scriptural quotation in v. 31b. "*bread* from heaven he gave them to eat". The Old Testament quotation in John 6:31b and its exposition in John 6:35a bear witness to Jesus.

In light of its immediate context, John 5:39 expresses the hope that the "Jews" might be able to receive testimony about the life available through Jesus, for they approach the Scriptures through learned exposition in the hope that in them they may have eternal life, and the Scriptures testify to Jesus. According to John, the learned study of the "Jews" and the testimony of the Scriptures seem to be in vain since they refuse to believe in Jesus.

Again, *Leg.* 3.208 provides an analogy to the conception of the "Scriptures" accredited to humans as witnesses. Using the exegetical method of

---

[59] Cf. also John 10:37–38. Cf. SCHNACKENBURG, *The Gospel*, 121.

[60] In *Mos.* 2.263 Philo characterizes the "sign" (σημεῖον) of manna falling from heaven as a testimony (μαρτυρία). Cf. also Josephus, *C. Ap.* 2.53.

[61] Cf. BORGEN, *Early Christianity*, 217.

confirming one reading of the biblical text against an alternative one,[62] Philo makes a distinction between God's own testimony and the witness of the divine word, which in the context of *Leg.* 3.207 is characterized as "the interpreting word" (τοῦ ἑρμησέως λόγου), accredited to human beings:

Moses too, let us observe, filled with wonder at the transcendency of the Uncreate, says, "and thou shalt swear by His name" [Deut. vi. 13], not "by Him," for it is enough for the created being that he should be accredited and have witness borne to him by the Divine word; but let God be His own most sure guarantee and evidence.

Moreover, in *Leg.* 3.162 there is a close parallel to John 5:39. There the transitional formulation with the verb μαρτυρέω is the key word: "That the food of the soul is not earthly but heavenly, we shall find abundant evidence in the Sacred Word (μαρτυρήσει διὰ πλειόνων ὁ ἱερὸς λόγος)." Thus, there is here a correspondence to the idea in John 5:39 that the "Scriptures" bear witness to Jesus, who, according to John 6:31–58, is "the bread of life" which came down from heaven.

Conclusion

The following points can summarize the observations of this study:

1. The parallel material in Philo, *Leg.* 3.205–208 provides documentation for the view that the controversy on self-testimony reflected in John 5:31–40 and 8:12–20 is a specifically "Christian" version of a discussion, which most probably also has existed among Jews in Alexandria.

2. The controversy reflected in John (John 8:12–20) and Philo (*Leg.* 3.205–208) follows the structure of a dialogue, including the form of "questions and answers". Philo's writings in general make it evident that the use of such a form is appropriate when John reports from a learned setting within Judaism, such as from the teaching activity that took place in the synagogues and in the temple courts.

3. In particular, the view represented by Philo, viz. that only God was capable of giving a self-authenticating testimony, may illuminate the Jewish background of the point made by the Evangelist that Jesus could testify in his own case because of his divine origin.

4. It is my proposal that the kind of a self-authentic witness by God and the reasoning behind it, which is documented by Philo, provides a further referential background for the statement in John 5:37–38. Thus, the words of John 5:37b state the reason for God's self-testimony by emphasizing the

---

[62] Cf. BORGEN, *Philo of Alexandria*, 155. Philo's use of this method (cf. e.g., *Migr.* 1 and 43) has parallels in examples found in rabbinic exegesis such as *Mek.* (Exod 15:11), and also in the New Testament, Gal 3:16.

principle of God's transcendency, viz. that the "form" and voice of God are not immediately accessible. Hence, other ways in which one might have expected God to witness are ruled out.

5. According to John 8:14 Jesus takes up God's role as an exception to the rule that no one can witness in his own case. The reason is then stated as an epistemological argument in terms of *knowing* where Jesus has *come from* and where he is *going*. In correspondence to John 8:14, Philo refers in *Leg.* 3.205–206 to the esoteric *knowledge* of God with regard to his essence, quality, state, and *movement* as the reason why God can testify to himself.

6. In John, the idea seems to be presupposed that God testifies to himself and his own works when it is stated that the "works" of Jesus testify to his divine origin. In Philo, *Leg.* 3.207, the idea is expressed that God testifies to himself and also to his own "deeds". Philo wrote: "God alone therefore is the strongest security first for Himself, and in the next place for His *deeds* also …"

7. In *Leg.* 3.208 the distinction is made between God's own testimony and the witness of the divine word given to human beings. Thus, we find here an analogy to the idea in John 5:39, that the "Scriptures" bear witness to the "Jews" about Jesus, who is the source of the life for which the "Jews" are searching. According to John, the learned study of the "Jews" and the testimony of the "Scriptures" seem to be in vain, since they refuse to believe in Jesus. Such observations support the conclusion that both Philo and John distinguish between testimonies at the divine level and testimonies accredited at a human level. According to John, both these levels of testimony attest to the "identity" of Jesus.

8. Since the "Nordic New Testament Conference 2007" has paid special attention to perspectives related to the formative forces of the identity of early Christians, an aspect of my study has been to focus on how a controversy about the biblical laws of testimony within Early Judaism might have contributed to the formation of a "high Christology" as part of the controversy between Early Judaism and the emerging Christian communities at the end of the first century A.D. In the Gospel of John, the distinction between the human and earthly level, on the one hand, and the divine and heavenly level, on the other hand, is apparent in the conflicts between Jesus and his interlocutors. Within the structure of the Fourth Gospel, the forensic and human and divine aspects involved in such debates might be explained and used in favor of the gospel about Jesus. Therefore, various forensic topics, such as the Law, the witnesses, the role of judgment, the healing works of Jesus, the claim of equality with God and so on are ambiguous motifs when they are seen from either a human or a divine level respectively. The motifs that served as accusations against Jesus at the

earthly level and within the jurisdiction of an earthly halakhah speak in favor of him when seen from the divine level and within the jurisdiction of a heavenly halakhah. In this way, the forensic issues, such as God's self-authenticating witness, the Law and the Scriptures become points of departure for the way in which John presents the gospel about Jesus. According to John, Jesus' adversaries are placed at the earthly and human level and they misunderstand the divine and heavenly relationships involved in the teaching and the activities of Jesus. Thus, from the position of Jesus' adversaries the case, the procedure, and the legal trial against Jesus, which led to his punishment as a crucified criminal seemed to be appropriate. However, from the perspective of the divine and heavenly jurisdiction, the account of the crimes – and the legal trial – and the punishment of Jesus were reinterpreted by John in order to become the gospel about Jesus as the Son of God. Thus, the Johannine forensic conflicts clarify the sense in which Jesus was for a certain circle of believers "equal to God."

Rituals of (Ex-)Communication and Identity:
1 Cor 5 and 4Q266 11; 4Q270 7

Tobias Hägerland

Paul provides us with the earliest evidence for a specific act of excommunication – the temporary exclusion or definitive expulsion of a deviant member – in Christianity. In the present study, the ritual of excommunication presupposed in 1 Cor 5:1–13 will be reconsidered in light of the Qumran material on exclusions and expulsions, especially 4Q266 11 and 4Q270 7, which present us with the most detailed description of how the rituals of expulsion were ideally carried out among the Qumranites. On the basis of this comparison, and with parallels from common (non-sectarian) early Judaism and primitive Christianity taken into due consideration, I will suggest that the ritual of 1 Cor 5 articulates and cultivates Paul's self-understanding and also reinforces certain aspects of the identity of the addressees.

Scholars have long since juxtaposed 1 Cor 5 with Qumran texts, noticing both commonalities and differences.[1] Heinz-Wolfgang Kuhn's contribution to the second meeting of the IOQS in 1995 is the most detailed treatment so far, providing an excellent list of parallels between 1 Cor 5 and passages from the scrolls. Kuhn concludes that these parallels are not extensive enough to presume a direct relationship between Qumran and Paul.[2] With the publication in 1996 of the *editio princeps* of a number of Cave 4 mss of the Damascus Document,[3] material that adds considerably to our knowledge of the details of the expulsion ritual at Qumran was made available in reliable transcription. Among these fragmentarily pre-

---

[1] Göran FORKMAN, *The Limits of the Religious Community: Expulsion from the Religious Community within the Qumran Sect, within Rabbinic Judaism, and within Primitive Christianity* (CBNTS 5; Lund: Gleerup, 1972); Adela Yarbro Collins, "The Function of 'Excommunication' in Paul", *HTR* 73 (1980): 251–63 (261–63).

[2] Heinz-Wolfgang KUHN, "A Legal Issue in 1 Corinthians 5 and in Qumran", in *Legal Texts and Legal Issues: Proceedings of the Second Meeting of the International Organization for Qumran Studies*, Cambridge, 1995 (ed. M. Bernstein, F. García Martínez, and J. Kampen; STDJ 23; Leiden: Brill, 1997), 489–99.

[3] Joseph M. BAUMGARTEN, *Qumran Cave 4.XVIII: The Damascus Document (4Q266–273)* (DJD XVIII; Oxford: Clarendon Press, 1996).

served copies are 4Q266 and 4Q270, which contain slightly different descriptions of this ritual. At the time when Göran Forkman authored his monograph on expulsions in Qumran, rabbinic Judaism and primitive Christianity, only vague ideas circulated concerning the contents of these texts.[4] Kuhn made use of photographs of the mss[5] as well as of the preliminary edition of the texts,[6] but some remarkable parallels in wording and contents seem nevertheless to have gone unnoticed. This calls for yet another investigation.

Analysis and comparison of the Pauline and Qumranite texts constitute the first part of this study. In the second part, the identity-shaping function of the ritual envisaged by Paul will be the focus of interest. Here two questions will be asked and answered. First, what can be said of the identity of the church expected to approve of the ritual and to participate actively therein? Secondly, what understanding of his own mission and relationship to the Corinthian church does Paul convey through prescribing this ritual? As will be shown, the identities underpinned by the Pauline ritual exhibit both affinities with and traits distinctive from those at Qumran.

1 Cor 5 and 4Q266 11; 4Q270 7

The Qumran fragments pertaining to the ritual of expulsion, understood as the formal and permanent dismissal of a deviant member,[7] are partly overlapping. Only 4Q270 preserves the heading that separates the order of expulsion from the penal code which precedes it.[8] It is also in this fragment that mention of the first step to be taken in case of a violation, that is to inform the "priest appointed over the many", is extant. Both fragments contain a short catena of scriptural quotations to legitimize the penalties to be inflicted on those who sin inadvertently. After the declaration that anyone who purposely rebels against the statutes cannot remain in the community, 4Q270 breaks off, and the main part of the ritual is preserved only in 4Q266. The ritual consists of an anamnetic prayer said by the priest, the

---

[4] See FORKMAN, *The Limits of the Religious Community*, 40, 84 n. 100.

[5] See KUHN, "A Legal Issue", 499.

[6] Ben Zion WACHHOLDER and Martin G. ABEGG, *A Preliminary Edition of the Unpublished Dead Sea Scrolls: The Hebrew and Aramaic Texts from Cave Four* (4 vols.; Washington: Biblical Archaeology Society, 1991–96), 1:21–22, 45–47. See KUHN, "A Legal Issue", 490 n. 4.

[7] Aharon SHEMESH, "Expulsion and Exclusion in the Community Rule and the Damascus Document", *DSD* 9 (2002): 44–74.

[8] 4Q270 7 I, 1–15 = 4Q266 10 I, 14–II, 1 = 4Q267 9 VI = CD XIV, 18–22; cf. 1QS VI, 24–VII, 25.

departure of the dissenter and his associates, and the ratification of the verdict in writing by the *mebaqqer*. Finally, 4Q266 stipulates a general assembly in the third month to curse anyone who deviates from the Law, and this was apparently also the original reading of the severely damaged second column of 4Q270 7.

Paul's instructions on how to deal with a member of the Corinthian church who is leading a sexually immoral life suggest a ritual[9] that corresponds to the Qumran order of expulsion at several points. Since the two rituals exhibit a remarkably similar structure, it will be convenient to comment on their components in the sequence of 1 Cor 5, from which the Qumran order seldom departs. A table of agreements between the rituals appears on the next page.

(a) Report (1 Cor 5:1)

An instance of unacceptable behaviour has been reported to Paul, evidently by word of mouth, as implied by the circumlocutionary "it is heard" (cf. 1:11; 11:18; contrast 7:1). The charge is fornication; specifically, a man is cohabiting with his father's wife, in violation of Jewish and Roman law.

The Qumran ritual stipulates that the "priest appointed over the many" is similarly to be informed in order that the one to be disciplined should receive his judgement (4Q270 7 I, 16), seemingly after the juridical process of rebuke before witnesses, frequently mentioned elsewhere,[10] has been completed. As the text is damaged, we do not know for certain who is expected to inform the priest,[11] but the report would certainly include a statement of what kind of crime had been committed. Sexual immorality, albeit not of the specific sort that Paul mentions, is listed in the penal code as warranting expulsion from the community: "He who approaches his wife for fornication, not in accordance with the rule, shall depart and never return" (4Q270 7 I, 12–13).

---

[9] Evan M. ZUESSE, "Ritual", *ER* 12:405–22 (405), provides a definition of 'ritual' useful for my purpose: "those conscious and voluntary, repetitious and stylized symbolic bodily actions that are centered on cosmic structures and/or sacred presences". Paul's assumption that the Corinthians will understand without further explanation what is meant by "handing someone over to Satan" indicates that they have previously been instructed about, and perhaps even performed, this action. It could therefore be added to the selection of "given elements of a sacred tradition or order" listed by Bengt HOLMBERG, *Paul and Power: The Structure of Authority in the Primitive Church as Reflected in the Pauline Epistles* (CBNTS 11; Lund: Gleerup, 1978), 186.

[10] 1QS V, 24–VI, 1; IX, 17–19; CD VII, 2–3; IX, 2–8, 16–18; XX, 4–5; cf. 4Q477.

[11] BAUMGARTEN, *Qumran Cave 4.XVIII*, 163, hesitatingly proposes a restoration of the first word in 4Q270 7 I, 16 as יתיסר. This would indicate that the one liable to penalty should report himself (ידע Hiphil) to the priest.

Table 1: Synopsis of 1 Cor 5 and 4Q266 11; 4Q270 7

1 Cor 5 (NRSV)	4Q266 11; 4Q270 7 (DSSSE2)
	[And these are the reg]ulations by which [shall be ruled] all those disciplined (4Q270 7 I, 15)
(a) Report	
It is actually reported (5:1)	everyone who [...] shall enter and inform the priest [who is appo]inted ov[er the Many] (4Q270 7 I, 15–16)
that there is sexual immorality among you (5:1)	(cf. 4Q270 7 I, 12–13)
(b) Repentance	
And you are arrogant! Should you not rather have mourned (5:2)	and in ano[ther place it is written:] "Tear your heart and not your clothes" and it is writt[en: "to return to God in tears and in fasting"] (4Q270 7 I, 18–19; cf. 4Q266 11 4–5)
(c) Judgement	
so that he who has done this would have been removed from among you? (5:2) I have already pronounced judgement ... on the man who has done such a thing (5:3)	In rebellion, he will be expelled from the presence of the Many (4Q266 11 7–8) And his sentence will be written down by the Inspector's hand, as an engraving, and his judgment will be complete (4Q266 11 16)
(d) Assembly	
When you are assembled (5:4)	And all [those who dwell in] the camps will assemble in the third month (4Q266 11 16–17 = 4Q270 7 II, 11)
you are to hand this man over to Satan for the destruction of the flesh (5:5)	and will curse whoever tends to the right [or to the left of the] law (4Q266 11 17–18 = 4Q270 7 II, 11–12)
(e) Consequence	
now I am writing to you not to associate with ... Do not even eat with such a one (5:11)	And the one who has been expelled will leave, and the man who eats from his riches, and the one who seeks his peace, and the one who is agreement with him (4Q266 11 14–15)

(b) Repentance (1 Cor 5:2)

Paul proceeds to accuse his addressees of being "inflated", when instead they should have "mourned". The choice of vocabulary is likely to express the sentiment that the Corinthians should have repented for the fornicator's sin, since the entire church shares in the guilt of its individual members.[12] In addition to this, they should have expelled the sinner.

In the corresponding place, the Qumran ritual also mentions repentance, but it must be pointed out that its function differs from that which Paul envisages. The scriptural quotations in 4Q266 11 2–5 = 4Q270 7 I, 17–19 apply to those who sin unintentionally and thus are willing to make amends for their transgression; such members of the community will accept their penalty as an act of repentance and as a substitute for the atoning sacrifices ordained by the Law,[13] and they are not expelled from the community. Only the one who commits a sin grave enough to show his complete disregard for the fundamental values of the community should be expelled.[14]

The notion of corporate culpability and repentance is not at all foreign to Qumran. In the order of the annual ritual for renewing the covenant prescribed by the Rule of the Community, a conventional penitential prayer[15] is recited by all prior to the cursing of those who despise the regulations of the covenant; as will be made clear below, this ceremony actually constitutes the completion of the expulsion ritual. Yet, this kind of communal repentance is not referred to in 4Q266 or 4Q270.

(c) Judgement (1 Cor 5:2–3)

As Paul again shifts the centre of interest, from the church's failure to deal appropriately with the problem to the fornicator himself, he immediately pronounces the sentence: the deviant member should be "removed from your midst" (5:2). This verdict, dressed in language closely paralleled in

---

[12] Brian S. ROSNER, "'Οὐχὶ μᾶλλον ἐπενθήσατε': Corporate Responsibility in 1 Corinthians 5", *NTS* 38 (1992): 470–73; Brian S. ROSNER, *Paul, Scripture and Ethics: A Study of 1 Corinthians 5–7* (AGJU 22; Leiden: Brill, 1994).

[13] SHEMESH, "Expulsion and Exclusion", 61–62.

[14] 4Q266 11 5–8 = 4Q270 7 I, 19–21; 4Q267 9 VI, 1–2 = 4Q270 7 I, 11; 4Q270 7 I, 7, 12–14; cf. 1QS VII, 16–17.

[15] 1QS I, 24–II, 1. See Rodney Alan WERLINE, *Penitential Prayer in Second Temple Judaism: The Development of a Religious Institution* (SBLEJL 13; Atlanta: Scholars Press, 1998), 135–38.

Qumran,[16] is then explained by Paul as the outcome of his already pronounced judgement of the offender (5:3; cf. 5:12–13).

In a similar vein, 4Q266 11 5–7 declares that anyone who refuses to
conform to the disciplinary system will be expelled "from the presence of
the Many". At the core of the ritual is the priestly prayer, which is formally
a blessing of the Deity, but which also refers to the curses inflicted on
those who transgress the boundaries set by the Law (9–14). After this, the
one who is being expelled departs (14). It is possible to take the subsequent enumeration of people, who hypothetically maintain good relations
with the expelled member (14–15), as the introduction of a new sentence,
thus making the *mebaqqer*'s writing down of the offence or the verdict
(16) concern the disloyal acts of these associates.[17] A construal that takes
the listing of associates as a continuation of the reference to departure, so
that the offence or verdict written down is that of the original offender is
however equally possible.[18] The latter alternative seems preferable, as the
notification in writing is said to complete the judgement.

A reading of 1 Cor 5:2–3 in comparison with this part of the Qumran
ritual reveals two similarities beside the obvious fact that both texts concern the expulsion of an errant member. First, the juridical and definitive
character of the decision is emphasized in both cases: Paul's irrevocable "I
have already judged" should be seen to parallel "his judgement is complete" in 4Q266. Secondly, in both texts the verdict is ratified in writing.
By contrast, Paul makes no reference to any prayer of the kind recorded in
the Qumran text.

(d) Assembly (1 Cor 5:4–5)

Now Paul states more directly the contents of his judgement: when the
Corinthian church is assembled, together with Paul's spirit and the power
of Jesus, they should hand over the fornicator to Satan. Leaving the question of Paul's spiritual presence for later, it is now sufficient to notice that
this handing over will take place when the Corinthian believers have assembled for worship. That a reference to the liturgical assembly is meant is

---

[16] 1QS II, 16; noted by KUHN, "A Legal Issue", 494.

[17] BAUMGARTEN, *Qumran Cave 4.XVIII*, 77, translates: "the one being expelled shall
depart. Anyone who eats from that which belongs to him, or who inquires about his wel-
fare, or derives benefit from him, shall have his action inscribed…".

[18] Florentino GARCÍA MARTÍNEZ and Eibert J. C. TIGCHELAAR, *The Dead Sea Scrolls
Study Edition* (paperback ed.; 2 vols.; Leiden: Brill, 2000), 1:597, translate: "And the one
who has been expelled will leave, and the man who eats from his riches, and the one who
seeks his peace, and the one who is agreement [sic] with him. And his sentence will be
written down…".

clear not only from the frequent use of συνάγεσθαι in this sense,[19] but also from the close affinities between this passage and Matt 18:20.[20] But what does it mean to hand somebody over to Satan? Needless to say, it involves the expulsion of the offender from the church, but it seems also to be a reference to the pronouncement of a curse that places the person actively in the diabolic realm.

That the expression can be construed as a curse formula was first observed by Adolf Deissmann on the basis of a magical papyrus.[21] Such an interpretation fits the wider context of Paul's letters quite well: these certainly alienate deviant members by anathematising them, that is, by excluding them, not only from the church, but also from all fellowship with Christ himself,[22] and this practice seems to be reflected also in 1 Cor 5:5. If the phrase 'in the name of the Lord Jesus' is taken to qualify 'hand over', it would seem to suggest that the curse was pronounced under the invocation of Jesus' name.[23] This is however far from evident. The convoluted syntax of 5:3–5 precludes any certainty,[24] and moreover there is no evidence either in Paul or in the rest of first-century Christian literature that Jesus' name was used for the purpose of cursing; this calls for restraint in attempting to reconstruct the shape of the curse. Nor should Paul's expression "destruction of the flesh" (5:5) be over-interpreted to mean that the expelled sinner would die as a result of the curse pronounced on him. James South has argued convincingly that Paul can hardly have expected the immediate death of the fornicator to result from his being handed over to Satan;[25] but South has not thereby disproved the involvement of a curse. There are curses entailing illness that does not necessarily culminate in death (2 Kgs 5:27), and for Paul, to be separated from Christ in a general sense certainly amounts to being accursed (Rom 9:3).

---

[19] Acts 4:31; 11:26; 13:44; 20:7, 8; *Did.* 14:1; 16:2; *1 Clem.* 34:7; *Mart. Pol.* 18:3.

[20] Matt 18:20 and 1 Cor 5:4 concern the topic of excommunication, employ συνάγεσθαι to refer to the liturgical assembly (for which Paul elsewhere uses συνέρχεσθαι; 1 Cor 11:17, 18, 20, 33, 34; 14:23, 26), and guarantee Jesus' presence among those assembled ("in his name" – certainly so in Matthew and possibly in Paul).

[21] PGM V. 335–36. See Adolf DEISSMANN, *Licht vom Osten: Das Neue Testament und die neuentdeckten Texte der hellenistisch-römischen Welt* (4th ed.; Tübingen: Mohr Siebeck, 1923), 256–57.

[22] Gal 1:8–9 (see Hans Dieter BETZ, *Galatians: A Commentary on Paul's Letter to the Churches in Galatia* [Minneapolis: Fortress, 1979], 320–21); 1 Cor 16:22; cf. Rom 9:3.

[23] FORKMAN, *The Limits of the Religious Community*, 142, draws attention to 4 Kgdms 2:24 (κατηράσατο ... ἐν ὀνόματι κυρίου).

[24] See Anthony C. THISELTON, *The First Epistle to the Corinthians* (NIGTC; Grand Rapids: Eerdmans, 2000), 393–94.

[25] James T. SOUTH, "A Critique of the 'Curse/Death' Interpretation of 1 Corinthians 5.1–8", *NTS* 39 (1993): 539–61.

Turning again to Qumran, an assembly is required here also for the purpose of cursing those who have been expelled, after the completion of the juridical process: "All the inhabitants of the camps shall assemble (יקהלו) in the third month and curse (ואררו) the one who turns to the right or to the left from the Law" (4Q266 11 16–18 = 4Q270 7 II, 11–12). The assembly referred to is the liturgy for the renewal of the covenant described in the Rule of the Community. During that liturgy, the priests and Levites pronounce, on behalf of the entire community, terrible curses on those who have entered the covenant but failed to comply with its regulations.[26] Thereby the community accomplishes its ambition to "confirm" or "fulfil" the divine curses,[27] which is expressed in the priestly prayer in conjunction with expulsion (4Q266 11 14); the expelled person now belongs to the realm of Belial, for "all the saints of the Most High have cursed him" (CD XX, 8).

The parallels with 1 Cor 5 are obvious. In Qumran as well as in Corinth, an assembly will take place in order to curse an expelled member whose judgement has already been completed. The very verb employed by Paul (συνάγεσθαι) is, in fact, one of those used in LXX to render קהל.[28] This insight, combined with the Qumranite-Pauline parallels in vocabulary already listed by Kuhn, such as the mention of destruction at the hand of Belial/Satan,[29] invites us to reconsider the nature of the relationship between these texts.

(e) Consequence (1 Cor 5:11)

Paul's directives concerning the formal expulsion of the fornicator are followed by a theological justification of the practice (5:6–8) and a clarification prompted by earlier correspondence between Paul and the Corinthians (5:9–13). In the latter passage, Paul spells out the social ostracism intended to follow on the ritual of excommunication, as he commands his addressees not to "associate with" (συναναμίγνυσθαι) and not to eat with these people. This is consonant with his admonition to the believers at Thessalonica to withdraw from, and not to "associate with" (συναναμίγνυσθαι) any member who does not comply with his halakhic tradition (2 Thess 3:6, 14).

---

[26] 1QS II, 1–18. See Russell C. D. ARNOLD, *The Social Role of Liturgy in the Religion of the Qumran Community* (STDJ 60; Leiden: Brill, 2006), 67–69.

[27] For this translation of קום Hiphil, see SHEMESH, "Expulsion and Exclusion", 47.

[28] קהל Niphal is rendered with συνάγεσθαι in Esth 9:15, 16, 18; Ezek 38:7; cf. ἐπισυνάγεσθαι in 2 Chr 20:26; קהל Hiphil is rendered with συνάγειν in Num 1:18; 8:9; 10:7; Ezek 38:13. This parallel seems to have been overlooked by KUHN; cf. "A Legal Issue", 494, 497.

[29] 1QS II, 6, 14, 15; CD VIII, 2; XIX, 14. See KUHN, "A Legal Issue", 494–95, 498.

In like manner, 4Q266 11 14–15 stipulates that anyone sympathetic to an expelled member will share in his punishment. To some extent, the three ways of associating with him agree with what Paul writes, in substance though not in wording: "he who eats from his belongings,[30] the one who seeks his peace,[31] and the one who consents with him".[32] But the function of the listing in 4Q266 is again somewhat different from its parallel in 1 Cor 5: whereas the Qumran text lays down a ruling that anyone who maintains good relations with an expelled member will himself have to leave the community, Paul is content to instruct the Corinthians not to associate with false brethren without any threat of excommunication levelled at those who might fail to heed his command. In this respect, the Pauline text actually comes closer to CD XX, 7–8, "a person should not consent with him[33] in belongings or labour, for all the saints of the Most High have cursed him".

Evaluation of the Parallels

The comparative analysis of 1 Cor 5 and 4Q266 11; 4Q270 7 has brought to light both similarities and differences. Among the differences to be noted, the distinctive features of Paul's and Jesus' spiritual presence being bracketed out for the moment, are the following: varying functions of repentance, lack of a Pauline counterpart to the Qumranite priestly prayer, and varying functions of the injunctions against associating with those expelled. On the side of similarities, in addition to those already listed by Kuhn, the following seem to be significant: the emphasis put on the definitive character of the judgement, the ratification of the sentence in writing, and above all the instruction to hold a liturgical assembly for the purpose of cursing the already judged and expelled member.

Let us now return to Kuhn's view of the relationship between Qumran and 1 Cor 5. He identifies Paul's use of the terms "destruction" and "spirit" in 5:5 as the strongest parallels to the scrolls, but concludes that these are not sufficient to demonstrate "a direct relationship". Instead,

---

[30] Cf. 1QS VII, 16; VIII, 17; CD IX, 21; 4Q270 7 I, 6.

[31] ידרוש שלומו. Sometimes taken to mean 'greets him' (see 2 John 10–11); cf., however, J. Duncan M. DERRETT, "The Reprobate's Peace: 4QDᵃ (4Q266) (18 v 14-16)", in *Legal Texts and Legal Issues: Proceedings of the Second Meeting of the International Organization for Qumran Studies*, Cambridge, 1995 (ed. M. Bernstein, F. García Martínez, and J. Kampen; STDJ 23; Leiden: Brill, 1997), 245–49 (247).

[32] יאות עמו (see n. 33 below). Cf. 1QS VII, 24–25; VIII, 23–24 (both יתערב); noted by KUHN, "A Legal Issue", 499. In LXX, ערב Hitpael may be rendered with μίγνυσθαι (4 Kgdms 18:23; Ps 105[106]:35; Isa 36:8) and ἐπιμείγνυσθαι (Prov 14:10).

[33] אל יאות איש עמו. In LXX, אות Niphal is rendered with ὁμοιοῦσθαι (Gen 34:15, 22, 23) and συμφωνεῖν (4 Kgdms 12:9).

Kuhn argues, a similar sociological situation and a shared Jewish heritage can account for the parallels.[34] However, whereas the development of ex-communication rituals among the Qumranites and the primitive Christians could in principle be credited to the sectarian character of these groups, it is difficult to see how some of the similarities in the details can be derived from a common dependency on the scriptures and on early Jewish tradi-tions. This holds true especially for the practice of assembling for the pur-pose of cursing the person being excommunicated, of which there is no mention either in the pertinent passages of Deuteronomy or in the (admit-tedly few) early Jewish texts, other than in those from Qumran, concerning expulsion. It is referred to only in the scrolls and in 1 Cor 5, and in very similar language.

Another solution therefore seems preferable. In an earlier article, Kuhn listed the "top ten" passages in Paul's letters which have parallels in the scrolls. He found here a real influence of notions and terminology from Qumran on Paul, and he concluded that "Paul must have had some contact [with Qumran theology], whether it was direct or, more probably, indirect before the 50s C.E.".[35] Influxes from Qumran into the Pauline letters can thus be considered "indirect", not in the sense that the similarities are due merely to a common background and to a sectarian orientation, but in the sense that they reached Paul through intermediaries. It seems most natural to assign also the contours of an excommunication ritual to this category of "indirect" influences from Qumran.

Identities Expressed by the Pauline Ritual

As the first part of this study has demonstrated, the rituals of expulsion in Qumran and 1 Cor 5 have several characteristics in common. In this sec-ond part, it will be shown that these features serve to express and reinforce aspects of an identity shared, to a large extent, by the Qumranites and Paul. However, attention will also be drawn to some elements in the Pauline rit-ual that are unparalleled in the scrolls and thus appear to establish a dis-tinctive set of identities.

It goes without saying that we cannot know if the historical Corinthian believers understood themselves along the lines that Paul wanted. Accord-ingly, the identity of the church, which will be dealt with first, is simply

---

[34] Kuhn, "A Legal Issue", 495–96.

[35] Heinz-Wolfgang Kuhn, "The Impact of the Qumran Scrolls on the Understanding of Paul", in *The Dead Sea Scrolls: Forty Years of Research* (ed. D. Dimant and U. Rap-paport; STDJ 10; Leiden: Brill, 1992), 327–39 (336).

the identity suggested for the Corinthians by Paul in 1 Cor 5. Subsequently the identity of Paul himself will be considered.

The Identity of the Church

Paul's understanding of the church, as it is expressed in the excommunication ritual, agrees with the Qumranite self-understanding on a fundamental point: the community and God's realm are fully identical. Expulsion entails separation from all spiritual life; outside of the community rules Belial and there is no forgiveness of sins but only utter destruction. This exclusivist mentality is expressed also in the expulsion practices of nonsectarian early Judaism discussed in detail by William Horbury,[36] but it is strongly emphasised in the Qumranite and Pauline rituals through the inclusion of active cursing in a context of worship. At the annual renewal of the covenant at Qumran, the curse pronounced by the Levites on "all men of Belial's lot" would include the imprecation "may (God) not forgive by atoning for your sins" (1QS II, 7). The priests would also join them in saying the curse that completes the expulsion ritual; God is invoked to "separate" these ex-members and anyone who might enter the community with insincerity, "for evil, so that he may be cut off from among all sons of light".[37] Physical death becomes a point of marginal interest in this perspective. While the Damascus Document prescribes capital punishment for some serious offences,[38] there are indications that the Qumranites were normally reluctant to execute fellow members[39] and deemed expulsion from the community to be a sufficient punishment, entailing both divine wrath and social ostracism.[40] By performing the ritual of excommunication, the members of the Corinthian church would uphold an identity substantially in agreement with that of the Qumran community, but also repre-

---

[36] William HORBURY, "Extirpation and Excommunication", *VT* 35 (1985): 13–38. As Horbury remarks (19–20), already Ezra-Nehemiah (Ezra 10:8 = 1 Esd 9:4; Neh 13:1–3) testify to expulsion being motivated through a combined reading of Deut 23:2–9; 29:20. Thus expulsion equals the blotting out of names and the evil things promised in Deut 29:19–20.

[37] 1QS II, 11–18; cf. Deut 29:19–20. See also CD VIII, 1–3.

[38] CD IX, 1, 6, 17; X, 1; XII, 3; XV, 4–5. See FORKMAN, *The Limits of the Religious Community*, 646–5.

[39] CD XII, 3–6. 1QS III, 5–6; CD VIII, 1–3; XIX, 13–14 do not appear to be expecting those under the curses to meet physical death rapidly.

[40] Gerald HARRIS, "The Beginnings of Church Discipline: 1 Corinthians 5", *NTS* 37 (1991): 1–21 (16–17), points out the dire social consequences of expulsion. Josephus, *B.J.* 2.143 mentions that an Essene expulsion could in itself result in death from starvation, although this effect would not have been primarily intended and seems even to have been undesired.

sented in common Judaism of the period and in other quarters of primitive Christianity:[41] the identity of belonging to the elect group, to the exclusive sphere of God.

Another common denominator is the shared ambition of the Qumran community and the Pauline church to maintain the purity and holiness of the collective. Association with an expelled member, especially commensality, is expressly prohibited. Neither the Qumranites nor the Corinthians are to be motivated primarily by the prospect that an errant member might repent and adapt to the standards of the community, although this may occasionally have been a secondary result,[42] but by zeal for the preservation of the holiness and sinlessness of the congregation. A deviant member of the Qumran community, which views itself as the true temple,[43] should be rebuked before witnesses, lest those who observed the breach should be partakers of his guilt; those who rebuke thus dissociate themselves from his sin, rather than attempting to bring him back to repentance.[44] In a similar vein, Paul expresses no concern for the fornicator but emphasizes the need for the Corinthians to have the evil person removed from their midst in order to purify themselves from the element that will otherwise infect them all.[45] This is so important because, as Paul points out in 1 Cor 3:16–17, the church is the holy temple of God, in which his Spirit dwells.[46] Again, the performers of the Pauline ritual would reinforce an aspect of identity which, although extant in broader Judaism,[47] is accentuated in Qumran and primitive Christianity:[48] that of belonging to a community

---

[41] 1 John 1:3, 6–7; 2:9–11; 3:14; 4:11–13. See Bernhard POSCHMANN, *Paenitentia secunda: Die kirchliche Buße im ältesten Christentum bis Cyprian und Origenes: Eine dogmengeschichtliche Untersuchung* (Theophaneia 1; Bonn: Hanstein, 1940), 65–66.

[42] Josephus, B.J. 2.143–144 mentions this as an occasional outcome of expulsions from among the Essenes.

[43] Bertil GÄRTNER, *The Temple and the Community in Qumran and the New Testament: A Comparative Study in the Temple Symbolism of the Qumran Texts and the New Testament* (SNTSMS 1; Cambridge: Cambridge University Press, 1965), 16–46.

[44] Florentino GARCÍA MARTÍNEZ, "La reprensión fraterna en Qumrán y Mt 18,15–17", *FilNeot* 2 (1989): 23–40.

[45] Barth CAMPBELL, "Flesh and Spirit in 1 Cor 5:5: An Exercise in Rhetorical Criticism of the NT", *JETS* 36 (1993): 331–42, argues convincingly that "the spirit" in 1 Cor 5:5 is not the fornicator's spirit, but the "spirit of the church". In 1 Tim 1:20, "handing over to Satan" has become a means of bringing deviant members to repentance, but this is likely a literary imitation of Paul's authentic voice (FORKMAN, *The Limits of the Religious Community*, 183).

[46] COLLINS, "The Function of 'Excommunication'", 259–60; ROSNER, *Paul, Scripture and Ethics*, 73–80.

[47] HORBURY, "Extirpation and Excommunication", 23, 25–30.

[48] See Eph 5:11; 1 Tim 5:20–22; 2 John 11.

which strictly maintains its moral purity by shunning those who do not comply with its standards.

There is one vital point at which the identity of the Corinthian Christians, as expressed in the Pauline ritual of excommunication, differs from that of the Qumranites, namely the conviction that they live in the messianic age. The people of Qumran also sensed strongly that the end of the ages was close at hand, but they were still looking forward to the coming of the Anointed One(s).[49] According to several passages in the scrolls, the Qumran community will, in the "latter days", have to be perfectly pure, since angels will then be present in the congregation.[50] Study of liturgical texts has shown that the community thought of itself as united with the angels in worship,[51] but there is no evidence that the Qumranites recognized an angelic presence with legal implications in the age in which it was presently living.[52] By contrast, Paul seeks to regulate the behaviour of Corinthian women by referring to the presence of angels,[53] and the excommunication ritual gains its force from the presence of an even more exalted spiritual being, the heavenly Jesus himself, in the assembly. His presence guarantees that the sinner is handed over to Satan in accordance with the divine will (cf. Matt 18:18–20), but it also signifies that the messianic age has commenced. No such notion of angelic or divine proximity can be found in the Qumran texts concerning expulsion, unless "the saints of the Most High" said to have cursed an expelled member (CD XX, 8) are angels. This cannot be excluded with absolute certainty, but the fact that none of the other texts that mention the curses (4Q266 11 16–18 = 4Q270

---

[49] 1QS IX, 11; CD XII, 23–XIII, 1; XIV, 19 (= 4Q266 10 I, 12); XIX, 10–11; XX, 1. See Johannes ZIMMERMANN, *Messianische Texte aus Qumran: Königliche, priesterliche und prophetische Messiasvorstellungen in den Schriftfunden von Qumran* (WUNT 2. Reihe 104; Tübingen: Mohr Siebeck, 1998).

[50] 1Q28a II, 3–10; 1QM VII, 4–7; CD XV, 15–17 = 4Q266 8 I, 9; cf. 4Q285 1 9 = 11Q14 1 II, 14–15. See Lawrence H. SCHIFFMAN, "Purity and Perfection: Exclusion from the Council of the Community in the Serekh Ha-'Edah", in *Biblical Archaeology Today: Proceedings of the International Congress on Biblical Archaeology, Jerusalem, April 1984* (ed. J. Amitai; Jerusalem: Israel Exploration Society, 1985), 373–89.

[51] Björn FRENNESSON, *"In a Common Rejoicing": Liturgical Communion with Angels in Qumran* (AUUSSU 14; Uppsala: Uppsala University, 1999); Esther G. CHAZON, "Liturgical Communion with the Angels at Qumran", in *Sapiential, Liturgical and Poetical Texts from Qumran: Proceedings of the Third Meeting of the International Organization for Qumran Studies, Oslo, 1998* (ed. D. K. Falk, F. García Martínez, and E. M. Schuller; STDJ 35; Leiden: Brill, 2000), 95–105.

[52] E. P. SANDERS, *Judaism: Practice and Belief 63 BCE – 66 CE* (London: SCM, 1992), 372.

[53] 1 Cor 11:10. See Joseph A. FITZMYER, "A Feature of Qumrân Angelology and the Angels of 1 Cor. XI.10", *NTS* 4 (1957): 48–58.

7 II, 11–12; 1QS II, 11–18) indicate that angels are involved speaks for seeing in the expression a designation of the members of the community.[54] The Pauline ritual expresses a distinctive trait of the church's identity as compared to that of the Qumranites: its members would conceive of themselves as already living in the messianic age and they would allow this condition to guide their handling of legal cases in the present.

The Identity of Paul

At Qumran the *mebaqqer*, by noting down the crime or verdict of the offender,[55] brings his judgement to completion. For the Corinthian church, Paul himself assumes this authority, even without a preceding trial of the person he judges. Similar expressions of this claim to full and nonnegotiable authority over the churches can be found in two other Pauline passages that deal with disciplinary questions. First, in 2 Thess 3:6–15 the believers at Thessalonica are commanded "in the name of the Lord Jesus Christ"[56] to withdraw from every "brother" who does not follow the tradition transmitted by Paul and his co-workers. This passage differs from 1 Cor 5 in several ways: it is phrased in conditional and general terms, suggests a temporal and partial exclusion, and perhaps delegates the authority to record the offenders in writing to the local church.[57] Yet Paul's confidence is hardly weaker here. Secondly, in 2 Cor 2:5–11 the apostle is encouraging the readmission of a person who had been subject to a "punishment by the majority", which should probably be understood as a temporal exclusion.[58] While the tenor is somewhat less self-confident here, perhaps by virtue of the humiliating experiences which Paul seems to have gone through, the

---

[54] See also GÄRTNER, *The Temple and the Community*, 128.

[55] 4Q266 11 16 involves several textual and interpretative uncertainties. דבר is variously translated as 'action' (BAUMGARTEN, *Qumran Cave 4.XVIII*, 77), 'sentence' (GARCÍA MARTÍNEZ and TIGCHELAAR, *The Dead Sea Scrolls Study Edition*, 1:597), or 'case' (SHEMESH, "Expulsion and Exclusion", 50). על יד המבקר 'by the hand of the mebaqqer' (WACHHOLDER and ABEGG, *A Preliminary Edition*, 1:21; GARCÍA MARTÍNEZ and TIGCHELAAR, 1:596; cf. CD IX, 18) seems preferable to על פני המבקר 'in front of the mebaqqer' (BAUMGARTEN, 76). Of less importance is the question whether כהרת should be translated as 'permanently' (BAUMGARTEN, 77) or 'as an engraving' (GARCÍA MARTÍNEZ and TIGCHELAAR, 1:597), or perhaps be seen as a corruption of בהרת in the sense 'with a graving tool' (BAUMGARTEN, 78) or 'with ink' (SHEMESH, 50).

[56] See 3:12; cf. Acts 16:18; Ign. *Pol.* 5:1.

[57] FORKMAN, *The Limits of the Religious Community*, 137–38, argues that σημειοῦσθαι (2 Thess 3:14) refers to the keeping of a protocol.

[58] FORKMAN, *The Limits of the Religious Community*, 179–80. The case is in all likelihood identical with the one mentioned in 2 Cor 7:12, but not with that of 1 Cor 5:1–11. See Victor Paul FURNISH, *II Corinthians: A New Translation with Introduction and Commentary* (AB 32A; New York: Doubleday, 1984), 164–66.

differences between the disciplinary procedures urged in 1 Cor 5 and 2 Cor 2 respectively should not be stressed to the point of declaring the former "authoritarian" and the latter "democratic", as has been done.[59] Behind different rhetorical strategies both passages presuppose that agreement between Paul and the Corinthians must and will be reached, and that this agreement will be in accordance with Paul's incontrovertible decision; the perfect form κεχάρισμαι (2 Cor 2:10), much like κέκρικα (1 Cor 5:3), signals that Paul has already made his decision and that he has no intention of altering it. Like Ezra[60] and the *mebaqqer* of Qumran, Paul views himself as authorized to lay down disciplinary rulings in the churches over which he claims jurisdiction in his capacity as their founding father (cf. 1 Cor 3:6, 10; 4:14–15).

However, Kuhn correctly points out that the procedure, which leads to excommunication in 1 Cor 5, is not only legal but also charismatic, as Paul is eager to stress his spiritual presence, both when judgement is passed and when the assembly takes place.[61] Since the Qumran expulsion ritual contains nothing that could correspond to this feature, one may expect it to say something about Paul's distinctive identity. His strenuously repeated claim to be "present in spirit" or "through the Spirit" at the assembly in Corinth, while his body remains on the far side of the Aegean, should be recognized as an expression of Paul's charismatic, indeed prophetic, self-understanding.[62] The Old Testament speaks of prophets who are transported by God's spirit, usually to gain knowledge of events that transpire in distant places. An expectation that the spirit of the Lord could "lift up" the prophet and transport him elsewhere bodily is voiced in the Elijah cycle.[63] By contrast, a translocation of the mind seems to be envisaged in the case of Elisha, whose "heart" went with Gehazi and thus saw his deceitful deed (2 Kgs 5:26). Similarly, Ezekiel's relocations from his dwelling-place in the Babylonian exile are not to be construed as bodily travels but as far-

---

[59] FURNISH, *II Corinthians*, 165.

[60] See ROSNER, *Paul, Scripture and Ethics*, 68–81.

[61] KUHN, "A Legal Issue", 492–93.

[62] Robert W. FUNK, "The Apostolic Presence: Paul", in *Parables and Presence: Forms of the New Testament Tradition* (Philadelphia: Fortress, 1982), 81–102 (98–99); repr. from *Christian History and Interpretation: Studies Presented to John Knox* (ed. W. R. Farmer, C. F. D. Moule, and R. R. Niebuhr; Cambridge: Cambridge University Press, 1967); Jerome MURPHY-O'CONNOR, "I Corinthians, v, 3–5", *RB* 84 (1977): 239–45 (243–44); Paul S. MINEAR, "Christ and the Congregation: 1 Corinthians 5–6", *RevExp* 80 (1983): 341–50 (342). Cf. also 1 Thess 2:17; Col 2:5; more distantly, 2 Cor 12:1–5.

[63] 1 Kgs 18:12; 2 Kgs 2:16; cf. the rationalizing rewriting of the former passage in Josephus, *A.J.* 8.333. See also Bel 33–39 (= Dan 14:32–38 Vulg.), where the Angel of the Lord carries the prophet Habakkuk in body from Judaea to Babylon "by the rush of his spirit" (36 Theod.).

sighted experiences.[64] These visionary, non-bodily transportations are frequently attributed to God's spirit.[65] Laying claim to such spiritual presence in Corinth, Paul depicts himself as the master prophet of the church and expects it to comply with his judgement on the errant member.

The judgement itself seems to be based on prophetic insight rather than on legal considerations.[66] Paul was bodily absent when he judged the fornicator and he cannot have conducted a tribunal. His formal list of members liable to expulsion: "a fornicator, a greedy person, an idolater, a slanderer, a drunkard, or a robber" (5:11; cf. 6:9–10) employs quite vague categories and is hardly sufficient to judge particular cases. This cannot be said of the Qumran documents, which provide detailed catalogues of offences and specify the punishment to be meted out for each crime.[67] The procedures to be taken, also described in detail, appear to be solely legal.[68] The same holds true for the little evidence we have of non-sectarian proceedings resulting in expulsion.[69] The church addressed by Paul is in a different position. It cannot make unrestricted use of the Mosaic Law and it has not developed a detailed Qumran-type casuistry, but must rely in individual cases on the presence of the Spirit of prophecy in the congregation. In 1 Cor 14:24–25, Paul approvingly depicts a hypothetical situation, in which an unbeliever is addressed personally by prophesying members of the assembly, who discern and expose the secret evils of his heart:[70] the outsider is convicted (ἐλέγχεται) and judged (ἀνακρίνεται) by all (14:25), for a spiritual person judges (ἀνακρίνει) everything (2:15). Since Paul, too, is spiritual (cf. 7:40), and the Corinthians have failed to deal properly with the fornicator, who pollutes the temple of God, he makes use of his prophetic competence to judge the offender. A regular court is superfluous.

Paul's prophetic self-understanding is not restricted to the ritual of excommunication, though he expresses it there with unusual force. That Paul did not only occasionally prophesy but also identified with prophetic characteristics and made use of prophetic forms of speech in his letters has

---

[64] Ezek 8:3; 40:2 speak of the travels taking place in visions, and 11:24 is especially clear: "the vision departed from me". See Daniel I. BLOCK, "The Prophet of the Spirit: The Use of rwḥ in the Book of Ezekiel", *JETS* 32 (1989): 27–49 (33–34).

[65] Ezek 3:12–15; 8:3; 11:1, 24; 37:1; 43:5. Only 40:1–3 does not mention the spirit.

[66] Ernst KÄSEMANN, "Sätze heiligen Rechtes im Neuen Testament", *NTS* 1 (1955): 248–60 (251–52).

[67] 1QS VI, 24–VII, 25; VIII, 16–IX, 2; CD X, 4–XII, 6; XIV, 18–22.

[68] CD IX, 16–X, 10; XX, 1–13.

[69] Ezra 9:1–10:44; Neh 13:1–3.

[70] See M. Eugene BORING, *Sayings of the Risen Jesus: Christian Prophecy in the Synoptic Tradition* (SNTSMS 46; Cambridge: Cambridge University Press, 1982), 117–18; Wayne A. GRUDEM, *The Gift of Prophecy in 1 Corinthians* (Washington: University Press of America, 1982), 199–200.

been acknowledged by several scholars.[71] It is nonetheless obvious that Paul does not explicitly label himself as a prophet, but as an apostle.[72] For Paul, the call to apostleship is a commission to evangelise (1 Cor 1:17; cf. 9:16) and to preach (Rom 10:15), a task centred on the transmission of received tradition (1 Cor 15:1–3). Prophecy is a kind of new revelation, independent of tradition and bound to specific situations. Such revelations must never be allowed to rival the received Gospel (Gal 1·8–9); thus, prophecy must yield to tradition, and the prophet to the apostle (cf. 1 Cor 12:28). But tradition does not provide the means by which to solve all individual problems that may arise in the church, and this leaves a gap that could be filled by prophecy, as mentioned above.

Accordingly, while "apostle" is the category by which Paul primarily identifies himself, he also sees himself as invested with unchallengeable prophetic authority. This prophetic identity has some very interesting parallels in non-Pauline primitive Christianity,[73] but sets Paul clearly apart from the Qumranites, who do not seem to have conceived of themselves as prophets. David Aune concludes:

Apart from the phenomenon of charismatic exegesis, prophecy (as direct revelation mediated through inspired speech or writing) does not appear to have been practiced by the Teacher of Righteousness or other members of the Qumran community. For the Qumran community charismatic exegesis played a functionally equivalent role to prophecy, yet it is readily apparent that the differences between the two phenomena are not small.[74]

---

[71] See, e.g., David E. AUNE, *Prophecy in Early Christianity and the Ancient Mediterranean World* (Grand Rapids: Eerdmans, 1983), 248–62; Karl Olav SANDNES, *Paul – One of the Prophets? A Contribution to the Apostle's Self-Understanding* (WUNT 2. Reihe 43; Tübingen: Mohr Siebeck, 1991); Helmut MERKLEIN, "Der Theologe als Prophet: Zur Funktion prophetischen Redens im theologischen Diskurs des Paulus", *NTS* 38 (1992): 402–29. For an argument that 1 Cor 5:1–8 displays formal features of prophetic speech, see Calvin J. ROETZEL, "The Judgment Form in Paul's Letters", *JBL* 88 (1969): 305–12 (309); but cf. Ulrich B. MÜLLER, *Prophetie und Predigt im Neuen Testament: Formgeschichtliche Untersuchungen zur urchristlichen Prophetie* (Gütersloh: Mohn, 1975), 181–83. The passage is more appropriately viewed as a statement partly about prophecy than as a prophetic utterance in itself.

[72] For a fresh assessment of Paul's notion of apostleship, see Samuel BYRSKOG, "The Apostolate in the Early Church: From Luke-Acts to the Pauline Tradition", in *The Chosen Lady: Scandinavian Essays on Emerging Institutions of the Church* (ed. S.-O. Back and T. Holmén; New York: T. & T. Clark, forthcoming).

[73] In my opinion John 20:22–23 is a commissioning of the disciples as prophets (see my forthcoming article "The Power of Prophecy: A Septuagintal Echo in John 20:19–23"), the implications of which for the understanding of excommunication in the Johannine literature cannot be dealt with here.

[74] AUNE, *Prophecy in Early Christianity*, 342. If the Qumranites are identified as Essenes, which is the most common opinion among scholars, the picture may be more complex. From Josephus, *B.J.* 2.159 it appears that charismatic exegesis was the means

Conclusions

Concerning the relationship between 1 Cor 5 and 4Q266 11; 4Q270 7, the first part of this study has shown that the structural agreement between the two expulsion rituals is more extensive than has hitherto been recognized. Without neglecting the fact that there are also points at which the rituals differ notably from each other, I have concluded that the ritual prescribed by Paul is likely to have been influenced by the Qumran ritual, to which the Cave 4 documents testify. Irrespective of the validity of my judgement on this point, it should be clear that the rituals have enough features in common to make a study of identities, based on a comparative analysis, potentially fruitful.

It has not been the aim of this study to uncover "new" aspects of primitive Christian identity, but rather to demonstrate how already known aspects would be expressed and confirmed through this kind of ritual, and how the ritual would create a sense of similarity with forms of early Judaism but also maintain the distinctiveness of the primitive church.

As for similarities, the ritual would strengthen the believers in Corinth – provided they adopted the perspective suggested for them by Paul – in their conviction that their group was the divine sphere, the pure temple of God at Corinth. Paul himself would be confirmed in his position at the top of the hierarchy. In these respects, the Corinthian identity would be quite comparable to the Qumranite type.

As for distinctive features, the ritual should have reminded the Corinthians that they were already living in the messianic age, to which the Qumranites were looking forward. The Pauline believers, through excommunicating the erring member, would themselves experience direct communication with the risen Lord. Paul too would be part of this communication through the Spirit, thus reinforcing the prophetic dimension of his identity.

---

by which Essenes would predict future events; however *A.J.* 15.373–379 (possibly also *B.J.* 1.78–81 = *A.J.* 13.311–313) seem to attribute prophecy in the stricter sense to Essenes.

Literary Strategies of Personification

Judith M. Lieu

"Personification is a meeting of linguistics, morality and religion in the house of rhetoric. Such a statement is, of course, highly rhetorical in itself."[1]

That quotation neatly frames the task set this paper, identifying the main players to be encountered. It also captures the self-mockery or even the self-deconstruction involved – not only is it a rhetorical statement but it also deploys personification itself, making present the association of what might otherwise be incommensurate terms, linguistics and religion. That they should meet "in the house", the place where women are supposed to belong, is something to which we shall return.

Introduction

"Personification", although not necessarily under that name, once searched for, proves to be found everywhere, and almost to defy interrogation. Even when constrained by academic debate and technical analysis the term remains a very slippery one, differently applied in different fields, resisting any agreed simple definition. Yet it has enjoyed something of a revival of interest and sympathy in recent years, perhaps because it is so open to a deconstructive reading. This renewed interest is notable for the way it encompasses both a reappraisal of the classical roots and expressions of the trope and a linguistic and philosophical analysis of the nature of discourse as representation.[2] It is this intersection that particularly invites exploration of how personification can function as a strategy of identification.

Although the practice of making something a person – *personam facere* – may be traced by historians of religion and of art to an early period, as a rhetorical topos, prosopopoiea (*prosōpon poiein*), it only receives close at-

---

[1] W. BURKERT, "Hesiod in context: abstractions and divinities in an Aegean-Eastern koiné," in *Personification in the Greek World: From Antiquity to Byzantium* (ed. Emma Stafford & Judith Herrin; CHS KCL Studies 7; Aldershot: Ashgate, 2005), 3–20 at p. 3.

[2] See, for example, James J. PAXSON, *The Poetics of Personification* (Literature, Culture, Theory 6; Cambridge: Cambridge University Press, 1994).

tention from the first century BCE.[3] Even then there is some inconsistency
in where the definitional centre lies. The *Rhetorica ad Herennium*, often
seen as the first to offer a definition, describes what the author labels as
conformatio, as when some person who is not present is represented as if
present or when a silent thing or one without form is made "eloquent"
(4.53.66); it distinguishes this from *notatio*, the Greek *ethopoiia*, the giving of imagined speech to an (fictional or real) individual in order to de-
lineate their character (4.50.63–52.65). Quintilian, who combines the two
modes and who introduces the Latin transliteration, *prosopopoeiae*, but
only alongside other equivalents (*forma, fictio personarum*), is most interested in the "imagined speeches of other individuals" as a powerful tool
in forensic oratory, for example in displaying the inner thoughts of opponents or in allowing victims to speak (*Inst.* 9.2; 6.1.25–27). More useful in
the present context is the oft-quoted example given by Demetrius *Style*:
"Another figure of thought – the so-called prosopopoeia – may be employed to produce energy of style, as in the words, 'Imagine that your an-
cestors, or Hellas, or your native land, assuming a woman's form, should
reproach you and say some such things'" (265).

This example, which is widely echoed,[4] suggests that it is necessary to
go beyond an initial, instinctive, definition of personification as "the process of animating inanimate objects or abstract notions".[5] Particularly useful here is the suggestion of an extension of the idea to an upward move on
an ontological scale.[6] Thus, when the sea roars, an activity usually associated with a lion, and equally when the lion aspires to kingship or initiates a
conversation with a human being. Yet these possibilities will also need
careful control; it may be that roaring has so much become something that
can be said of the sea that its original association with creaturely vocal

---

[3] This is widely discussed; see PAXSON, *Poetics*; Emma STAFFORD, *Worshipping Vir-
tues: Personification and the Divine in Ancient Greece* (London: Duckworth, 2000), 3–9;
Jon WHITMAN, *Allegory: The Dynamics of an Ancient and Medieval Technique* (Oxford:
Clarendon Press, 1987), 269–272.

[4] *Rhetorica ad Herennium* 4.53.66; Quintilian, *Inst.* 9.2.

[5] Morton W. BLOOMFIELD, "A Grammatical Approach to Personification Theory,"
Modern Philology 60 (1963): 161–171, "Personification allegory is the process of animating inanimate objects or abstract notions, and [that] a personification is the animate
object thereby created". This distinction between the mode and the result has not been
sustained in recent discussion.

[6] I owe this to conversation with and an unpublished paper by Willard McCarty. See
also W. MCCARTY, *Humanities Computing* (Basingstoke, UK: Palgrave Macmillan,
2005), 53–71, 57, "Any rhetorical act that transgresses normal ontology by investing an
entity with a human imaginative component, whether or not the result is anthropomor-
phic". I am grateful to Dr McCarty for initial bibliographical suggestions, which set me
on the path for this paper.

chords is now obsolete. Some will be inclined to protest that the roaring sea belongs only to the sphere of metaphor, or the kingly lion to that of anthropomorphism.[7] Another category whose relationship to personification is much discussed is allegory.[8] Although some have tried to distinguish sharply between these modes and to set up mutually exclusive categories, such efforts seem doomed to failure, and it is perhaps better to envisage a spectrum of overlapping modes. It is more productive to follow James Paxson who sets out a range of what he labels "figural translations" whereby members of one ontological category are translated figurally into another; his ontological categories or domains are 1) human; 2) non-human life form (plant or animal); 3) inanimate object; 4) place; 5) abstract idea; 6) deity.[9] Not all translations from one category to another will come under even a broad umbrella of "personification" but the glossary demonstrates just how variegated an exercise personification is, or belongs to. It also exposes the extent to which such strategies are almost unreflecting – adopted quite naturally in ordinary style as well as in more self-conscious discourse.

Finally, it is discourse, literary strategies, with which we are here concerned. Personification is common in art, both two-dimensional and plastic, and much has been written about this, particularly in the classical and medieval periods. Art and literature cannot be separated from each other; understanding personification in one medium often demands an appeal to the other.[10] At the same time, each medium offers possibilities unavailable to the other; whereas the visual form is primary in art but may demand interpretation, explicit or implicit, literary strategies have to make that form present to "the mind's eye" of the reader or the hearer.

---

[7] See PAXSON, *Poetics*, 14–17 for these debates already in the classical period. By "anthropomorphism" here is meant the representation of the non-human as human, but not of the divine as human.

[8] PAXSON, *Poetics*, 29–34; WHITMAN, *Allegory*; Marina WARNER, *Monuments and Maidens: The Allegory of the Female Form* (London: Weidenfeld and Nicholson, 1985), 82, "Although personification can exist outside allegory, as in the poetry of Baudelaire, allegory requires personification to function as drama, both in the mind's eye and before the eye of the body."

[9] PAXSON, *Poetics*, 42–43.

[10] See Colum HOURIHANE, ed., *Virtue and vice: the personifications in the Index of Christian art* (Princeton: Princeton University Press, 2000).

Forms of Personification

Although, as this introduction indicates, personification can be utilised in a number of settings, what follows will focus on some key examples within the biblical and postbiblical tradition, and particularly on their relevance for the shaping of identity. These start with the appropriate move from the inanimate to the animate.

i. Inanimate and Abstracts

The obvious starting point, in light both of the rhetorical discussion and of actual practice is the treatment of abstracts or of inanimate things as sentient beings, having ontological existence.[11] One very common form of this in the ancient world is when worship is directed to natural or to geographical features or else to abstract ideas – a distinction that may be alien to the ancient context.[12] Already in the classical period the rationality of and behind this practice was much discussed; in more recent times there have been vigorous debates as to the direction of development in the origins of primitive religion – namely, whether the personification of natural forces is a primary stage in the development of religious cult or whether it is a secondary rationalisation. In these cases the marker of personification is the act of worship, which presupposes that a response can be expected from that which is worshipped and addressed.[13] Although there are more traces of this than might be anticipated within the biblical tradition, a concern with literary strategies will need to look beyond cult to the attribution of any unusual ontological activity. Some examples will help frame the discussion:

An example from nature would be, "Sing for joy, O heavens, and exult, O earth; break forth, O mountains, into singing" (Isa 49:13). It is important to note how the personification is established: first, the address ("apostrophe") to the natural spheres treats them as beings who can respond, and, secondly, the activity – singing – is peculiar to sentient beings; hence it is the combination of subject and predicate that confirms personification,[14]

---

[11] *Rhetorica ad Herennium* 4.53.66 "Haec conformatio licet in plures res, in mutas atque inanimas transferatur."

[12] See STAFFORD, *Worshipping*, 2.

[13] See generally STAFFORD, *Worshipping*. WHITMAN, *Allegory*, 271–272, distinguishes between giving an abstract a "real personality" (as gods) and the giving of a "fictional personality" to an abstraction, although there may be more overlap between these than he admits.

[14] So, BLOOMFIELD, "Grammatical Approach", and MCCARTY, *Humanities Computing*, 57, who emphasises the combination of markers.

while speech, distinctive to human beings, is often seen as particularly determinative. For abstracts consider, "Steadfast love and faithfulness will meet, righteousness and peace will kiss each other": here only the attributed actions create the personification and the following line may demonstrate the consequent instability of the figure, "faithfulness will spring up from the ground, and righteousness will look down from heaven" (Ps 85:10–11).[15]

Because these may seem little more than the language of poetry – although poetry is a natural home for personification[16] – it may be difficult to discern any further strategy in them. However, when the personification is brought into direct contact with human persons, the transformation between literal and figurative creates powerful illusions of presence. So, for example, "*Who* (masculine/ feminine, not neuter) will separate us from the love of Christ? Will hardship or distress, or persecution, or famine, or nakedness, or peril, or sword?" (Rom 8:35).[17] Romans 5–8 is particularly rich in such personification; thus, "death reigned ... those ... shall reign"; "when you were slaves of sin ... being freed from sin (you) have been enslaved to God"; "sin deceived me" (Rom 5:14, 17; 6:20, 22; 7:11). In each of these cases it is the verbal predicate that establishes personification; but in addition these are relational activities involving human participants, and so they create a sense of unity and communication between personified subject and human object. The cumulative effect across these chapters is to set readers on a stage that is *peopled* by multiple forces, creating illusions of presence.[18] This sense is intensified by other personifications, such as "creation waits with eager longing", "the whole of creation has been groaning in labour pains until now ... and we also groan" (Rom 8:19, 22–23): here disparate categories are endowed with an (imagined) shared ontology addressed to the human subjects. One effect is that the language of power and control excludes neutrality by those human subjects; at the same time, it also encourages readers to join in a common cause, excluding any doubt as to where they are to position themselves.[19]

---

[15] BURKERT, "Hesiod", 9 gives this example; A. A. ANDERSON, *Psalms (73–150)* (NCB; London: Marshall, Morgan and Scott, 1972), 612, describes this as personifications.

[16] See the robust defence by D. DAVIE, "Personification," *Essays in Criticism* 31 (1981): 91–104.

[17] Even though the following nouns are masculine or feminine, *tis* should be translated as "who" in continuity with the repeated "who" of the previous verses (8:31, 33, 34).

[18] Note how this raises the question of human agency: see below.

[19] Similarly, Gal 5:16, "what the flesh desires is opposed to the spirit. And what the spirit desires is opposed to the flesh", personifies an opposition which readers are bound to internalise.

A further effect is that abstracts, normally timeless, become part of a narrative; in so doing they cross the divide into what is the normal form of human existence, while at the same time they also avoid the need for specific definition or analysis.[20] Something similar is achieved by Gal 3:24, which describes the law as our "disciplinarian" (*paidagōgos*) until Christ came. Again this goes beyond a metaphor: personification serves to oppose law, essentially an abstract concept, to Christ, a person.[21] In so doing it effectively sidesteps the debates that exercise more prosaic modern scholars as to whether Jesus obeyed the law or whether people in Christ still have to do things enjoined in the law, approaches that return law to an impersonal object.

A different exercise in personification may be found in 1 Corinthians 13 where the one who is patient, kind, and is not jealous, is not the one who loves but is love itself.[22] With reference to a later text and period James Paxson has explored whether there is a relationship between personification and what he calls "the moralized landscape" of early Christian literature;[23] the phenomenon that provokes such a question may already be found in Paul and is quickly developed, as shall be seen in Hermas. It carries with it the problem of the place of human agency here; the problem is a recurring one in the topos of personification, for when "abstract" forces or entities are endowed with personal attributes do they over-ride the human persons who experience them to assume ultimate accountability?[24]

At this point it will be useful to recall the long-lived topos of virtue and vice encountered as women. This is found first in the story of Heracles attributed by Xenophon to the fifth-century BCE philosopher Prodicus (*Mem.* 2.1.21–34):

The one was fair to see and naturally free; and her body was adorned with purity, her eyes with modesty; her appearance was sober and her robe was white. The other was well nourished, and so plump and soft. Her face was made up to heighten its natural white and

---

[20] See PAXSON, *Poetics*, 166–167, "Abstract intellectual qualities have, naturally, no form, substance, or temporal dimensions. They are ontologically and phenomenologically alien to living persons and substantial objects" (166). Hence Paxson calls this effect "substantialization".

[21] In discussion following this paper Lone FATUM made the intriguing suggestion that Christ should here also be considered a personification; this might certainly be the case understanding personification as the process of giving form to an imagined (but not necessarily fictional) character, but whether and to what extent Christ should be considered a personification in terms of this paper is more contentious. Galatians assumes that Christ refers to a historical personage in the recent past (Gal 4:4).

[22] The KJV translates 1 Cor 13:5 as "seeketh not *her* own".

[23] PAXSON, *Poetics*, 63–81, 169 with reference to Prudentius, *Psychomachia*.

[24] See WHITMAN, *Allegory*; modern discussions of the personification of the state face similar challenges: see below.

pink, her figure to exaggerate her height. Open-eyed was she, and she was dressed so as to disclose all her charms. Now she eyed herself; then looked whether any noticed her; and often stole a glance at her own shadow. (*Mem.* 2.1.21–22).[25]

The topos is taken up and developed in later Christian discourse (and art), and it is perhaps best known from Prudentius' *Psychomachia*, which, as the title shows, exploits the war between the virtues and vices over the human soul.[26] There are, however, earlier anticipations of this, albeit partly externalized, for example, when the account of the persecution at Lyons describes it as the work of the devil or "adversary", against whom was arrayed "the grace of God who protected the weak" (Eusebius, *Hist. eccl.* 5.1.5–6), or when Hierax declares that "Christ is our true father and our mother faith (*pistis*) in him" (*Mart. Just.* B 4.8). However, it is Hermas' vision of the seven young women around the tower, identified as the church under construction, which best develops the theme (Herm. *Vis.* 3.8.2–8): these women are identified as Faith, Continence, Simplicity, Understanding, Innocence, Seemliness and Love. Later these become twelve virgins (*parthenoi*) and there they are matched by twelve others – women (*gynaikes*), not virgins – still beautiful but tellingly dressed in black with unbound hair (Herm. *Sim.* 9.2; 9.9.5).[27] Here, these female personifications are developing a life of their own, becoming subjects of sustained, as it were "conscious", activity.[28] Although Hermas also sees a number of young men interacting with these maidens, and although these young men are no less beautiful, they are not personifications; they have no life outside the vision. The women, however, may indeed belong to the fictionalised world of a dream or parable, and yet Hermas, the seer of the visions, interacts extensively with them. Consequently, personification here not only represents the emotion or virtue but actively stimulates it in the hu-

---

[25] WHITMAN, *Allegory*, 22–24 argues that this is not yet a fully developed personification because we know that Heracles is considering his options, and the two do little more than speak: "the figures have not yet fully emerged from rhetorical flourishes into agents of interpretive force" (p. 24).

[26] See S. Georgia NUGENT, "*Virtus* or Virago? The Female Personifications of Prudentius' *Psychomachia*," in HOURIHANE, *Virtue and vice*, 13–28; M. VERDONER, "Cultural Negotiations in the Psychomachia of Prudentius," in *Beyond Reception: Mutual Influences between Antique Religion, Judaism and Early Christianity* (ed. D. Brakke, A. C. Jacobsen, J. Ulrich; Frankfurt a. M.: P. Lang, 2006), 227–243.

[27] See C. OSIEK, *The Shepherd of Hermas* (Hermeneia; Minneapolis: Fortress, 1999), 77, who notes that "the personification of virtues and vices in feminine form is traditional in Greco-Roman mythology" but does not examine in depth the significance of this.

[28] For this distinction between a more generalised personification figure and a personification character see PAXSON, *Poetics*, 35–37. Continence is the daughter of faith: family relationship is another marker of personification (MCCARTY, *Humanities Computing*, 57).

man participant, producing an identity or relationship between concept and individual.[29]

On the surface a very different personification of this "abstract" type is that of Wisdom, who appears already in Proverbs (8–9) and who acquires a variety of characteristics in subsequent literature.[30] Wisdom, *hokhmah; sophia*, is not one among a number of interchangeable and malleable virtues but is a figure with a unique place whose initial identity is determined first by her relationship with God and only then with humankind (or Israel) (Wis 7:22–30; 10–11).[31] The tired debate as to whether wisdom in such literature is *only* a personification or represents a real entity or hypostasis may misunderstand the very nature of personification.[32] That debate is of evident importance for the Christological appropriation of wisdom.[33] However, more pertinent here is the undoubted way in which wisdom functions as the personification of culturally appropriate norms and values; she becomes a means by which the distinctive character of the people within a wider world can be explored and maintained (Sir 6:18–31), while the contrast with or opposition against folly, also personified, helps draw the boundaries which define the identity of the community (Prov 7:4–23; 9:13–18; cf. 4Q184, 185 and below). Yet as one who encounters and addresses the individual she similarly inspires imitation or internalisation (Wis 6:12–25; Sir 38:34–39:11; 51:13–30).

ii. The State and Collectives

A second form of personification is also ubiquitous, namely, the representation of a state and perhaps also of some other collective as a woman. Although a state is not strictly speaking inanimate or abstract but is made up of persons, as a personification it is viewed as a concept independent of those who constitute it. This is seen as paradigmatic in Demetrius' definition of personification, "your native land assuming a woman's form", and Quintilian vividly quotes Cicero, "Indeed if my native land, which is much

---

[29] WARNER, *Monuments and Maidens*, 83, "Myths, written or pictured, enflesh abstractions and, by incarnating imaginary beings, they reproduce the very process they narrate."

[30] The literature is extensive: see Alice M. SINNOTT, *The Personification of Wisdom* (SOTSMS; Aldershot: Ashgate, 2005);. PAXSON, *Poetics*, 36–37 is too restrictive in seeing Wisdom as an extended figure (see n. 28) and not as a character.

[31] Her relationship with divine figures elsewhere cannot be discussed here.

[32] See SINNOTT, *Personification of Wisdom*; Carole R. FONTAINE, *Smooth Words: Wisdom, Proverbs and Performance in Biblical Wisdom* (JSOTSup 356; Sheffield: Sheffield Academic Press, 2002), 2–3; 94–95.

[33] The re-appropriation of Wisdom in the Johannine prologue by the *logos*, incarnated in Jesus, might be seen as a depersonification.

dearer to me than my life, if all Italy, if the whole republic were to speak thus, 'Marcus Tullius, what are you doing?'" (*Inst.* 9.2 quoting Cicero, *Cat.* 1.27).

Biblical examples of this type are familiar: Second Isaiah provides some of the best examples with Zion as the mother bereft of her children (Isa 54:1; 66:7–10). Again she becomes the subject of speech, "Zion said, 'The Lord has forsaken me'" (Isa 49:14), and it might be possible to create out of the scattered references in Second Isaiah a whole narrative of desertion, despair and restored fecundity.[34] To some extent this woman's story carries echoes of the story of the barren matriarchs, Sarah and Rebekah, perhaps composed at a similar date, and, if the "patriarchal narratives" explore the identity of the community, it would be interesting to explore how these two different styles of personification cross-fertilise each other. There are numerous other examples within the prophetic writings; in anticipation of what is to come we should note, on the one hand the characteristic themes of suffering, barrenness and transformed fertility, on the other those of uncleanness and unfaithfulness, vividly represented by the two women Oholah and Oholibah in Ezek 23, while starkly disturbing is the harsh treatment that God enacts against a personified Nineveh in Nahum 3, especially verses 4–6.

This trajectory is itself particularly rich, and a list of examples will have to suffice: these would include the weeping woman of Ezra's vision who is herself transformed into what she already represents, a city (*4 Ezra* 10); the woman clothed with the sun in Rev 12 or the holy city prepared as a bride in chapter 21 (what does that look like?), who in turn recalls the church as loved by Christ in Eph 5:25–33. Later there is Hermas' vision of the lady who is also identified as the church (Herm. *Vis.* 1.2–2.4); in subsequent appearances the woman subtly changes, although only retrospectively, first old, then younger despite retaining her grey hair (Herm. *Vis.* 3.10–13). One of the possibilities of personification is its instability, and hence its potential for undermining apparently stable categories.[35]

On the other hand, there is the woman clothed in purple and scarlet in Revelation 17. She is not just a woman who has gone astray, like Oholah and Oholibah, but is one who is by nature a prostitute and who cannot be

---

[34] Edith M. HUMPHREY, *The Ladies and the Cities: Transformation and Apocalyptic Identity in Joseph and Aseneth, 4 Ezra, the Apocalypse and The Shepherd of Hermas* (JSPSup 17; Sheffield: Sheffield Academic, 1995), 21–23 uses the term "symbol" but personification would be better. We might note how once again the Fourth Gospel redefines if not depersonifies that story (John 16:21).

[35] "Very little if anything is what it seems, and whatever that may seem to be does not persist for very long. Personification, which by nature violates ontology, is apt for this undermining" (MCCARTY, *Humanities Computing*, 55–56)

anything other than one. In a perversion of all that is proper she is drunk, on blood, and she is sitting on a beast with seven heads representing seven Kings – another inversion of sexual propriety. The woman is "the great city that rules over the kings of the earth", a mocking parody of a long and widespread tradition of the personification of the city as *Roma* – a further demonstration of the way in which personification can be manipulated to challenge familiar identities.

These latter examples belong to the imagery of vision as a literary genre, although, as in Hermas, boundaries are dissolved as the seer converses with symbol. Yet, this provides no grounds for drawing too sharp a distinction from other forms of personification. Hence, before long the representation of *ecclesia* and *synagoga* as two women will become common, first textually and later in art and in sculpture.[36] City, or in this case *synagoga*, *ecclesia* personifies people, and in turn is itself personified as a woman.[37]

The rhetorical and emotional effect of this topos was already evident to Demetrius and Quintilian, and it has been sustained into the present age. Particularly in war or under other pressure political rhetoric quickly takes up the imagery of the *mother*land; such language inspires a determination to protect *her* against despoliation and against rape, and it evokes deep fears of the destruction of the family unity, and of the violation of the security of home. In these contexts personification necessarily infers the threat of the outsider, the other, who may intrude. Concomitant with this is that such personification obscures the actual complexities of belonging and identity; it projects a unitary image perhaps built out of a limited set of characteristics.[38] If self-identity on the individual level is a continuous exercise in differentiation from the other, then such personification of the collective adopts the same binary model, the same desire to suppress internal difference in the interests of a homogenous self, opposed to the threatening other. In addition, in recent debate in political philosophy and international relations this has provoked intense debate as to how moral and legal accountability is to be understood when the subject is a personified entity (state).

---

[36] See Judith M. LIEU, "The Synagogue and the Separation of the Christians," in *The Ancient Synagogue from its Origins until 200 C.E.* (ed. B. Olsson & M. Zetterholm; ConB NT 39; Stockholm: Almqvist & Wiksell, 2003), 189–207, 190–92.

[37] Another level is added by Justin Martyr's identification of Leah and Rachel as synagogue and church (*Dial.* 134.4).

[38] Compare in a different way the rhetoric of "the West", "Islam".

iii. The Logo

On this basis it may be justified to include a third form of personification, best illustrated by a quotation from the internet – for this is surely a characteristically modern or post-modern use of the trope, although not unrelated to that which has just been explored:

The Swinburne University of Technology logo translates our identity into a visual language. It is the personification of who we are and what we stand for and is the public demonstration of our brand. The identity must be used on everything produced by the organisation, both internal and external, and in line with style guidelines. No other logos or marks will be allowed.[39]

This may appear to be the very inverse of personification; yet what it does is to expose the extent to which personification in practice depersonifies. It is, as James Paxson has noted, never separable from reification.[40] Although relentlessly contemporary, there may be early equivalents to this: the image of Britannia, still on British coins, perhaps comes between the last category and this, and others have pointed to the figure of John Bull or of Uncle Sam, particularly in patriotic contexts such as recruiting for the army, or perhaps to that of the Statue of Liberty. An earlier example might be provided by the visual effect of *Judaea capta* on Roman coins, although this is but an extension of the normal personification of virtues and of places. Yet these older examples claim personal qualities for the collective; the modern ones do not: instead personal qualities are subsumed or obliterated, and heterodoxy is explicitly denied.

iv. Abstracts Once More

The final three categories shall be more speedily dealt with, and to some extent they may appear to be the inverse of those already discussed; they indicate more how the language of personification has come to be used in contemporary thought and may reflect the different perceptions of the nature of the individual. The first of these is when individuals are perceived as the "personification" of something that is not animate, for example when an individual, whether historical or fictional, is said to be the personification of a particular characteristic, of ruthlessness, gentleness, or even wickedness. This too could be classed more as "reification", although again each perhaps implies the other.[41] While this could be seen as a more

---

[39] http://www.swinburne.edu.au/ims/style/web_intro/ accessed 27/08/2007.

[40] *Poetics*, 50.

[41] PAXSON, *Poetics*, 50 sees reification as the obverse of personification; yet each is contained in the other. Or this may come closer to his category of "ideation" (p. 43). BLOOMFIELD, "Grammatical Approach", 170 would perhaps call this symbolism.

modern conceit, from the ancient world a different example would be Philo's treatment of characters from the biblical narrative;[42] for example, Abraham's journeys are not only those of the man but also those of the "virtue-loving soul" (*On the Life of Abraham* 14.62–18.88). Comparable would be the way in which in Christian exegesis and art biblical women become personifications of virtues or of the church, losing their individual characteristics in the process.[43]

In such examples personification becomes an interpretive strategy, not a compositional one. The presence of and distinction between these two modes, interpretive versus compositional, demands recognition within discussion of personification, just as in the case of allegory more generally. By extension, it is perhaps arguable that this is what "the Jews" become in the Fourth Gospel, the "personification" of unbelief, for example. Here (as elsewhere) interpreters would differ as to whether this is an intended, compositional, personification, or only one created by the interpreter.

v. The Individual and the Collective.

If the fourth category is the inverse of the first, then the fifth is the inverse of the second. This is when an individual is presented as the "personification" of a collective or of some aspect of it. In recent times Nelson Mandela was perhaps seen as the personification of the oppression and struggle of the victims of South African apartheid, and Arafat as the personification of the Palestinians: this was true of them not just as individuals, but in that their stories *were* the stories of thousands of others. More contentiously this could be extended, for example, to seeing a particular political figure as, for example, the personification of American foreign policy, although here Paxson's category of "ideation" might serve better – and yet, as he notes, one may merge into the other.[44] Here relevant examples for the current discussion are more difficult to identify, although this might provide a framework for seeing the Beloved Disciple as the personification of the Johannine community.[45] More ambiguous is the case of Aseneth who is told that she will be a city of refuge (*Jos. Asen.* 15:7; 16:6).[46]

---

[42] See L. BAYNES, "Philo, Personification, and the Transformation of Grammatical Gender," *The Studia Philonica Annual* 14 (2002): 31–47.

[43] See n. 37.

[44] PAXSON, *Poetics*, 43. At the time of delivery the example given was Condoleezza Rice.

[45] This is not synecdoche since it is not simply the use of a part, which could be replaced by some other part, to represent the whole. Again, commentators will disagree as to whether this is intentional (compositional) or merely an interpretive choice.

[46] See HUMPHREY, *Ladies*, 51.

vi. Shifting Personifications

Finally, and in part balancing the third category, are the post-modern games with personification. Particularly challenging is the creation in cyber space of avatars as personifications of self and as providing ways of exploring identity.[47] In contrast to the imposed uniformity of brand logos this projects the possibility of multiple personifications, of the themes of carnival and of the instability and disruption of identity; even of identity theft and hence of false personification. This might have seemed to have abandoned any proper academic analysis of the topic and its relevance to ancient literature. Yet at the same time it exposes the precise problem that lies at the heart of personification, and indeed that provides the reason for the bad reputation prosopopoiea came to have after the mediaeval period. For, as already indicated by Quintilian's terminology of *"forma"*, *"fictio"*, *"ficta"*, personification is an exercise in the adoption of masks; of presenting something by what it is not – even if, as many would argue, this is the only way in which we can speak and think.[48] Personification hides at the same time as it manifests, and it does this in order to persuade, not by reason but by the potentially more questionable *amplificatio*.

Personification and Gender

This introduces the third section of this paper. The exploration of personification so far has identified a number of points relevant to any discussion of identity and the strategies through which it is explored. Rather than develop those, the focus here will be on a question that has received widespread attention. Although it is not the case that all personifications in the ancient world are feminine, the vast majority are, and this has been the case in the analysis above. In most of these gender has not been a peripheral matter but has been exploited in the strategies adopted. Although some have ascribed this phenomenon to the fact that most abstract nouns are feminine in ancient languages, this is evidently inadequate, for why this should be so is itself a matter of debate. It is not my task – neither am I qualified – to enter the fray as to the nature and origins of grammatical

---

[47] One might ask whether this is a continuation of the diary – who is the one who is addressed therein? (A question asked, reportedly, by Beatrix Potter). At the time of writing the prime example was Second Life (www.secondlife.com) "a 3D digital world, imagined, created, & owned by its residents", which on 27/08/2007 had more than 9 million residents.

[48] This is thoroughly explored by James J. PAXSON, "Personification's Gender," *Rhetorica* 16 (1998): 149–179

gender, but most would now agree that it is not independent of the structures and the values of society.[49] Moreover, there is no reason why the
grammatical gender could not be subverted, as it is by the Wisdom of Solomon's celebration of the barren woman and the eunuch as models of
wisdom (Wis 3:12–14), and even more explicitly by Philo, who states that
although wisdom is feminine its nature is masculine (*Fug.* 51–52).[50] Easier
than explaining *why* most personifications are female, is analysing *how*
their female character functions – although it may be that where the same
answers to the "how" recur, there is evidence also of the "why".

Out of the many general discussions of the problem in classical and medieval sources two insights in particular emerge. First, as pithily formulated by Emma Stafford:

> While the very fact that women have a low profile makes the female form a practically
> suitable vehicle for abstract ideas in search of an incarnation, psychologically their desir-
> able form conveys the desirability of the abstract values they embody.[51]

– that is, the cultural status of women makes them more useful for, or open
to, personifactory manipulation than would be males, in whom so much
normativity is invested. The female combines the unstable, the malleable,
and the desirable – perhaps startlingly expressed in the instability of the
woman who appears to Hermas.[52] Secondly, and perhaps as a consequence,
James Paxson wonders to what extent the personification of negative qualities as women reinforces women as the epitome of negative qualities,
while even the positive qualities engender a certain ambiguity.[53] From
these two perspectives, four particular issues may be identified within the
texts discussed here.

---

[49] See generally, PAXSON, "Personification's Gender"; also STAFFORD, *Worshipping
Virtues*, 27–35; WARNER, *Monuments and Maidens*, 66–70; BAYNES, "Philo", 34–39 for
the classical debate

[50] BAYNES, "Philo"; see also Diana BURTON, "The gender of Death," in Stafford &
Herrin, *Personification*, 45–68.

[51] STAFFORD, *Worshipping Virtues*, 35; cf. FONTAINE, *Smooth Words*, 97, "Abstraction is understood as in some sense 'female' precisely because the *male* experience is the
ontologically 'really Real' against which language measures all else." Conversely, PAX-
SON, *Poetics*, 50 "Along with abstractions, animals, and objects that can be translated
into a personifier, we find suppressed in the domain of the personified all categories of
Otherness: infants and children, women, the aged, the feeble-minded, insane, or infirm,
and members of ethnic, religious, occupational, or racial minorities".

[52] First, there is the problem of her relationship with Rhoda whom Hermas secretly
desired; next there is here changing age, in addition to her being at once woman and
tower (Herm. *Vis.* 3.2.4; 10–13).

[53] See PAXSON, "Personification's Gender".

i. Paired Women

A common pattern is that in which female personifications only appear when paired with their counterpart: virtue and vice in Heracles' encounter and the tradition that ensues; Wisdom and Folly in Proverbs and its followers, perhaps *ecclesia* and *synagoga*. The relationship between them is ambiguous: at once dichotomous and yet one incomplete without the other; although decidedly different, requiring some skill to be able to identify them and to decide which to follow. In Heracles' encounter "vice" (*kakia*) is only so-called by others, she names herself "happiness" (*eudaimonia*); she is not unattractive – "Her face was made up to heighten its natural white and pink, her figure to exaggerate her height" – although the hero will not need much guidance in order to recognise the path that he should choose. In Proverbs wisdom "takes her stand at the crossroads and cries out besides the gates in the front of the town" (Prov 8:1–3); clearly a contrast is intended, but there seems little externally to distinguish her from the loose woman who is "Loud and wayward; her feet do not stay at home; now in the street, now in the squares, and at every corner she lies in wait" (7:11–12).[54] The twelve women in Hermas' parable who lead others astray can indeed be recognized because of their black garments, but they are still beautiful even if Hermas does say, "I thought they had a savage look" (Herm. *Sim.* 9.9.5). Those who follow them are "deceived by their beauty" (Herm. *Sim.* 9.13.9), but of course the virtues can be no less beautiful.

This is the familiar pattern which Carol Fontaine calls the "good girl/ bad girl syndrome" of the biblical and post-biblical tradition;[55] the "whore/ virgin", "bride/ wanton wife". There is, indeed, a sense, in which the one demands or always carries the shadow of the existence of the other. The ambiguity entailed in this dialectic is made possible because as the primordial "other" "woman"/ women can be configured and reconfigured, at once attractive and to be feared. Seduction, presenting oneself as something that one is not by the adoption of an altered persona – make-up, hair-style, clothing – is what women do; indeed, this is the attraction and the danger, the dangerous attraction or the attractive danger of women. Personification projects the ambiguities and the demand for decision and choice, and perhaps it also sustains an unresolved anxiety.

---

[54] This is recognised by M. AUBIN, "'She is the beginning of all the ways of perversity:' Femininity and Metaphor in 4Q184," *Women in Judaism: A Multidisciplinary Journal* 2 (2001) [48] (https://jps.library.utoronto.ca/index.php/wjudaism/article/view/ 182/257 accessed 27/08/2007). See also Benjamin G. WRIGHT, "Wisdom and Women at Qumran," *DSD* 11 (2004): 240–261.

[55] FONTAINE, *Smooth Words*, 149.

ii. The Threat of the Seductress

Secondly, the negative female figures and their dangerous potential is developed intensively. This is not unique to the Jewish and Christian tradition: Quintilian includes *voluptas* in his brief list of abstract personifications, and Diana Burton notes that female representations of death are more aggressive and voracious than the masculine *thanatos*, which largely stands for a good death.[56] The negative counterpart to wisdom, folly, however, is developed in extreme terms, both in the Jewish tradition (4Q184; 11QPs[a] XXI,11–17), and in the Christian (the Apocalypse), to represent the dangers of heresy, apostasy, or any form of deviation from the communal norm. Of the former, Melissa Aubin remarks:

For any patriarchal discourse in which the self is defined as male, woman qua woman is the quintessential other. For the Qumran community, mightily consumed by self-imposed social boundaries, the concerns are easily transcribed on the body of a seductress.[57]

As the language of perversion and seduction becomes more extreme, so too does the repudiation of any alternative way of living or believing. Inevitably, what this does is to reinforce the (male) characterization of "real" women by the way they exercise their sexuality in relation to males, and the double-edged attraction and danger that holds for men. The consequence is that it becomes almost impossible to determine from these texts the actual status and role of real women.[58] A further question, and one equally resistant of easy answer, would be how women could read this except by the erasure of their own gender or, perhaps better, by internalizing the threats of their own being?[59]

iii. The Male Viewer

Thirdly, as just noted, what is assumed here is that the viewer is constructed as male. This is already true in the female personification of Zion. Tivka Frymer-Kensky writes:

The image of Zion is also the image of connectedness, for Zion is a focus for intense passion and longing for the men of Israel. They can express their love directly to this

---

[56] BURTON, "The gender of Death".

[57] AUBIN, "'She is the beginning'" [7].

[58] This is widely recognised more generally in the textual construction of women; here see WRIGHT, "Wisdom and women", 257–258

[59] AUBIN, "'She is the beginning'" [31]. However, see Rosemary Muir WRIGHT, "The Great Whore in the illustrated Apocalypse Cycles," *Journal of Medieval History* 23 (1997): 191–210, for how the illustrations in texts owned by women were made acceptable to them.

female figure in a way they cannot have towards the remote, invisible, and masculine God.[60]

While there may be some truth in this, the images associated with Zion are particularly to do with vulnerability, transformation, barrenness, fertility. Sirach 14:20–27, however, uses startlingly erotic language of the pursuit of wisdom (cf. Sir 51:13–19). By contrast the images associated with the church emphasise purity, virginity, even when combined with motherhood – the virgin mother who welcomes as living her aborted apostates (Eusebius, *Hist eccl.* 5.1.45; cf. 2.8).

This takes a particular and distinctive form in Hermas' parable; there, in a strange scene, Hermas is persuaded to stay the night with the twelve virgins – not, of course with the *women*. He sleeps with them "as a brother and not as a husband", but this does not prevent him becoming "as it were a young man" as he begins to sport (*paizein*) with them, and as they kiss him (*Sim.* 9.11). Certainly they do nothing but pray all night, although the next morning the shepherd asks whether they have done him any insult; later, the provisions made for the virgins to remain in his house "in purity" are immediately followed by the exhortation "Behave manfully (*viriliter*) in this ministry" (*Sim.* 10.4.1).[61] As Carol Osiek notes "His sexual honor is at stake, with or without celibacy".[62] It is unmistakable that the normative identity that is being constructed here, as in other early Christian and indeed in classical literature in general, is a masculine identity. Yet here female personification is manipulated in such a way in order to achieve a reconstruction of Christian normative identity that entails the reconfiguration of sexuality and its exercise. Masculinity is reconfigured so that, although not the active figure as penetrator, Hermas is still *the man*.[63]

iv. The Manipulation of Gender

Conversely, when Hermas' virgins first appear, seven in number, the second, *Encrateia*, is described as "girded about and like a man" (*andrizome-*

---

[60] T. FRYMER-KENSKY, *In the Wake of the Godesses: Women, Culture, and the Biblical Transformation of Pagan Myth* (New York: The Free Press/ Macmillan, 1992), 178. See also, H. EILBERG-SCHWARTZ, "The Problem of the Body for the People of the Book," in *People of the Body: Jews and Judaism from an Embodied Perspective* (ed. H. Eilberg-Schwartz; Albany, NY: SUNY, 1992), 17–46.

[61] Only the Latin is extant here but this probably represents the Greek *andreiōs* which figures as a theme in the *Shepherd*: the lady's parting words after her first appearance are, "Be the man, Hermas" (*Vis.* 1.4.3). See Steve YOUNG, "Being a Man: The Pursuit of Manliness in *The Shepherd of Hermas*," *JECS* 2 (1994): 237–255.

[62] OSIEK, *Hermas*, 228, although she does not develop this.

[63] YOUNG, 'Being a Man', 252–253 notes how the revelatory women are replaced by the masculine shepherd, while the virgins become Hermas' assistants.

nē) (Herm. *Vis.* 3.8.4). Later, all twelve were "girded", albeit "in a seemly fashion", and had their right shoulders exposed "as if they were about to carry a load" – which is precisely what they do. Although delicate (*tryphera*), they take their stand "like a man" (*andreiōs*) (Herm. *Sim.* 9.2.4– 5).[64] Similar transformations are familiar elsewhere in early Christian literature – in the *Gospel of Thomas* 114, or the *Martyrdom of Perpetua* 10.7; what they achieve is by no means obvious, although at the very least the topos avoids any celebration of independent femininity.

Beyond the period covered here this ambiguity about gender takes a distinctive form in Prudentius *Psychomachia* where the virtues have no qualms about the military techniques they adopt nor about the blood with which they are splattered.[65] Georgia Nugent draws attention to the transsexuality of the female figures/ virtues who take on both the clothing and some of the attributes of male warriors, but with a viciousness that in women would be deeply culturally unacceptable; she concludes that "what Prudentius effects, through his elaboration of the personifications, is a mode in which these female figures do indeed 'give birth' to Christian progeny (i.e., the doctrinal lessons embodied in the allegory), while at the same time the bodies of the women are both explicitly sexualised, and that sexuality is – in violent and bloody terms – repudiated".[66]

This is far from the result that Hermas intends, but it surely arises from a similar dilemma, one that is rooted in the inherent tension in the symbolic representation of women within the Christian, and in part within the earlier Jewish, tradition, compounded by the centrality that sexuality was to play in Christian self-construction.

Such a conclusion may seem far distant from the heavens singing and the earth exulting. It helps explain why personification acquired so bad a reputation, itself attractive and yet dangerous.[67] Yet personification also allows that which cannot be logically examined to be said and to be explored while at the same time providing the means for it to be undermined. It both mimics cultural values and so reinforces them, while also allowing us to imagine a "second life", another possible world.

---

[64] See OSIEK, *Hermas*, 77, 221.

[65] See NUGENT, "*Virtus* or Virago?" Such military cross-dressing has a long history: see Kristen SEAMAN, "Personifications of the Iliad and Odyssey in Hellenistic and Roman art," in Stafford and Herrin, *Personification*, 173–189, 179.

[66] NUGENT, "*Virtus* or Virago?", 25.

[67] See PAXSON, "Personification's Gender", which exploits the feminine gender of *prosopopoiea*.

The Antagonists – Rhetorically Marginalized Identities in the New Testament

Lauri Thurén

One group in the New Testament has been completely, and at least to some extent, unjustly marginalized. These individuals have been misrepresented and unfairly treated, not only in innumerable religious talks, but also in academic commentaries and studies. Pastors and scholars seldom bother to ask what these people really taught and how they actually lived, but rely blindly on the one-sided negative criticism found in the New Testament. This group deserves a fair hearing, not only in order to rehabilitate their memory, but also because this distorted picture has prompted biased interpretations of several historical and theological issues.

No, I am not referring to the Pharisees. They were in fact called "healthy" by Jesus,[1] and Paul boasted of his Pharisaic background.[2] Far worse treatment is meted out to the antagonists in the New Testament epistles. Only one fact can to a certain degree alleviate this historical injustice, from which they have suffered: perhaps some of them never even existed. But others, such as Diotrephes in 3 John or Hymenaios and Philetos in 2 Tim, held central positions in the early congregations, and they would certainly not approve the description of their thoughts and behavior.

Since correct information concerning Paul's, and other NT writers', opposition is crucial for understanding the thinking of these authors, I will discuss the question of how and why these individuals were marginalized.

For inspiring discussions and observations on this topic I should like to thank the 2006–2007 New Testament seminar at Joensuu University, especially Antti Kurkola, Hanne-Mari Karjalainen, Seija Helomaa, and Markus Partanen.

[1] Luke 5:29–31. The statement as such does not contain irony or sarcasm, on the contrary. The overall tone toward the Pharisees in Luke is rather optimistic.

[2] Phil 3:4–6. In this section Paul compares his new life in Christ with the best he knows, not the worst. See Lauri THURÉN, "*EGO MALLON* – Paul's View of Himself," in *A Bouquet of Wisdom* (ed. K.-J. Illman et al.; Åbo Akademi University, 2000), 202; Lauri THURÉN, *Derhetorizing Paul: A Dynamic Perspective on Pauline Theology and the Law* (WUNT 124; Tübingen: Mohr, 2000), 168–169.

Introduction: Conflict-Oriented Documents

Many New Testament authors seem to be constantly at odds with a certain group, or at least with certain individuals. In the epistles in particular, theological formulations, as well as practical guidelines and counsels, are typically articulated in argumentative terms, by which the author seeks, through suppression of his opponents, to present his own point of view as the only viable alternative.

But who are these alleged or real antagonists? Why are they so vividly present in the New Testament? According to a standard explanation, the epistles were provoked by critical situations, in which certain individuals threatened the theological or practical influence of the author, and thus vehement counteraction was necessary. The epistles are thought to reflect the true identity, doctrine, and behavior of these *personae non gratae*. This solution has dominated the exegetical discussion for centuries.[3] Typically, the scholars admit that some exaggeration and simplification may have occurred, but with sufficient diligence and practical training in reading between the lines, at least a rough picture of these antagonists can be obtained. In fact, a great deal of New Testament exegesis has been devoted to descriptions of the historical and theological backgrounds and the identity of these antagonists.

Nevertheless, among recent scholars, severe criticism of the standard position has been voiced, mostly due to methodological dissatisfaction with earlier research. But even in the documents themselves we can observe some annoying facts, which cast doubt on all descriptions of the antagonists. Thus, in this paper, I shall focus on four problems that are essential to the study of the opposition in the New Testament.

First, in some epistles the antagonists are described with too many, mutually exclusive attributes, as if they were, for example, Jewish Christians who were strictly obedient to the Torah and simultaneously libertine Gnostics. In other texts, the antagonists lack all specific contours.

Secondly, the labels given to the antagonists tend to be stereotyped and to follow a fixed pattern known from other Hellenistic and Jewish sources: they are outsiders, who have infiltrated the community, and they are licentious and ludicrous gluttons with evil intentions.

Thirdly, the main method, *mirror-reading,* which has been used in order to gain information about the antagonists, lacks validity, since the texts

---

[3] It is interesting to compare the study of Paul's antagonists with the attempt to identify the historical Jesus. Whereas the latter topic is associated with deep skepticism and sophisticated methodology, Pauline studies seem, in this respect, to be almost in a pre-critical phase.

were not written in order to share information about these villains. The aim in the epistles was to modify previous assessment of these opponents by the addressees, of which we have no knowledge

Fourthly, since the description of the antagonists is so problematic in some epistles, that it is almost impossible to attain a reliable view of them, other solutions must be found. We need to reassess their function in the text, especially if the antagonists were misrepresented or entirely imaginary. Why were these individuals so necessary that, if they did not exist, they had to be invented? An answer could perhaps explain and justify the New Testament authors' biased representation of the real antagonists as well. Towards the end of this paper I will discuss this issue and propose two possible solutions.

Too Many Identities

First, a basic mistrust of any description of the opponents arises, since the suggestions are too numerous. In some cases not even a faint *opinio communis* has been reached. The disunity can rarely be explained by referring to natural diversity among scholarly opinions. For example, in Galatians, Colossians, or 2 Tim, suggestions concerning the opponents' historical or ideological identity are based on a wide range of almost all heresies imaginable.[4] On the one hand, the assumption about the presence of most of these heresies can be supported by clues in the text and our knowledge of the context. On the other hand, they cannot all be true at the same time. Moreover, in order to choose one explanation, many contradictory expressions and hints in the text must be neglected.

Concerning *Galatians*, Mitternacht argues that, when dictating the epistle, Paul did not fully understand the situation. Actually, he makes no attempt to describe the opponents' propaganda or behavior, but is more interested in presenting and discussing other conflicts, which have allegedly occurred in Jerusalem or in Antioch.[5]

---

[4] For Gal, see Lauri THURÉN, "Paul Had No Antagonists" in *Lux Humana, Lux Aeterna – Essays on Biblical and Related Themes* (ed. A. Mustakallio, FS Lars Aejmelaeus, Finnish Exegetical Society, Helsinki; Vandenhoeck & Ruprecht, Göttingen 2005), 268–288; for Col and 2 Tim see below.

[5] Dieter MITTERNACHT, *Forum für Sprachlose, ein kommunikationspsychologische und epistolär-rhetorische Untersuchung des Galaterbriefes* (ConBNT 30; Stockholm: Almquist, 1999), 62. According to Vouga, however, the vague contours of the antagonists are due to the nature of the document as a circular letter (Francois VOUGA, "Der Galaterbrief: Kein Brief an die Galater? Essay über den literarischen Character des letz-

The shortage of specific, explicit descriptions of the antagonists in Galatians does not mean that the letter lacks hints about their identity. By mirror-reading Paul's claims, they have been identified as intruding Jewish- Christian teachers[6] or as local Jewish-Christians who were loyal to the Torah,[7] or as libertine Gnostics.[8] Some scholars find in Galatia Gentile Christians with a Judaizing tendency,[9] or a combination, i.e. Gnostics with a Judaizing tendency.[10] There may have been a double front,[11] or perhaps the local community simply wanted the addressees to define their identity?[12] The antagonists have also been identified as various syncretists.[13] Some scholars emphasize the recipients' internal questions, such as their theological frustration[14] or their desire to avoid persecution.[15] Moreover, it could be claimed that the addressees in the text represent a general model, or they are imaginary for some reason, so that definition of the situation is impossible.[16] The abundance of suggestions[17] cannot be explained solely as the result of by the vivid imagination of scholars or by poor methodology, since they are mostly based on textual evidence. It is not easy to create a general explanation, which would include all the data available in the text.

---

ten grossen Paulusbriefes," in *Schrift und Tradition* (ed. K. Backhaus and F. Untergaßmair; Wien: Schöningh, 1996), 245–246.

[6] Franz MUSSNER, *Der Galaterbrief* (HTKNT 9. Freiburg: Herder, 1974), 25, represents this traditional view.

[7] Joseph B. TYSON, "Paul's Opponents in Galatia," *NovT* 10 (1968): 252.

[8] Walter SCHMITHALS, *Paul and the Gnostics* (trans. J. Steely; Nashville: Abingdon, 1972).

[9] Emanuel HIRSCH, "Zwei Fragen zu Galater 6." *ZNW* 29 (1930): 192–97.

[10] Klaus WEGENAST, Das Verständnis der Tradition bei Paulus und in den Deuteropaulinen (Neukirchen: Neukirchener, 1962), 36–40.

[11] Wilhelm LÜTGERT, Gesetz und Geist, eine Untersuchung zur Vorgeschichte des Galaterbriefes (BFCT 22.6.; Gütersloh: Bertelsman, 1919), 11.

[12] Mark NANOS, "The Local Contexts of the Galatians: Toward Resolving A Catch-22," June 2003, 1–17 [cited 19 October 2007]. Online: http://marknanos.com/ Galatians-LocalContext-6-03.pdf.

[13] E.g. Frederic C. CROWNFIELD, "The Singular Problem of the Dual Galatians," *JBL* 64 (1945): 491–500; Dieter GEORGI, *Die Geschichte der Kollekte des Paulus für Jerusalem* (Hamburg: Reich, 1965), 35–38; Helmut KOESTER, "Häretiker im Urchristentum," in vol. 3 of *RGG* (ed. K. Galling; 7 vols, 3d ed.; Tübingen, 1957–1965), 18–21.

[14] Hans Dieter BETZ, *Galatians: A Commentary on Paul's Letter to the Churches in Galatia.* (Hermeneia; Philadelphia: Fortress, 1979), 8–9.

[15] Robert JEWETT, "The Agitators and the Galatian Congregation," *NTS* 17 (1979): 198–212; MITTERNACHT, *Forum*, 314–320.

[16] VOUGA, "Kein Brief," 245–254; George LYONS, *Pauline Autobiography: Toward a New Understanding* (Atlanta: Scholars Press, 1985), 104.

[17] Cf. Mark NANOS, ed., *The Galatians Debate: Contemporary Issues in Rhetorical and Historical Interpretation* (Peabody, Mass.: Hendrickson, 2002).

In *Colossians*, it is even more difficult, if not virtually impossible, to create a coherent picture of the antagonists based on the multifaceted accusations against them in this letter. They could not simultaneously be law-abiding Jews,[18] Jewish syncretists,[19] syncretistic god-fearers,[20] Gnostic Jews[21] with or without Gentile elements,[22] Phrygian Jews interested in mystery cults,[23] Gentiles fascinated by mystery cults,[24] individuals influenced by local and Jewish ideas,[25] Pythagoreans interested in mystery cults and Judaism,[26] Gnostic syncretistic philosophers,[27] Hellenistic syncretists,[28] Judeo-Christian mystic ascetics,[29] and elitist Christians.[30]

The situation in *2 Timothy* follows the same pattern. According to current scholarship, the antagonists were law-abiding Jewish-Christians,[31]

---

[18] Markus BARTH and Helmut BLANKE, *Colossians*. AB 34B (New York: Doubleday, 1994), 29.

[19] Stanislas LYONNET, S.J.,"Paul's Adversaries in Colossae" in *Conflict at Colossae* (ed. F. O. Francis and W. A. Meeks; Missoula: Scholars Press, 1975), 147–153.

[20] Lars HARTMAN, *Kolosserbrevet* (Kommentar till Nya Testamentet 12; Uppsala: EFS, 1985), 121–125.

[21] Peter T. O'BRIEN, *Colossians, Philemon* (WBC 44; Waco, Tex.: Word, 1982), xxxii–xxxiii.

[22] Günther BORNKAMM, "The Heresy of Colossians" in *Conflict at Colossae* (ed. F. O. Francis and W. A. Meeks; Missoula: Scholars Press, 1975), 123–135.

[23] See O'BRIEN, *Colossians, Philemon*, xxxvi.

[24] Martin DIBELIUS, "The Isis Initiation in Apuleius and Related Initiatory Rites" in *Conflict at Colossae* (ed. F. O. Francis and W. A. Meeks; Missoula: Scholars Press, 1975), 82–101.

[25] Martin HENGEL and Anna Maria SCHWEMER, *Paul Between Damascus and Antioch* (Louisville: John Knox, 1997), 162–63.

[26] Eduard SCHWEIZER, *Der Brief an die Kolosser* (EKKNT; Zürich: Benziger, 1976).

[27] Eduard LOHSE, *Der Brief an die Kolosser – Die Briefe an die Kolosser und an Philemon* (KEK; Göttingen: Vandenhoeck & Ruprecht, 1986), 118–20, 127–131.

[28] Esko HAAPA, *Kirkolliset kirjeet* (Suomalainen Uuden testamentin selitys 9; Helsinki: Kirjapaja, 1978), 49–55.

[29] Fred O. FRANCIS, "Humility and Angelic Worship in Col 2:18," in *Conflict at Colossae* (ed. F. O. Francis and W. A. Meeks. Missoula, MT: Scholars Press, 1975), 163–185; O'BRIEN, *Colossians, Philemon*, xxxvi–xxxviii; cf. LOHSE, *Kolosser*, 118–119 n. 36.

[30] BARTH & BLANKE, *Colossians*, 384–386.

[31] Michael GOULDER, "The Pastor's Wolves: Jewish Christian Visionaries behind the Pastoral Epistles," *NovT* 38 (1996): 256.

Jewish Gnostics,[32] libertine ascetics,[33] or Hellenistic Jews, but not Gnostics,[34] pure Gnostics,[35] outsiders[36] or insiders,[37] and so forth.

To choose one of the options while rejecting the others would do violence to strong hints in the text. Nor does an attempt to combine all these doctrines and heresies sound viable either, since this would be excessive in one congregation. How then can we know which heresy the author did refute?

Perhaps even the author himself did not know? Why not admit that he was not omniscient? Perhaps he needed to combat different heresies, just in case, since he was poorly informed about the situation?[38] Thus, he would condemn all possible movements and ideas that were opposed to his Christian doctrine in order to hit at least one target. The author's limited knowledge of the situation provides an interesting explanation.

According to Vorster, it is a typical fault of modern scholars that they envisage axiomatically that the New Testament authors did know all the details of the congregation and that they had a good overall picture of the situation. But when Paul in *Romans* 16 names more individuals than in any other epistle, this does not prove that he was particularly well aware of the situation. On the contrary,[39] this rhetorical device ("name-dropping") could be used in order to hide the fact that he was not personally familiar with the congregation. Actually, we may know more, or at least different, historical facts about Rome than Paul ever did.[40]

---

[32] John N. D KELLY, *A Commentary on the Pastoral Epistles, 1 Timothy, 2 Timothy, Titus* (BNTC; London: Black, 1983), 10–12. 44.

[33] Ian H. MARSHALL, *A critical and exegetical commentary on the Pastoral Epistles* (in collaboration with Philip H. Towner; ICC; Edinburgh: T&T Clark, 1999), 41–51.

[34] Gordon D. FEE, *1 and 2 Timothy, Titus* (NIBCNT; Grand Rapids: Eerdmans, 1988), 7–9.

[35] Walter SCHMITHALS, "Judaisten in Galatien?" *ZNW* 74 (1983): 27–58.

[36] Philip H. TOWNER, *1–2 Timothy & Titus* (IVP; Downers Grove: InterVarsity, 1994), 23–42.

[37] Lloyd PIETERSEN, "Despicable Deviants: Labelling Theory and the Polemic of the Pastorals," *Sociology of Religion* 58 (1997): 345. Cf. also Lloyd PIETERSEN, *The polemic of the Pastorals: a sociological examination of the development of Pauline Christianity* (JSNTSup 264; London, New York: T & T Clark, 2004).

[38] Concerning 1 Peter, I have suggested that the strikingly adversative picture of the recipients can be explained by the type of the document as a circular letter and different psychological reactions even by the same person. See Lauri THURÉN, *The Rhetorical Strategy of 1 Peter, with Special Regard to Ambiguous Expressions* (Åbo: Åbo Academy Press, 1990), 81–83.

[39] Johannes VORSTER, "The context of the letter to the Romans: a critique on the present state of research," *Neot* 28 (1994): 137–138.

[40] THURÉN, *Derhetorizing*, 96–101.

Barclay and Lyons criticize the thesis of a non-omniscient author by stating that it would cause more problems than it solves, and it would open the door to uncontrollable suggestions.[41] Naturally, the assumption of the author's limited knowledge must not be exaggerated, as if he possessed no information whatsoever about the situation of the addressees. Something must have triggered the letter after all. However, it remains a fact that we do not know the limits of his knowledge. This puts us, as historians, in an unsatisfactory situation. Despite our willingness to know and to say as much as possible about the situation, our limitations must be taken seriously.

The epistle of *Jude* provides opposite material, which however leads to a similar result. The document contains next to no specific information about the opponents. For that reason it could be used – at least in its canonical form – as a model epistle, in which everybody could fill in the blanks for themselves.[42] *2 Peter* proves that Jude has in fact been used as such a model. But even there, no consensus on the identity of the antagonists has been achieved.[43] Nevertheless, 2 Pet and other texts, which contain more specific data, later became more popular than the original and general Letter of Jude. Perhaps details and proper names make the text more interesting, even if these individuals and specific circumstances otherwise remain unknown and irrelevant for us.

To summarize so far we can state that in some cases, either too much or too little information about the antagonists is provided, so that it is impossible to create a solid portrayal of them. Of course the author had always a certain view of the situation in mind. However, his text does not easily convey that view to us. The reason is obvious: The New Testament epistles were not written in order to provide modern readers with information about the adversaries. We do not possess all the information that their historical or implied recipients did. On the other hand, we may know things about the historical situation, for example in Rome, that Paul did not know. Thus, even if some of our guesses were correct, they would be useless for interpreting the text if the author did not share our knowledge.

---

[41] John BARCLAY, "Mirror-reading a Polemical Letter: Galatians as a Test Case," *JSNT* 31 (1987): 76; LYONS, *Autobiography*, 98–99.

[42] Lauri THURÉN, "Hey Jude! – Asking for the Original Situation and Message of a Catholic Epistle," *NTS* 43 (1997): 465. It is possible that the original Jude contained more particular information about the antagonists.

[43] Cf. Jerome H. NEYREY, *2 Peter, Jude: a new translation with introduction and commentary* (New York : Doubleday, 1993), 207 and Richard BAUCKHAM, *Jude, 2 Peter.* (WBC 50; Waco, Tex.: Word, 1983), 155–157.

Heavy Rhetoric Should Not be Misunderstood

If we examine the way in which the antagonists are described, they seem to be strikingly *stereotypical*. To name but a few examples, the antagonists typically come from outside; they have intruded into, or infiltrated, the community of the addressees (Gal 2:4; 2 Pet 2:1, Jude 4).[44] They are lying hypocrites (Gal 2:13; 2 Cor 11:13; 1 Tim 4:2, cf. *1 Clem* 15:1; 2 Cor 11:13–15; Rev 2:2), often with ψευδ-prefix 2 Cor 11:13, Gal 2:4, 2 Pet 2:1; 1 John 4:1), they are filled with hubris (Jas 4:16; 2 Tim 3:2; 2 Pet 2:10; Rom 2:17, 23; Gal 6:13; Jude 7–8), sorcery (Gal 3:1; 2 Tim 3:13), moral depravity (Gal 2:4; 6:12–13; 2 Pet 2:3, 10, 14, 18; Jude 7–8, 12; Rev 2:14, 20–22), gluttony (Rom 16:18, Phil 3:19; 2 Pet 2:13, Jude 12), perverting influence (Gal 1:7; 5:10, 12; 2 Tim 2:18), and they are ludicrous (Gal 5:12). The author reveals their secret intentions (Gal 2:4; 6:13) and threatens them with eschatological judgment (Gal 1:8–9; 5:10; 1 Thess 2:16; 2 Thess 1:8; 2 Pet 2:3–22; Jude 4–16).[45]

Such stereotyped negative labeling of the antagonists, or *vituperatio*, is by no means restricted to the New Testament. On the contrary, it was a standard rhetorical *topos*.[46] The accusations presented above were well known and utilized in Roman and Greek speeches and literature as well as in Jewish texts.[47] The goal was not to introduce the antagonists, their behavior, or their reasoning. There was no need to do so, since they lived among the addressees and were well known to them. Instead, by using familiar, fixed negative expressions, the author could label his antagonists as villains in order to dissociate them from the addressees. Both the author and the original recipients were usually aware of the nature of these accusations: no correspondence with actual facts was necessary, although it could be useful. Corresponding language is known from modern political discourse as well.[48] By vilification, the *ethos* of the antagonists is dimin-

---

[44] See Rickhard LONGENECKER, *Galatians* (WBC 41; Waco, Tex.: Word, 1990), 51.

[45] For more detailed studies of the stereotypical labeling or *vituperatio* of the antagonists, see Robert J. KARRIS, "Background and Significance of the Polemic of the Pastoral Epistles," *JBL* 92 (1973): 549–564; Andrie DU TOIT, "Vilification as a Pragmatic Device in Early Christian Epistolography." *Bib* 75 (1994): 408–13 and THURÉN, "Jude," 456–462; Thurén, *Derhetorizing*, 65–67.

[46] See Heinrich LAUSBERG, *Handbuch der literarischen Rhetorik (*2d ed.; München: Hueber, 1973); § 55. 131–38. 205–206. 546; Cicero, *De or.* 2.79.321; *Rhet. Her.* 1.5.8; Quintilian, *Inst.* 4.1.6–29.

[47] See DU TOIT, "Vilification," 403–412; Luke Timothy JOHNSON, "The New Testament's Anti-Jewish Slander and the Conventions of Ancient Polemic," *JBL* 108 (1989): 419–431; MITTERNACHT, *Forum*, 286–291; THURÉN, *Derhetorizing*, 65–69; THURÉN, "No Antagonists," 273–276.

[48] For example, the word *fascist* has been used in such a way in many countries.

ished. Moreover, it serves to reveal their secret intentions, which are not even claimed to be visible.

The perception of many details attributed to the antagonists as stereotyped *vituperatio* by no means proves that the accusations are not historically true. On the contrary, confirmation would be provided if the addressees were able to observe any correspondence with the visible reality, at least to some degree.[49] However, it is hard to assess how much of this is factual, since recognition of the rhetorical device drastically reduces our possibilities to obtain reliable historical information. Of course it is possible, that the antagonists were invariably obscure intruders, filled with depravity, gluttony, and evil intentions. But this cannot be proven by the text. They may well have used words similar words to the words of the author who accuses them. It is a serious mistake to think that the true historical identity of the antagonists can be found by a reduction of the accusations against them, at least to some extent.[50]

There are even more rhetorical and epistolary devices and strategies in the NT epistles, which may lead us astray.[51] To name but a few, the standard epistolary opening phrases in Jude have led to fanciful descriptions of the situation and of the antagonists.[52] In several other documents, in which the author actually describes the situation, scholars have overlooked the fact that such a description belongs to the category of *narratio*, which was one of the most effective devices of ancient rhetoric, and one which still carries weight in modern persuasion.[53] The author describes the situation in seemingly neutral terms, but in fact he manipulates the scene for his own purposes. Another, especially Pauline, device was *hyperbole*.[54] As exaggeration was typical of his language, we must be aware of the difficulties inherent in retrieving objective information from Paul's statements. This is particularly true when he describes his antagonists.

To summarize this section, we must conclude that since most of the information about the antagonists is affected by heavy rhetoric, it is difficult

---

[49] Du Toit, "Vilification," 411, and Thurén, *Derhetorizing*, 274.

[50] Also, if the early Christians were stereotypically blamed for eating their children, this does not mean that they did so, at least to a certain degree. Or if the Church Fathers constantly accuse the Gnostics of heavy libertinism, this does not mean that they were immoral at lest to some extent.

[51] See closer Thurén, "No Antagonists," 276–277.

[52] See Thurén, "Jude."

[53] Cf. John D. O'Banion, "Narration and Argumentation: Quintilian on *Narratio* as the Heart of Rhetorical Thinking," *Rhetorica* 5 (1987): 325–351.

[54] Lauri Thurén, "'By Means of Hyperbole' (1 Cor 12:31b)" in *Paul and Pathos* (ed. Thomas Olbricht and Jerry Sumney; SBLSymS 16, Atlanta: SBL, 2001), 104–110. See also Thurén, "*EGO MALLON.*"

to obtain any neutral data about them. It is inadvisable to take at face value statements, which even the original addressees presumably understood as rhetorical devices.

No More Mirror-Reading

To misunderstand rhetorical devices is but one of the problems inherent in scholarly attempts to mirror-read the documents in order to identify the opponents in the New Testament. John Lyons argues that such a technique is in principle wrong because it automatically adds much extratextual data the text. According to Lyons, we can never know what information is based on facts and what is mere rhetorical.[55] Correspondingly, John Barclay argues that mirror-reading necessarily distorts the historical information because polemical expressions are overinterpreted and too hastily seen as sources for the opinion of the antagonists. Johannes Vorster is even more critical. According to him, the text should not be seen as a reflection of its historical context. We must reject the ideas that we ourselves attribute to the situation and remember that they have emerged from scarce and haphazard historical data. The author does not necessarily comment on all, or even some central, factors of the exigency of the text.[56]

I could add that the original purpose of the text, including all references to the opposition, must be acknowledged. The New Testament epistles were not dictated in order to provide objective information about some unpleasant Christians to their original addressees, let alone to us. All the data presented are designed to reform the previous attitudes, values and behavior of the original recipients.

Scholars who take this criticism seriously have nevertheless attempted to define the true identity of the opponents. Barclay believes that it is possible to avoid some problems by following certain criteria.[57] Mitternacht, who affirms that the opponents remain mute, hopes to provide a "forum" for them after all.[58] I have suggested that since rhetorical polemics is one of the main sources of our problems, identifying these devices and *derhetorizing* them might enable us to look behind them. For example, if we find among classical stereotyped accusations some atypical, surprising

---

[55] LYONS, *Autobiography*, 97. 104; Klaus BERGER, "Die impliziten Gegner. Zur Methode des Erschliessens von 'Gegnern' in neutestamentlichen Texte," in *Kirche* (ed. D. Lührmann and G. Strecker; Tübingen: Mohr, 1980), 372–400.

[56] VORSTER, "Context," 127–145; THURÉN, *Derhetorizing*, 97–98.

[57] BARCLAY, "Mirror-Reading," 73–93.

[58] MITTERNACHT, *Forum*, 61–64.

claims, they could convey a glimpse of the actual situation. Thus, in the Epistle of Jude, unconventional references to speech and verbal denigration of other individuals – the very same thing as the author himself employs – may represent real internal problems, discontent and criticism within the community.[59] Similarly, when the author alleges that the antagonists "deny Christ," this is not a typical Hellenistic accusation. However, even when we attempt to elicit some data through these methods, Vorster's warnings should be borne in mind.

To summarize this section, we must admit that our unspoken axiomatic assessments of the nature of the text may impede our search for historically reliable information. An epistle was not written in order to inform outsiders like us about the situation; the original purpose was to influence the audience, which was well aware of its own context. Thus, the existing pieces of information may lead us astray.

Despite all these *caveat*s, we still want to know at least something about the historical situation and the antagonists. It seems necessary, especially when we attempt to understand the author's own point of view, to know against whom and against what kind of thinking or behavior he is writing. But this necessity should not impel us to find information where none is actually provided.

Opponents for a Purpose

We have seen hitherto that it is arduous to gain reliable historical information. The original addressees did not share this difficulty, as they often knew the "antagonists" personally, or were actually identical with them. Indeed, some scholars have argued, that we should not emphasize the difference between the author and the antagonists. It is possible, that the diversity was minor, and that the alleged antagonists agreed with the author on most issues. Perhaps they were surprised when they heard the criticism.[60] Actually, Paul himself gives support to this thesis when he indicates, that the explicit impetus for the Letter to the Galatians can be called "a little yeast" (Gal 5:9; cf. 1 Cor 5:6), which is dangerous only because it "leavens the whole batch of dough."

---

[59] THURÉN, "Jude," 462–464.

[60] Jerry L. SUMNEY, *"Servants of Satan", "False Brothers" and Other Opponents of Paul* (JSNTSup188; Sheffield : Sheffield Academic, 1999), 15–20; BARCLAY, "Mirror-Reading," 78, 80, MITTERNACHT, *Forum*, 63; George HOWARD, *Paul's Crisis in Galatia* (SNTSMS 35; Cambridge: Cambridge University Press, 1979), THURÉN, "No Antagonists," 273.

For what reason were these individuals so often discussed and opposed? Why were they accursed[61] even if they hardly existed? Obviously, the description has a purpose. The antagonists, as they appear in the text, *represent* opposite values, alternative thinking or inappropriate behavior, which the author condemns. Thus, the standard explanation for the basic setting of a New Testament epistle – the author struggles against a crisis created by real opponents – is not always true. In fact, it has at times been suggested that the opponents may be purely fictional, possibly in Gal, Rom, Col, and 2 Tim.[62] Indeed, there was a constant need for antagonists, regardless of whether or not they ever existed.

Thus, instead of focusing on historical antagonists, we should study them as they appear in the texts. Such a study is not restricted by the problems discussed above, so long as we bear in mind that they are not identical with their historical counterparts. Since in Romans, the interlocutor is clearly imaginary, he enables us to see why an opponent was needed. It is my thesis that they served both the formation of Paul's theology and his presentation thereof, viz. his rhetoric.

Serious Persuasion Requires Antagonists

In Romans, Paul creates an opponent, who poses provocative questions and statements. This imaginary partner is utilized in order to express rebuttals and criticism, which the apostle can then reject, or at least attempt to reject. For example, in Romans 3:3, 5, 7, 8; 6:1 we meet this nasty interlocutor: "Will their lack of faith nullify God's faithfulness? Is God unjust in bringing his wrath on us? For if the truth of God has increased through my denial of His glory, why am I also still judged as a sinner? Let us do evil in order that good may come!"; 6:1.15: "Shall we continue in sin so that grace may abound? Shall we sin because we are not under the law but under grace?"; 7:7, 13: "Is the law sin? Has what is good become death to me?"

The interlocutor does not directly refer to any existing person. He is more like a hand puppet, which can be heavily at odds with the puppeteer. We witness a heated discussion between Paul himself and this character. In

---

[61] Cf. Romans 3:8: "Their condemnation is just."

[62] Concerning Galatians, see THURÉN, "No Antagonists"; for Colossians, see Morna D. HOOKER, "Were there False Teachers in Colossae?" in *Christ and Spirit in the New Testament* (ed. B. Lindars and S.S. Smalley; Cambridge: Cambridge University Press, 1973), 315–331; for 2 Tim see Helmut KOESTER, *Introduction to the New Testament. Vol 2. History and Literature of Early Christianity* (New York: Walter de Gruyter, 1982), 297–305; Martin DIBELIUS and Hans CONZELMANN, *Pastoral Epistles.* Translated by P. Buttolph and A. Yarbro. Hermeneia. Minneapolis: Fortress, 1989; for Romans see below.

fact, the puppet's provocative questions are more intriguing for Paul than the heresies that he meets in Galatia. At times, it seems that the apostle lacks any convincing rational arguments and therefore he has to resort to threats or condemnations, Rom 3:8c.[63]

The imaginary opponent in Romans is well suited to Paul's habit of using the *diatribe* style.[64] It could be assumed that in other letters, where at least some real people could be suspected to oppose Paul's thinking, he puts correspondingly well-tailored criticism into their mouths, or at least shapes the real utterances of the antagonists into a suitable form.

Therefore, in Galatians, Paul makes use of heavy rhetoric and theology in order to attack individuals, who are planning or preaching circumcision and thereby to ruin Pauline theology in its entirety. To be sure, we do not know whether Paul's historical "antagonists" ever represented the theology that he opposes... Yet they appear in the text as evil theologians. It is important to ask what the function of such straw men may have been in the text... For what purpose did the Apostle struggle against them?

A simple explanation may be found in his rhetorical praxis. The presentation of complicated theology to an illiterate audience, or in an oral version, required the personification of real or imaginary opponents, who represented abstract ideas. The creation of villains could have been necessitated by Paul's eagerness to discuss difficult theological matters in a way that would interest the audience and make the topic easy to understand.

This technique, which is called *prosopopoiia,* was a well-known pedagogical device in antiquity. When abstract and ideological matters are discussed, it is convenient to personify them, so that they can be fully comprehended by the audience.[65] The speaker presents theoretical standpoints as if they were advocated by real people. A well-known corresponding convention is to report events in world history through prominent per-

---

[63] To be sure, modern requirements for fair discussion cannot be automatically applied to ancient presentation.

[64] See Rudolf BULTMANN, *Der Stil der paulinischen Predigt und die kynisch-stoische Diatribe* (Göttingen: Vandenhoeck, 1910).

[65] Walter BÜHLMANN and Karl SCHERER, *Stilfiguren der Bibel: Ein kleines Nachschlagewerk.* (BibB 10; Fribourg: Schweizerisches Katholisches Bibelwerk, 1973); Joseph MARTIN, *Antike Rhetorik: Technik und Methode* (Handbuch der Altertumswissenschaft 2.3.; München: Beck, 1974), 292–293. Cf. also Chaim PERELMAN and Lucie OL-BRECHTS-TYTECA, *The New Rhetoric: A Treatise on Argumentation* (trans. J. Wilkinson and P. Weaver. Notre Dame, Ind.: University of Notre Dame, 1969), 330–31. 294. A good example is the early apologetic novel *Octavius* by Minucius Felix. *Prosopopoiia* is traditionally but misleadingly referred to when discussing Romans 7. See closer Lauri THURÉN, "Motivation as the Core of Paraenesis – Remarks on Peter and Paul as Persuaders" in *Early Christian Paraenesis in Context* (ed. J. Starr and T. Engberg-Pedersen; BZNW 125, Berlin: de Gruyter, 2004), 368.

sons.[66] This technique served the central aim of general rhetorics, namely *perspicuitas* (clarity) and communicability.

The proclamation of ideas in a litigious, cantankerous way not only yields clarity and helps to refute possible counterarguments.[67] Such polarization and *synkrisis* (comparison) made it easy for Paul to emphasize "righteousness through works of law" as opposite to "through faith/ through Christ." It did not matter whether or not somebody actually represented the former. Paul presents such a sharp and absolute version of "legalistic" soteriology, that it exceeds any contemporary Jewish text. Based on our current knowledge, it is plausible that it was composed by Paul himself.[68] It reflects a pedagogically purposeful, overstated line of thought, which Paul forcefully rejects. By driving the counterpart *ad absurdum*, the Apostle could illuminate his own model.

As I have argued above, the image of the antagonists is in many cases incoherent and difficult to combine with external information about them, at least if the exaggeration is not reduced. It is rather the case that the antagonists, as they appear in the text, fit well into general rhetorical customs and especially into Paul's own persuasive techniques. Moreover, the antagonists' opinions asserted in the text serve well Paul's theological aims. I therefore want to put forward a hypothesis, that many antagonists, in the form they appear in Pauline text, are *fictional imaginations,* who were created by the apostle himself. To be sure, they certainly had some contact with real historical people, Paul invariably give a wrong impression of those individuals, at least in our eyes. They were marginalized without justification.

Theologically Necessitated Antagonists

A profound explanation of the strong presence of antagonists in the New Testament is, as argued above, a theological requirement. In Galatians, Paul expands some seemingly minor, rather practical issues into a crucial theological topic. He informs his addressees that among them, there are individuals, who represent an Anti-Gospel, which they do not yet recognize.

This purposeful definition of their theology corresponds to Paul's historical presentation. The description of his contacts with Jerusalem in the beginning of Galatians shows that the information he gives is hard to combine with 1 Cor 15:1–11. The contrast is stark if we take both these texts as

---

[66] This technique is called "The Great Man Theory," originally developed by Thomas Carlyle. See further http://en.wikipedia.org/wiki/Great_Man.

[67] See THURÉN, *Derhetorizing*, 68–69.

[68] THURÉN, *Derhetorizing*, 143–148.

neutral historical presentations. Not until the different rhetorical purposes of the texts have been observed, does their relationship become easier to understand: in Galatians, the main purpose of Paul's narration was to promote his ethos, especially his theological independence. But if we intend to use Paul's narration as a basis for an historical presentation, additional data are required.[69]

Moreover, when Paul fights for "justification through faith," this does not mean that the idea was rejected or even questioned among the addressees. However, the implied antagonists, i.e. the opponents as they appear in the text, function nicely as a counterpart to Paul's own teaching. Both the interlocutor in Romans and the mute antagonists in Galatia help Paul to formulate his own theological reasoning. Irrespective of whether the antagonists ever existed physically, they help the apostle to emphasize his own theories. Later on at least, when the text was read in new situations and the historical Galatia had lost its relevance, this became their sole function.

It is hardly probable that somebody in Rome actually propagated the idea of that more sin should be committed in order to multiply the grace, nor that somebody in Galatia preached a theological system based on "works of the law." Yet, these ideas may have been there, and, on that basis Paul might have inferred such heresies. The interest in circumcision in Galatia may well have been such "yeast."

Traditionally, scholars assume that the problems arrived in Galatia from outside, and that Paul therefore had to defend himself and his theology. His "doctrine of justification" is consequently often interpreted as a "Kampfeslehre," which does not reflect Paul's principal theological aims. However, our picture of Paul as fighting against other theologians is based on his own presentation of the conflicts in Jerusalem and Antioch, especially described in Gal (2:1–14). But it has been claimed that he was so belligerent only in the epistles.[70] A description of his deep conflict with the other apostles and the conveyance of his self-portrait as a person filled with pathos were needed for the sake of his theology,[71] but his theology was not necessarily a reaction against conflicts with actual individuals.

In Galatians, his theological zealotry is an explicit, text-internal reason for Paul's attack.[72] This black-and-white theology, clearly visible in Galatians, permitted no exceptions. It is hard to believe that there were *no* theo-

---

[69] See further THURÉN, "No Antagonists."

[70] Cf. 2 Cor 10:10 "For they say, 'His letters are weighty and strong, but his bodily presence is weak, and his speech contemptible.'"

[71] See Lauri THURÉN, "Was Paul Angry? Derhetorizing Galatians." *The Rhetorical Interpretation of Scripture, Essays from the 1996 Malibu Conference* (JSNTSup 180; ed. D. Stamps and S. Porter; Sheffield: Sheffield Academic, 1999), 302–320.

[72] See also MITTERNACHT, *Forum*, 149–152.

logical differences between Paul and some members of his audience.[73] And
individuals who did not share this intransigence were probably surprised
by Paul's vehemence.[74]

Irrespective of whether or not Paul's recipients were theologically motivated, the apostle himself certainly was. He needed to formulate a solid,
clear principle – justification by faith – for himself and for his recipients.
For this purpose, the antithesis and its representatives were needed.

It is my thesis that Paul needed antagonists because of his theology, not
vice versa. Reaction to social challenges is a too simple explanation of his
theological thinking.[75] The man was obviously driven by his passion for
theological issues, and the way in which he presents his antagonists in Galatians derives from his own theoretical consideration of the Torah. I have
argued earlier that Paul was provoked, either by the theological tensions,
which he perceived within the Holy Scriptures themselves, or by a general
problem with human boasting before God.[76] Be these hypotheses true or
not, Paul's theological opponent, the real antagonist in Galatians, was Paul
himself. To a certain degree this is also true of many of his other antagonists.

Since the picture of the antagonists that Paul conveys in Galatians is
rhetorically and theologically purposeful, the same may well apply to other
New Testament epistles as well: the doctrine and behavior of the opposition are described in a purposeful, biased way. Like the one-sided portrayal
of the Pharisees in Matthew or of the Jews in John, they have served well
to highlight the message of the author. The historical "antagonists" may
however have suffered as vicarious victims.

Conclusion: Is Rehabilitation Necessary?

In conclusion, we must ponder the ethical consequences of our results.
Were the New Testament authors dishonorable when creating these fictional men for their own purposes? Insofar as no actual person was involved, which seems to be the case in Romans, no harm was done. Furthermore, when the caricature of the antagonists was created by the use of
standard rhetorical devices, such as *vituperatio*, the only people led astray

---

[73] It is difficult to tell, which goal was more important to the apostle. See THURÉN,
Derhetorizing, 72 n. 93.

[74] THURÉN, *Derhetorizing*, 68–72.

[75] See THURÉN, *Derhetorizing*, 8–18.

[76] I have discussed these hypotheses in more detail in THURÉN, *Derhetorizing*, 138–
178.

are the latter-day users of the text, who are unaware of these techniques. But even then the memory of the historical antagonists may have been stained in vain.

Even so, the original "antagonists" were presumably distressed to hear the texts, in which they were unjustly denigrated and marginalized. And as Biblical texts are still authoritative in many ways for many individuals, echoes of this technique are not always pleasant either.

In academic circles, a correct understanding of expressions that refer to the antagonists is not merely an ethical question. As I have hinted above, several historical and theological questions are related to this issue. Therefore, a reassessment of the opposition is necessary, not only for the sake of their reputation, but because of our search for a more realistic view of the New Testament documents and their immediate context. The marginalized antagonists deserve a fair treatment.

Son of Man and Early Christian Identity Formation

Thomas Kazen

Introduction

The lack of consensus in interpreting the Son of Man in the New Testament is still being characterized as embarrassing.[1] Nonetheless scholars seem unable to keep away from the question. In two recent articles I have argued in detail for a "collective" interpretation of the expression, at the level of the historical Jesus, suggesting that Jesus used "Son of Man" as kingdom imagery, following the obvious meaning of the symbol in Daniel.[2] This line of interpretation was championed by Thomas W. Manson, C. F. D. Moule and Lloyd Gaston, and is worth more than a file among others in the archives of research historians.[3] Although Manson's idea of corporate personality, borrowed from Wheeler Robinson, as well as his speculative grand narrative ending, in which he reads Mark too chronologically, may be criticized,[4] these flaws should not obscure the basically sound idea of Jesus following Daniel in referring to the Son of Man as a symbol or an embodiment of the faithful remnant. That interpretation merits consideration and may be further developed.

---

[1] Cf. Frederick H. BORSCH, *The Son of Man in Myth and History* (NTL; London: SCM, 1967), 15, with James D. G. DUNN, *Jesus Remembered*, 725.

[2] Thomas KAZEN, "Son of Man as Kingdom Imagery: Jesus Between Corporate Symbol and Individual Redeemer Figure", in *Jesus from Judaism to Christianity: Continuum Approaches to the Historical Jesus* (ed. T. Holmén; ESCO; LNTS [JSNTSup], 352; London: T & T Clark, 2007), 87–108; Thomas KAZEN, "The Coming Son of Man Revisited", *Journal for the Study of the Historical Jesus* 5 (2007): 157–176.

[3] T. W. MANSON, *The Teaching of Jesus: Studies of Its Form and Content* (Cambridge: University Press, 1931), 211–236; T. W. MANSON, *Studies in the Gospels and Epistles* (ed. M. Black; Manchester: University Press, 1962), 123–145; C. F. D. MOULE, *The Phenomenon of the New Testament: An Inquiry into the Implications of Certain Features of the New Testament* (SBT, 2:1; London: SCM, 1967), 21–42 (For further references to Moule, see articles in note 2); Lloyd GASTON, *No Stone on Another: Studies in the Significance of the Fall of Jerusalem in the Synoptic Gospels* (NovTSup, 23; Leiden: Brill, 1970), 370–409.

[4] Cf. the criticism of GASTON, *No Stone*, 394.

In the present essay I enquire into the significance of the Son of Man imagery for identity formation, in particular in early Christ-believing communities. In doing this I draw on my previous work, understanding "Son of Man" as collective kingdom imagery. A full argument for this mode of interpretation cannot be outlined here, but the present discussion will also lend support to previous conclusions. I suggest that while the Danielic image was very soon transferred to Jesus as an individual re-deemer figure, it continued to provide an impetus for Christian collective identity formation, not least through the original apocalyptic context to which it belonged: a powerless remnant people of God, subject to trial and suffering, soon to be vindicated and exalted at the inbreaking of the divine kingdom. We will see that the extent to which the Son of Man plays a role for group identity differs between various communities.

Son of Man

While "Son of Man" soon came to designate an individual redeemer figure, all three categories of Son of Man sayings (present, suffering and coming) in the Synoptic gospels are easily read and interpreted in a collective sense. I have previously argued that sayings from all three categories could have originated with Jesus himself, and that Son of Man imagery was em-ployed as Danielic kingdom language for the ongoing process of prophetic change and restoration to which Jesus and his disciples belonged and in which they saw themselves as playing an initiating or inaugurating role, although without referring to a present or future individual redeemer fig-ure.[5]

The significance of this imagery for early Christian identity formation is inherent in such an interpretation; the point with a collective reading is that a Son of Man typology provided possibilities of identification for the early Jesus movement – for disciples as well as for Jesus. The correspondence between the life-style and fate of the Son of Man and that of the disciples has been repeatedly observed.[6] Just as the circles responsible for the for-

---

[5] For detailed arguments, see KAZEN, "Son of Man" and "Coming Son of Man".

[6] Cf. MANSON, *Teaching*, 201–211, 231–232; Gerd THEISSEN, *Sociology of Early Pal-estinian Christianity*; Philadelphia: Fortress, 1978), 24–30; Gerd THEISSEN, *Die Jesus-bewegung: Sozialgeschichte einer Revolution der Werte* (Gütersloh: Gütersloher Verlag-shaus, 2004), 91–98; Aarto JÄRVINEN, "The Son of Man and his Followers", in *Charac-terization in the Gospels: Reconceiving Narrative Criticism* (eds. D. Rhoads and K. Syreeni; JSNTSup, 184; Sheffield: Academic Press, 1999), 180–222, (189–90); Aarto JÄRVINEN, "Jesus as Community Symbol in Q", in *The Sayings Source Q and the His-torical Jesus* (ed. A. Lindemann; BETL, 158; Leuven: University Press, 2001), 515–521.

mation of Daniel looked at the fifth non-monstrous and human-like being as an inspiring visionary or heavenly mirror image of their own faithful and martyred remnant, soon to be given power over the kingdom, so Jesus and his early followers made use of the same image to anticipate final vindication and victory in spite of current homelessness and suffering.

The Son of Man continued to play a role for early Christian identity formation *in spite of* rapid transmutation into a messianic title. Although this change is more or less apparent in all New Testament documents where the designation occurs, we still find enough remnants of an originally collective interpretation, which can contribute to our understanding of how early Christian identity was formed. In the following, we will analyse not only New Testament evidence reflecting various groups of early Christ-believers, but also the Book of Daniel and the Parables of *1 Enoch*, to establish the Son of Man's significance for group identity in various recipient communities.

Identity Formation and Group Identity

Ancient Christian identity formation has been in focus in recent years.[7] The concept of identity is somewhat problematic when dealing with ancient texts, as it can easily be used anachronistically. The distinction between individual and corporate or group identity is not as straightforward as one might first believe. Furthermore, identity in terms of labelling is not entirely the same thing as identity in terms of self-definition.[8]

In social psychology, the concept of *social identity* has become a commonplace, going back to Henri Tajfel[9] and John C. Turner.[10] It is dependent on social categorization, "in which distinctions are made between the individual's own group and the out-groups which are compared or con-

---

For further references, see KAZEN, "Son of Man", 98–99, n. 60; "Coming Son of Man", 166, n. 40.

[7] See the Norwegian project "Construction of Christian Identity in Antiquity" (http://www.tf.uio.no/antikk/) and the Swedish project "Christian Identity – the First 100 Years" (http://www.teol.lu.se/nt/ identitet/eng.html).

[8] For an introducing discussion, see Judith M. LIEU, *Christian Identity in the Jewish and Graeco-Roman World* (Oxford: University Press, 2004), 1–26.

[9] Cf. Henri TAJFEL, *Differentiation Between Social Groups: Studies in the Social Psychology of Intergroup Relations* (London: Academic Press, 1978); Henri TAJFEL, *Human Groups and Social Categories: Studies in Social Psychology* (Cambridge: University Press, 1981).

[10] John C. TURNER, *Rediscovering the Social Group: A Self-Categorization Theory* (Oxford: Blackwell, 1987).

trasted with" it.[11] Tajfel defines social identity as limited to "that *part* of an individual's self-concept which derives from his knowledge of his membership of a social group (or groups) together with the value and emotional significance attached to that membership".[12] There is a paradoxical focus on *individual* identity in the sense of the individual's relationship to the group and his/her categorization of "us" and "them".[13] An alternative would be to focus on generalized group behaviour and beliefs that relate to how the group is experienced and characterized not only by its own members but also by out-groups. This could be defined as *group identity*.[14] A precise distinction is, however, not always possible.

In New Testament studies, the concept of social identity has been used and developed in particular by Philip Esler. He employs it in his study on Galatians to analyse inter-group conflicts.[15] In his study of Romans, Esler complements social identity with its "cousin", self-categorization theory, in discussing intra-group tensions.[16] In both cases, the aim is to find tools for analysing and interpreting conflicts.

In the present essay, the focus is not on group conflicts, but on adherents' relationships to groups and on group behaviour. Son of Man imagery seems to have had an influence on both, although to different extents in the various contexts. We will thus talk of *group identity* in a very general and non-technical sense, as the experience of shared characteristics, rather than individual self-concepts. We will, however, take particular note of some of Tajfel's observations concerning group membership and identity formation: even when group membership may be in some ways disadvantageous for individuals, many will stick to it if it is associated with "important values which are themselves a part of [their] acceptable self-image". In such cases

at least two solutions are possible: (i) to change one's interpretation of the attributes of the group so that its unwelcome features (e.g. low status) are either justified or made

---

[11] TAJFEL, *Human Groups*, 254.

[12] TAJFEL, *Human Groups*, 255.

[13] Cf. Stephen WORCHEL *et al.*, "A Multidimensional Model of Identity: Relating Individual and Group Identities to Intergroup Behaviour", in *Social Identity Processes: Trends in Theory and Research* (eds. D. Capozza and R. Brown; London: SAGE, 2000), 15–32 (20).

[14] This is a gross simplification, but sufficient for our present purposes. WORCHEL *et al.* ("Multidimensional Model", 17–21), discuss four dimensions of identity: person characteristics, group membership (similar to traditional social identity), intra-group identity and group identity.

[15] Philip ESLER, *Galatians* (London & New York: Routledge, 1998).

[16] Philip ESLER, *Conflict and Identity in Romans: The Social Setting of Paul's Letter* (Minneapolis: Fortress, 2003).

acceptable through a reinterpretation; or (ii) to accept the situation for what it is and engage in social action which would lead to desirable changes in the situation.[17]

As we will see, the Son of Man typology facilitates both of these strategies.

Daniel

The influence of the book of Daniel in various strands of Second Temple Judaism is considerable, and Daniel played a decisive role for eschatological development and identity formation not only among early Christians.[18] What role, then, did Son of Man imagery play for the early recipients of the Book of Daniel?[19]

In Dan 7:13–14, the human-like figure symbolizes a final and eternal kingdom, given to the saints of God, while the previous beasts symbolize four successive oppressive kingdoms. This is made explicit in the subsequent explanation (cf. vv. 18, 22, 27). While the four beasts are said to represent "kings" (7:17), the fifth non-monstrous figure is never interpreted as an individual, but only as "the holy of the Most High" (*qaddîšê ʿelyônîn*). A similar ambiguity is found in chapter 2. There is no king mentioned in the final kingdom, represented by the little stone (2:44–45).

There is a certain fluidity: the animal/human imagery symbolizes kingdoms, and kingdoms are represented by rulers and/or people. The Son of Man thus becomes a symbol of the eternal kingdom and its representatives. No individual messianic leader or royal figure is implied, however. The Son of Man is in all respects a collective symbol with whom readers regarding themselves as a faithful remnant are supposed to identify themselves.[20]

Nevertheless, this figure was later interpreted as an individual redeemer. Some impetus was found in the subsequent text. In Dan 9:21, Gabriel is somewhat oddly called "man" (*hāʾîsh gabrîʾēl*); in 10:5 a man (*ʾish-ʾehād*), dressed in linen, speaks to Daniel; in 10:16 and 18 someone "like a man", touches him/his lips and gives him strength. Two different expressions are used in Daniel 10: *kidmût běnê ʾādām* in v. 16 and *kěmarʾēh*

---

[17] TAJFEL, *Human Groups*, 256.

[18] For details and references, see KAZEN, "Son of Man", 91–94 with notes; "Coming Son of Man", 160–162, especially n. 20.

[19] The *religionsgeschichtliche* background of the image will not be discussed here. Its interpretation must be determined by its function and context, not by its supposed origin.

[20] Cf. Mogens MÜLLER, *Der Ausdruck "Menschensohn" in den Evangelien: Voraussetzungen und Bedeutung* (Acta Theologica Danica, 17; Leiden: Brill, 1984), 14–24.

ʾādām in v. 18, both reminding of *dĕmût kĕmarʾēh ʾādām* in Ezek 1:26, the former, however, supplying a possible association with the Son of Man in Dan 7:13. These figures are different: in Dan 7 the Son of Man is a symbol or metaphor, referring to a collective reality; in Dan 10, the man-like figure is "real", although "of a higher, probably angelic nature".[21] John Collins finds human imagery consistently portraying angelic figures in Daniel,[22] and identifies the Son of Man in Dan 7 with Michael, the angelic prince of Israel.[23] While angelic princes, representing peoples in their capacity as heavenly counterparts, do belong to the close context,[24] these figures are not intervening in human terrestrial affairs but, according to a world-view then current, carry on their own battle above, parallel to what happens below. Michael is no more a messianic figure than the angelic princes of Persia and Greece. Whether equated with the Son of Man in ch. 7 or merely lending his attributes to him, he is nevertheless no individual redeemer but a heavenly counterpart ("symbol") of the Israelite people.[25]

If, however, subsequent interpreters came to see the man-like figures of chapter 7 and 10 as identical, they had to differentiate him from Michael, since Michael assists him in his warfare against the angelic princes of Persia and Greece (10:21–11:1). This might easily have spurred imagination: who could this Son of Man be, if not the angelic double or representative of Israel? Perhaps some kind of celestial Messianic redeemer figure?

While such interpretations go beyond the plain meaning of Dan 7, they did evolve with time and seem to go together with a re-interpretation of Daniel's kingdom scheme as referring to Babylon, Media-Persia, Greece and Rome, respectively.[26] Somewhere in this process the Son of Man ac-

---

[21] Sabino CHIALÀ, "The Son of Man: The Evolution of an Expression", in *Enoch and the Messiah Son of Man: Revisiting the Book of Parables* (ed. G. Boccaccini; Grand Rapids: Eerdmans, 2007), 153–178 (158–159).

[22] John J. COLLINS, "Enoch and the Son of Man: A Response to Sabino Chialà and Helge Kvanvig", in Boccaccini, *Enoch and the Messiah Son of Man*, 216–227 (217).

[23] Cf. John J. COLLINS, *Daniel: A Commentary on the Book of Daniel* (Hermeneia; Minneapolis: Fortress, 1993), 304–310.

[24] Apart from Michael (the angelic prince of Israel), angelic princes of Persia and Greece are mentioned (Dan 10:20–11:1; 12:1).

[25] Cf. John J. COLLINS, "The Heavenly Representative: The 'Son of Man' in the Similitudes of Enoch", in *Ideal Figures in Ancient Judaism: Profiles and Paradigms* (eds. G. W. E. Nickelsburg and J. J. Collins; SBL Septuagint and Cognate Studies, 12; Chico: Scholars, 1980), 111–133 (114–116).

[26] An original interpretation continued to be reflected for some time in what Maurice Casey calls the "Syrian tradition". Maurice CASEY, *Son of Man: The Interpretation and Influence of Daniel 7* (London: SPCK, 1979), 51–98.

quires the traits of an individual redeemer. In Daniel, however, this process has not yet begun.

The Son of Man figure in Dan 7 provided a type that was well suited to the reinforcement of the group identity of early recipients in the middle of the second century BCE They had been crushed and trampled by the fourth beast, but were now hoping to be vindicated as power relationships swiftly changed. The Son of Man imagery confirmed them as the people of the kingdom, the true Israel, reinforced their common values and assured them that their low status in relation to the "Hellenizers" was not a disadvantage, but would soon be reversed as they – the faithful and observant – would be finally rewarded.

1 Enoch

The significance of *1 Enoch* for the development of the Son of Man figure has been debated for two centuries. A pre-Christian date used to be generally accepted, and the Son of Man was often understood as a pre-existent and heavenly messianic figure.

When it was realized that the Aramaic fragments in Qumran lacked the Parables (*1 En.* 37–71), this section was increasingly regarded as a post-70 document, of little use for interpreting christological development during the Second Temple period. The idea of an apocalyptic Son of Man gave way to other explanations, notably generic ones.[27]

Today, a growing number of scholars argue that the absence of the Book of Parables in Qumran cannot settle the issue, and some suggest a date during the reign of Herod the Great.[28] Claims for a near consensus are, however, overstated.[29] A number of scholars prefer a date close to the fall of Jerusalem.[30] We must remember that no external evidence for the Parables exist before the Ethiopic text. Suggestions of patristic allusions have been made for a century, but none is decisive or even convincing.[31]

---

[27] Cf. CASEY, *Son of Man*, and more recently, *The Solution to the 'Son of Man' Problem* (LNTS 343; London: T & T Clark, 2007).

[28] See several of the essays in Boccaccini, *Enoch and the Messiah Son of Man*.

[29] Cf. Gabriele BOCCACCINI, "The Enoch Seminar at Camaldoli: Re-entering the Parables of Enoch in the Study of Second Temple Judaism and Christian Origins", in Boccaccini, *Enoch and the Messiah Son of Man*, 15–16.

[30] Paulo SACCHI, "The 2005 Camaldoli Seminar on the Parables of Enoch: Summary and Prospects for Future Research", in Boccaccini, *Enoch and the Messiah Son of Man*, 499–512.

[31] Daniel C. OLSON, "An Overlooked Patristic Allusion to the Parables of Enoch?" in Boccaccini, *Enoch and the Messiah Son of Man*, 492–496; cf. David W. SUTER, "Enoch

As for internal evidence, numerous attempts to trace historical events in the text have been implausible and overly speculative.[32]

It is more promising to locate the Parables within a social context and a historical development of ideas.[33] According to Boccaccini, they testify to "a stage in which the encounter and merging of the Sapiential, Messianic, and Apocalyptic Paradigms were still at their inception".[34] Still, this provides no exact dating.

A detailed comparison of the text of the Parables with New Testament material may provide another avenue. Johannes Theisohn and, more recently, Leslie Walck[35] compare Matthew 19:28 and 25:31, where the Son of Man is described as sitting on the "throne of glory", with the same phrase in *1 En.* 62.5; 69.27, 29. In both instances in Matthew, the Son of Man is obviously redactional, and reflects a Matthean development in which this figure is more clearly identified with Jesus than in the other Synoptics.[36] Walck concludes that "the influence of the Parables on Matt 19:28 is quite likely".[37] Elsewhere, there is no evidence for any direct literary relationships between the Parables and the Gospels, but only general similarities suggesting a shared world of ideas.[38] Hence, a date near 70 CE seems just as possible as an earlier one. The Parables remain important for the study of messianic and apocalyptic ideas – including the Son of Man – in the gospels, but not necessarily as a source or a premise.

What role does the Son of Man figure play, then, for the readers of the Parables? While focus is usually placed on the messianic figure, called the "Righteous One", the "Chosen One" and the "Son of Man",[39] the text is

---

in Sheol: Updating the Dating of the Book of Parables", in Boccaccini, *Enoch and the Messiah Son of Man*, 415–443.

[32] Several examples are found in BOCCACCINI, *Enoch and the Messiah Son of Man*. There is, however, no room to discuss them further here.

[33] Lester L. GRABBE, "The Parables of Enoch in Second Temple Jewish Society", in Boccaccini, *Enoch and the Messiah Son of Man*, 386–402; Gabriele BOCCACCINI, "Finding a Place for the Parables of Enoch within Second Temple Jewish Literature", in Boccaccini, *Enoch and the Messiah Son of Man*, 263–289.

[34] BOCCACCINI, "Finding a Place", 288.

[35] Johannes THEISOHN, *Der auserwählte Richter: Untersuchungen zum traditionsgeschichtlichem Ort der Menschensohngestalt der Bilderreden des Äthiopischen Henoch* (Göttingen: Vandenhoeck & Ruprecht, 1975); Leslie W. WALCK, "The Son of Man in the Parables of Enoch and the Gospels", in Boccaccini, *Enoch and the Messiah Son of Man*, 299–337; cf. Leslie W. WALCK, "The Son of Man in Matthew and the 'Similitudes of Enoch'" (Ann Arbor: UMI Dissertation Services, 1999; not seen).

[36] Cf. KAZEN, "Coming Son of Man", 168, 171.

[37] WALCK, "Son of Man", 324.

[38] WALCK, "Son of Man", 336.

[39] "Righteous One" (38.2; 47.1, 4; 53.6); "Chosen One" (39.6; 40.5; 45.3, 4; 48.6; 49.2, 4; 51.3, 5; 52.6, 9; 53.6; 55.4; 61.5, 8, 10; 62.1); "Son of Man" (*walda sab'*: 46.2,

just as concerned with the identity, character and fate of the community that is supposed to find this writing appealing, "the congregation of the righteous" (38.1). This group of faithful people are, just like the key figure, designated as "righteous", "chosen" and "sons of men".[40] The Righteous and Chosen One, the Son of Man, clearly functions as a heavenly type for the righteous and chosen ones, the sons of men, to identify with. This is basically similar to Daniel, where the Son of Man represents the faithful Israelite remnant, the saints. In the Parables this Son of Man is "chosen and hidden in his [the Lord of Spirits'] presence before the world was created" (48.6; cf. v. 3; 62.7). This may be understood as pre-existence but just as well as election. In Daniel, the vindication of the saints is still in the future from the standpoint of the narrator ("I, Daniel") and their identity is at present still hidden; hence things must be revealed in a dream vision. Similarly, in the Parables, the elect Son of Man, corresponding to the elect remnant, is hidden at present, to be vindicated only in the future. The "Son of Man" that belongs to the "hidden things" will overturn persecuting kings and kingdoms (ch. 46) for the sake of the holy and righteous martyrs (ch. 47). On the other hand, his revelation to the holy and righteous (48.7) *means* that these kings and "strong" will fall into the hands of the "chosen ones" (48.9).

The Son of Man that was named/chosen/hidden before creation (48.3, 6) thus symbolizes the elect people, pre-determined for future victory (cf. 62.7–8).[41] As in Daniel, he can be taken as their heavenly counterpart or

---

3, 4; 48.2; *walda be'si*: 62.5: 69.29; 71.14; *walda 'eg^wala 'emma-ḥeyāw*: 62.7, 9, 14; 63.11; 69.26, 27; 70.1; 71.17). This figure is also, although not so often, called the "Anointed One" (*mas/šiḥ/h*: 48.10; 52.4). For detailed discussion, see J. C. VANDERKAM, "Righteous One, Messiah, Chosen One, and Son of Man in 1 Enoch 37–71" in *The Messiah: Developments in Earliest Judaism and Christianity* (ed. J. H. Charlesworth; Minneapolis: Fortress, 1992), 169–191.

[40] E.g. "righteous" (38.2, 3, 4, 5; 39.4, 6, 7; 41.8; 45.6; 47.1, 2, 4?; 48.7, 9; 50.2; 51.2, 5; 53.7; 56.7; 58.1, 2, 3, 4; 60.2, 8; 61.3; 62.12, 13, 15); "chosen" (38.2, 3, 4; 39.1, 6, 7; 40.5; 41.2; 45.3, 5; 48.9; 50.1; 51.5; 56.6; 58.1, 2, 3; 60.8; 61.4, 12; 62.7, 8, 11, 12, 13, 15); "sons of men" (42.1). They are also less frequently called "holy" (39.4; 43.4; 45.1; 48.9; 51.2; 58.3; 62.8), although more often the expression "holy ones" refers to angelic beings (39.1, 4; 41.2?; 47.2, 4?; 50.1; 58.5; 61.8, 10, 12), corresponding to "the Holy One" as a divine attribute.

[41] This was pointed out already by MANSON (*Studies*, 140). The material was written in 1949, before the significance of the Qumran findings was apparent. Other early voices for collective interpretations even for such texts as *1 Enoch* and *4 Ezra* include Nils Messel and H. H. Rowley. See D. S. RUSSELL, *The Method and Message of Jewish Apocalyptic 200 BC – AD 100* (OTL; London: SCM, 1964), 344–345, 350–352. Cf. THEISSEN, *Jesusbewegung*, 96–8. See also the views of VANDERKAM, "Righteous One", 179–182, warning against reading pre-existence into *1 Enoch* 62.7; and of Collins, interpreting the Son of Man in *1 Enoch* as "the supernatural double not of the individual Enoch but of all

angelic double; what he does the chosen do, and what happens to him will happen to the righteous saints. Although on his way to become an individual messianic figure, partly because of amalgamation of the human-like figures of Dan 9 and 10 with the Son of Man of Dan 7 (cf. *1 En.* 46.1), he still retains his character as a collective symbol.[42] We can thus conclude that the Son of Man still functions as a collective symbol, although he is becoming more and more individualized. While a symbol does not automatically become instrumental for identity formation just because it is collective, the *repeated parallelism* between this figure and the righteous or elect ones suggests that he represents the *content* and *character* of the community's behaviours and beliefs. He provides a perspective through which they look at themselves. The problem is that we know too little of the people associated with the Parables.[43] The composite and complicated history of the text makes any attempt at contextualising a hazardous enterprise. Nevertheless, similarities with Daniel and suggestions of martyrdom, together with the emphasis on present hiddenness and future vindication, imply a group identity in which low status is being made acceptable through apocalyptic re-interpretation.

---

righteous human beings", and as "the heavenly counterpart of the righteous on earth"; John J. COLLINS, *The Scepter and the Star: The Messiahs of the Dead Sea Scrolls and Other Ancient Literature* (New York: Doubleday, 1995), 181–182.

[42] Manuscript evidence suggest that at an early stage, the distinction between the Son of Man and his corresponding earthly reality was not always very clear; in a few places there are variant readings for the "Righteous One" and the "Chosen One", making the text refer to the righteous and the chosen instead: 39.6 (cf. the variant *"their* dwelling" in 39.7); 45.4; 47.4; cf. 38.2.

[43] The problems in associating apocalyptic texts with communities or circles have been discussed by a number of scholars; cf. John J. COLLINS, "Pseudepigraphy and Group Formation in Second Temple Judaism", in *Pseudepigraphic Perspectives: The Apocrypha and Pseudepigrapha in Light of the Dead Sea Scrolls* (eds. E. G. Chazon and M. Stone; Leiden: Brill, 1999), 43–58; Lester L. GRABBE, "The Social Setting of Early Jewish Apocalypticism", *JSP* 4 (1989): 27–47; Matthias HENZE, "Enoch's Dream Visions and the Visions of Daniel Reexamined", in *Enoch and Qumran Origins: New Light on a Forgotten Connection* (ed. G. Boccaccini; Grand Rapids: Eerdmans, 2005), 17–23; Patrick TILLER, "The Sociological Context of the Dream Visions of Daniel and 1 Enoch", in Boccaccini, *Enoch and Qumran Origins*, 23 *Group Dynamics* 26. While one must be cautious in associating apocalyptic texts with specific communities, the repeated parallelism just mentioned strongly suggests a group or groups of recipients modelling their identity on the text's main figure.

Q

Among Q scholars, the Son of Man has usually been assigned to a stratum (Q^2) that emphasizes judgment, in distinction to an earlier stratum intent on wisdom teaching.[44] This idea is, however, being increasingly questioned,[45] as is the validity of detailed stratification.[46]

Several scholars have suggested that Dan 7 had no influence on the Son of Man sayings in Q.[47] This fits with the supposition that the Son of Man on the lips of Jesus carried a merely generic meaning and that an apocalyptic interpretation was only added at some later stage. Tuckett, however, points out that

the theme of the rejected prophets is part of a broader complex of motifs in Q. The prophets who suffer violence are messengers of Wisdom (cf. Q 11,49–51; also 7,31–35). Further, a number of passages which allude to this complex of motifs, whether together or separately, refer to Jesus as "SM" (Q 6,22; 7,34; 9,58). In a number of these texts, the experience of Jesus serves as a prototype for the suffering and hostility experienced by his later followers.[48]

Among Tuckett's examples, we find the last beatitude (Q 6:22–23), the comparison with the Baptizer, implying a similar fate to Jesus and his disciples (Q 7:29–36) and the saying about homelessness (Q 9:58), which functions as an interpretive key to the mission charge (Q 10).[49] Tuckett also points out that the judging activity of the coming Son of Man in Q (12:8–10) is not restricted to Jesus alone, but expected to be shared by his disciples (cf. Q 22:30). We thus have a far-reaching analogy between Jesus

---

[44] For a convenient summary, see John S. KLOPPENBORG, *The Formation of Q: Trajectories in Ancient Wisdom Collections* (Studies in Antiquity and Christianity; Philadelphia: Fortress, 1987), 317–328.

[45] Cf. JÄRVINEN, "Son of Man", 180–222; Jens SCHRÖTER, "The Son of Man as Representative of God's Kingdom: On the Interpretation of Jesus in Mark and Q", in *Jesus, Mark and Q: The Teachings of Jesus and Its Earliest Records* (eds. M. Labahn and A. Schmidt; JSNTSup, 214; Sheffield: Academic Press, 2001), 34–68; Christopher M. TUCKETT, "The Son of Man and Daniel 7: Q and Jesus", in *The Sayings Source Q and the Historical Jesus* (ed. A. Lindemann; BETL, 158; Leuven: University Press, 2001), 371–394. Tuckett points out that an *interest* in the Son of Man sayings is not equal to *creating* them and argues for several of these sayings being "pre-redactional" ("Son of Man", 381–388).

[46] Cf. the scepticism of Christopher TUCKETT, "On the Stratification of Q", *Semeia* 55 (1991): 213–222. Some material common to Matthew and Luke but with a low degree of literal correspondence could better be explained by an oral relationship. Cf. DUNN, *Jesus Remembered*, 147–158, 234–238.

[47] E.g. Maurice Casey, Leif Vaage, etc. See TUCKETT. "Son of Man", 371, n. 2.

[48] Tuckett, "Son of Man", 373.

[49] TUCKETT, "Son of Man", 373–374.

and his followers, governed by a Son of Man typology. This has already been argued by Theissen, in his *Sociology of Early Palestinian Christianity*; the Son of Man sayings provide a "structural homologue" between the life and fate of Jesus and his disciples.[50] The Son of Man is the most important referential figure for the members of the early Jesus movement as reflected in Q, shaping their social practice,[51] as well as their understanding of themselves, and is thus instrumental in forming their group identity.

Similar conclusions have also been drawn by other scholars.[52] Sayings concerning suffering and hardship, such as Q 7:34 and 9:58, make little sense when interpreted generically, as if referring to human beings in general. The homelessness and renunciation of family they describe characterize the kingdom announced by Jesus and are typical of the Jesus movement, i.e., Jesus *together with* his disciples.[53]

In coming Son of Man sayings like Q 12:39–40, the Son of Man can be read as originally referring to the kingdom that the faithful represent and to which they belong. This is a possible reading, in line with Daniel, and not implausible when we realize that Luke does not, like Matthew, clearly signal an individual reinterpretation by inserting this saying into Jesus' eschatological discourse.

Similar considerations apply to the saying about confessing or denying, in Q 12:8–9. There is an overlapping Markan tradition and Luke includes both, as he frequently does (Mark 8:38 / Luke 9:26).[54] In both variants, however, it is obvious that Jesus cannot without great difficulty be understood as fully identical with the Son of Man. Matthew's reworking of the Q version attests to this apparent problem, as he has simply substituted

---

[50] THEISSEN, *Sociology*, 24–30. Theissen's analysis is made from a sociological perspective (analysis of roles, social role-taking). From a literary point of view, this connection has been pointed out by JÄRVINEN, "Son of Man", 189–190. While I agree with Järvinen that the (limited) characterization of Jesus has the effect of contemporising the situation of Jesus for the readers, making it possible to step inside the text, I would not regard the connection between Jesus and the disciples as *created* by the narrator of Q. It is present throughout the gospel tradition (thus already MANSON, *Teaching*, 201–211, 231–232) and must be regarded as an historical one.

[51] THEISSEN, *Jesusbewegung*, 91–98. Theissen suggests that "der Menschensohn die zentrale Bezugsgestalt der Jesusbewegung war. Seine Situation entsprach ihrer Situation: Glauben und Praxis bildeten hier eine unauflösliche Einheit" (98).

[52] E.g. JÄRVINEN, "Son of Man"; "Community Symbol"; SCHRÖTER, "Son of Man".

[53] For a more detailed argument, see KAZEN, "Son of Man", 100–102.

[54] The Markan and Q versions are obviously variants of one saying. Cf. H. J. de JONGE, "The Sayings on Confessing and Denying Jesus in Q 12:8–9 and Mark 8:38", in *Sayings of Jesus: Canonical and Non-Canonical: Essays in Honour of Tjitze Baarda* (eds. W. L. Petersen, J. S. Vos and H. J. de Jonge; SupNovT, 89; Leiden: Brill, 1997), 105–121 (117–118).

"the Son of Man" for "me" and "I", in order to make the embarrassing discrepancy disappear and the text conform to an identification of the Son of Man with Jesus, which must be taken for granted in his context. Both variants of this tradition, however, reveal an earlier understanding in which the Son of Man who might confirm or deny people was interpreted according to the Danielic image of the kingdom and of its saintly representatives taking part in divine judgment. The idea would have been that one's future status in the kingdom depends on one's present response to Jesus and his message, and the role of the Son of Man suggests the function of Jesus and his disciples as kingdom representatives in the judgment of Israel.[55]

That the judgment activity of the Son of Man is collectively shared by the Jesus movement is attested in Q 22:30.[56] Thus Tuckett's conclusion that "in Q, as in *1 Enoch*, the SM figure seems to be a single individual" seems insufficiently supported.[57]

Although there are clear tendencies towards the individualization of the Son of Man figure in Q, we find much ambiguity. The Son of Man provides a typology that shapes the group identity of early followers living within the Q tradition. An itinerant life-style, poverty, serving, suffering and persecution were part of this identity. Like the homeless, suffering and denied Son of Man, they expected future vindication, a reversal of values and a turnover of power structures, since they would partake in the coming eschatological judgment. This made their present low status acceptable and meanwhile they engaged in activities associated with Jesus and effecting at least symbolic change. Thus they could maintain a positive view of themselves as a faithful remnant.

Mark

Two Markan Son of Man sayings have often been regarded as prime examples of an originally generic meaning: 2:10 and 2:28.[58] They may, however, just as well be interpreted in a collective sense. The Son of Man's

---

[55] For an alternative interpretation, see KAZEN, "Coming Son of Man", 171, n. 54.

[56] This saying might have concluded Q, and may be considered a major editorial theme. Cf. John S. KLOPPENBORG VERBIN, *Excavating Q: The History and Setting of the Sayings Gospel* (Edinburgh: T & T Clark, 2000), 118.

[57] TUCKETT, "Son of Man", 379. The statement that "Q gives no indication that the term 'SM' itself refers to anyone other than to Jesus (e.g. to a corporate group of Jesus and his followers)" (379–380) is not corroborated by evidence.

[58] For a better example of an originally truly generic use of Son of Man, we can turn to the blasphemy saying in Mark 3:28 / Matt 12:32 / Luke 12:10. See KAZEN, "Coming Son of Man", 165, n. 37.

authority to forgive sins corresponds to similar claims for the disciples: they are given power and sent out to preach and heal (Mark 6:7–13; a task later interpreted as forgiveness, Luke 24:47). This is not a task for everyone, as a generic interpretation would imply, but for Jesus and the disciples as kingdom representatives. Similarly, lordship over the Sabbath is not claimed indiscriminately for human beings. Rather, the needs of the disciples are of higher importance than a strict interpretation of Sabbath *halakhah*. The common kingdom mission of Jesus and his followers takes priority, expressed as lordship.[59] As a symbol of the coming kingdom, the Son of Man provides group identity for Jesus and his disciples; through their practice they identify with and represent the reality associated with this figure. Their practice furthermore effects changes for deprived individuals included in their group, thus strengthening the group identity of the movement, re-interpreting its low status character.

While an individual identification of Jesus with the Son of Man is usually presupposed in the three predictions of his suffering (Mark 8:31; 9:31; 10:33 pars.), they, too, may be taken in an originally collective sense, with the Son of Man as a typological model for the Jesus movement at large. I have elsewhere demonstrated how the conspicuous terminology in the second and third sayings (*paradidonai* etc.), which recurs in the tradition of the last supper (Mark 14:21) and at the very betrayal itself (Mark 14:41), echoes Dan 7:25 (LXX).[60] A suffering Son of Man is implied in Daniel: he represents faithful Israel, the kingdom of saints, vindicated after persecution and suffering. This fits with numerous synoptic sayings, warning disciples that suffering and contempt and violent death will be theirs too, and frequently referring to the kingdom or to the Son of Man.[61] The suffering Son of Man interprets the present experience of Markan recipients and provides a frame of reference for a common identity; his experience is theirs too as they identify with him. The hope of the Son of Man's future *vindication* is crucial for justifying the sufferings and persecutions that threaten them, but their apocalyptic vision of future glory (Mark 9:2–8) remains in a sense "hidden" and must not be proclaimed in full until the

---

[59] Cf. other incidents when Jesus' disciples are criticized for not adapting to the halakhic interpretation of dominant groups. Cf. Mark 2:18 pars.; Mark 7:1–2 pars.; Luke 5:30.

[60] καὶ παραδοθήσεται πάντα εἰς τὰς χεῖρας αὐτοῦ ἕως καιροῦ καὶ καιρῶν καὶ ἕως ἡμίσους καιροῦ. Cf. Mark 9:31: ὁ υἱὸς τοῦ ἀνθρώπου παραδίδοται εἰς χεῖρας ἀνθρώπων, καὶ ... μετὰ τρεῖς ἡμέρας ἀναστήσεται.

[61] Matt 5:10–11; 10:23; Mark 13:9–13, 19 pars.; Luke 6:22 (Q; in Matthew's version, 5:11, "Son of Man" is replaced by "me". In Luke 6:22, "Son of Man" could just as well be replaced by "kingdom"). Cf. early Christian expectations of suffering and persecution: Rom 8:17; 1 Thess 3:4; 2 Thess 1:5; Acts 9:16; John 15:20.

Son of Man is raised from the dead (9:9), i.e. until the kingdom comes with power (9:1) and the elect are vindicated.[62]

An acceptance of lowly conditions paired with an expectancy of future reversal of the honour-shame code is illustrated by the injunction to become everybody's slave (Mark 10:42–44). This shocking reversal of values is motivated by the Son of Man as a type or model for believers (10:45) and redefines the Danielic idea of dominion, power, and all people serving the Son of Man (cf. Dan 7:14, 27).[63] Although he has certain powers even in the present (Mark 2:11) and his vindication is associated with power and glory (Mark 13:26; 14:62), the image of the servant and martyr Son of Man is innate in the Markan Jesus tradition and constitutive for Markan theology. It is designed to influence the group identity of adherents, not only in terms of self-concept but also in shaping their common behaviour. Servanthood is prescribed and defined in such a way that its positive value overshadows its negative consequences and low-status character.

Finally, the Markan coming Son of Man sayings may be read as a confirmation of the final victory of God's kingdom wholly in line with Daniel's vision, after the suffering that now lies before Jesus and his disciples. As I have discussed these sayings in more detail elsewhere, they will only be briefly mentioned.[64] Although Mark 14:62 is shaped by subsequent developments and expectations, nothing is actually said about a personal return of Jesus. Even Mark 13:26–27, although given its present shape within the context of the eschatological discourse, may have originated as a reference to the kingdom and its representatives, who see themselves as faithful martyrs, to be vindicated and restored in the future.[65] Mark, however, creates an association with the "Day of the Lord" by prefacing this saying with vv. 24–25, and identifies the Son of Man with Jesus, returning as an individual redeemer. In Mark 8:38 the author intends the coming Jesus to be identified with the Son of Man, in spite of the awkward combination of first and third person references in one sentence, which suggest an original saying with a different sense.[66]

---

[62] The picture of Mark as aimed at communities threatened by suffering and persecution is commonplace.

[63] Cf. DUNN, *Jesus Remembered*, 814–815.

[64] For a detailed discussion of the following passages, see KAZEN, "Coming Son of Man".

[65] The apocalyptic flavour of this saying does not require an end-of-the-world perspective, not even in its present shape. See further KAZEN, "Coming Son of Man", 168–169.

[66] Cf. de JONGE, "Confessing and Denying", 105–121; Matthias KREPLIN, *Das Selbstverständnis Jesu: Hermeneutische und christologische Reflexion. Historisch-kritische Analyse* (WUNT, 2:141; Tübingen: Mohr Siebeck, 2001), 159–165.

It is unlikely that early recipients of Mark's gospel identified themselves with the coming Son of Man in a straightforward manner. Nevertheless, all three categories of Son of Man sayings in Mark show signs of an underlying collective interpretation. It is likely that the Son of Man as a *role model* continued to influence the common identity of Markan Christians. In Mark, this role is intimately tied to Jesus and in some sayings it is more clearly individualized than in Q; sayings like 14:21 or 14:41 are framed and placed in contexts by Mark that make them unambiguously refer to the known fate of Jesus. Many of the sayings are, however, utilized in Mark's theology to shape the group identity of present believers in an imitation of the Son of Man typology embodied in Jesus.

Luke-Acts

Luke transmits both Markan and Q Son of Man sayings, at times even two variants of the same saying (Q 12:8–9 and Mark 8:38 / Luke 9:26), as already mentioned above. In 11:30 he has retained a version that can be read in a collective sense. We also noted that, unlike Matthew, Luke has not inserted Q 12:39–40 into Jesus' eschatological discourse, thus making it possible to read this as a reference to the imminent kingdom. Similar considerations apply to Q 17:22–30. While Matthew talks of the *parousia* of the Son of Man, Luke's language betrays a more complex background to this tradition, revealing an earlier understanding of the Son of Man as more than an individual title.[67]

Looking at traditions particular to Luke, we note the question in Luke 18:8 (but then will the Son of Man find faith on earth when he comes?), which fits with other sayings about people's (lack of) response to the kingdom and to the message of Jesus and his disciples.[68] The concluding line in the Lukan story of Zacchaeus (19:10: *elthen gar ho huios tou anthrōpou zētēsai kai sōsai to apolōlos*) is conspicuously similar in content to the ending of the call of Levi (Luke 5:32: *ouk elēlutha* [Mark 2:17: *ēlthon*] *kalesai dikaious alla hamartōlous*[69]), which Luke took over from Mark. One may wonder whether these were originally two versions of the same tradition, which Mark has individualized, replacing an original Son of Man

---

[67] Note the unique and repeated use of the expression "day(s) of the Son of Man" (17:22, [24,] 26, 30). In spite of Q interpretation and Lukan redaction, this may be read as a reference to the inbreaking kingdom with its concomitant judgment, as understood in prophetic tradition. See KAZEN, "Coming Son of Man", 169–170.

[68] Cf. Luke 4:23; 8:9–10; 9:5, 41; 10:10–16; 11:29–32; 13:34; 14:16–24.

[69] Here Luke adds εἰς μετάνοιαν to the Markan text.

with the verb in 1st person singular; the surrounding Markan traditions – often thought of as a pre-Markan block – speak of the Son of Man. In the preceding narrative, the Son of Man has power to forgive sins. In the subsequent story, the Son of Man has authority over the Sabbath. Thus the point of the story of Levi's calling might initially have been the mission of the *Son of Man* to call or heal sinners, or, as in the Lukan Zacchaeus version, to save the lost. "Son of Man" would then have referred in all these cases to the kingdom, and it comes as no surprise that this is most easily traced in Luke, as he emphasizes this vision of the kingdom's purpose and scope in particular.[70]

In spite of clear signs in Luke of an *underlying* interpretation of the Son of Man as kingdom imagery, he does not avoid individualizing this designation. The message of the two bright men at the empty grave (24:7) leaves no doubt as to who is meant by the Son of Man. This is an explicit reference to the suffering Son of Man sayings, and the explanation concerning Messiah's suffering, that is given to the two disciples on their way to Emmaus in the following section, leaves no doubt that the author of Luke's gospel saw the Son of Man symbolism as epitomized and fulfilled in Jesus, according to early christological interpretation of the prophets in the light of Jesus' death.

To what extent, then, does the Son of Man constitute an identity-shaping typology for early hearers or readers of Luke? Although capable of being interpreted as general kingdom imagery, the Lukan sayings that are added to those inherited from Mark and Q do not particularly invite participatory readings. While the son of Man typology in Mark, and particularly in Q, clearly functions to shape the identity of followers, Luke hardly develops this aspect, suggesting that in his context Son of Man typology plays hardly any role for group identity. This conclusion may, however, need one or two caveats.

The disciples in Luke identify with the kingdom and function as judgmental witnesses against non-receptive people through their actions (5:14; 9:5). Similarly, early recipients of Luke could have identified with the Son of Man, constituting a sign (*sēmeion*) against this generation (11:30), by proclaiming the kingdom in view of the coming judgment.

In Acts, traits of the Son of Man surface in Luke's description of the practice of the early Jerusalem community, and seem constitutive for their group identity: authority to promise forgiveness, power to heal, inclusive fellowship, serving of the needy, loyalty in the face of persecution, readiness to suffer, perhaps also itinerancy (although not immediately in Luke's

---

[70] Cf. other Lukan expressions of this, such as Luke 7:36–50; 9:2, 11; 10:9; 15:1, 6, 9, 24, 32; 16:16; 18:13–14; 23:42.

description) and, possibly, eschatological judgment (Peter's condemnation of Ananias and Sapphira). These traits all suggest that the *content* of the Son of Man typology provided building blocks for early Jerusalem believers' way of life, as Luke envisages them, although this would be implicitly, since the expression is utilized neither for motivating their behaviour, nor for enhancing their social identity. In Stephen's speech we encounter homelessness, exposure and the powerlessness of an oppressed people. Towards the end, when the asymmetrical power relationship between a faithful and righteous minority and those opposing them is highlighted, Stephen is described as having a vision of the Son of Man at the right hand of God (Acts 7:56). This is evidently intended as a fulfilment of Jesus' predictive words to the High Priest (Luke 22:69 / Mark 14:62)[71], and functions as a vindication of Stephen and the early Christians in the context of Acts. The Son of Man imagery thus retains some of its character as an identity-creating type or role model, not only for the narrative Stephen, but also for the readers of Acts.

These caveats, however, are hardly decisive. They only serve to remind us that in the Lukan writings, some Son of Man traditions are bearers of collective traits that may have influenced the identity formation of the readers. The effect was probably limited.

Matthew

The author of Matthew's gospel consistently identifies Jesus as an individual redeemer figure with the Son of Man and often redacts his source materials to that effect. In the first suffering Son of Man saying, Matthew *omits* the Son of Man, making Jesus talk about himself only (Matt 16:21). The same procedure is followed in redacting Q 6:22 (Matt 5:11 has *emou*). The individual identification of the Son of Man with Jesus is self-evident for the author. Thus he elsewhere *inserts* Son of Man as an unambiguous reference to Jesus as part of his redaction (e.g. 16:13; 26:2). One of the most flagrant examples of this is Matt 16:27–28, where Mark's "kingdom of God coming with power" has become "the Son of Man coming with his kingdom". Hence the special Matthean saying in 10:23, urging persecuted disciples to flee from one town to another, assuring them that "you will no way finish the towns of Israel until the Son of Man comes", must be intended as a reference to Jesus as an individual, although it could very well be envisaged as having originally referred to the coming of the kingdom.

---

[71] This partly explains the occurrence of the expression outside of the gospels, i.e. Acts 7:56; Heb 2:6; Rev 1:13; 14:14.

The Matthean version of the sign of Jonah saying (12:40) is best explained as a clarification, in view of post-resurrection interpretation of the fate of Jesus. Its ambiguity is thus lessened.[72] Similarly, ambiguity is replaced by a neat device in 17:9–13. While the Markan text (Mark 9:9–13) not only identifies the Baptizer as Elijah, but also subsumes him under the Son of Man paradigm, Matthew's emendations result in a clear distinction between Elijah and the Son of Man, i.e. between the Baptizer and Jesus, one following the other.[73] Such conscious editing could, however, suggest that the identification of the Son of Man was not as clear-cut among all strands of the Jesus movement as it was in Matthew's mind.

Re-writing Mark's eschatological discourse, Matthew follows the same pattern. He enhances those traits which allude to judgment, reinforcing the apocalyptic imagery (sign of the Son of Man, tribes will grieve, great trumpet).[74] He inserts a number of Q sayings (Matt 24:26–28; 37–51), which Luke places in quite different contexts, transforming the Markan ending into a clearer reference to Jesus' personal return.

Most conspicuous in Matthew is the explicit image of the Son of Man as judge.[75] Four passages stand out.[76] First, the Matthean allegorical interpretation of the parable of the tares (13:37–43) understands the Son of Man as both sower and reaper, sending out his angels in what is unmistakably a judgment scene. Secondly, the Markan saying of the Son of Man coming in his father's glory with the holy angels (Mark 8:38) is complemented by Matthew (Matt 16:27) using a scriptural phrase: coming with *his* angels, the Son of Man will "reward each one according to his deeds".[77] Thirdly, in response to Peter's enquiry about a recompense (Mark 10:28–30 / Matt 19:27–29 / Luke 18:28–30), Matthew has inserted a reference to the *palingenesia*, when the Son of Man will sit "upon the throne of his glory" (*epi thronou doxēs autou*; 19:28). Then the disciples will also sit on twelve thrones and judge the twelve tribes of Israel. The promise to sit on thrones and judge the twelve tribes comes from Q. In Luke it belongs to a different context, however, when after the last supper the disciples are promised that they will eat and drink in the coming kingdom (Luke 22:30). There is no

---

[72] See above, n. 62.

[73] Cf. KAZEN, "Son of Man", 103–105.

[74] Cf. Matthew's use of apocalyptic imagery in the narrative of Jesus' death and resurrection (Matt 27:51–53; 28:2–3).

[75] Not so in Mark; Mark 13 mainly describes a gathering in. The "sitting" at the right hand of the power in Mark 14:62 may be taken as a slight intrusion of royal enthronement language into a saying otherwise intent on the vindication and reversal implied in the Danielic quotation: ἐρχόμενον μετὰ τῶν νεφελῶν τοῦ οὐρανοῦ.

[76] Cf. CHIALÀ, "Evolution of an Expression", 166–168.

[77] Cf. Ps 28:4; 62:12; Prov 24:12; Isa 3:11; Jer 25:14; Hos 4:9; 12:12.

corresponding individual Son of Man in the Lukan version. Fourthly, in Matt 25:31–46 the author redacts a parable of the last judgment, in which "the king" figures as judge, introducing it with a Son of Man formula similar to that of 19:28: "When the Son of Man comes in his glory and all the angels with him, then he will sit upon the throne of his glory" (*epi thronou doxēs autou*).

The last two passages are somehow related to the Parables in *1 Enoch*. Theisohn argues that the *Sitz im Leben* of the formula "sitting on the throne (of glory)" is the prophetic vision of Yahweh.[78] The expression "throne of glory" is common neither in the Hebrew Bible, nor in intertestamental texts, except for the Parables. The image of the "Elect One" or the Son of Man sitting or being seated on the throne of glory is thus unique. Theisohn finds a possible background in a messianic reading of Ps. 110, together with influences from the Isaianic Ebed-Yahweh tradition.[79]

The idea of the righteous elect taking part in divine judgment is sometimes found elsewhere in Jewish literature; the mention of "thrones" in plural in Dan 7:9 has triggered speculative interpretations.[80] While such a context applies to Luke 22:30, Matthew supplements this image by uniquely describing the Son of Man as sitting on the throne of glory (Matt 19:28; cf. 25:31). According to Theisohn, this combination of elements strongly suggests an influence from the Parables of *1 Enoch*. This influence could be oral, since the formula is short and pregnant, and must be assumed to have taken place at the level of Matthean redaction.[81]

Theisohn's arguments have been accepted by a number of scholars.[82] Leslie Walck comes to essentially similar conclusions in a more recent study.[83] Like Theisohn, Walck finds only general similarities between the Synoptic tradition and the Parables, except for Matthean future Son of Man sayings. Walck, however, considers all four passages above, as well as the Matthean redaction in 24:30–31 and 26:64, as material consciously shaped

---

[78] E.g. 1 Kgs 22:19; Isa 6:1–2; Ezek 1:26; Dan 7:9–10; *1 Enoch* 14.18–20. THEISOHN, *Der auserwählte Richter*, 82–85.

[79] THEISOHN, *Der auserwählte Richter*, 31–143.

[80] For a comparison with some intertestamental material, see Christian GRAPPE, "Le logion des douze trônes: Eclairages intertestamentaires", in *Le Trône de Dieu* (ed. M. Philonenko; WUNT, 69; Tübingen: Mohr Siebeck, 1993), 204–212. See also Jacques DUPONT, "Le logion des douze trônes (Mt 19,28; Lc 22,28-30)", *Bib* 45 (1964): 355–392.

[81] THEISOHN, *Der auserwählte Richter*, 149–175.

[82] Cf. SUTER, "Enoch in Sheol", 434–435; WALCK, "Son of Man"; Matthew BLACK, "The Messianism of the Parables of Enoch: Their Date and Contribution to Christological Origins", in *The Messiah: Developments in Earliest Judaism and Christianity* (ed. J. H. Charlesworth; The First Princeton Symposium on Judaism and Christian Origins; Minneapolis: Fortress, 1992), 145–168.

[83] WALCK, "Son of Man in Matthew" (not seen).

by Matthew "in the direction of the Parables of Enoch".[84] While other synoptic future Son of Man sayings may share some general characteristics with the Parables, these "could be explained as deriving from Dan 7, or from the general conceptions of an eschatological judge and deliverer current in the milieu of the first century CE as well as in the Parables".[85]

Even in Matthew, the Son of Man in one sense provides believers with a common identity. As he will appear as an eschatological judge, so they too will be vindicated and share in his judgment. He is, however, no typological model, but an individualized redeemer figure only, fully identified with Jesus. In Matthew, neither Jesus, nor his followers, identify with the Son of Man; rather, the Son of Man is identified with Jesus. While Jesus is crucial for Matthean communities, the Son of Man imagery does not seem to play an important role in their identity formation.

Paul

Paul never uses the expression Son of Man. If, as some have suggested, it was first applied to Jesus by the authors of the gospels, and is thus a later creation of early Christian communities, we need not wonder.[86] Since, however, Paul rarely quotes Jesus, and Son of Man is almost exclusively found on Jesus' lips, we should not be surprised.[87]

Perhaps the roots of the expression "Son of Man" made it difficult to comprehend and lessened its relevance for predominantly gentile believers. Its Greek translation might have further complicated matters in the West. In time, it became quite popular in gnostic circles. Paul may have avoided it for its hazardous potential. Possibly, "Son of Man" was seen as too lowly a designation during the second half of the first century CE, when christology developed. Such explanations are, however, speculative and

---

[84] WALCK, "Son of Man," 299–337, quote p. 337.

[85] WALCK, "Son of Man," 331.

[86] E.g. Bousset, Käsemann, Vielhauer, and Perrin. Cf. Delbert BURKETT, *The Son of Man Debate: A History and Evaluation* (SNTSMS, 107; Cambridge: University Press, 1999), 50–56. This is, however, extremely unlikely for a number of reasons. Cf. the frequency and consistent use of "Son of Man" on the lips of Jesus in Mark and Q, as well as in John, but its virtual non-existence elsewhere (see n. 71 above). Why should early believers have created this self-designation for Jesus when they never used it themselves? See KAZEN, "Son of Man", 90–91.

[87] There is no room here to discuss questions of genre and Paul's relationship to the Jesus tradition.

somewhat arbitrary; they do not all fit together and they presuppose a certain christological or dogmatic development.[88]

If Jesus and his earliest followers used the Son of Man as an essentially
collective symbol of the expected kingdom, which they represented and
identified with, and if this designation only subsequently became individualized and restricted to Jesus alone, we may expect a state of flux during
Paul's time that would hardly render Son of Man an obvious christological
title for Paul to use. The image would not have been readily accessible to
his Hellenistic congregations.[89] Hence, Paul does not use "Son of Man",
although he develops his particular christology, including the idea of a
personal coming of Christ. While his eschatology is informed by a reading
of Daniel, this does not include a straightforward individualized interpretation of the Son of Man.

This explanation would be plausible were we to find signs in Paul of the
content of a collective interpretation being transmitted, but without the Son
of Man imagery as *vehicle*, but nevertheless juxtaposed with an anticipation of Jesus appearing as an eschatological redeemer figure. This is precisely what we do find in Paul's apocalyptic interpretation of Daniel, in his
theology of suffering and eschatological redemption, and in his particular
participatory language.

To begin with, in 1 Thessalonians, Paul refers to what seems like common belief: Jesus' coming from heaven (1:10). From later texts, capable of
being interpreted in "realized" ways, we gather that previous traditions
must have allowed for diversity in development.[90] Even in 1 Thessalonians, Jesus' coming is a *parousia* rather than a return, and as in Acts it is a
direct continuation of his task: God's vindication of Jesus necessitated the
completion of his prophetic-messianic mission. The book of Daniel entered
into this re-interpretation, not least as an important source for belief in a
resurrection. The fluid character of early conceptions is evident in the description of Jesus' coming in 1 Thess 4:13–18, because *Jesus* is not
equated with the Danielic Son of Man, but it is actually the *believers* that
are, like the Son of Man, carried with the clouds to meet "the Lord", i.e.

---

[88] Cullman, for example, argues that Paul's use of ἄνθρωπος in 1 Cor 15, Rom 5 and
Phil 2 is a development of the Son of Man tradition. The argument, however, presup-
poses a pre-existent heavenly man concept. Oscar CULLMANN, *The Christology of the
New Testament* (2nd ed; London: SCM, 1963 [German original 1957]), 166–181.

[89] Cf. Coppens who, although denying any influence of the Danielic Son of Man on
Paul whatsoever (contra Cullmann), finds the imagery of little use in a Gentile context,
offering too many ambiguities and risks with regard to gnosticising tendencies. Joseph
COPPENS, *La relève apocalyptique du messianisme royal*, vol. 3: *Le fils de l'homme
néotestamentaire* (Leuven: Peeters, 1981), 23–44 (esp. 36–8, 43–4).

[90] E.g., Luke 24:46–53; Acts 1:6–11; 2:1–4, 14–21; John 14:1–21; 16:1–24; 20:19–22.

Daniel's Ancient of Days.[91] The imagery is employed in a context of the vindication of the elect, similar to its use in Daniel. Daniel's Son of Man thus provides typological material that Paul uses for shaping the beliefs of his congregations. Although the Son of Man is not mentioned, the *content* of the collective symbol is appealed to in strengthening the group identity and common outlook of the Thessalonian congregation, assuring them of future vindication in view of present hardships.

Paul's overall theology of suffering and eschatological redemption is furthermore congruent with the Danielic Son of Man paradigm, although decisively modified by Stoic ideals.[92] The sonship conferred on believers is linked to the sonship of Christ[93] and results in co-inheritance, including both co-suffering and co-vindication (Rom 8:17). Suffering is shared; it is not only Christ who suffered for his followers, but believers are thought to suffer for Christ, too (Phil 1:29; cf. Col 1:24). Suffering, however, means nothing in comparison to the glory to be revealed. This glory is explicitly described not as the glory of God's Son only, but as that of God's *sons*; they as a collective will be revealed; the yearning of creation is for their collective *apokalupsis* (Rom 8:19). As part of their vindication, Paul envisages the believers participating in the final judgement: "the holy ones will judge the world" (1 Cor 6:2). Here, as in 1 Thess 4, we have another example of how one of the *attributes* of the Son of Man is ascribed to faithful followers collectively in a sense that corresponds to the Jesus tradition.

This theology of shared suffering, subsequently followed by shared glory, is part of Paul's general paradigm of participation.[94] Christ becomes a first fruit, guaranteeing the future vindication of the rest of the collective, which still has to undergo suffering and death. We could read this as evidence for a Danielic Son of Man typology exercising its influence on Pauline ideas through the Jesus tradition. Although, in Paul's theology,

---

[91] Does this meeting in the air belong to the content of the λόγος κυρίου referred to in v. 15? Cf. Traugott HOLTZ, *Der erste Brief an die Thessaloniker* (EKK, 13; Zürich/Neukirchen-Vluyn: Benziger/Neukirchener, 1986), 184–185, 194–198. Holtz suggests that the reference is limited to v. 15b, but it is reasonable to assume that Paul refers to a saying similar to Mark 13:26–27, although in a version more akin to Matt 16:27–28 and 24:30–31. Cf. E. P. SANDERS, *The Historical Figure of Jesus* (London: Penguin, 1993), 180–182.

[92] Cf. 1 Thess 3:4; 2 Thess 1:4–8; 2 Cor 1:3–7; 4:10–13, 17; Phil 3:10; often in an eschatological context, including future vindication. Cf. Col 1:24–27. In Rom 5:3–4, suffering is juxtaposed to a list of Stoic virtues (ὑπομονή, δοκιμή, ἐλπίς).

[93] Gal 4:4–7; Rom 8:14–23.

[94] Cf. Paul's portrayal of Christ as the new man or a second Adam, into whom believers are somehow incorporated. Rom 5:12–21; 1 Cor 15:21–22, 45–49; 2 Cor 5:17–21. Cf. Eph 2:14–22.

Jesus has in a sense "emancipated himself" from the collective, it is mostly as a precursor, a facilitator for those following close behind. Everything that Christ is, the believer may become, at times proleptically, *in* Christ. This is not so much a question of "mystical union" as of participation in a common identity.

As the Markan Jesus tradition reverses the Danielic idea of all peoples serving the Son of Man, Paul similarly portrays a humble and serving behaviour as constitutive for believers. This idea is intimately tied to Paul's participatory perspective, being *in* Christ, as parts of one body (Rom 12:3–21; 1 Cor 12–13).

While Christ, not the Son of Man, is the figure with which believers identify in Paul, one may legitimately ask whether Son of Man imagery may have contributed in providing building blocks for the common identity of Christ and Christians alike. We could, of course, posit such an influence directly from Daniel, in view of the deep knowledge and creative use of Old Testament traditions which Paul frequently displays, without the Son of Man of the Jesus tradition as a mediating link. We could also think of different sources for Paul's participatory theology, such as various types of martyr ideology, the Isaianic suffering servant, etc. While this is admittedly speculative, it is possible, however, to look at Paul's "corporate" christology as an expression, albeit further developed, of a collective understanding of the Son of Man, in which Jesus is seen as the foremost of a larger group of kingdom representatives.[95] Paul would then have developed the "collective content" of the Son of Man imagery of the Jesus tradition in his own way, abandoning the Semitic terminology in his Hellenistic context, while other traditions, like that of Matthew, individualized the expression further, reserving it for Jesus only. The paradoxical result is that Son of Man *imagery* plays no explicit role as a typological model for Pauline Christians, while Son of Man *ideology* is implicitly relayed by the image of a corporate Christ. Paul's corporate Christ becomes paradigmatic for his recipients' self-conception, group belonging and common behaviour *insofar as* he shares crucial traits with the Son of Man figure of, in particular, Markan and Q tradition. Present hardships are accepted in view of an eschatological reversal of honour and shame.

Conclusions

We have suggested that the Son of Man initially functioned as a typological figure, a role model, which provided an eschatological group identity in

---

[95] Cf. MOULE, *Phenomenon*, 21–42.

a number of contexts. The imagery bonded individuals to a movement through enforcement of superior values; it re-interpreted negative consequences and made low status characteristics acceptable; it shaped common beliefs and behaviour, sometimes including engagement for social change.

Son of Man imagery particularly contributed to Jewish apocalyptic and early Christian identity-formation with regard to attitudes to suffering and persecution. By identifying with the Son of Man, suffering and hardship could be viewed as a necessary prelude to eschatological vindication, including a reversal of status or power. The expectation of future vindication, even taking part in divine judgment, compensated for present lack of position and power. The traditional value scale could thus be reversed; honour could be attributed to servanthood, poverty, weakness and death.

The above is true in particular of early readers of Daniel, as well as recipients of Q and Markan traditions. We may suppose a similar function for the Son of Man in the Parables of *1 Enoch*, although the evidence is not sufficient safely to construe the social context of the early recipients. As a heavenly double he functions as a typological model, corresponding to the elect people, providing them with group identity.

In circles associated with the Q tradition, aspects of the Son of Man imagery that are crucial for their identity formation include a reversal of values and future vindication, even partaking in divine judgmental activity. Such aspects concern Markan recipients, too, but in their context, servanthood and suffering play a primary role. These experiences become paradigmatic for their identity as believers and are charged with positive value as they are incorporated in early Christian identity. Of crucial importance in this process is the Markan reversal of the Danielic expectation; instead of all people serving the Son of Man, his role is defined as that of a servant. The image of the *coming* Son of Man in Q as well as in Mark does not directly influence group identity to the same extent, but as the image still displays ambiguous traits, it serves as a challenge to early recipients to identify with, and integrate, the kingdom vision of Jesus.

In Luke, several Son of Man traditions in the inherited material retain collective traits, which could have influenced the identity formation of early readers. We may doubt the effect, however, since the author of Luke and Acts does not develop his traditions in this direction, but clearly identifies the Son of Man with the individual Jesus in his special material. Even more pointedly, Matthew redacts his traditions in order to avoid ambiguities with regard to the Son of Man. He is consistently identified with Jesus and in some instances an influence from the Parables in *1 Enoch* seems reasonable. To some extent, the Son of Man provides Matthean readers with a common identity, as some analogies remain, but he has no clear function as a typological model. He is rather an individual redeemer figure.

In Paul, the Son of Man is never used as a *vehicle*, but the *content* of the Son of Man typology continues to inform Pauline ideas, as transmitted to the recipients of his letters, through his participatory christology. This applies to suffering and martyrdom, serving behaviour, reversed value scales and expectations of eschatological vindication. While we should reckon with other sources, too, for Paul's theology of servitude and suffering, his knowledge of the Son of Man tradition can be argued from his use of Danielic and apocalyptic material. Since the expression was still in a state of flux and not necessarily reserved for Jesus only, it would not have been an obvious choice in writing *about* Jesus, besides possibly being problematic in a Hellenistic context.

As long as collective traits were registered, the Son of Man tradition had direct influence on early Christian identity formation, just as it shaped group identity in such eschatological or apocalyptic communities as those represented by Daniel and the Parables of *1 Enoch*. In contexts and communities using texts and traditions that did not favour a collective understanding, possibilities for identification decreased. It is somewhat of a paradox that Paul, in spite of not using the terminology at all, provides more opportunity for early believers to identify with the "collective content" of the Son of Man imagery than does, for example, Matthew. As Matthew became the dominant gospel, the Son of Man figure lost his influence as a typological figure. The collective implications of the Son of Man imagery, complemented by traditions about discipleship and Pauline participatory theology have, however, never ceased to influence subsequent readers or followers.

Social Identity and a Stereotype in the Making: The Pharisees as Hypocrites in Matt 23

Raimo Hakola

In contemporary English, the word "pharisee" has become a common noun that denotes "a person who thinks they are very religious, but who does not care about others;"[1] or "someone who pretends to be religious or morally good, but who is not sincere;"[2] or simply "a self-righteous or hypocritical person."[3] In this article, I will try to explain how and why the Pharisees first came to be seen as archetypical hypocrites. The identification of the Pharisees as hypocrites derives, of course, from the New Testament gospels where it is developed in the most consistent way in the gospel of Matthew. I will first give an overview of Matthews presentation of the Pharisees as hypocrites and how scholars have responded to this presentation. Then I will use some insights from social psychology to explain the function of Matthew's portrait of the Pharisees. I propose that the portrait of the Pharisees as hypocrites served to construct and maintain the social identity of a group, whose members may sometimes themselves have had difficulties with practicing what they preached.

The Pharisees and Hypocrisy in Matthew 23

An overview of the Gospel material reveals that although Matthew was not the first to connect the Pharisees with hypocrisy. This connection is most comprehensively developed in Matthew 23, where the scribes and the Pharisees are repeatedly addressed as hypocrites.[4] In chapter 23, Matthew has expanded Jesus' condemnation of the scribes, found in Mark 12:38–40.

---

[1] Cambridge Dictionaries Online (http://dictionary.cambridge.org/).

[2] Longman Dictionary of Contemporary English Online (http://www.ldoceonline.com)

[3] Oxford Dictionaries Online (http://www.askoxford.com/dictionaries/?view=uk)

[4] The noun ὑποκριτής appears in the NT 17 times, only in the Synoptic Gospels: Matthew 13, Mark 1, Luke 3. The related word ὑπόκρισις appears 6 times, 3 times in the Synoptic Gospels: once each in Matthew, Mark and Luke. These words are connected to the Pharisees in the following passages: ὑπόκρισις: Mark 12:15; Luke 12:1; Matt 23:28; ὑποκριτής: Mark 7:6 (= Matt 15:7); Matt 22:18; Matt 23:13, 15, 23, 25, 27, 29 [x14].

In addition to Mark, Matthew has used the series of woes, which has a parallel in Luke 11:37–53 and which originates from the Q-source.[5] Matthew has made several editorial changes to his sources. One of the most important concerns the target group that Jesus attacks. While Mark speaks in this connection only of scribes and Luke applies the woes alternately to Pharisees or to Lawyers, Matthew consistently refers to Jesus' opponents as the scribes and the Pharisees. This is in line with Matthew's tendency to place the opponents of Jesus together in groups of two.[6] Furthermore, neither Mark nor Q mentions the charge of hypocrisy in this connection; this charge probably derives from Matthew, who has organized Jesus' attack around this charge by repeating it six times. It may be concluded that the charge of hypocrisy is "the overriding accusation in ch. 23."[7]

The significance of the charge of hypocrisy is underscored in a saying at the beginning of the chapter, where Jesus says to the crowds and his disciples: "The scribes and the Pharisees sit on Moses' seat; therefore, do whatever they teach you and follow it; but do not do as they do, for they do not practice what they teach" (23:2–3).[8] The interpretation of this saying has been a constant problem for scholars, because here Jesus seems to encourage both the crowds and his disciples, who are Jesus' audience, to follow all the teaching of the Scribes and the Pharisees. This is odd because earlier in the gospel Jesus himself has spoken against the teaching of the Pharisees, based on the "tradition of the elders" (15:1–9).[9] Despite the problems in the first part of the saying, the conclusion clearly identifies Jesus' opponents as those who fail to live according to their own teaching. This theme is later illustrated in a series of woes, which provide actual examples of how both the scribes and the Pharisees fail to live according to their own standards. It seems, therefore, that it is Matthew, who is to a

---

[5] For Matthew's reworking of Q-material in Matt 23, see Patrick J. HARTIN, "The Woes against the Pharisees (Matthew 23,1–39): The Reception and Development of Q 11,39–52 within the Matthean Community" in *From Quest to Q: Festschrift James M. Robinson* (ed. J. M. Asgeirsson, K. de Troyer and M. W. Meyer; BETL 146; Leuven: Leuven University Press, 2000), 265–283.

[6] Cf. Sjef van TILBORG, *The Jewish Leaders in Matthew* (Leiden: Brill, 1972) 1–7; Ulrich LUZ, *Matthew 1–7: A Continental Commentary* (transl. by W. C. Linss; Minneapolis: Fortress Press, 1989), 170. The Scribes and the Pharisees appear as a one group also in Matt 5:20, 12:38 and 15:1.

[7] Cf. David E. GARLAND, *The Intention of Matthew 23* (NovTSup 52; Leiden: Brill, 1979), 95.

[8] The quotations from Scripture contained in this chapter are, unless otherwise stated, taken from the New Revised Standard Version.

[9] For these problems, see, e.g., Mark Allan POWELL, "Do And Keep What Moses Says (Matthew 23:2–7)," *JBL* 114 (1995): 419–435; Ulrich LUZ, *Matthew 21–28: A Commentary* (transl. by W. C. Linss; Hermeneia; Minneapolis: Fortress Press, 2005), 100–101.

large extent responsible for creating a portrait of the Pharisees as the standard of hypocrisy. The first part of Matthew's expression "the scribes and
the Pharisees" was soon dropped in subsequent Christian tradition and
even in Christian scholarship, where Matthew's description was – more
often than not – taken as an adequate description of the Pharisees.

Scholarly Responses to Matthew 23

In a recent article, Susannah Heschel has demonstrated how Christian –
mainly German – scholarship on the Pharisees prior to World War II was
quite often infused with political and cultural bias toward Judaism. The
depictions of the Pharisees in the gospels were generally accepted without
question. The echoes of Matthew's description of the Pharisees are clearly
seen in, for example, a comment by Gustav Volkmar, one of the members
of the Tübingen School of the nineteenth century: "The Pharisees represent
a wish to deceive oneself, and on top of it, God, [a wish] which turned out
to be no more than an ever-growing despair; the tighter and more hardened
the shackles of the idolatrous power, which one hoped to evade through
hypocrisy."[10]

This standard Christian view of the Pharisees was challenged with the
commencement of modern Jewish scholarship on ancient Judaism. According to Heschel, serious German scholarship on the Pharisees began
with the works of Abraham Geiger. By applying critical and historical methods to various sources, Geiger presented the Pharisees as a liberalizing,
progressive movement and described Jesus as a Pharisee.[11] These views
were completely rejected by the majority of Christian scholars. The views
of Geiger and some other Jewish scholars were deemed to be unhistorical
and baseless because these writers "are themselves nothing but Pharisees
and do not intend to be anything else."[12] Julius Wellhausen was among the
most vehement critics of Geiger's views. He criticized Geiger's use of rabbinic sources and defended the accuracy of the gospels' portrait of the
Pharisees. With regard to Matthew 23, Wellhausen says that "doubts con-

---

[10] Quoted by Susannah HESCHEL, "The German Theological Tradition," in *In Quest of the Historical Pharisees* (ed. J. Neusner and B. Chilton; Waco, Texas: Baylor University Press, 2007), 353–373, esp. p. 354.

[11] See HESCHEL, "The German Theological Tradition," 357–360. Cf. also Anthony J. SALDARINI, "Pharisees," *ABD* 5 (1992): 289–303, esp. p. 290. According to Saldarini, "Geiger's work on the Pharisees set the terms for the debate in the 19th and 20th centuries."

[12] Thus Heinrich Ewald as quoted by HESCHEL, "The German Theological Tradition," 363.

cerning the historical accuracy of Matthew 23 would only be justified if it transfers a foreign type onto the Pharisees."[13] However, this is clearly not the case, since Wellhausen elsewhere describes the Pharisees as the "most outstanding representatives of Jewish educational arrogance," who become "very unattractive as soon as they set themselves up as models for everyone."[14] Wellhausen admits that, "in Matthew 23, wrath holds the brush; without doubt, it favors dark tones and applies them assertively." But he continues: "Even a Jew will not deny that the wrath in Matthew is justified: the Pharisees are perhaps only disadvantaged by the fact they have fallen into the hands of this connoisseur who, at the same time, expresses a sentiment that still compels the reader."[15]

Even though Christian scholars, with a few exceptions, followed Wellhausen and rejected Geiger's views, Geiger's description of the Pharisees was later advanced by many Jewish scholars, who wrote against dominant Christian understandings of the Pharisees. A major tendency among Jewish historians was to demonstrate that the Pharisees were the very opposite of what Christians say about them.[16] For example, in 1924 Israel Abrahams wrote:

---

[13] Julius WELLHAUSEN, *The Pharisees and the Sadducees: An Examination of Internal Jewish History* (transl. M. E. Biddle; Mercer Library of Biblical Studies; Macon Georgia, Mercer University Press, 2001; transl. of *Die Pharisäer und die Sadducäer: Eine Untersuchung zur inneren Geschichte*; 3rd Edition; Göttingen: Vandenhoeck & Ruprecht, 1967), 112.

[14] WELLHAUSEN, *The Pharisees*, 16.

[15] WELLHAUSEN, *The Pharisees*, 112–113. For Wellhausen's portrait of the Pharisees, see HESCHEL, "The German Theological Tradition," 363–368. Heschel shows that Wellhausen did not have any independent knowledge of rabbinic sources in his criticism of Geiger's views. Furthermore, Wellhausen's views on the Pharisees reflect his own bias toward Judaism. For a very different appraisal of Wellhausen's views on the Pharisees, see Roland DEINES, *Die Pharisäer: Ihr Verständnis im Spiegel der christlichen und jüdischen Forschung seit Wellhausen und Graetz* (WUNT 101; Tübingen: Mohr-Siebeck, 1997), 40–67. Deines concludes: "Wellhausens Darstellung bleibt vielmehr in ihren Grundzügen bei aller nötigen Detailkritiken bis heute gültig" (p. 67). Deines also seems to accept Wellhausen's defense of the historical accuracy of Matt 23. Wellhausen (*The Pharisees*, 113) excuses Jesus' polemic by remarking that "it is not the task of the repentance preacher to depict the most flattering image possible of his time." According to Deines, Wellhausen has formulated here, in passing, a fundamental methodological principle that has not lost its significance.

[16] For this apologetical scholarly tradition on the Pharisees, see Jacob NEUSNER, "The Anglo-American Theological Tradition to 1970," in *In Quest of the Historical Pharisees* (ed. J. Neusner and B. Chilton; Waco, Texas: Baylor University Press, 2007), 375–394. As Neusner shows, scholarly apologies for the Pharisees were based on an uncritical presupposition that everything in diverse rabbinic and other Jewish sources written even centuries after the destruction of the temple could be applied to the pre-70 Pharisees. Of course, the same could be said of a large amount of older Christian portraits of the Phari-

Much of Matt xxiii ... belongs to a period later than Jesus, and reflects an antipathy, which grew during the struggle of the new faith to find a home in the abode of the old. ... The attack is too indiscriminate to be effective. It has been often pointed out how forcibly Pharisaic leaders themselves satirized and denounced hypocrisy. ... One would have imagined that the Pharisaic exposure of hypocrisy ... could only have one significance, viz. that hypocrisy was abhorrent to the 'scribes', the authors of the exposure. It is disappointing to have again and again to argue this point.[17]

Abrahams and many other Jewish scholars before World War II may have been motivated, at least partly, by apologetic intentions, but their views that Christian theology in general, and Matthew 23 in particular, gives a distorted picture of the real-life Pharisees has also become widespread among Christian scholars.[18] Especially since the appearance of E. P. Sanders' *Paul and Palestinian Judaism*, the majority of scholars have become increasingly sensitive to the polemical nature of the traditional Christian picture of pharisaic or rabbinic Judaism.[19] Today mainstream Christian scholarship agrees with Abrahams in situating Matthew's attack against the scribes and the Pharisees in a period later than Jesus. It has become very common to situate Matthew in the context of a conflict between Matthew's Jewish-Christian community and the post-70 rabbinic movement.[20] This scenario helps to explain Matthew's polemic against the Pharisees as a reflection of the alleged rise and influence of the emerging rabbinic movement. The situation in which Matthew's community is seen to struggle with the rabbinic movement, which is claiming a new leadership for

---

sees. Neusner ascribes the introduction of the critical agenda in the study of the Pharisees to himself and remarks that his own contribution "was to render obsolete nearly all historical scholarship on the Pharisees of the preceding two hundred years" (p. 376).

[17] Israel ABRAHAMS, *Studies in Pharisaism and the Gospels* (2nd Series; Cambridge; Cambridge University Press, 1924; repr., Eugene, Oregon: Wipf & Stock, 2004), 30–31.

[18] There are still – and there will probably still be also in the future – scholars who defend Matthew 23 as a historically accurate portrait of the Pharisees. Cf. Noel S. RABBINOWITZ, "Matthew 23:2–4: Does Jesus Recognize the Authority of the Pharisees and Does He Endorse Their *Halakhah*?" *JETS* (46 (2003), 423–447, esp. p. 447: "On a deeper level, however, the inner motives of the Pharisees often betrayed them, and their zeal for the Torah frequently became self-serving. When Jesus rebukes the Pharisees in the woes section of Matthew 23, he reveals that their wrong teachings were a manifestation of their wrong motives. In their heart, these Pharisees yearned for the praise of people, but in their minds, they believed they honored God."

[19] E. P. SANDERS, *Paul and Palestinian Judaism: A Comparison of Patterns of Religion* (Minneapolis: Fortress Press, 1977).

[20] See, e.g., W. D. DAVIES, *The Setting of the Sermon on the Mount* (Cambridge: Cambridge University Press, 1964; J. Andrew OVERMAN, *Matthew's Gospel and Formative Judaism: The Social World of the Matthean Community* (Minneapolis: Fortress Press, 1990; Anthony J. SALDARINI, *Matthew's Jewish-Christian Community* (Chicago Studies in the History of Judaism; Chicago/ London: University of Chicago Press, 1994).

the Jewish communities, offers a rationale for Matthew's vilification of the
Pharisees and makes it at least understandable – if not acceptable – to our
eyes.

Another important factor in recent approaches to Matthew's attack on
the scribes and the Pharisees has been the growing awareness among New
Testament scholars of the conventions of ancient polemic. In an important
article, Luke Timothy Johnson has collected evidence, which places the
New Testament's slander against the Jews in the context of ancient rhetoric. Johnson shows how such standard categories of vice as vainglory, love
of pleasure or money and hypocrisy were quite often attributed to any opponents. Johnson concludes:

First-century Jews, who disputed with each other, used language conventional to their
world. These conventions provide the appropriate context for properly assessing the polemic of the NT. If by definition sophists are hypocritical, and philosophers of all opposing
schools are hypocritical, and philosophers in general are hypocritical, and Alexandrian
pagans are hypocritical, and Apion is a hypocrite, are we really surprised to find scribes
and Pharisees called hypocrites?[21]

By placing Matthew 23 in an appropriate historical context and by comparing Matthew's polemics with ancient rhetorical conventions, current
scholarship has taken a significant step in explaining Matthew's fierce attack against the scribes and the Pharisees. However, some questions still
remain.

First, despite its popularity and heuristic usefulness, the theory of a conflict between Matthew's community and the emerging post-70 rabbinic
movement lacks any substantial external evidence. This idea is, to a large
extent, based on a portrayal of early rabbis that has been seriously questioned in recent scholarship. Many scholars have revised their views con-

---

[21] Luke Timothy JOHNSON, "The New Testament's Anti-Jewish Slander and the Conventions of Ancient Polemic," *JBL* 108 (1989): 419–441 esp. p. 440. In addition, other
scholars have compared the charge of hypocrisy in Matthew 23 to ancient rhetorical conventions. Cf. Steve MASON, "Pharisaic Dominance before 70 CE and the Gospels' Hypocrisy Charge (Matt 23:2–3)," *HTR* 83 (1990): 363–81, esp. p. 380–381. Mason notes
that the accusation of hypocrisy was well established in the ancient world and "it was
considered the special task of the philosopher to expose and denounce such activity."
Mason defends the authenticity of Jesus' – not Matthew's – hypocrisy charge by saying
that Jesus "joined others in denouncing the apparent hypocrisy of the policy makers."
This is in line with Mason's conclusion that "leaders and policy-makers invariably attract
the charge of hypocrisy from disaffected groups. Since the accusation results from a perceived dissonance between one's avowed principles and one's actions, only those who
advocate principles – politicians and preachers – make themselves eligible for the label
of hypocrisy." But if the charge of hypocrisy was as common in debates between different philosophical schools as Johnson claims, it can hardly be taken as evidence of the
political status or influence of the targeted groups.

cerning the influence and power of the early rabbinic movement.[22] According to recent studies, the early rabbinic movement may well have been a relatively powerless group. This position emerges from the study of the earliest layers of Mishnaic Law as well as from the study of stories of legal cases connected to rabbis of different eras.[23] As Jacob Neusner has concluded, the rabbis "enjoyed no documented access to power of any kind" and were "unable to coerce many people to do very much." Thus, rabbinic ideals never "attained realization in the structure of actual institutions and in the system of a working government and ... never actually dictated how people would do things."[24] In light of these developments, Douglas Hare is right in stating that "because this [Matt 23] is not a church history ... we cannot safely conclude that this hostile contact [with Pharisaic Judaism] is continuing into the period in which Matthew is completing his gospel. Persecution by the scribes may belong to a past chapter in Matthew's life, or it may not. Nothing in the text permits certainty on this issue."[25]

Secondly, even though it is helpful to compare Matthew's polemic to ancient rhetorical conventions, these conventions do not really explain why Matthew picked specifically on the scribes and the Pharisees and described them as hypocrites. Matthew's deliberate design of ch. 23 implies that there were some actual reasons for him to attach the charge of hypocrisy to the scribes and the Pharisees. In what follows, I propose that some social psychological theories could prove helpful in explaining Matthew's reasons for doing so.

Matthew 23 and Social Identity of the Matthean Community

I am not the first to apply social-scientific approaches to Matthew's polemics against the scribes and the Pharisees. As Anthony Saldarini has stated,

---

[22] For a full discussion with references, see Raimo HAKOLA, *Identity Matters: John, the Jews and Jewishness* (NovTSup 118; Leiden: Brill, 2005), 55–65.

[23] Jacob NEUSNER, *Judaism: The Evidence of the Mishnah* (Chicago: The University of Chicago Press, 1981), 76–121; Catherine HEZSER, *The Social Structure of the Rabbinic Movement in Roman Palestine* (TSAJ 66; Tübingen: Mohr-Siebeck, 1997), 360–68; Shaye J. D. COHEN, "The Rabbi in Second Century Jewish Society," in *The Cambridge History of Judaism, Volume Three: The Early Roman Period* (ed. W. Horbury, W. D. Davies and J. Sturdy; Cambridge: Cambridge University Press, 1999), 922–990, esp. pp. 961–71. Many other rabbinic scholars (e.g., Martin Goodman, Lee I. Levine, Hayim Lapin, Günter Stemberger) have also made observations pointing in the same direction.

[24] Jacob NEUSNER, *The Mishnah: Social Perspectives* (HO, Section One vol. 46; Leiden: Brill, 1999), 265–266.

[25] Douglas R. A. HARE, "How Jewish is the Gospel of Matthew," *CBQ* 62 (2000), 264–277, esp. p. 266.

it is not difficult to see that some basic characteristics of intergroup dynamics are present in Matthew's polemical portrait of Jesus' opponents:
"From a sociological point of view, vilification and misrepresentation of
the opposition can serve to establish the identity and boundaries of the po-
lemicist's group and weaken the power and attraction of the opposing
group."[26]

In order to explain Matthew's polemics more fully, Saldarini takes up
the concept of legitimacy from the theory of the sociology of knowledge
developed by Berger and Luckmann. According to Saldarini, Matthew is
engaging in the de-legitimizing the symbolic universe of his opponents,
who form "the dominant leadership group in his Jewish community" and
who are "strongly influenced or partly constituted by a rival reform
movement, which was on its way to becoming rabbinic Judaism."[27] Matthew 23 can be seen as "an attempt to de-legitimize them in the eyes of the
whole Jewish community."[28] Matthew still continues to dispute with the
Jewish leadership in his environment and this is in line with Saldarini's
contention that Matthew does not deny the legitimacy of Israel and its traditions, but rather affirms the purity laws, tithing, and the Sabbath observance.[29]

In his reconstruction, Saldarini is well aware of recent progress in rabbinic studies and he presents his arguments in a nuanced way, but his reconstruction of the situation in Matthew's gospel still presupposes to a
large extent that the early rabbinic movement was the dominant social institution in Matthew's surroundings. Furthermore, it is controversial
whether Matthew really confirms the legitimacy of Israelite institutions, as
Saldarini maintains (see below). However, Saldarini's general observations
concerning the way in which Matthew's vilification of the Jewish leadership serves to establish the group identity of his community are valuable
and deserve further investigation.

While Saldarini, in his reconstruction of the situation in Matthew's gospel, refers only briefly to social psychological explanations of stereotypes
and prejudice, Ulrich Luz explicitly uses a social psychological perspective in order to explain Matthew's polemic in his commentary on Matthew.

---

[26] Anthony J. SALDARINI, "Delegitimation of Leaders in Matthew 23," *CBQ* 54
(1992): 659–680, esp. p. 659. In this connection, Saldarini refers in passing to some so-
cial psychological studies associated with prejudice, see Gordon ALLPORT, *The Nature of
Prejudice* (Reading, MA: Addison-Wesley, 1954) and Ervin STAUB, *The Roots of Evil:
The Psychological and Cultural Origin of Genocide and Other Forms of Group Violence*
(New York: Oxford University, 1989).

[27] SALDARINI, "Delegitimation," 665.

[28] SALDARINI, "Delegitimation," 667.

[29] SALDARINI, "Delegitimation," 666, 668. Cf. also SALDARINI, *Community*, 124–164.

According to Luz, this perspective makes Matthew's polemics, which "historically is unjust and theologically contradicts the message of Jesus," understandable. Social psychology explains how important it is, "on the one hand, to define one's boundaries against outsiders and, on the other hand, to have inner stability through strengthening one's own identity and group cohesion." In addition, "verbal aggression that focuses the frustration outward is a way of coping with failure and suffering" and "prejudice against people who do not belong to one's own group also increase the stability of the group."[30]

Following Luz's lead, I here pursue the study of Matthew's polemics in the light of social psychological theories connected to intergroup relations. What is particularly relevant in this connection, is the so-called "social identity theory."[31] The social identity theory was first developed by the social psychologist Henri Tajfel and his colleagues in Great Britain in the late 1960s and early 1970s.[32] One of the key ideas behind the theory was formulated by Tajfel as the "minimal group paradigm."[33] This paradigm seeks to find out necessary and sufficient reasons for the emergence of intergroup conflict. In a series of experiments, Tajfel and his colleagues

---

[30] Luz, *Matthew 21–28*, 176–177. Luz refers in this connection to U. Six, "Vorurteile," in *Sozial-psychologie: Ein Handbuch in Schlüsselbegriffen* (2nd ed; Munich: Psychologie Verlagsunion, 1987).

[31] This theory has already been applied to Matthew 23 by Steve Black in an unpublished seminar paper, see Steve Black, "The Construction of Christian Identity through Stereotyping of the Pharisees in the Gospel of Matthew." A Paper Presented at the SBL Annual Meeting in Washington DC, 2006.

[32] For applications of the social identity perspective to ancient Jewish and Christian writings, see Philip Esler, *Galatians*, London and New York: Routledge, 1998; *Conflict and Identity in Romans: The Social Setting of Paul's Letter*. Minneapolis: Fortress Press, 2003; Jutta M. Jokiranta, "Identity on a Continuum: Constructing and Expressing Sectarian Social Identity in Qumran *Serakhim* and *Pesharim*." Ph. D. Diss., University of Helsinki, 2005; Raimo Hakola, "Social Identities and Group Phenomena in the Second Temple Period," in *Explaining Early Judaism and Christianity: Contributions from Cognitive and Social Science* (ed. P. Luomanen, I. Pyysiäinen and R. Uro; Biblical Interpretation Series 89. Leiden: Brill, 2007), 259–276. The last-mentioned collection also contains articles from Philip Esler, Jutta Jokiranta and Petri Luomanen applying the social identity perspective. For an application of the social identity perspective to John's portrait of the Pharisees, see Raimo Hakola and Adele Reinhartz, "John's Pharisees," in *In Quest of the Historical Pharisee* (ed. J. Neusner and B. Chilton; Waco, Texas: Baylor University Press, 2007), 131–147.

[33] Henri Tajfel, *Human Groups and Social Categories: Studies in Social Psychology* (Cambridge: Cambridge University Press, 1981), 233–38, 268–76; Henri Tajfel and John Turner, "An Integrative Theory of Intergroup Conflict," in *The Social Psychology of Intergroup Relations* (ed. by W. G. Austin and S. Worchel; Monterey California: Brooks/Cole Publishing Company, 1979), 33–47, esp. pp. 38–40.

found out that, even in minimal groups where there is neither any conflict of interest nor any previously existing hostility, people tend to favor in-group members over outgroup members. These findings connected with minimal group studies resulted in the formulation of the concept of social identity, which is understood as "that part of an individual's self-concept, which derives from his knowledge of his membership of a social group (or groups) together with the value and emotional significance attached to that membership."[34] Tajfel also proposed that human social behavior varies along the "interpersonal and intergroup continuum."[35]

The social identity theory is based on the observation that cognitive, emotional and motivational processes connected to intergroup relations cannot be seen as an extension of interpersonal relations, nor can they be explained simply in terms of personal psychology. The distinction between personal and social identity is further clarified by the self-categorization theory developed in particular by John Turner and his colleagues.[36] The self-categorization theory is based on the observation that social categorization is a fundamental aspect of group behavior. When we define our-selves in relation to other people, we experience ourselves as similar to one clearly-defined category of people and therefore as different from those in other categories. This process helps us to orientate ourselves in variable social environments by making those environments more predictable and meaningful. Social categorization, however, results in exaggeration and a polarization of perception. Individuals, who belong to different groups, are viewed as being more different from each other than they really are, while individuals, who belong to the same group, are perceived as more simi-lar.[37] Categorization has been described as "a cognitive grouping process that transforms differences into similarities, and vice versa."[38]

---

[34] TAJFEL, *Human Groups*, 255.

[35] Henri TAJFEL, "Interindividual Behaviour and Intergroup Behaviour," in *Differenti-ation between Social Groups: Studies in the Social Psychology of Intergroup Relations* (ed. H. Tajfel; European Monographs in Social Psychology 14; London: Academic Press, 1978), 27–60; TAJFEL, *Human Groups*, 228–53.

[36] John TURNER *et al.*, *Rediscovering the Social Group: A Self-Categorization Theory* (Oxford: Blackwell, 1987); John. C. TURNER, "Some Current Issues in Research on So-cial Identity and Self-Categorization Theories," in *Social Identity: Context, Commitment, Content* (ed. N. Ellemers, R. Spears and B. Doosje; Oxford: Blackwell, 1999), 6–34.

[37] Penelope J. OAKES, S. Alexander HASLAM and John C. TURNER, *Stereotyping and Social Reality* (Oxford: Blackwell, 1994), 95–6; Penelope J. OAKES, S. Alexander HASLAM and Katherine J. REYNOLDS, "Social Categorization and Social Context: Is Stereotype Change a Matter of Information or of Meaning?," in *Social Identity and So-cial Cognition* (ed. D. M. Abrams and M. A: Hogg; Oxford: Blackwell, 1999), 55–79, esp. pp. 57–61.

[38] OAKES, HASLAM and REYNOLDS, "Social Categorization," 62.

According to the social identity perspective, categorization is a natural part of all perception, even though it often results in the emergence of social stereotypes. Unlike in some other psychological or social psychological theories, stereotypes are not seen as products of a perverted mind or extreme circumstances. This has consequences for Matthew's stereotyped portrait of the scribes and the Pharisees. As was mentioned above, Matthew's polemical portrait is quite often conncctcd to a real-life conflict between Matthew's Jewish-Christian community and the emerging rabbinic movement, even though the external evidence for this kind of a conflict is meager, if not non-existent. This procedure echoes the so-called realistic conflict theory, according to which intergroup conflicts arise if groups are in competition with each other for limited resources.[39] However, the social identity perspective maintains that it is not necessarily incompatible group interests that provoke intergroup discrimination, but "the mere perception of belonging to two distinct groups – that is, social categorization per se – is sufficient to trigger intergroup discrimination favoring the ingroup."[40] The need for social differentiation between groups "is fulfilled through the creation of intergroup differences when such differences do not in fact exist, or the attribution of value to, and the enhancement of, whatever differences that do exist."[41] Therefore, the polarization of attitudes between an ingroup and its pertinent outgroups does not by itself provide evidence for the ongoing real-life conflict between the groups in question.

The principal idea of self-categorization theory is that we categorize ourselves just as we categorize others, and thus we depersonalize ourselves. Therefore, the process of categorization concerns both the self-conception of an individual in relation to his or her ingroup and people who are perceived as different from the ingroup. This depersonalization makes group behavior possible and means that the behavior of individual group members "assimilates or conforms to the relevant ingroup prototype in terms of attitudes, feelings, and actions." Group prototypes "capture not only similarities within groups but also differences between groups," which means that "prototypes can often be extreme or polarized relative to the central tendency of a specific group."[42] The biased portrait of the Jewish leaders in Matt 23 is a case in point.

---

[39] For conflict theory, see M. SHERIF, *Group Conflict and Cooperation: Their Social Psychology* (London: Routledge, 1966).

[40] TAJFEL and TURNER, "An Integrative Theory," 38.

[41] TAJFEL, *Human Groups*, 276.

[42] Michael A. HOGG, "Social Categorization, Depersonalization and Group Behavior," in *Blackwell Handbook of Social Psychology: Group Processes* (ed. M. A. Hogg and R. S. Tindale; Oxford: Blackwell, 2001), 56–85, esp. p. 60.

In a series of woes, Matthew refers to such religious activities of the scribes and the Pharisees as their missionary activity (23:15), religious oaths (23:16–22), tithing (23:23–24), purity rites (23:25–26), and the building of the memorials of the prophets (23:29–33). Matthew's intention here is not a detailed, legal discussion of these various parts of pharisaic piety, but these references serve to illustrate the corrupt nature of Jesus' opponents. For Matthew, religious practices associated with the scribes and the Pharisees betray that they are "children of hell" (23:15), "blind fools" (23:17), "full of greed and rapacity (23:25), "full of hypocrisy and lawlessness" (23:28), descendants of murderers (23:31), and "brood of vipers" (23:33). Many scholars have noted how the description of Jesus' opponents in Matthew 23 forms an antithesis to the description of Jesus' ideal followers in the beginning of the Sermon on the Mount. K. C. Hanson remarks that the makarisms in Matthew 5 and the reproaches in Matthew 23 bracket Jesus' public ministry, and that "the antithetical character of the makarisms and the reproaches is not only formal, but semantic as well."[43] For example, Jesus' ideal followers are promised the kingdom of heaven (5:3, 10) while the scribes and the Pharisees "lock people out of the kingdom of heaven" (23:13), Jesus' followers hunger and thirst for righteousness (5:6), while the scribes and the Pharisees only "look righteous to others" (23:28), Jesus' followers' receive mercy, while the scribes and the Pharisees neglect mercy (23:23), Jesus' followers are "pure in heart" (5:8), while the scribes and the Pharisees are impure (23:27), Jesus followers are called the children of God (5:9), while the scribes and the Pharisees are "children of hell" (23:15), Jesus' followers are persecuted in the same way as the prophets (5:12), while the scribes and the Pharisees are "descendants of those who murdered the prophets" (23:31). From a social identity perspective, this antithesis between an idealized ingroup and a denounced outgroup is an example of extreme and polarized group prototypes typical of the process of social categorization.

---

[43] K. C. HANSON. "How Honorable! How Shameful! A Cultural Analysis of Matthew's Makarisms and Reproaches." *Semeia* 68 (1994): 81–111, esp. p. 102. Cf. also SALDARINI, "Delegitimation," 673 n. 39. Saldarini notes that "Matthew brackets his account of Jesus' deeds and teaching with a vision of a new society (chaps. 5–7) and an attack on an alternative program (ch. 23). It should be noted that both have succeeded quite well for almost 2000 years."

Matthew 23 and Cognitive Dissonance

The social identity theory explains quite well how Matthew's polemical portrait of the scribes and the Pharisees results from a process of social categorization, but can we explain in more detail why Matthew selected these groups and turned them into exemplary hypocrites? Again, Ulrich Luz has made an ingenious proposal. Luz takes Matthew 23 as an example of the so-called "post-decision conflict." According to him, "with the separation from the synagogue comes dissonance – that is, regrets over the negative consequences of a decision that has been made. Therefore it is necessary to portray the rejected alternative as bad in order to legitimate one's own decision."[44] Here Luz makes a reference to the phenomenon which, since the publication of Leon Festinger's classic book on the subject,[45] has become known as cognitive dissonance In his study, Festinger claimed that an aversive psychological state called dissonance arises when a person's two cognitions are inconsistent, which leads to attempts to reduce this dissonance. Dissonance may occur "when people evaluate their own behavior and find it discrepant from some standard of judgment. This standard can be based on personal considerations and self-expectancies or on social factors such as the normative rules and prescriptions used by most people in a culture."[46]

Recently, the role of social groups in the dissonance arousal and dissonance reduction has gained new interest also among social identity theorists.[47] While Luz refers to this phenomenon on a general level and con-

---

[44] LUZ, *Matthew 21–28*, 176. Luz refers here to Werner HERKNER, *Einführung in die Sozialpsychologie* (Berne: Huber, 1991), 90–91.

[45] Leon FESTINGER, *The Theory of Cognitive Dissonance* (Stanford, CA: Stanford University Press, 1957).

[46] David C. MATZ and Wendy WOOD, "Cognitive Dissonance in Groups: The Consequences of Disagreement," *Journal of Personality and Social Psychology* 88 (2005), 22–37, esp. p. 22.

[47] Blake M. MCKIMMIE *et al.*, "I'm a Hypocrite, but So Is Everyone Else: Group Support and the Reduction of Cognitive Dissonance," *Group Dynamics: Theory, Research, and Practice* 7 (2003), 214–224. These writers note that, although Festinger's original monograph foreshadowed the role of group processes in dissonance arousal and reduction, subsequent dissonance research has focused on individuals rather than on groups and overlooked the importance of group-derived cognitions. Tajfel already recognized the potential of cognitive dissonance theory for the study of social groups. Cf. TAJFEL, *Human Groups*, 39. Tajfel says that cognitive dissonance theory is useful because the "concepts of commitment and of justification are inherent in it" and "these concepts are as social as they are psychological."

nects it to the separation from the synagogue, I think that the concept of cognitive dissonance helps us to explain more specifically why Matthew portrays the Pharisees as hypocrites. This portrait is closely related to their role in Matthew's gospel.

It is generally accepted that Matthew has inserted the Pharisees into more narrative situations than his sources had done. Most recently, Martin Pickup has described the role of the Pharisees in Matthew's gospel and concluded: "It appears that the author of Matthew tried to identify Jesus' opponents as Pharisees (on) every opportunity that he could. ... The emphasis that Matthew's gospel gives to the Pharisees ... seems intended to show that halakhic approach to the Torah that conflicted so seriously with the teaching of Jesus was that of the Pharisees."[48] In Matthew's gospel, therefore, the Pharisees are Jesus' main opponents in different conflict stories that focus on the role and interpretation of the Mosaic Law. As also Mark Allan Powell has stated: "Matthew's Gospel presents disputes over interpretation of Mosaic Law as the most serious of all Jesus' conflicts with the religious leaders. Furthermore, Matthew never records any instance in which the scribes and the Pharisees are represented as interpreting Moses in a way that Jesus finds acceptable."[49]

The Pharisees and the Law of Moses are thus closely related in Matthew's gospel. Matthew's own understanding of the Law is one of the most controversial issues in recent studies. This issue is closely related to the question concerning Matthew's relationship to Judaism in general. It is today almost universally accepted that Matthew and his community are deeply rooted in diverse first century Judaism, but this is where the scholarly consensus ends. Some scholars agree with Anthony Saldarini (cf. above) and describe the Matthean community as a Law-observant community, representing Christian Judaism and they interpret Matthew's polemics against the scribes and the Pharisees as an intra-Jewish debate.[50] Other scholars emphasize the newness of Matthew's description of Jesus as the

---

[48] Martin PICKUP, "Matthew's and Mark's Pharisees," in *In Quest of the Historical Pharisee* (ed. J. Neusner and B. Chilton; Waco, Texas: Baylor University Press, 2007), 67–112, esp. p. 95.

[49] POWELL, "Do And Keep," 428.

[50] For the discussion, see Warren CARTER, "Matthew's Gospel: Jewish Christianity, Christian Judaism, or Neither?" in *Jewish Christianity Reconsidered: Rethinking Ancient Groups and Texts* (ed. Matt Jackson-McCabe; Minneapolis: Fortress Press, 2007), 155–179. Carter finds some problems even in Saldarini's description of Matthew as an example of Christian Judaism, but still regards this description as more appropriate than the one emphasizing the gospel's newness and the christological displacement of the Torah (see the next note).

sole authoritative interpreter of the Torah and claim that Matthew signals a break with different strands of first century Judaism.[51]

Space here does not permit the full discussion of this complex issue, but even some cursory observations suggest that the Torah was a possible candidate for arousing cognitive dissonance in Matthew's community. Saldarini has presented thus far the most compelling arguments for the view that Matthew does not suggest in any way that Jesus denounced or superseded the Torah.[52] Saldarini's nuanced arguments show how Matthew and his community wanted to understand themselves as a Law-fulfilling community, whose righteousness is greater than that of the scribes and the Pharisees (5:20). We may be quite sure, however, that not everyone in Matthew's environment agreed with this description. Recurrent conflicts in Matthew's gospel over the Law betray that the significance of the Law and its individual commandments for daily life were disputed matters in his community. Saldarini argues that Matthew has edited, or even left out, some sayings, which appear in Mark's gospel (e.g., Mark 2:27; 7:17–23), that could be interpreted as promoting laxity towards the Torah.[53] Even if this were the real motive for Matthew's redactional changes, it clearly shows that Matthew was consciously aware of those disturbing problems connected to the keeping of the Torah in the early Christian communities.

At the end of the day, however, it may be that Matthew was not only aware of these problems but deeply involved in them himself. The end of the gospel (Matt 28:16–20) clearly indicates that Jesus' message, as rendered by Matthew, is meant for all people – not only for Israel, that baptism is crucial for those who become disciples – circumcision is not mentioned at all – and the disciples should obey all that Jesus has commanded – the Torah is not mentioned. Given the fact that circumcision is not mentioned at all in Matthew's gospel, it could be maintained that Matthew presupposes that gentile converts, who are baptized, are also circumcised. However, even Saldarini admits that the opposite may be true and Matthew's group may indeed have accepted gentile members without demand-

---

[51] See Petri LUOMANEN, *Entering the Kingdom of Heaven: A Study on the Structure of Matthew's View of Salvation* (WUNT, 2. Reihe 101; Tübingen: Mohr-Siebeck, 1998); "The 'Sociology of Sectarianism' in Matthew: Modeling the Genesis of Early Jewish and Christian Communities," in *Fair Play: Diversity and Conflicts in Early Christianity. Essays in Honor of Heikki Räisänen* (ed. Ismo Dunderberg, Christopher Tuckett and Kari Syreeni; SupNovT 103; Leiden: Brill, 2002), 107–130; HARE, "How Jewish," 264–277; Donald W. HAGNER, "Matthew: Apostate, Reformer, Revolutionary?," *NTS* 49 (2003): 193–209.

[52] SALDARINI, *Community*, 124–164.

[53] Cf. SALDARINI, *Community*, 131, 138.

ing circumcision.[54] Saldarini refers to cases, which suggest that there were male Jews, who were not circumcised, but who did not cease to be Jews sociologically, even though he admits that the evidence for such cases is weak and controversial.[55] Even if circumcision was not a universal marker of Jewishness, the decision not to circumcise some members of the community would surely raise anxiety, not only among Matthew's Jewish opponents but also among the members of the community.

Many scholars think that Matthew's relationship to the Torah is a lot more ambiguous than Saldarini suggests and that those who follow him are ready to acknowledge. Even though Matthew's Jesus insists that "not one letter, not one stroke of a letter, will pass from the Law until all is accomplished" (5:18), this is not necessarily the whole picture. Ulrich Luz has noted that, in spite of Matthew's insistence on keeping the whole Law, "in practice the Matthean community has subordinated the many individual commandments of the Torah to the commandment to love, which is the center. In theory, they probably were not able to see a tension."[56] As also Petri Luomanen has remarked, the words in Matthew 5:16–20 "are exactly what we would expect to find in a foundation document of a deviant group. They aim at the impression that nothing new has come into existence."[57] Luomanen has also aptly noted that "a proper description of dissenting religious groups will not pay attention only to their self-understanding. Groups also have to be compared with each other, tracing items that separate or unite them both socially and ideologically."[58]

If regarded not only from Matthew's own point of view, it seems that there were major ambiguities in Matthew's understanding of the Torah even though we may not be able to say in detail how different commandments were interpreted and what practices were followed by Matthean Christians. It is probable that the ambiguous role of the Torah was the main source for arousal of cognitive dissonance among the members of his community. Matthew's assertion, that Jesus has come to fulfill the Law and not to abolish it, demonstrates that Matthew and his community were quite reluctant to admit that their faith in Jesus was in any way a contradiction to the Law.

I propose that one way to reduce the dissonance between the principle of emphasizing the keeping of the whole Law and the more liberal reli-

---

[54] SALDARINI, *Community*, 157.

[55] For the problems in the evidence suggesting that circumcision was not practised by all Jews, see the discussion and references in HAKOLA, *Identity Matters*, 27–28, esp. n. 100.

[56] LUZ , *Matthew 1–7*, 270.

[57] LUOMANEN, *Entering*, 88.

[58] LUOMANEN, "Sociology," 118.

gious practice of the community was to externalize the dissonance by making it a main characteristic of those who represent the most virulent defenders of the Law in Matthew's gospel, namely the Pharisees.[59] Instead of seeing the beliefs of his own community as dissonant, Matthew promoted its social identity by producing the portrait of the Pharisees as hypocritical teachers, who do not practice what they teach. This portrait does not reflect any alleged failure of some real-life Pharisees in Matthew's environment, but the ambiguous self-understanding of a community, who preached that they fulfill the whole Mosaic Law, but who were about to realize how difficult it was to comprehensively follow their own teaching in their daily lives. Matthew's portrait of the hypocritical Pharisees reflects quite well what William Scott Green has said of the way in which religious communities represent "others" in the light of their own self-understanding:

In so constructing "otherness," religions do not see the outsiders' whole. Rather, a religion mistakes some part of the outsider for outsider and a piece of itself for itself, and it construes each in terms of the other. Each negation of the "other" is simultaneously an affirmation of self, in terms of some particular trait. This means that "otherness" is as much about the naming of religion as it is about outsiders named. ... "Otherness", therefore, is at least as much a reflection of the religious community's self-understanding as it is a response to actual conflicts with the real other.[60]

---

[59] Cf. Joel COOPER and Jeff STONE, "Cognitive Dissonance and the Social group," in *Attitudes, Behavior and Social Context* (ed. by D. J. Terry and M. A. Hogg; Applied Social Research; Mahwah, New Jersey: Lawrence Erlbaum Associates, 2000), 227–244 esp. p. 235: "One source of negative affect to which group members can misattribute their dissonant state is the outgroup. A group whose purpose and identity is not only different from, but contradictory to, a person's ingroup is likely to cause negative affect. As such, if it is salient when people are in the throes of cognitive dissonance, the outgroup may serve as a convenient source of misattribution. Placing additional negative arousal (due to dissonance) onto a group that already is unattractive and the source of its own negative affect is likely to lead to additional derogation of, and hostility toward, the outgroup and its members."

[60] William Scott GREEN, "Heresy, Apostasy in Judaism," in *The Encyclopaedia of Judaism, vol. I* (ed. J. Neusner, A. J. Avery-Peck & W. S. Green; Leiden: Brill, 2000), 366–380, esp. p. 366.

Act as a Christ-Believer, as a Household Member or as Both? – A Cognitive Perspective on the Relationship between the Social Identity in Christ and Household Identities in Pauline and Deutero-Pauline Texts

Rikard Roitto

Introduction

In everyday life we often find ourselves in situations in which we have to decide whether to identify with this or that social identity (role) and, as a consequence, act in this or that capacity. Should I act as a customer, as a Ph.D. student or as a father? This was also true for the first Christ-believers.[1] Should I handle this situation as a Christ-believer or as a slave? Or perhaps as a slave in Christ? In this article, I will present a cognitive perspective on social identities and on self-categorisation theory, and I will focus on the cognitive ordering of these categories. This will be followed by a very brief discussion of social identities in the Mediterranean world of the first century. I will then use self-categorisation theory, complemented with other strands of cognitive psychology, to argue that, while Paul himself saw household identities and the identity in Christ as different and potentially conflicting identities that were meant to function in different spheres of life, the deutero-Pauline authors saw household identities as a subcategory to the identity in Christ and not as mutually conflicting. I will then argue that ideology cannot explain this change in cognition fully, but that this change can be understood as a reflection of a historical develop-

---

[1] In this article the phrases "identity in Christ", "Christ-believer" and "Christ-movement" will replace "Christian identity", "Christian" and "Christianity". This terminology is inspired by terms which are recurrent in Pauline and deutero-Pauline literature. The term *christianos* is rare in the New Testament (Acts 11:26; 26:28; 1 Pet 4:16) and does not appear in the Pauline or deutero-Pauline literature. The term *Christianismos* does not appear until Ignatius (Ign. *Magn.* 10:1, 3; Ign. *Rom.* 3:3; Ign. *Phld.* 6:1). Terms such as *en Christō* and *ho pisteuōn (epi Christō)* are however very frequent self-designations in Pauline and deutero-Pauline literature.

ment, by which households, in which just about everyone belonged to the community in Christ, became increasingly common.[2]

Categorising Ourselves and One Another

The identity in Christ and household identities will in this article be analysed as social identities, i.e. as cognitive categories, by which people categorised themselves and others.

To be able to categorise is basic to our ability to handle the complexity of life.[3] The mental representation of a category in our brains, our category schemata, centre on an ideal, i.e. on the prototype, flanked by a list of examples, which belong to the category and fit more or less well into the prototype.[4] Through processes of analogical thinking we then fit new experiences into existing schemata, even though these new experiences might not fit exactly into the prototype.[5] Imagine for example our very flexible per-

---

[2] In a way this argument revisits some of the historical insights from Elisabeth SCHÜSSLER FIORENZA, *In Memory of Her: A Feminist Theological Reconstruction of Christian Origins* (New York: Crossroad, 1994) and rephrases the development into cognitive categories. The cognitive perspective will however hopefully reveal other aspects of this socio-historical development. Some commentators of Schüssler Fiorenza have criticised her for being overtly optimistic about which theological and historical conclusions can be drawn from Paul about gender equality and the prominence of women in the first generation of Christ-believers, see e.g. Lone FATUM, "Image of God and Glory of Man: Women in the Pauline Congregations." in *The Image of God and Gender Models: In Judaeo-Christian Tradition* (ed. Børresen: Oslo: Solum Forlag, 1991); Ross Shepard KRAEMER, *Her Share of the Blessings: Women's Religions among Pagans, Jews, and Christians in the Greco-Roman World* (New York: Oxford Univ. Press, 1992), 128–56. While this critique is relevant, I still find that Schüssler Fiorenza is able to present a plausible historical reconstruction of a lived reality where at least some women had influence and prominence in the congregations. This article will however not appraise Schüssler Fiorenza's (or any other scholar's) work in a systematic way. Rather, the cognitive track will be followed quite strictly. I do nevertheless recognise that some of the conclusions, which arise from a cognitive perspective, confirm some of the suggestions of Schüssler Fiorenza. The purpose of this article is however not to revisit the question of exactly how strong women's positions were. The focus is not gender but household identities (although these overlap). The purpose is to reflect upon which social circumstances might have allowed men, women, masters and slaves in the Christ-movement to act out of their household identities or might have prevented them from doing so.

[3] George LAKOFF and Mark JOHNSON, *Philosophy in the Flesh: The Embodied Mind and Its Challenge to Western Thought* (New York: Basic Books, 1999), 17–20.

[4] Susan T. FISKE and Shelley E. TAYLOR, *Social Cognition* (New York: Random house, 1984), 146–48.

[5] Robert S. WYER and Thomas K. SRULL, *Handbook of Social Cognition* (Vol. 1, Hillsdale, N.J.: Lawrence Erlbaum, 1984), 53.

ception of dogs. The categories are often ordered into hierarchies, in which a category at a level "above" is more inclusive than a category at a level "below"; e.g. entity, thing, furniture, chair, kitchen chair.[6] The more specific levels are typically modelled on the characteristics of the more general level, and more specific characteristics are added; e.g. a chair is made to sit on, while a kitchen chair is made to sit on in the kitchen. Since categories centre on prototypes and hold no strictly defined boundaries, we are able to reflect on whether an object belongs to this or that category, how prototypical it is etc.[7] Imagine for example how the categories of vase, cup and bowl tend to have no strict boundaries towards each other as long as we only discuss their shape. In a particular context we can, however, negotiate what a particular object should be categorised as, depending on our dispositions (e.g. goals, needs) in that situation.

We do not only categorise things, but also ourselves and one another into groups. According to self-categorisation theory, John Turner's development of Henry Tajfel's social identity theory, "cognitive representations of the self take the form, amongst others, of self-categorizations, i.e. cognitive groupings of oneself and some class of stimuli as the same ... in contrast to some other class of stimuli."[8] This self-categorisation has the effect that we perceive ourselves and others as more like the prototype of the group, i.e. as the ideal group member.[9] With which of all our possible social selves we identify in a certain situation depends on a) how well the identity fits the situation and b) how easily accessible that identity is in our current cognitive disposition.[10]

Just like any other category, these social identities are often hierarchically structured;[11] e.g. I am a scholar, a scholar of humanities, a historian, a New Testament historian, a New Testament historian who uses cognitive

---

[6] John R. TAYLOR, *Linguistic Categorization* (Oxford: Oxford University Press, 2003), 48–53.

[7] TAYLOR, *Linguistic Categorization*, 63–83.

[8] John C. TURNER, *et al.*, *Rediscovering the Social Group: A Self-Categorization Theory* (Oxford: Blackwell, 1987), 44.

[9] Stephen D. REICHER, *et al.*, "A Social Identity Model of Deindividuation Phenomena," *European Review of Social Psychology* 6 (1995); Dominic ABRAMS, "Social Identity, Social Cognition and the Self" in *Social Identity and Social Cognition* (ed. Abrams and Hogg: Oxford: Blackwell, 1999); Michael A. HOGG and Dominic ABRAMS, *Social Identifications: A Social Psychology of Intergroup Relations and Group Processes* (London: Routledge, 1988); John C. TURNER, *et al.*, "Self and Collective: Cognition and Social Context," *Personality and Social Psychology Bulletin* 20 (1994).

[10] Penelope J. OAKES, "The Categorization Process: Cognition of the Group in the Social Psychology of Stereotyping" in *Social Identity Theory: Constructive and Critical Advances* (ed. Abrams and Hogg: London: Harvester Wheatsheaf, 1990).

[11] TURNER, *et al.*, *Rediscovering the Social Group*.

theory. Just like any category, the more specific social identity is typically modelled on the characteristics of the more inclusive category; e.g. if it is virtuous for a scholar to be aware of his or her dispositions, then the same is virtuous for a historian. In situations where we have to choose between social identities which are not hierarchically subordinated to each other, e.g. between father and scholar, it becomes more difficult to identify with both roles in the same situation, although we can be aware that the actions we perform now in one role may affect us in another role; e.g. a politician who loves soccer might avoid some of the more aggressive and offensive possible expressions of a soccer fan in order to maintain his credibility as a politician. We can be aware that we are in an ambiguous situation where it is unclear in what capacity we should act. However, in ambiguous and conflicting situations, there is a strong tendency to identify with one social identity and to suppress the other.[12] In practice, it is often necessary to choose whether to act in the capacity of this or that social identity.

Social Identities in the First Century Mediterranean World

It is fairly safe to claim that the culture[13] in which the Christ-movement was born was on average a more collectivistic culture than large portions

---

[12] Theresa K. VESCIO, *et al.*, "Percieving and Responding to Multiple Categorizable Individuals: Cognitive Processes and Affective Intergroup Bias" in *Social Identity and Social Cognition* (ed. Abrams and Hogg: Oxford: Blackwell, 1999). Regarding two identities in the same hierarchy, self-categorisation theory originally proposed that we can only identify with one identity at one level of identification at the time. This position has received critique, and experiments have shown that people can identify on different levels of a hierarchy of identities simultaneously; e.g. I can identify as a scholar and a New Testament historian simultaneously. See M. CINNIRELLA, "Towards a European Identity? Interactions between the National and European Social Identities Manifested by University Students in Britain and Italy," *British Journal of Social Psychology* 36 (1997); P. P. MLICKI and Naomi ELLEMERS, "Being Different or Being Better? National Stereotypes and Identifications of Polish and Dutch Students," *European Journal of Social Psychology* 26 (1996).

[13] I follow cognitive anthropologists, such as Bradd SHORE, *Culture in Mind: Cognition, Culture, and the Problem of Meaning* (New York: Oxford Univ. Press, 1996); Dan SPERBER, *Explaining Culture: A Naturalistic Approach* (Cambridge: Blackwell, 1996); Claudia STRAUSS and Naomi QUINN, *A Cognitive Theory of Cultural Meaning* (Cambridge: Cambridge University Press, 1997), who understand "culture" to be more or less shared cognitive patterns among interacting people. With this definition, it is possible to avoid to reidentify "Culture" and yet still to speak about cultural phenomena. A thought pattern does not need to be universally shared or to have definitive boundaries in its distribution among a population in order to be cultural. It just needs to be fairly commonly used in interaction in order to qualify as culture.

of our 21ˢᵗ century western culture.[14] From a social identity perspective, "collectivistic culture" means a culture in which people tend to identify more often with social identities, such as father, mother, Christ-believer etc., and in which there is a stronger social pressure to act according to one's social identities.[15] We might need to beware of stereotyping "them" as the entirely collectivistic others and "us" as entirely individualistic, but there is and there was a more collectivistic tendency in the Mediterranean culture than in our own culture.[16]

When we describe the collectivistic nature of the first century Mediterranean culture, it might be tempting to paint a picture of a world in which the social identities available were primarily concentric circles of kinship belonging. For instance, I belong to a household, which belongs to a clan, which belongs to a tribe. In terms of self-categorisation theory, kinship is a hierarchy of identity categories. In such a hypothetic society, the self would always be determined by the same social identity hierarchy at different levels of inclusion. The individual would then be entirely destined by his or her social kinship situation, and would always identify with his or her family roles. However, although the household and the kinship hierarchy would certainly have been important, this view is just too simple, at least for the cities. Such an overtly uniform view of social identities would make it a mystery that the early Christ-movement actually had some success, in spite of its frequent collision with the household structure. In order to make the expansion of the Pauline Christ-movement understandable, we must remember that the web of embedded social identities was not uniform

---

[14] E.g. Bruce J. MALINA, *The New Testament World: Insights from Cultural Anthropology* (Louisville: Westminster/John Knox Press, 2001); Bruce J. MALINA and Jerome H. NEYREY, *Portraits of Paul: An Archaeology of Ancient Personality* (Louisville, Ky.: Westminster/John Knox Press, 1996).

[15] The stronger tendency in collective cultures to identify with groups is attested in social identity research, see Fransisco J. MORALES, *et al.*, "Discrimination and Beliefs on Discrimination in Individualists and Collectivists" in *Social Identity: International Perspectives* (ed. Worchel, *et al.*: London: SAGE, 1998); Dario PAEZ, *et al.*, "Constructing Social Identity: The Role of Status, Collective Values, Collective Self-Esteem, Perception and Social Behaviour" in *Social Identity: International Perspectives* (ed. Worchel *et al.*: London: SAGE, 1998).

[16] Louise Joy LAWRENCE, *An Ethnography of the Gospel of Matthew: A Critical Assessment of the Use of the Honour and Shame Model in New Testament Studies* (Tübingen: Mohr Siebeck, 2003) scrutinises the different aspects of Mediterranean culture as described by MALINA, *The New Testament World*. Although her main critique, that Malina "reifies" culture, might be unfair, Lawrence's study offers many important insights on certain points where Malina has chosen to be more categorical than is perhaps justifiable. One of these insights is that Malina might have painted a too collectivistic picture of the Mediterranean mind.

and simple. The first century Roman Empire offered a complex system of possible social identities, especially in the cities, where one identity was not always a subcategory of the other. Religious groups (Christ-believers, mystic cults, Pharisees etc.), burial societies, schools, philosophical sects (Epicureans, Cynics etc.), associations based on occupation, patron-client-networks etc. provided an ambiguous web of possibilities for social identi-fication in any given situation.[17] The individuals in such a society would have to make decisions about which social identity to adopt in different situations. In short, in the cities, where the Pauline version of belief in Christ had its greatest success,[18] there was already an established pattern by which people used to join various groups, which did not coincide with the family structure.

The Relationship between Being a Christ-Believer and Being a Household Member according to Paul

In 1 Cor 7 Paul's focus is on resolving potential conflicts between the identity in Christ and the identity as a spouse. He must resolve the problem of how to handle household duties in a way which does not compromise devotion to Christ. Paul realises that a spouse has duties as a spouse, which will sometimes conflict with the duties of a Christ-believer (vv. 3–4, 33–34). His main proposal is to avoid the conflict as far as possible by avoid-ing marriage entirely (vv. 1, 25–40). He does however realise that this is not realistic for everyone, since many are already married (vv. 12–13) and since many people would be tempted to extramarital sex if they did not marry (v. 2). His insistence on avoiding divorce does not seem to be mis-sionary tactics (v. 16).[19] Rather, both sex and marriage have bearings be-fore the eyes of God in their own right according to Paul (6:16–18; 7:2, 8–10, cf. Matt 19:5–6). In spite of his ascetic ideals, he obviously does not believe that God has dispensed with the institution of marriage. Both ex-tramarital sex and divorce break God's order. Paul can therefore not rec-

---

[17] MALINA and NEYREY, *Portraits of Paul*, 158–64 for an overview over different so-cial groupings. Neyrey and Malina do not, however, reflect upon what it meant for the individual that s/he had to make decisions about which social identity was the most ap-propriate in a given situation.

[18] Wayne A. MEEKS, *The First Urban Christians: The Social World of the Apostle Paul* (New Haven: Yale University Press, 1983), 9–50.

[19] I take v. 16 to mean "For how do you know, wife, whether you can save your hus-band?" rather than "For who knows, wife, if you [just might] save you husband? ...", since the former understanding makes sense more easily as a continuation of the advice to allow divorce if the unbelieving partner so wishes in v. 15.

ommend divorce on the initiative of the Christ-believer, even though this advice probably would have made life as a fully committed Christ-believer in Pauline fashion much simpler. Thus he must construct a compromise between the two social identities which does not violate his beliefs about sex and marriage, and which nevertheless secures the Christ-believer's status before God. A central portion of the problem-solving in 1 Cor 7 pre-supposes that one member of the household is not a Christ-believer (vv. 10–16, and probably also vv. 17–24 about slaves).[20] In order to resolve the conflict, he must therefore employ the seemingly ad hoc idea that the un-believing spouse has been sanctified through the marriage (vv. 12–14). He also tries to reduce conflict by allowing several exceptions to the rule that one should not divorce. He does not prohibit divorce on the initiative of the unbelieving spouse (v. 15) and reluctantly allows believing women to separate as long as they do not remarry (v. 11a). In this way he relieves the anxiety over divorces, which the Christ-believer might not be able to avoid, and he gives women a last escape from maybe unbearable conflicts between different obligations. Moreover, he orders that new marriages should be intra-group, at least for women (v. 39), and thus he seeks to pre-vent future problems.

In sum, Paul sees these two social identities as separate and as poten-tially conflicting. He seeks to find a compromise in the areas where the two identities clash in practice. In terms of cognitive categories, this indi-cates that the two social identities do not belong to the same hierarchy in Paul's cognition. For Paul, it is of course the identity in Christ which should be most important and any negotiation between different duties should not compromise anyone's devotion to Christ. This priority does however not mean that he sees household identities as hierarchically sub-ordinate to the identity in Christ, only that he finds the identity in Christ the most important one.

We can see the same attitude when Paul deals with slave issues in 1 Cor 7:20–23. "Called as slave, it should not bother you" (v. 21). He then goes on to speak metaphorically about being free and being a slave in relation to Christ (v. 22), which creates the impression that earthly and heavenly slav-ery or freedom has nothing to do with each other. Therefore, your identity

---

[20] Perhaps also vv. 36–38 about what a man should do with his *parthenos*, who could either be his fiancé (who he may marry) or his daughter (who he may give away in mar-riage). In this discussion both parties are Christ-believers, and in the latter interpretation part of the same household. Assuming the latter interpretation, there might be a perceived danger that the daughter might end up in a non-Christ-believing household. Vv. 8–9, 25–40 discusses potential future marriages, which could principally be to either Christ-believing or non-Christ-believing spouses, but v. 39 seems to suggest that Paul thinks that future marriages should be to Christ-believing spouses.

in Christ does not have anything to with your social identity as a slave. The only advice he can give is what to do if offered freedom (v. 21b). Unfortunately the advice, "rather utilize (*mallon chrēsai*) [freedom/slavery]", is so cryptically phrased that there is no consensus as to what his advice is.[21] Paul seems to be surprisingly insensitive to the possible identity conflicts of the slaves, since many slaves were in fact expected to have sex with their masters.[22] This insensitivity might however be the result of Paul's use of the slaves as an example of the principle that everyone should remain in the position in which he was when he was called (vv. 17, 20) and he therefore sees the situation of the slaves as secondary compared to the point that he tries to bring home.

In the letter to Philemon, Paul feels the need to negotiate between the social identity as a master and the social identity in Christ. Rather than exhorting Philemon to handle the situation as a Christ-believing master, he asks him to let his identity in Christ take priority over his social identity as a master. Philemon should receive Onesimus "no longer as a slave, but as [something] above a slave, a beloved brother" (v. 16). Although the situation could have been handled perfectly well if household identities had been subordinated to the identity in Christ, Paul thinks in terms of separate categories.

Both in the case of spouses and in the case of slaves and masters, we have seen that Paul sees household identities as separate from the identity in Christ. When he writes that, in Christ, there is "neither slave nor free, neither male nor female" (Gal 3:28), this formulation probably reflects the social experience that these social identities could be temporarily left aside in the community of Christ-believers.[23] However, both Paul's complicated compromises on marriage and the Onesimus-incident show that Paul's solution to keep these identities separated became problematic at times. I will return to why in which this became problematic in the section below, in which I try to reconstruct a possible historical development in the Pauline congregations. Already at this stage we might suspect that these identity conflicts were perhaps one of the reasons for the deutero-Pauline authors

---

[21] Carolyn OSIEK and David L. BALCH, *Families in the New Testament World: Households and House Churches* (Louisville, Ky.: Westminster John Knox Press, 1997), 179–82.

[22] Jennifer A. GLANCY, *Slavery in Early Christianity* (New York: Oxford University Press, 2002), 48–50, 67–69.

[23] FATUM, "Image of God and Glory of Man". Fatum is quite right that, in the light of 1 Cor 11:2–16, Gal 3:28 cannot be seen as a Paul's theological programme for gender equality, but that any status of women in the Christ-movement was dependent on disregarding their gender. The main result of her analysis confirms the finding of this article that Paul is trying to separate household-identities from the identity in Christ.

to rearrange the cognition of the relationship between identity in Christ and household identities. In the long run, no compromise could resolve the problems for women and slaves, who in the end did not always have a choice in certain situations.

The Relationship between Being a Christ-believer and Being a Household Member According to the Deutero-Pauline Authors

The absence of the experience of conflict and negotiation between household identities and the identity in Christ in the household code of Col 3:18–4:1 is striking. Household relationships are regulated with reference to the members' identity in Christ. The content of the regulations is quite mainstream in the Graeco-Roman context,[24] but the motivations for these regulations are nevertheless related to their identity in Christ. Women should submit "as is fitting in the Lord" (v. 18). Children should obey, "for it is pleasing in the Lord" (v. 20). Slaves should serve "fearing the Lord ... from the soul ... as for the Lord and not for men" (v. 23). Doing right or wrong in the context of the household will cause reward or punishment from the Lord himself (vv. 24–25).

In this text it is quite clear that household identities are considered to be subcategories of the identity in Christ. Household behaviour is motivated on the basis of the ideals of a prototypical Christ-believer and with reference to the judgement narrative, which is related to the identity in Christ. To be a good household member is part of what it means to be a good Christ-believer. As discussed above, a subordinate category inherits the characteristics of the superior category. In this case, the argument in favour of the subordinate category of the household member is based on ideals and narratives that belong to the superior category of the Christ-believer. Further, there is not a single trace in this text of any expressed conflict between these two identities, just as there should not be when one identity is the foundation of the other.[25] In Colossians, the household member is not just any household member, but a household member in Christ. In the case of slaves, it even seems likely that the author subtly contrasts a slave in Christ with other non-Christ-believing slaves, who

---

[24] SCHÜSSLER FIORENZA, *In Memory of Her*, 251–59.

[25] However, the cognitive non-conflicting solution *in the text* does not necessarily correspond to the *historical situation which has inspired the text*. The emphasis in the text might quite plausibly reflect a situation in which the author seeks to convince for example slaves, who still think that there is a tension between their identities, to change their perception. See the historical reconstruction section below.

supposedly are eye-serving in order to please men (v. 22). Other slaves are outgroup if they are not "in Christ."

The reasoning in Eph 5:22–6:9 largely corresponds to that in Colossians. There is however a difference in the rhetoric. The author of Colossians mainly makes use of a quite straightforward rhetoric, by which he appeals to ideals from the prototypical Christ-believer and refers to the will of God and the judgement narrative. The author of Ephesians combines these kinds of arguments with analogy arguments in order to suggest that the relationship between husband and wife and between master and slave are analogical to certain aspects of the identity in Christ. Analogical thinking and blending is a still developing field within cognitive research, which describes how we take a pattern of knowledge from one cognitive domain and use it in new domains or mix patterns from different domains in order to create something new.[26] Through this capacity we can transfer beliefs and emotions from one cognitive domain to another or mix domains in order to resolve new situations.[27] Cognitive anthropologists argue that in every culture, people tend to share cognitive patterns, which are easily accessible for the brain, and which therefore have a tendency to be reused in new situations in order to resolve hitherto unresolved problems.[28] In the culture of the Pauline Christ-movement, we should therefore expect patterns from the central narrative about Christ to be reused analogically to resolve issues which were considered to be essential to the identity in Christ. In Eph 5:22–33, we see how one domain, i.e. the narrative of Christ as the self-sacrificing and loving head and master of the *ekklesia*, is used to transfer patterns of subordination, love and respect to the domain of marriage. In Eph 6:5–9 the ideal of submission to Christ is used to transfer patterns of honesty, fear, subordination and respect to the domain of slaves and masters. This is exactly what one would expect if household identities

---

[26] Keith James HOLYOAK, *et al.*, "Introduction: The Place of Analogy in Cognition" in *The Analogical Mind: Perspectives from Cognitive Science* (ed. Gentner, *et al.*: Cambridge, Mass.: MIT Press, 2001), 9–10; Mark TURNER and Gilles FAUCONNIER, "Conceptual Integration and Formal Expression," *Metaphor and Symbolic Activity* 10 (1995).

[27] On analogical transfer of emotions, see Paul THAGARD and Cameron SHELLEY, "Emotional Analogies and Analogical Inference" in *The Analogical Mind: Perspectives from Cognitive Science* (ed. Gentner, *et al.*: Cambridge, Mass.: MIT Press, 2001). On transfer between narrative and real life see e.g. Arthur C. GRAESSER, *et al.*, "How Does the Mind Construct and Represent Stories?" in *Narrative Impact: Social and Cognitive Foundations* (ed. Strange, *et al.*: Mahwah, N.J.: Lawrence Erlbaum, 2002); Roger C. SCHANK and Tamara R. BERMAN, "The Persuasive Role of Stories in Knowledge and Action" in *Narrative Impact: Social and Cognitive Foundations* (ed. Strange, *et al.*: Mahwah, N.J.: Lawrence Erlbaum, 2002).

[28] SHORE, *Culture in Mind*; SPERBER, *Explaining Culture*; STRAUSS and QUINN, *Cultural Meaning*.

were experienced as a subcategory of the identity in Christ. If household identities are subordinate to the identity in Christ, then your identity in Christ should be the model for your behaviour in the household.

In 1 Tim 3:1–13 the transfer of norms goes in the opposite direction. While in Eph 5:22–6:9 the relationship to Christ becomes a paradigm for relationships in the household, in 1 Tim 3:1–13 competence in the household becomes a condition for competence as a leader of the congregation. Both *episkopoi* and *diakonoi* must be able to govern their households (3:5, 12). Further, the wife's household duty to bear children is salvatory (2:15). Again, the sphere of the household identity and the sphere of the identity in Christ are so integrated that the duties of the household becomes the duties of the Christ-believer. The congregation is like a household. As 1 Tim 1:4 and Elisabeth Schüssler Fiorenza put it, the congregation is now "the household of God".[29] First Timothy represents the most complete integration of household identities with the identity in Christ. They are now so integrated that the duties of the household gives status before God and before the congregation. It is as if the identity in Christ has not only subordinated the household identities, as in Ephesians and Colossians, but that the cognitive pattern of the household identities has become the leaven that has leavened the entire identity in Christ. Once the household identities were subordinated to the identity in Christ, the thought patterns from these household identities became part of the cognitive resources in Christ and were transferred to the thinking about other spheres of the identity in Christ as well.

Perhaps surprisingly, the rhetoric in Tit 2:1–10 expresses less integration of the two identities than 1 Tim 3:1–13. The reasons given in Tit 2:1–10 to be a good household member are largely strategic, i.e. they aim to protect the reputation of the congregation in society (vv. 5, 8, 10). The household advice is presented as "sound teaching" (v. 1), but there are no analogies to the narrative of Christ in order to motivate this behaviour; no references to the will of God, to future judgement or to what is fitting in Christ. But even though the author is perhaps less enthusiastic than the author of First Timothy about integrating the two identities, we do not get the impression that the author sees the identity in Christ as potentially conflicting with household identities, as in 1 Cor 7 and Philemon. Further, if we consider what virtues are mentioned in Tit 2:1–10, we can see how virtues associated with the identity in Christ are mixed with virtues associated with the household. Elderly women, who should have various virtues not specifically associated with the household, should teach the younger women specific household virtues (vv. 3–5). Elders need to lead a virtuous

---

[29] SCHÜSSLER FIORENZA, *In Memory of Her*, 287.

life within their believing household in order to qualify as elders (1:6). In short, for some reason Tit 2:1–10 is more restrained about the rhetoric of integration than 1 Tim 3:1–13, but nevertheless sees no conflict between these two spheres of identity.

Summary of Cognitions of the Relationship between Identity in Christ and Household Identities

Paul:

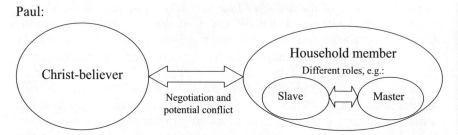

The identity in Christ is separate from household identities and the relationship between them is marked by negotiation and potential conflict.

The deutero-Pauline authors:

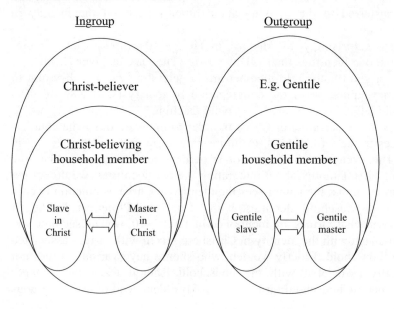

According to this view, being a household member is a subcategory of being a Christ-believer. For example, a Christ-believing slave should not be like a Gentile slave. The cognitive system purports that being a good Christ-believer entails being a good household member, and being a good household member is part of what it means to be a Christ-believer. Being a Christ-believer should govern the interpretation of all household identities.

A Historical Reconstruction of Why a Change in Cognition Took Place

So far, I have looked at the texts and how they order social identities. The next step, which necessarily is more speculative, is to try to reconstruct a plausible historical development, which would make these changes understandable.,In her analysis of Christian identity, Judith Lieu expresses scepticism as to whether one can really know anything beyond the textual constructions of identity.[30] In spite of her recognition that the texts were situated in a social context, she draws the methodological conclusion that it is safer to concentrate on the constructions of the text.[31] While I fully appreciate the efforts to analyse texts as literary constructions and not only as straightforward reflections of the past, perhaps this linguistic awareness has overemphasised how impenetrable and arbitrary the relationship between the text and the social reality is.

Cognitive research has made it more and more obvious how our minds are closely interrelated to human biology, i.e. how our cognitive experience is founded in our bodies. First, evolutionary cognitive research has emphasised that the brain has domain-specific capacities, which have evolved for the purpose of handling specific tasks that help us to survive as biological beings.[32] As human beings, these inherited skills do not only help us to survive physically, but also to handle social interaction. Secondly, cognitive linguists have emphasised that although we construct our

---

[30] Judith LIEU, *Christian Identity in the Jewish and Graeco-Roman World* (Oxford: Oxford University Press, 2004).

[31] Lieu exemplifies how the so called "linguistic turn", which has been around for decades in many other disciplines, has reached at least some biblical scholars during the last two decades or so. Elizabeth A. CLARK, *History, Theory, Text: Historians and the Linguistic Turn* (Cambridge, Mass.: Harvard University Press, 2004) makes an impressive presentation of the development during the 20th century of the philosophy of history and suggests that the awareness which comes with linguistic turn is beneficial for the historian.

[32] Ilkka PYYSIÄINEN, *How Religion Works: Towards a New Cognitive Science of Religion* (Leiden; Boston: Brill, 2003), 197–233.

subjective experience of reality through metaphorical (analogical) thinking, the basic metaphors come from our biological experience of being
bodily creatures, and these basic metaphors are valid across different cultures.[33] This suggests that cognition, as expressed in texts, does usually
have a relevant relationship to lived material and social circumstances,
even if this relationship is not straightforward. It is reasonable to assume
that texts, which attempt to resolve lived experience, do articulate a cognitive representation of a lived social reality – a representation which attempts to order this reality in practical and feasible ways.

The text is in dialogue, not only with other texts, but also with the social
experience of everyday life. While I admit that speculation about the relationship between text and the lived experience of the past can never become more than more or less plausible, I believe that it is valuable for a
historian, who aims to gain an inter-subjective understanding, and at least
to try to say something about the social history that has caused the cognitive patterns reflected in these texts, since these texts were most probably
written in dialogue with a specific social context. Such a reconstruction
draws lines between the dots, and necessarily construes something more
simplistic than the reality of the actual past.[34] However, without such
speculation, the risk of misunderstanding the text increases rather than de-
creases.

When we try to make such a reconstruction, a cognitive approach has
the advantage of starting from how people, as biological beings, usually
perceive reality. Many basic cognitive skills, such as the categorisation of
people, are the same across time and cultures. Although cultures may di-
verge considerably, they are all formed by our biologically inherited cognitive skills.[35] In this way, the cognitive sciences can be an aid to the reconstruction of a plausible historical development of a reality which is admit-
tedly no longer there to be observed.

The commonly suggested chronological order of the texts in the analysis
above is a) First Corinthians and Philemon by Paul, b) Colossians and
Ephesians in the generation after Paul, and c) First Timothy and Titus at
the beginning of the second century.[36] Assuming that this is correct, we

---

[33] LAKOFF and JOHNSON, *Philosophy in the Flesh*.

[34] John Lewis GADDIS, *The Landscape of History: How Historians Map the Past* (Oxford: Oxford University Press, 2002) emphasises how the historian puts a perspective on
the past rather than describes it as it was.

[35] Maurice BLOCH, *How We Think They Think: Anthropological Approaches to Cognition, Memory, and Literacy* (Boulder, Colo.; Oxford: Westview, 1998); LAKOFF and
JOHNSON, *Philosophy in the Flesh*.

[36] E.g. Stephen L. HARRIS, *Understanding the Bible* (Boston: McGraw-Hill, 2006),
496–503. Even though some commentators dispute these dates, these commentators usu-

find the following chronological development of the Pauline Christ-movement:

a) Identity in Christ and household identities are separate identities.

b) Household identities become cognitively subordinated to the identity in Christ.

c) The identity in Christ becomes permeated by thought patterns from the household sphere in First Timothy. Titus is however less integrated in its argument.

Why would Paul handle household identities as identities not subordinated to the identity in Christ? After all, Paul was a Jew and most branches of Judaism held that household identities were governed by their ethnic and religious identity as the people of God. A central thought in the Jewish identity was that God himself had promised that they would be a chosen people, i.e. an ethnic group with a self-understanding which certainly involved the household. God had given the laws about marriage, sexual relationships, slavery, food production and other typical household issues. They cultivated a wisdom tradition and an oral *Torah*-tradition which dealt with practical household issues. Of course, some Jews who were less committed to their Jewish heritage were not always too happy to let their Jewish identity govern their behaviour (1 Macc 1:11–15), but Paul's background was rather at the other end of the spectrum of commitment (Gal 1:13–14). One would imagine that these thought patterns were deeply embedded in Paul's mind. To a certain extent we can see this in Paul's reasoning: a) One of the reasons for Paul to see a potential conflict between household identities and the identity in Christ in 1 Cor 7 is that he thinks that improper sexual activity and divorce affects a person's status before God. b) Paul does not let go of the traditional construction of gender differentiation as intrinsic to God's creation and to the asymmetrical relationship between husband and wife (1 Cor 11:2–16). But we nevertheless see how he treats the duties, which arise from these two identity spheres, as conflicting. He even does his best to minimize the effects of one identity sphere on the other. Why, then, does he construe the relationship between these social identities in this way?

We can quite easily lay aside the theory that Paul gives his advice out of some general concern for gender equality, since he construes woman as principally subordinate to man in 1 Cor 11:2–16. Fatum suggests the oppo-

---

ally assume that Eph, Col and the pastorals are written late in Paul's career in order to explain the shift in theology. This means that the chronological order of these texts is still intact even if Paul really is their author.. However, this article shows that the letters differ fundamentally in basic cognitive organisation. It seems quite unreasonable to imagine that Paul changed his cognition as radically as this while in prison when he had only a distant contact with the social reality of the congregations.

site, i.e. that the advice in 1 Cor 7 is a consequence of Paul's thinking that a woman can only have full access to Christ by denying her female gender, and that the negotiations in 1 Cor 7 is the fruit of Paul's dualistic view of women as either married and unequal or as unmarried and desexualised.[37] Only the unmarried woman, who denies her sexuality, can become "male" in the eschatological sphere in Christ and thus have direct access to Christ. This suggestion does however mainly treat Paul as an ideologist, who is stuck in between his eschatological conviction and his convictions about the order of creation, a suggestion which implicitly makes him insensitive to the lived experience of the recipients. Further, this explanation fails to explain why Paul largely chooses to express himself symmetrically about men and women in 1 Cor 7 in spite of his asymmetrical view of men and women at the theoretical level. Why would he advocate that men should not remarry if marriage is mainly an obstacle for women? It seems to me that 1 Cor 7 cannot be adequately understood as only a compromise between these two conflicting ideological convictions, even though these convictions are certainly part of the problem.

That Paul's acute eschatological expectations (1 Cor 7:28–31) made him see household duties as an obstacle can perhaps serve as a partial explanation of his attitude. But why does it need to be an obstacle? And in what way? Is it an obstacle to the missionary efforts in Corinth? The advice to stay within marriages and within slavery would then be part of the missionary tactics in order not to disturb the congregation by giving them a bad reputation in society and perhaps also in order to spread the gospel within the household sphere. While it is certainly true that it would be good short term missionary tactics not to interfere with the household structures more than necessary, and that the household might work as a contact area for missionary work, this explanation fails to explain a number of features in the texts. Paul does not mention even once any concerns about their reputation among non-believers in 1 Cor 7, even though he expresses such concern when he deals with speaking in tongues (1 Cor 14:15–25). It seems as if the explanation of missionary tactics would impose the strategy of 1 Pet 2:13–3:6 and the concerns of the Pastoral Letters (e.g. 1 Tim 3:7; Tit 1:5, 8, 10) on 1 Cor 7. When Paul brings up the "shortened time" (v. 29) he argues in favour of the advantage of not being married, and not for any strategic reason to remain within a marriage. Paul certainly has an eschatological expectation, but he does not seem to think that the relationship within the household should be determined by any missionary tactics (v. 16). One could even argue that eschatology is not Paul's primary reason to give advice, but rather an argument which he

---

[37] FATUM, "Image of God and Glory of Man", 85.

adds in order to give weight to his advice. The eschatological argument is brought into the discussion with only few words and fairly late in the discourse in 1 Cor 7, while the argument about the potential conflict between the identity in Christ and household identities is one of the main themes. Besides, Col 4:5, Eph 5:16, 1 Tim 4:1 and 2 Tim 3:1–2, 4:3, 8 for example show that the eschatological expectations had not vanished in the deutero-Pauline literature, and yet these authors have no problem about integrating the household with the identity in Christ. Eschatological expectation does not necessarily produce Paul's separating attitude. To sum up, eschatological expectation, missionary tactics and gender constructions, i.e. Paul's ideology, cannot explain the features of the texts satisfactorily. Speculation about social reality seems necessary in order to make sense of these texts. Perhaps such speculation might shed light on Paul's thinking.

A more straightforward answer to the question why he did not subordinate household identities to the identity in Christ is that his cognition was adjusted to the social reality, in which the first Christ-believers in Corinth (and perhaps elsewhere as well) lived, and not only to his own ideology. Perhaps it simply did not fit the experience of the Corinthians to see household identities as a subcategory to the identity in Christ. Under what circumstances then would it be cognitively dysfunctional to see household identities as a part of the identity in Christ? If you, as the only person in your household who had joined the new Christ-cult, it would not match your social reality to think in the traditional Jewish way about the way in which the household identities were subordinated to the religious identity. As noted above, a lot of problem-solving in 1 Cor 7 presupposes that one household member is not a Christ-believer. The social reality was that the two identities filled up different spheres of life. Different people, with different ideals, belonged to each identity category. Neither the elements of the categories, nor the prototypical traits, matched. When the congregation met, you could lay your household role aside and worship with the other Christ-believers, but as soon as you left the gathering, you would have to return to a different social reality. We can therefore conclude from Paul's cognition that it is not probable that entire households converted very often during the Pauline era.[38] We may also be confident about the social stratification expressed in 1 Cor 1:26 and assume that those who joined the Christ-cult in the Pauline generation were not very often in a position to

---

[38] The conversion of entire households in Acts, suggested in 11:14; 16:15, 31; 18:8, seem to reflect the situation in the post-70 generation of the author rather than the situation of the first generation of believers.

convince their entire households to join.[39] Asymmetries in 1 Cor 7 affirm this assumption. Paul only gives advice to slaves, not to masters. Moreover, the minor asymmetry in v. 10, where he opens up for the possibility that a wife – but not a husband – may divorce if she remains unmarried, reveals that he has some idea that it might be more difficult for a wife than for a husband to stay within a marriage to a non-Christ-believer. This would explain why Paul's tactic is to let the identity in Christ cause as little problems as possible in the household sphere and vice versa. It was cognitively and pragmatically more functional to see the two social identities as separate. Whatever one may say about Paul's theology, this social situation in the congregations probably meant that the social patterns, which were formed in this generation of Christ-believers, could scarcely have been entirely based on household hierarchies. Schüssler Fiorenza's enumeration of strong women in the first generation, of which we have some knowledge, affirms this.[40]

But as we have seen, Paul's cognitive solution caused problems occasionally. Sometimes the practical duties of different identities clashed. But more importantly, as time progressed, it seems to have become increasingly common that several members of the same household became Christ-believers (cf. 1 Tim 6:2). This was the case with the Onesimus-incident in the letter to Philemon. It probably became increasingly awkward to treat each other in one way in Christ and then in another way in the household. As the social reality progressed in this direction, the traditional Jewish way of subordinating household identities to the identity as the people of God became increasingly functional. In the end, this meant that the conventional household patterns made their way into the identity in Christ. As unfortunate as this might have been for women, slaves and children, this modified cognition managed to correspond to the changed social reality in a way which the Pauline cognition could not.

We do not need to imagine that at first, entire households never joined the community in Christ and then, suddenly, only entire households joined. This would not be very plausible. Shared cognition within a group does not match the situation of every individual perfectly. It is rather a consensus which is reached trough intragroup processes of negotiation.[41] The lengthy

---

[39] Gerd THEISSEN, *The Social Setting of Pauline Christianity: Essays on Corinth* (Philadelphia: Fortress Press, 1982), 69–119 suggests a majority of members from the lower strata, and only a few from the higher strata, in Corinth.

[40] Cf. note 2.

[41] E.g. Aaron M. BROWER and Judith L. NYE, *What's Social About Social Cognition? Research on Socially Shared Cognition in Small Groups* (Thousand Oaks, Ca.: Sage Publications, 1996); Jean DECETY and Jessica A. SOMMERWILLE, "Shared Representa-

argument on the subject of slaves in Col 3:22–25 and the extended argument on the subject of wives and husbands in Eph 5:22–33 suggest that the texts might have been written as a response to diverging perception within the community. Groups rarely have perfectly shared cognition, but nevertheless tend to converge in their cognition. Social identity research suggests that those who are perceived as leaders have more influence over the shared self-perception of the group than other members do.[42] This means that a plausible reconstruction of why a change in cognition took place should claim that those who had the greatest influence increasingly found it beneficial and functional to see household identities as subordinate to the identity in Christ. If we imagine that such influential people increasingly had households, in which just about everyone was a Christ-believer, including the slaves, it would be most functional and beneficial for these influential persons to rearrange the cognition of household identities as a subcategory of their identity in Christ. Therefore the change in cognition probably reflects a development during the deutero-Pauline generations, when an increasing part of the congregations consisted of households with a majority of Christ-believers, led by a Christ-believing *paterfamilias*, and that these households exerted strong influence over the ingroup consensus. Such a scenario fits well into those reconstructions, which suggest that the heads of households played a key role in the Christ-movement around the turn of the century, both as providers of money for the poor and as providers of a place for worship and teaching.[43] Their influence would also explain why the thought patterns from the household spheres began to permeate the interpretation of the identity in Christ.

Why did the congregation tend to converge with the household? One reason might be that the household is a network of contacts, through which it is easy to introduce one's newly found interest in the Christ-cult to other household members.[44] Paul himself does not seem to have much confidence in that network (as discussed above), but later generations might have seen the potential of the household contacts (1 Pet 2:12; 3:1). A good guess is however that evangelisation within this network worked best when

---

tions between Self and Other: A Social Cognitive Neuroscience View," *Trends in Cognitive Science* 7 (2003).

[42] John C. TURNER, "Explaining the Nature of Power: A Three-Process Theory," *European Journal of Social Psychology* 35 (2005).

[43] E.g. Harry O. MAIER, *The Social Setting of the Ministry as Reflected in the Writings of Hermas, Clement and Ignatius* (Ontario: Wilfrid Laurier UP, 1991).

[44] Rodney STARK, *The Rise of Christianity: A Sociologist Reconsiders History* (Princeton, N.J.: Princeton Univ. Press, 1996) sees the synagogues as a social network where the Christ-movement could reach new people easily. The household might have been another such social network.

the superior tried to influence the inferior, since it would have been a great shame for a free man to become influenced by the foreign superstition of a wife or a slave.

Another possible reason why the household converged with the congregation is that Paul himself encouraged this development when he recommended that Christ-believers should only marry within the group. Judging from the deutero-Pauline texts, his advice seems to have been followed. In this way it did not take many generations before the congregation and the household coincided. Since Paul was convinced that the end was near, he had no reason to imagine the consequences of his advice in future generations. In his own time it did not benefit the congregation to try to see household identities as subordinate to the identity in Christ. Nevertheless, the combination of leaving household relationships aside and at the same time recommending intragroup marriage inevitably lead to a situation in which the household identities and the identity in Christ had to be integrated, and this is exactly what later generations did.

Speculation about the Further Consequences of the Subordination of Household Identities to the Identity in Christ

What consequences might this subordination of the household identities to the identity in Christ have had for the development of the Christ-movement? Many, and most famously Schüssler Fiorenza, have pointed out the obvious consequence of the permeation of the patriarchal structures of the household into the Christ-movement. As the previous section shows, a cognitive perspective affirms such a conclusion and also gives a new perspective on the reasons why this was almost unavoidable. But I would like to suggest that there was also another consequence – namely that the identity in Christ became increasingly capable of interpreting new spheres of everyday life.

As the identity in Christ became salient in the household, the identity in Christ took priority in more and more situations related to the household. A larger and larger part of life was to be handled as a Christ-believer. Other investigations could probably show that, as time went by, not only did the household identities but also the identities as a citizen, a business man, a worker etc. became subordinated to the identity in Christ, thus making the identity in Christ salient in just about every situation in life for a committed believer. There seems to have been a historical development, by which the identity in Christ became increasingly dominant for the entire cognition of a committed Christ-believing person. As a result, the identity in Christ became cognitively more and more inescapable. And the cognitive resources (narratives, norms etc.) associated with the identity in Christ would have surfaced in more and more situations.

As discussed above, the cities of the Roman Empire were complex environments with a multitude of possible social identities with which to identify. In such a society, it was not obvious that the identity as a Christ-believer would surface in every situation. But texts such as Colossians, Ephesians, and First Timothy show an ambition to let the identity in Christ become a superior identity which subdued the household identities and also any other social identities. It is of course a very sweeping proposition, but might it be that this ambition to usurp every aspect of life is part of the explanation of how Paul's successors managed to maintain the Pauline Christ-movement so efficiently?[45] If there was little escape from the cognition in Christ, then it would have been difficult to find any meaningful alternatives to the identity in Christ. Just as John's disciples asked "To whom could we go?" (John 6:68) later generations of Christ-believers would have asked "How else could we think and act?"

---

[45] By "to maintain efficiently" I mean that the Christ-movement grew in numbers and did not whither away, not that they managed to form a uniform movement.

Body, Gender and Social Space: Dilemmas in Constructing Early Christian Identities

Halvor Moxnes

The title of Stephen Moore's book, *God's Gym*,[1] may strike us as strange, even irreverent, as it juxtaposes God and the gym, the most striking image of modern body culture associated with the cult of human, especially male bodies. The gym embodies the strong encouragement to become your own creator. It encourages you to shape your own body into that image of worship and object of desire that you wish.

It is tempting for those of us who find little promise for our own bodies in the gym to find in the eagerness to regard the body as something to be redesigned and manipulated a modern version of the golden calf. The body becomes an indication that modern men and women have exchanged the image of God for an image of themselves. A typical Christian attitude to physical exercise has been that it may be useful, but it should not be turned into idolatry. This attitude seems to find support in the words of pseudo-Paul in 1 Tim 4:17–18: "Train yourself in godliness; for while bodily training is of some value, godliness is of value in every way, as it holds promise for the present life and also for the life to come."

I use this humorous little introduction to point out that significant changes have taken place with regard to the role of the body in religious studies, not least in studies of antiquity in recent years. First of all, the body has become part of what is now studied. William R. LaFleur says that "The fact that 'body' has become a critical term for religious studies, whereas 'mysticism,' for instance, has largely dropped out, can itself signal significant change in how we study religion."[2] To verify his judgement, in the handbook entitled *Critical Terms for Religious Studies,* in which LaFleur's article on "The Body" appears, there is no essay on "Mysticism." The article on the body is followed by one on gender and also one on territory, which includes a discussion of space, that is, the concepts that are combined in the discussion in this essay.

---

[1] Stephen D. MOORE, *God's Gym: Divine Male Bodies of the Bible.* New York: Routledge, 1996.
[2] William R. LAFLEUR, "The Body" in *Critical Terms for Religious Studies* (ed. Mark C. Taylor; Chicago: Chicago University Press, 1998), 36.

LaFleur does not explain why "the body" has become an important term in recent research. Amy Richlin, however, makes a suggestion in her essay "Towards a History of Body History." Within the large field that a history of the body might encompass, Richlin focuses on "the body as sexual, gendered, and marked," that is again largely similar to our focus on the relations between body, gender and social space. According to Richlin, "history has rarely been a language for talking about bodies. Today it seems as if that is changing, and the 'history of the body' and the 'history of sexuality' seem to be turning into recognized fields of history."[3] She introduces her essay by a literary quotation that refers to the concentration camp at Dachau and to Hiroshima, and asks whether the screams from bodies at Dachau are different from those in Hiroshima. Richlin finds that this question "suggests how rooted body history is in the specific agonies of the twentieth century; and (hence?) how embroiled it is in moral and epistemological issues."[4] The question whether bodies are different or similar is part of the larger discussion of whether history consists mostly of continuity or mostly of change. Scholars are divided on this issue. But Richlin finds that both groups of scholars of the history of the body "are united at some point by their consciousness of human suffering and their urge to end it."

Let us sum up the importance of the change that has taken place with regard to body in religious studies. First, LaFleur suggests that there has been a shift away from an interest in spiritual issues to an interest in the body. This signals a significant change in scholarly perspective. In early Christian studies, the study of godliness (*eusebeia*) has been more important than studies of the body. The Norwegian professor H. P. L'Orange, an influential scholar on late antiquity, characterised this development within early Christian culture as a move from "body to symbol."[5] This position implied that the transition was not just in the eye of the beholder, but in the material itself: the early Christians themselves were less interested in the body than in the spirit. Consequently, a change in scholarly perspective must be followed by new investigations of the ancient material. What do we see when we look at bodies, not just as symbols, but as physical and social realities? A new perspective requires new research strategies.

Secondly, Richlin's suggestion that the new scholarly focus on the body is a result of the experiences of suffering bodies in our own times, points

---

[3] Amy RICHLIN, "Towards a History of Body History" in *Inventing Ancient Culture* (ed. Mark Golden and Peter Toohey, London: Routledge, 1997), 16.

[4] RICHLIN, "Body History," 16–17. The following quotations are from p. 17.

[5] Cf. the first chapter ,"Fra legeme til symbol," in H. P. L'ORANGE, *Mot Middelalder* (Oslo: Dreyer, 1963), 1–48.

to the moral responsibility of a history of human bodies. This involves going beyond the spiritualised interpretations of terms such as suffering, punishment, being a slave etc. that abound in interpretations of early Christian texts. It means to go beyond constructions of early Christianity, primarily in terms of religious ideas and ideologies, and to raise the question that Wayne Meeks has made the basis for his monograph *The First Urban Christians:* what did it mean to be an ordinary Christian in the Roman Empire?[6] That is, what did it mean to be a woman or a man with bodily needs, involved in social relationships, mostly in the non-elite sections of society in a city in the Eastern Mediterranean? To read ancient texts with a moral responsibility has consequences for hermeneutics. When texts are read and studied in their context "from below" in ancient societies the result must be a hermeneutics of involvement in the suffering and vulnerability of human bodies even today.

Finally, a focus on the body requires an integrated perspective. "The body" is not just another topic in addition to a list of topics that are interesting. Bodies are never abstract; they are always gendered and always placed. They represent men or women, and they are placed in biological, social and cosmological hierarchies, as well as in spaces that have different characters: domestic, public, ritual and cultic.[7] It is this that is indicated by the title of this essay, "Body, gender and social space." But this is not just a list of issues in a social history of early Christianity, updated with regard to Meeks' study 25 years ago. The interrelationship between these categories suggests that we are looking for an integrated methodological approach to the study of early Christian identities, thus combining gender studies and space studies.

For a brief overview of the various perspectives included in this essay, let us start with that concerning the body. Studies of the body in New Testament studies that went beyond presentations of concepts such as *sōma*[8] were inspired by the British social anthropologist Mary Douglas and her influential books *Purity and Danger* and *Natural Symbols.*[9] In her studies, the body is not the physical, individual body, but rather the body as a symbol of society. However the term "natural symbol" is in one way misleading. Douglas is interested in the body, not as a natural, but as a cultural

---

[6] Wayne A. MEEKS, *The First Urban Christians* (New Haven: Yale University Press, 1980), 2.

[7] Jorunn ØKLAND , *Women in Their Place: Paul and the Corinthian Discourse of Gender and Sanctuary Space* (JSNTSup 269, London: T&T Clark, 2004), 39–77.

[8] John A. T. ROBINSON, *The Body. A Study in Pauline Theology* (London: SCM, 1952).

[9] Mary DOUGLAS, *Purity and Danger* (London: Routledge & Kegan Paul, 1966); *Natural Symbols* (New York: Pantheon, 1970).

symbol, i.e. as an expression of the social attitudes to the body. The body
is a microcosm of society. Attitudes to the body reflect society's attitude to
itself. Social control within a society is reflected in the control of the body.
Douglas' works inspired many New Testament studies, especially in the
1980s.[10] Later studies of the body have also focused primarily on the social and cosmological function of the metaphor of the body. In *The Corinthian Body*[11] Dale B. Martin investigates how various medical views of the
body in the Greco-Roman world are reflected in Paul's communication
with the Corinthian community. In *Body and Belly in the Pauline Epistles*,
Karl Olav Sandnes studies Paul's use of the body metaphor in the context
of Greco-Roman philosophy.[12] But none of these studies are concerned
with concrete, physical bodies or with their relationships to gender.

Feminist studies have moved from the social history of a group to study
the New Testament and early Christianity in feminist perspectives. But for
a long time these studies had blind spots. Both feminist and "male-stream"
scholars took the role and identity of men for granted as something that
was not in need of investigation. Thus, the gender perspective has only
recently been extended to the study of masculinity.[13] We may now speak
of early Christian gender studies that are concerned, not only with the social roles and histories of women and men, but with the formation and the
upholding of their identities.

The most recent approach is the study of space. Space has often been
overlooked within a Western culture that has put the emphasis on time, and
also increasingly on the social structures and relationships involved without grounding them in any particular place. The awareness of the importance of space in the study of the early Christian movement and its context
started as part of studies of history, of localities and of geography, as archaeology and architecture. But space and place are more than physical
settings. Houses with household and families, located in a village or an
urban district are places of identities. Identities are located, developed and
sustained within in a place. To be "placed" does not only imply geographi-

---

[10] See Jerome H. NEYREY, *Paul in Other Words: A Cultural Reading of his Letters*
(Louisville: WJK, 1990); Halvor MOXNES, "Kropp som symbol. Bruk av sosialantropologi i studiet av Det nye testamente," *NTT* 84 (1983), 197–217.

[11] Dale B. MARTIN, *The Corinthian Body* (New Haven: Yale University Press, 1995).

[12] Karl Olav Sandnes, *Body and Belly in the Pauline Epistles* (SNTSMS 120; Cambridge: Cambridge University Press, 2002).

[13] See the integration of perspectives in Marianne BJELLAND KARTZOW, *Gossip and
Gender: Othering of Speech in the Pastoral Epistles*. Thesis for the degree of Dr.Theol.,
Faculty of Theology, University of Oslo, 2007. For the growing number of studies of
masculinity, see the collection of essays in *New Testament Masculinities* (SemeiaSt 45,
ed. by Stephen D. MOORE and Janice C. ANDERSON: Atlanta, SBL, 2003).

cal locations. Physical locations, such as a house and a household, represent social, ideological and mental places[14] and, as places of identity, they are differentiated according to gender, age, wealth and power.[15]

Thus, it is not possible to gain a picture of the identities in early Christianity by applying only a single perspective. We need to employ and to integrate the perspectives enumerated above in order to study the strategies of identification.

Bodies – Given or Constructed?

Within this broad range of areas for a study of bodies in early Christianity I must concentrate on one small question. I propose to go back to our starting point: the criticism of the modern attempt to design or re-design one's own body. Both because of my own interest in constructions of early Christian masculinities, and because of the nature of the material, I will concentrate on the male body. LaFleur suggests that the question of how religions have reacted to the question of redesigning the human body is an important issue. To what extent have religions considered the body as a given, which should not be altered, and to what extent have they regarded alterations or changes to the body as necessary signs of religious identification?

By pointing to the fact that both Jews and Muslims put circumcision at the centre of their religious identities, LaFleur undercuts the notion that the so-called Western religions embraced the "natural" body and refrained from modification.[16] Among the first Christ-followers the question of circumcision caused strong controversies. Paul's letters are the main sources of information about this discussion. In this argumentation in Romans, Paul is respectful of the tradition of circumcision of the male body, even if he does not consider it sufficient in itself. He seems to have accepted circumcision for Jews (Rom 2:25),[17] but he reduces its significance by calling it a "sign" (*sēmeion*, 4:11).[18] As a bodily marker ("in the flesh, *sarx*" Rom 2:28), it is not sufficient if it is not accompanied by "circumcision of the heart" (2:29), i.e. by a spiritual attitude that follows the will of God. In an earlier letter to the Galatians, Paul is however much more polemical

---

[14] Halvor MOXNES, *Putting Jesus in His Place. A Radical Vision of Household and Kingdom*. (Louisville: WJK, 2003).

[15] A good illustration is Jorunn ØKLAND , *Women in Their Place*.

[16] LAFLEUR, "The Body," 39.

[17] Joseph A. FITZMYER, *Romans* (AB 33; New York: Doubleday, 1993), 321.

[18] FITZMYER, *Romans*, 380–81.

against circumcision. Here the conflict concerns whether non-Jewish converts, who became Christ followers should be circumcised, i.e. take on a
Jewish identity marker for males. Thus, the question of circumcision seems
to underlie Paul's aggressive attacks upon "the Law" in this letter.

It appears that the early Christ-followers, especially those of a non-
Jewish background, by and large rejected or did not find circumcision necessary as a bodily marker of their identity. But that does not mean that they
were uninterested in their bodies as expressions of identity. If we raise the
question of how bodily changes, or forming and shaping of the body, was
part of the expression of their identities as Christ-followers, we might see
links between texts and issues that are not normally studied together. The
issues we shall look at are the relationship between sexual ethics and bodies in 1 Corinthians 6:12–20; the question of voluntary castration in Matthew 19:12 and the reaction to involuntary pain suffered by slave's bodies
in 1 Peter 2:18–25.

Male Bodies and Questioned Identities, 1 Cor 6:12–20[19]

In this passage, Paul argues that Christian men in Corinth should not engage in sexual relationships with prostitutes. For modern readers, it is not
strange that Paul is against this sexual practice. But with a closer look at
the passage, we must say with E. P. Sanders: "Everyone agrees so easily
with Paul's conclusion … that it is easy to miss how strange the logic behind it is for us and how natural it is to Paul."[20] The first observation we
make is that Paul addresses his readers as "body" (*sōma*) eight times in this
brief passage. His argumentation evolves around the question of relationships to the body and the relationships of the body to other bodies. Thus,
an issue that we would consider one of sexual morality appears as a question concerning the physical body. In Paul's view, a man is not only responsible for how he uses his physical body, but he *is* **his** body, so that the
sexual ethics of the body is an issue where male identity comes into play.

Wayne Meeks has suggested that the main question in early Christian
ethics is not "What shall we do?" but "Who shall we become?"[21] In order
to grasp the relevance of this suggestion for Paul, we shall look at how
Michel Foucault views the discussion of sexual ethics in the Greco-Roman

---

[19] For a full discussion of this passage, see H. MOXNES, "Asceticism and Christian
Identity in Antiquity: A Dialogue with Foucault and Paul," *JSNT* 26 (2003), 3–29.

[20] E. P. SANDERS, *Paul and Palestinian Judaism* (London: SCM, 1977), 455.

[21] Wayne A. MEEKS, *The Moral World of the First Christians* (Philadelphia: WJK,
1986), 11–17.

world as formation of the male subject. In his *History of Sexuality*, Foucault argues that sexuality is not the same across the centuries; it is a modern concept that is not found in the same way in antiquity. In antiquity, he argued, the concept that came closest was *desire*, and Foucault wanted to study the "hermeneutics of desire," i.e. how individuals handled desire.[22] This perspective opened up for a much broader field than sexuality as a topic. It became part of what Foucault termed "the formation of the subject," that is, the formation of identity. In some of his later writings he contrasted this ethical model, this "self-formation of the (male) subject," with Christian ethics, which he regarded critically as obedience towards a set of rules.[23] This negative view may be a result of Foucault's limited interest in Jewish and early Christian sources. His studies in this area appear to be limited to a few authors in late antiquity, especially to Cassian and Augustine and to early medieval handbooks on penitence. Therefore he compares "ethics as self-formation" according to Greco-Roman philosophers of the Hellenistic and early Roman period with a more codified system from a much later period. I suggest, therefore, that it is more appropriate to use Foucault's approach on Paul, who belongs to the same period as Plutarch and Musonius Rufus, who are Foucault's main examples when he discusses ethics as the formation of the self.

With his discussion in 1 Corinthians 6 of men who visit prostitutes, Paul addresses both a well known practice in society and a common topic among moral philosophers. In the male dominated slave societies of the Greco-Roman world, prostitution was common and at least partly socially acceptable. Sexual ethics was part of the social structure; the social standing of the free man was expressed also in his sexual rights over all subordinates, regardless of their sex. Thus, it was not regarded as shameful for free men to use prostitutes, but male and female prostitutes incurred shame because of their profession. In some instances, however, moral philosophers might also take a negative view of men who visit prostitutes, expressed by arguments that they should show regard for their wives, or that excessive use of prostitutes showed a lack of control of their bodies. And, since self-control was the main masculine ideal, this was a severe fault.

This male superiority is reflected in Paul's text. The female prostitute does not come into view as a person of concern. In Paul's view, she appears only as a threat to the man's identity. And if Paul addresses married Christian men in Corinth in this section of the letter, he shows no regard for their wives. The saying "the two will become one flesh" from Genesis

---

[22] M. FOUCAULT, *The Use of Pleasure* (New York: Vintage, 1985), 5–6.
[23] M. FOUCAULT, "An Aesthetics of Existence," in M. Foucault, *Politics, Philosophy, Culture* (Ed. L. D. Kritzman: New York, Routledge, 1988).

2:24, which is used in the gospels about a married couple (Mark 10:8 par), is here used about the relationship between the man and a prostitute in order to emphasize the dangerous consequences of a sexual relationship with a prostitute. "To be joined" (*kollaomai*) to a prostitute is compared with "to be joined" to Christ: in both cases a man enters with his body into a union that determines his identity. Therefore sexual unions are so fateful compared to other sins (6:15–17). Other sins are "outside" the body, but sexual sins are "against his own body" (6:18). Therefore, sins with one's male body affect one's identity.

The relationship between body and identity is a complex one. Paul does not seem to think that a man's body represents a fixed or a permanent identity. The body can be shaped; it has a fluid character and receives its identity by entering into relationships with other bodies. Paul's starting point for his argument is not that of the moral philosophers, that the free man must show that he is in control of his own body. Paul presents his male addressees with a totally different perspective. He points to his previous teaching and to their own experience, but then he goes on to draw consequences that probably would seem quite strange to Corinthian free men. He uses the reminder phrase "do you not know" twice to point out how they should understand themselves and their bodies: "Do you not know that your bodies are members of Christ? (6:15) "Do you not know that your body is a temple of the Holy spirit within you, whom you have from God?" (6:19). These explicit mentions of their bodies may point to the bodily experiences that they had when Paul's addressees became Christians by baptism, and maybe to their speaking in tongues (1 Cor 14). These examples are in themselves honourable expressions of a new identity within a Christian worldview. But then Paul draws the consequence: "You are not your own, for you were bought with a price" (6:19–20). This is a saying that appears to create a conflict with the cultural context of free men in Corinth. Here Paul compares the bodies of free men with those of slaves who were sold and bought at the market place. A slave did not own his or her own body; it belonged to the slave master. Paul uses a mixture of honourable and shameful categories about the bodies of the Corinthian men and the result is that a man's identity, focused on the body, is destabilized. The body is not within a man's own control, it is determined by the relationships into which it enters.

For Paul, the Christian body is determined by its union with Christ[24] and therefore Christ is also described in bodily terms, i.e. as the resurrected body (6:14). And since a Christian man lives in a bodily union with Christ, to enter into a bodily, sexual union with a prostitute is fateful, as

---

[24] SANDERS, *Paul and Palestinian Judaism*, 452–63.

Dale Martin has pointed out in *The Corinthian Body*.[25] The prostitute represents *porneia,* a cosmic category that stands against God. A sexual union with a prostitute means to expose Christ to *porneia.*

We may think – and Corinthian Christian men most likely thought – that a man's relationship to a prostitute was a relatively limited moral issue. However, Paul places it in a larger context, although he is himself limited by his male perspective when he focuses only on the man in the sexual union. He does place the body of the Christian man within the broader perspective of Christian narratives of identity. These narratives are told with a focus on the body. The bodies of Christian men are addressed as members of the dead and resurrected body of Christ, which they have become by baptism and by speaking in tongues, and as participants in the coming resurrection. It is this unity that is threatened by sexual unions with prostitutes since such unions destroy this Christian cosmology. Therefore bodily relationships have great consequences. The promises that they will be a temple of God and sharers in the resurrection are significant (6:14, 19). But they come at a price. The free Corinthian man, who considered himself to be in command of his body, is reminded by Paul that his body is not his own. He is like a slave, bought at the market place (6:20). His body tells him that his identity is always determined by his relationships.

Eunuchs – Castrated Male Bodies or Metaphors of Bodily Control in Matt 19:12?

Paul's argumentation in 1 Corinthians 6 broke with one of the most characteristic elements of male identity in the Greco-Roman world: self-control, expressed by a man's control of his own body, his sexuality and his passions. But this understanding of what it is to be a man was so strong that, despite Paul's criticism, the traditional view prevailed in most early Christian scriptures. Studies of masculinity in late antiquity clearly show how Christian writers shared views on masculinity typical of the Roman elites.[26] By and large they took over the standpoints of Roman authors. When they encountered difficulties, especially in relation to the words of Jesus, images were transformed to fit early Christian ideals into the later context of masculine ideology.

One of the important areas was of course sexual renunciation, not just of contact with prostitutes, but of sex altogether. Paul was one of the main

---

[25] MARTIN, *Corinthian Body*, 174–79.

[26] See esp. M. KUEFLER, *The Manly Eunuch: Masculinity, Gender ambiguity and Christian Ideology in late Antiquity* (Chicago: Chicago University Press, 2001).

sources for the ideals of asceticism in early Christianity. In 1 Corinthians 7 he puts forth his own status as single as an ideal and he portrays marriage as the second best option, designed to contain sexual desire. In *Body and Society: Men, Woman and Sexual Renunciation in Early Christianity* Peter Brown narrates how important this trend of asceticism was in early Christianity,[27] and Elizabeth A. Clark traces how asceticism was forced into many Biblical texts in her *Reading Renunciation: Asceticism and Scripture in Early Christianity.*[28]

The masculine ideal of self-control and control of the male body was one of the major presuppositions that shaped ideals and determined the interpretation of Scripture. This is an example of how concepts and ideals, such as self-control and courage, are given male personifications; they are gendered as male virtues. In contrast, the lack of self mastery, softness and servility were gendered as female, "unmanly" qualities, whether they occurred in women or in men. We find such descriptions of ascetic life as a result of male self-control in Philo's presentation of the Therapeutae in *De vita contemplativa* 68–69 and in Josephus' descriptions of the Essenes in *Bellum judaicum* 2.120–21 and *Antiquitates judaicae* 18.18–22. Among the Therapeutae there were also women, but Philo describes them as having renounced their femaleness to become "virgins." Other women are described in negative terms, as selfish, jealous, untrustworthy, and therefore not able to live a communal, ascetic life.

The conviction that renunciation of sexuality required male self-control and steadfastness also determined the paradigm of the interpretation of one of the most difficult sayings of Jesus, the word about the eunuchs in Matt 19:12: "For there are eunuchs who have been so from birth, and there are eunuchs who have been made eunuchs by men, and there are eunuchs who have made themselves eunuchs for the sake of the kingdom of heaven. Let the one who is able to receive this receive it."[29]

The plain reading of this word is that it speaks of men who have made the most drastic trans-formation imaginable of their bodies by castrating themselves. This was apparently done as a way of shaping their bodies "for the sake of the kingdom of heaven." When I suggest that this is the "plain" reading of Matthew 19:12, it is because of the parallel terminology of *eunuchs* in all three cases, and of *eunouchisan* "making (oneself) a eunuch" in the two last ones. The first group refers to boys, who were born

---

[27] Peter BROWN, *Body and Society: Men, Woman and Sexual Renunciation in Early Christianity* (New York: Columbia University Press, 1988).

[28] Elizabeth A. CLARK, *Reading Renunciation: Asceticism and Scripture in Early Christianity* (Princeton: Princeton University Press, 1999).

[29] For a broader presentation of this passage, see MOXNES, *Putting Jesus in His Place*, 72–90.

with destroyed or imperfect genitals and who could therefore not beget children. The other group refers to young boys, or men, who were castrated, e.g. as slaves, to be sold into prostitution, or as an act against prisoners taken in wars. There can be no doubt that the word *eunuch* and *eunouchizein* refers to destroyed genitals that are not physically able to beget children.

Why should it not be understood in the same way in the third part, which refers to self-castration among the followers of Jesus? It is not an impossible idea. In *Apologia* I.29 Justin Martyr speaks about a young Christian in Alexandria in the 2nd century, who wanted to be castrated. He was stopped by a Roman decree, i.e. by one of several decrees issued by Roman emperors, who wanted to put an end to this practice associated with Eastern religions. But such decrees cannot have stopped everyone. The first canon from the Council of Nicaea in 325 condemned self-castration and barred self-castrated eunuchs from the priesthood.[30]

The eunuch was an ambiguous person. He represented renunciation of sexuality, but even more a forced renunciation of masculinity, and that made it difficult to define his position. He did not have a fixed identity, but was described by what he was *not:* not a "real man", but "half-man" (*semi-vir*), and when he was described as "soft" or "feminine," he was again described by what hat he was not, i.e. as a woman.

It is clear from the interpretation of Matt 19:12 in antiquity that the very notion of physical castration caused great problems. Most interpreters rejected the possibility that this could be the meaning of the statement by Jesus. Instead it was interpreted in line with the masculine ideals of asceticism as an expression of self-control. Justin told the story of the young man who was denied his wish to be castrated in a passage dealing with *sōphrosynē*, moderation and self-control. This was the line of interpretation followed by later writers, such as Clement of Alexandria, Origen and Jerome. They all emphasized that the word of Jesus required chastity, but that physical castration was to go too far. Their ideal of male self-control was expressed in a way that made voluntary chastity superior to physical castration. Clement said that the true eunuch was not the one who did not have the generative power because he was castrated, but the one who had the will-power to make a conscious decision to live a chaste life.[31] Origen uses a strange picture when he speaks of the ideal eunuch as the one who takes "the sword of the Spirit" to cut out the passions from the soul, with-

---

[30] *The Seven Ecumenical Councils*, Nicene and Post-Nicene Fathers Ser 2.14 (ed. H. R. Percival, Edinburgh: T&T Clark, 1991), 8.

[31] Clement of Alexandria, *Paed.* 3.4.26.

out touching the body.[32] Thus, instead of the eunuch as an emasculated man, the spiritual eunuch was a real man who had a heightened masculinity. Modern interpreters follow the same line, comparing Jesus' "eunuchs for the Kingdom of heaven" to Spartan warriors and Greek athletes, who disciplined themselves in preparation for the fight or the competition.[33] It appears that today, as in early Christianity, masculinity is the predominant value, and it is unimaginable that Jesus should break with that ideal.

But there are indications that just that might have been the case. Several scholars have suggested that Matt 19:12 originally was a separate Jesus' logion that only later was put in the context of the discussion of divorce and re-marriage, 12:1–9.[34] It is this passage that provides a context for the interpretation that the last mention of "eunuch" refers to a single life without re-marriage. A plausible context for Matt 19:12 as a separate Jesus' logion is that it could be a response to slander and accusations that Jesus and his followers was a "bunch of eunuchs." To his critics Jesus and his group of followers might appear as groups of galli, i.e. as male castrates associated with Dea Syria or Cybele, who were wandering around the countryside, begging and proclaiming their goddess. Jesus and at least some of his disciples had left their households, and thereby their male places as responsible for the upkeep of families and for social power. In short, they had left their male roles in some of the same ways as eunuchs had. Therefore, it is possible to understand this saying as Jesus taking up the accusation and turning it around, thereby presenting the eunuch as an ideal figure for the Kingdom, even if, or just because, he did not conform to masculine role patterns.

Tertullian was the only author in early Christianity who seemed to grasp the ambiguity of this saying and who did not try to force eunuchs into a masculine pattern. When he discusses levirate marriage in Deut 25:5–6, he gives as a reason for this custom that "eunuchs and the unfruitful were despised." But now the situation has changed. Tertullian argues that "no longer are eunuchs despised; rather, they have merited grace and are invited into the kingdom of heaven."[35] This is clearly a reference to Matt 19:12. In another reference to that saying, he describes Jesus in a way that must have been shocking to his readers: "For the Lord Himself opened the Kingdom of heaven to eunuchs, he himself being a eunuch."[36] Tertullian is

---

[32] Origen, *Comm. Matt.* 15.1.

[33] Dale C. ALLISON, *Jesus of Nazareth: Millenarian Prophet* (Minneapolis: Fortress, 1998), 202.

[34] ALLISON, *Jesus of Nazareth*, 183–84; the first to make the suggestion probably was J. BLINZLER, "*Eisin eunouchoi*," *ZNW* 48 (1957), 254–70.

[35] *Mon.* 7.3–4.

[36] *Mon.* 3.1.

the only ancient writer to use the term eunuch about Jesus, by applying to him the Latin term *spado*, a common word for a castrated or impotent man.

Tertullian was an exception in early Christian interpretation of Matt 19:12. With Clement, Origen and Jerome, the interpretation of this passage became stabilized within a Greco-Roman pattern of masculinity. The term "eunuch" was spiritualised to mean voluntary chastity, and the emphasis was put upon male will-power to choose chastity. Eventually, as Kuefler points out, the monk became the ideal picture of the eunuch.[37] But I suggest that Tertullian represents an earlier interpretation that has preserved some of the first controversies of the eunuch saying and its ambiguity. This is also a matter of context. The "stabilizing" interpretation of Matt 19:12 reads it in the context of 12:1–9, which deals with divorce and remarriage. But it is also possible to read it together with the following section, 12:13–14. This saying, which proclaims that the children are those to whom the kingdom of heaven belongs, provides a context for a de-stabilizing reading of the eunuch saying. The sayings about eunuchs and children as true members of the kingdom of heaven reverse the social structures of a society in which adults and "real" men had a privileged place.

Taken together, these sayings give a picture of the Kingdom that was very different from the ideal patriarchal household. The male world, in which everybody knew their place, is turned upside down. The eunuch and the child are lifted up and into a Kingdom, which becomes an alternative to the surrounding society. It may be that in chapter 19, the author of Matthew preserved sayings of Jesus that were upsetting and de-stabilizing, and that he combined them in such a way that renunciation became integrated into a social pattern, which was not so culturally upsetting as the emasculation of the body. Physical castration, as a marker of Christian identity, was most likely a fringe phenomenon in early Christianity, but the eunuch saying may originally have represented a challenge that had been lost in the spiritual interpretation with its conformity to male Roman ideals.

Slave Bodies and the Beaten Body of Christ in 1 Pet 2:18–25

The abnormal body of the eunuch introduces us to the structures of the normal male body. It is therefore interesting that there has been quite some interest in eunuchs lately, even if they were a marginal phenomenon in earliest Christianity. By contrast, it is surprising that the large numbers of slaves in early Christian groups have been almost invisible in social studies of early Christianity. Until recently, studies of slaves and slavery have

---

[37] KUEFLER, *Manly Eunuch*, 273–82.

been few and far between. In most cases they were of the same type as the early studies of women, focusing on a few texts that expressly speak of slaves, presenting them as a special group and as an addition to the general history of early Christianity. This approach is now beginning to change. Substantial studies treat early Christian groups as part of the Greco-Roman world, which was a slaveholding society, and all early Christian scriptures may be read as documents about slavery.[38] Moreover, slaves are no longer studied as a gender-less, that is as a male group, but as male and female slaves. Recent studies include major works by Albert Harrill and Jennifer Glancy,[39] as well as shorter ones and also works underway, especially on female slaves.[40] In a Nordic context, Jesper Svartvik has taken up the study of slavery especially with regard to the history of interpretation and hermeneutics.[41]

Glancy's work, *Slavery in Early Christianity,* is especially valuable for the question of the body in social space, since she undertakes "a social-historical analysis of early Christianity through the lens of the ever-present reality of slaves as 'bodies'."[42] She starts from the observation that "the Greek word for body, *sōma,* served as a euphemism for the person of a slave,"[43] and therefore all discussions of the various aspects of slavery, their work, the treatment by their masters, the ideology and rhetoric of slavery are all expressed with reference to the body. Slavery consists of the disempowerment of the subject and the loss of control of one's body. One of the section headings of her book is entitled "Bodies Without Boundaries." Her discussion of slaves illustrates the connection between body, gender and social space. Glancy says that "since slavery was identified with the body it is not surprising that the experience of slavery was condi-

---

[38] Cf. also the role of slavery as metaphor, see Dale B. MARTIN, *Slavery as Salvation: The Metaphor of Slavery in Pauline Christianity* (New Haven: Yale University Press, 1990).

[39] Jennifer A. GLANCY, *Slavery in Early Christianity* (Oxford: Oxford University Press, 2002); Albert J. HARRILL, *Slaves in the New Testament* (Minneapolis: Fortress, 2006).

[40] Carolyn OSIEK and Margaret Y. MACDONALD with Janet H. TULLOCH, *A Woman's Place: House Churches in Earliest Christianity* (Minneapolis: Fortress, 2005), Margaret Y. MACDONALD, "Slavery, sexuality and house churches: a reassessment of Colossians 3.18–4.1 in light of new research on the Roman family," *NTS* 53 (2007), 94–113; Bernadette Brooten, Brandeis University, is writing a book on early Christian women who were enslaved or who owned enslaved laborers.

[41] Jesper SVARTVIK, *Bibeltolkningens Bakgator: Synen på judar, slavar och homosexuella i historia och nutid.* (Stockholm: Verbum, 2006).

[42] F. E. UDOH , Review of Glancy, *Slavery, RBL* 7:2 (2007).

[43] GLANCY, *Slavery,* 10.

tioned by gender and sexuality,"[44] and the social space in which they lived is clearly indicated by the perspective of the texts, which always reflect the position of the slaveholder.

First Peter 2:18–25 explicitly illustrates how slavery consists in the loss of control of one's body and how the bodies of slaves were exposed to involuntary formations in the form of beatings. This text raises the question of the relationship between such beatings and the formation of Christian identity. This passage, which addresses household slaves, is part of a larger group of texts with instructions for household management (2:18–3:7; 5:1–5), with parallels in Eph 5:22–6:9 and Col 3:18–4:1.[45] The admonition to slaves in 1 Peter 2 has distinctive characteristics, compared to other Christian exhortations to masters and slaves. It is alone in only addressing the slaves, exhorting them to be submissive to their masters, without addressing the master and articulating his responsibilities. First Peter is also unique among Christian texts in that it does not only mention suffering in general terms, but speaks explicitly of cruel masters and of beating of slaves. It is taken for granted that slaves are beaten. There is no distinction between kind and reasonable masters and cruel masters in this regard; the only difference is between the reasons why they are being beaten, i.e. whether these reasons appear to be just or unjust. Earlier in the letter there are references to sufferings, probably caused by verbal insults, but in the passage in 2:18–25 it is the beatings inflicted upon the slave bodies that speak.

How did the beaten bodies of slaves speak in the context of the Roman Empire? Jonathan Walters has studied similarities between beatings and sexual penetration as language inscribed upon male bodies in Roman culture.[46] The central point was that a free man was protected against violations of his body, since his body was protected by boundaries that should not be crossed. Not so with slaves. The boundaries around the body depended on social status. Compared to the elite, men lower down in the social hierarchy had less protection and slaves had none at all. From a position higher up in the hierarchy, a man could penetrate the boundaries of someone lower down, be it a woman, a child, a man of lower status and in particular a slave, male or female. This penetration could both be sexual

---

[44] GLANCY, *Slavery*, 9.

[45] See the early study by David L. BALCH, *Let Wives be Submissive: The Domestic Code in 1 Peter.* SBLMS 26 (Chico, CA.: Scholars Press, 1981), and a different perspective by John H. Elliott, most recently in John H. ELLIOTT, *1 Peter*, The Anchor Bible 37B (New York: Doubleday, 2000), 484–617.

[46] Jonathan WALTERS, "Invading the Roman Body: Manliness and Impenetrability in Roman Thought" in *Roman Sexualities* (ed. J. P. Hallett and M. B. Skinner: Princeton, Princeton University Press, 1997), 29–43.

and in the forms of beatings. The similarity between these two acts, which we might consider to be of a different character, lay in the fact that they were both expressions of power-relations between a free man and a subject. Thus, sexual penetration and beatings were expressions of a common language, used by a slave master to inscribe his power upon a slave body.

The passage in 1 Peter 2 takes for granted that slaves are beaten both by good and by cruel masters, both with justice and unjustly. Moreover, it even urges the slaves to accept their position by saying "be subordinate" (*hypotassomenoi*, 2:18). Has the power and position of the slave owners co-opted the discourse, so that it functioned to support even cruel beatings inflicted upon the slaves' bodies? First Peter is an exceptional text, even when compared to Greek and Roman moral philosophers, in that it makes no attempt to address slave masters and to urge them to treat their slaves fairly. It appears to accept the slave owners' ideal of "the good and faithful servant" and urges the slaves to act in this way,[47] even in the face of unjust cruelty. This ideal provides the cultural pattern behind the admonition to "endure patiently" even unjust beatings. This cultural pattern is strengthened by bringing in God to legitimize willing subordination (2:19–20). The most plausible reading of the passage is that God, as the highest authority, is thrown fully behind the slave system and the master's role.

We mentioned earlier Foucault and his focus on how the free man could shape his own body and so to speak create his own subjectivity. The criticism directed against Foucault, especially from feminists, was that this perspective included only free males. There was no room for women or other subordinates. In the light of this criticism, we may ask whether the author of 1 Peter opens in any way for a role for slaves to act as subjects with regard to their own bodies. Could they react to the afflictions they suffered as subjects? This is the question we must address to the continuation of the discourse in 2:21–24, now with a description of Christ to support the admonition to slaves to be submissive.

There are striking similarities between the description of the suffering Christ in this section and that of the slaves in the previous passage. The description of Christ employed the same terminology and appears to reinforce and legitimate the slave system. The description of Christ's suffering combines elements from the passion narratives in the gospels with the portrait of the suffering servant in Isaiah 53. Christ is portrayed as exposed to the power of hierarchical domination, just as the slaves were; he was insulted and suffered (2:20, 23), even if he, like the slaves, had done nothing wrong (2:20, 22). Moreover, the way in which Christ acted by not respond-

---

[47] GLANCY, *Slavery*, 115–118.

ing to insults corresponded to the attitude that the slaves were encouraged to follow: "to endure patiently" (2:20).

So far the example of Christ seems to function in support of submissiveness under a cruel slave system. But is it also possible to read it in a different way. It was said that Christ suffered and left them an example (*hypogrammon*, 2:21). Rather than fighting back, Christ "committed his cause to the one who judges justly" (2:23). The suffering Christ, who trusted God as the just judge (*dikaios*), is the guiding image for the slaves who suffers unjustly (*adikos*). In the social universe of a slaveholding society, the just God has replaced the unjust slave master as the judge over both Christ and the slaves. Their hope may now be put in what the just judge will do, and this is described several times in the letter. Just as God brought Christ from suffering to glory, so he will do with the faithful, including the slaves (1:11; 5:10). The example that Christ left to the slaves is more than a moral exhortation. It is an example that includes their bodies in the fate of the body of Christ. The writer presupposes that slaves also can become subjects in their own lives. The discourse with the example of Christ will shape an "inner person" by a life characterised by suffering.

But the presentation of Christ does not deal only with an inner person, it returns to the physical sufferings. Among the more general descriptions of salvation and the righteous life, there is one term that seems to refer directly to the situation of the slaves. It builds on the image of the suffering servant in Isa 53:5: "By his bruise you have been healed" (2:24). "Bruise" (*molops*) refers to the damage on the body caused by a blow or a whip, most likely a reference to the scourging of Jesus before the crucifixion (Matt 27:26; John 19:1), and it brings to mind the beatings of the slaves. This saying from Isaiah has often been taken in a figurative meaning, as "healings from sins," but together with the description of the slaves' suffering, the physical meaning of this image of the beatings of the body of Christ stands out. It seems that the word has a performative effect. The image of Christ, with its bruises, is inscribed upon the bodies of the slaves and ensures that they will also share his glory, which God has prepared. In this way Christ becomes more than an example to follow.

The admonition to slaves in 1 Peter 2 is a text full of complexities and contradictions. It is a text which requires a reading that openly criticizes the way in which the knowledge of God, even the image of the suffering Christ, may be employed in order to support hierarchy, power and a cruel slave system.[48] From one perspective, 1 Peter 2 is a discourse that supports the destruction of human bodies and accepts that slaves are bodies without any protecting boundaries. It may be a slight consolation that slaves are

---

[48] Cf. Glancy's similar evaluation in GLANCY, *Slavery*, 148–151.

addressed as subjects, and that Christ's body is portrayed in an identical way. The image of God as a just judge brings hope of an end to unjust suffering. But the problem remains: The victory over injustice is put forth without any criticism of the cruel system, which has produced it.

Conclusion: Shaping Christ's Body

We started out with the image of the self-shaping of the human (especially the male) body as an example of human *hybris,* and asked if changes or alterations of the body had any role in the formation of identities among the early Christians. Three different texts reflected various locations and periods: Paul's admonition to Corinthian male citizens, the eunuch-saying from an early Jesus tradition in Matthew 19 and finally the address to slaves in the household code in 1 Peter 2. These texts showed similarities in the way they combined body, gender and social space.

All texts participated in a common discourse of the male role in a hierarchical society. Paul addressed free Corinthian men, who had a privileged position with powers over men and women in subordinate places, and who considered that they exercised self-control over their bodies. In the Jesus-word about eunuchs, the social context was the household, in which the generative power of the father's body, protected by his male honour, provided the security for the continuity of the family. First Peter presupposes, as the social world of its addressees, a slaveholding society in which the bodies and authority of the masters were protected, but where the bodies of the slaves had no physical and social protective boundaries whatsoever.

To start with the body and the question of voluntary or involuntary shaping of the body reveal how the formation of a Christian identity affected gender roles and the structures of social space. In all these texts, the privileged role of the free man and his position in the social hierarchy are questioned. In 1 Corinthians 6, the free man is directly addressed and the unquestioned control over his own body and the way in which he could use it to express his social power are deconstructed. In Matthew 19 and in 1 Peter 2, eunuchs and slaves, whose bodies place them in a subordinate position, are brought directly into view and promised or challenged to take a new place. In all these discourses it is the mention of Christ that brings about these changes. That is in itself not surprising in discourses about identity for Christ-believers, but the way in which it is done is worth noticing. The texts portray Christ as a body and with a bodily relationship to the addressees. The Corinthian Christian man enters into a bodily union with Christ that represents a new social space, which confuses all the old structures. It is a privilege to be united with Christ but, at the same time, the free man is not different from a slave. In Matthew 19, instead of the ordered structures of a household, to which mutilated men were outsiders, the Kingdom is introduced as a social space, in which the privileged role of procreation is suspended.

The power of the traditional structures of body, gender and social space came to the fore in the address to the beaten slaves in 1 Peter 2. There is a real danger that the identification with Christ, also portrayed as beaten and suffering, can be manipulated to support subservience under cruel slave masters, so that the old structures could remain in place. But their powers are partly deconstructed by the way in which the slaves are addressed as subjects, who can shape their selves, even if they cannot protect their bodies against beatings. Furthermore, the image of God as the just judge opens a future space for slaves, who are currently enclosed in a space dominated by cruel masters.

Body, gender and social space are all constituent elements in the shaping of identities that are never abstract or only mental, but always placed in a context. It was within such specific contexts that the first Christ-followers lived, and where they attempted to integrate their new faith into their lives. In this process their relationships to their body, to their gender and to their social space were questioned. To follow the experiences of their bodies and how they reacted to them points to the way in which faith in Christ initiated the formation of a specific Christian identity that also affected gender roles and the structures of social space.

A Man has to Do What a Man has to Do: Protocols of Masculine Sexual Behaviour and 1 Corinthians 5–7

Fredrik Ivarsson

First Corinthians 5–7 is the most extended discussion of sexuality and marriage in the Bible, and as such important for modern discussions of Christian ethics and theology. The same chapters are also crucial for our understanding of the aim of 1 Corinthians, as Paul here refers to his earlier correspondence with the Corinthian congregation.[1] In a previous letter, Paul has urged them not to associate with *pornoi* (5:9). The Corinthians have responded with a letter that raised the question whether a man should 'touch a woman' at all (7:1). In 1 Corinthians 5–7, Paul explicitly elaborates on this ongoing discussion. Therefore, commentators have often tried to understand Paul's argument by reconstructing the Corinthian position to which Paul is responding. The Corinthians can be seen as libertines, claiming that everything is permissible (6:12), including incest (5:1–2). Or they can be assumed to be ascetics, abstaining from sex even in marriage (7:1, 5). Quite often these hypotheses are combined, which requires the small Corinthian community to harbour two diametrically opposed positions simultaneously.[2] Thus, it is often supposed that Paul occupies the middle ground in a discussion on sexuality over against two extremist positions in Corinth.

The reading that I propose here is based on a different set of assumptions. First, I will not try to reconstruct 'the Corinthian position', since doing so is both impossible and unnecessary. It is impossible, since the original communicative situation of 1 Corinthians is irrecoverable. We simply do not know the arguments of Paul's Corinthian interlocutors. Mirror reading Paul's letter for the Corinthian position will only blur the reading of Paul's argument – or project our own image into the text. Fortu-

---

[1] An earlier version of this paper was presented at the Nordic New Testament Conference in Lund, 2007. I would like to thank the seminar chair Marianne Bjelland Kartzow, my respondent Halvor Moxnes, and all the participants in the seminar group on gender for their helpful comments. I am also grateful to The Royal Society of Arts and Sciences in Göteborg for their generous support.

[2] See any standard commentary on 1 Cor. In this paper, I will focus on my own reading of Paul and keep the discussion of secondary literature at a minimum.

nately, mirror reading is not only impossible but also unnecessary, as Paul's argument can be read within the context of more general socio-rhetorical patterns in the Graeco-Roman world. Paul's argument makes sense without the postulation of extremist positions.[3] Secondly, I will assume that the main issue is not sexuality but masculinity. In 1 Corinthians 5–6, Paul does not discuss sexual behaviour in general, but the behaviour of free men. He wants the Corinthians to expel *men* who are involved in *porneia*. The women involved are not discussed at all. And the Corinthians have raised the question of how a *man* should behave in relation to women. This emphasis on masculine behaviour fits with the immediate literary context, where Paul has threatened to 'come with a stick', and to measure the power of those arrogant ones who do not heed him as their 'father' (4:14–21). Paul does not only respond to questions and rumours, but also to a challenge of his authority.[4] Therefore, Paul both discusses masculine behaviour and, at the same time, exhibites masculine behaviour in his argument. Paul plays the man, and the Corinthians must imitate him (4:16).

Thus, the context, in which I want to read Paul's argument, is Graeco-Roman constructions of masculinity in general and norms for masculine sexual behaviour in particular. Therefore, we will first have to say something about masculinity and sexuality before we turn to Paul.

Protocols of Masculine Sexual Behaviour

In the last two decades, sexuality in Greek and Roman cultures has emerged as a field of research in its own right.[5] Unfortunately, this re-

---

[3] This the first of my assumptions is shared by Alistair SCOTT MAY, *'The Body for the Lord': Sex and Identity in 1 Corinthians 5–7* (JSNTSup 278; London: T&T Clark International, 2004). However, although he is clearly aware of Graeco-Roman constructions of masculinity, he does not let this awareness inform his interpretation of Paul's views on sexual behaviour.

[4] The question of whether Paul's authority was challenged in Corinth is widely debated. Again, I do not mean to say anything about the real situation in Corinth. What I claim is that Paul is posing *as if* his authority was challenged.

[5] A good introduction to this field of investigation is provided by Marilyn B. SKINNER, *Sexuality in Greek and Roman Culture* (Malden, Mass.: Blackwell, 2005). Important contributions have been made by Michel FOUCAULT, *The History of Sexuality* (trans. R. Hurley; 3 vols.; New York: Pantheon, 1978–1986); Amy RICHLIN, *The Garden of Priapus: Sexuality and Aggression in Roman Humor* (New Haven: Yale University Press, 1983); John J. WINKLER, *The Constraints of Desire: The Anthropology of Sex and Gender in Ancient Greece* (New York: Routledge, 1990); David M. HALPERIN, *One Hundred Years of Homosexuality: And Other Essays on Greek Love* (New York: Routledge, 1990); David M. HALPERIN, John J. WINKLER, and Froma I. ZEITLIN, eds., *Before Sexuality: The*

search has not yet been brought into dialogue with the main stream of New Testament studies.[6] One aim of this paper is to argue for the necessity of taking ancient constructions of sexuality and gender into account when studying the letters of Paul.

The notion of ancient Greek erotic protocols was introduced by John Winkler,[7] and has been developed and adapted to Roman circumstances by Craig Williams.[8] Protocols are fundamental conventions, i.e. cultural ground rules that are generally taken for granted. At least they are so in theory – a social protocol describes the official truth, but not necessarily what is going on behind closed doors. Protocols are concerned with appearance and reputation.

Masculine sexual behaviour is restricted by two main protocols: Dominance and self-restraint.[9] These protocols must be respected – or, at least, *seem* to be respected – by every man who aspires to some status and honour. If a man is respected, he will be said to conform to these protocols, while allegations of non-conformity are typically intended to dishonour a man. Failure to abide by the protocols is seen as a sign of effeminacy. A man has to do what a man has to do. And if he does not, he is womanish and 'soft' (*mollis* in Latin, *malakos* in Greek).[10]

Graeco-Roman constructions of sexuality do not allow for equality and mutuality. Sexual relations are necessarily hierarchical. There is always someone in control of somebody else. Therefore, dominance is the first protocol of masculine sexual behaviour. A man is supposed to be 'on top' in all sexual relations. Masculine sexual behaviour means penetrating a

---

Construction of Erotic Experience in the Ancient World (Princeton: Princeton University Press, 1990); and Judith P. HALLETT and Marilyn B. SKINNER, eds., *Roman Sexualities* (Princeton: Princeton University Press, 1997).

[6] In Pauline studies, references to research on Graeco-Roman sexuality are most often found in discussions of homosexuality.

[7] WINKLER, *Constraints of Desire*. Winkler's erotic protocols state that 'sexual contact is understood in public contexts as male-initiated, phallus-centered, and structured around the act of penetration' (43).

[8] Craig A. WILLIAMS, *Roman Homosexuality: Ideologies of Masculinity in Classical Antiquity* (New York: Oxford University Press, 1999). Williams's first protocol is that 'a self-respecting Roman man must always give the appearance of playing the insertive role in penetrative acts, and not the receptive role' (18). The second protocol concerns the status of the partners: 'freeborn Roman males and females were excluded as acceptable partners, thus leaving slaves, prostitutes, and noncitizens of either sex as persons (other than his wife) with whom a Roman man could have sexual relations' (19).

[9] My formulation of these protocols of masculine sexual behaviour is intended as an expanded version of Williams's protocols (see note 7). His version is the core, around which I have organised related values and conventions.

[10] WILLIAMS, *Roman Homosexuality*, 125–159; Catharine EDWARDS, *The Politics of Immorality in Ancient Rome* (Cambridge: Cambridge University Press, 1993), 63–97.

socially inferior person, whether a woman or a boy. A man must not be penetrated himself. Nor must he seem to be submissive in any other way. The most flagrant deviance from this protocol is a man who desires and finds pleasure in being penetrated by other men. This despised scare-figure is called a *cinaedus*.[11] But there are many other degrees of sexual submission. A man can be considered to be dominated by his wife or his mistress, if he seems to be too dependent on her, or too concerned about pleasing her, or if he just spends too much time in her company.[12] A man can even be ridiculed for being 'too much in love with his wife'.[13] The protocol of dominance is related to a man's control over his own body. Suffering penetration, or other kinds of sexual submissiveness, is conceptually similar to being the victim of humiliating physical abuse. A man must be able to defend the integrity of his own body.[14]

The second protocol is self-restraint (*enkrateia*). According to the first protocol, a man must not be sexually dominated by anyone else. The second protocol states that he must also not be dominated by his own passions and desires. Excess must be avoided. A man can visit the brothel, but he should not be seen there all the time.[15] Excessive womanising is seen as a sign of softness.[16] And the young man, who squanders his patrimony on mistresses and prostitutes is a commonplace. Such unrestrained and irresponsible behaviour is supposed to be accompanied by other vices of excess, such as drinking, partying, gambling, theft, assault, etc. Another aspect of this protocol is that a man must avoid partners that are forbidden.

---

[11] WILLIAMS, *Roman Homosexuality*, 160–224.

[12] Whether a young man can marry an older and richer woman without being dominated by her is a central issue in Plutarch's *Amatorius* (see e.g. Plutarch, *Amat.* 752e–754e). The political propaganda against Marc Anthony portrayed him as dominated by Cleopatra. See Horace, *Epod.* 9.11–14; cf. Paul ZANKER, *The power of images in the Age of Augustus* (trans. Alan Shapiro; Jerome Lectures 16; Ann Arbor: University of Michigan Press, 1988), 45.

[13] EDWARDS, *Politics of Immorality*, 85; Suzanne DIXON, 'Sex and the Married Woman in Ancient Rome', in *Early Christian Families in Context: An Interdisciplinary Dialogue* (ed. David L. Balch and Carolyn Osiek; Grand Rapids: Eerdmans, 2003), 111–129, here 122–125.

[14] Jonathan WALTERS, 'Invading the Roman Body: Manliness and Impenetrability in Roman Thought', in *Roman Sexualities* (ed. Hallett and Skinner), 29–43.

[15] Cato, the archetypical defender of traditional Roman values, is said to have commended a youth for going to the brothel rather than seducing married women (Horace, *Sat.* 1.2.31–35). But after seeing the same man coming out of the brothel a number of times, Cato's evaluation of his behaviour changes: 'Young man, I commended you on the understanding that you were coming here occasionally, not living here!' (Acro's commentary on the passage in Horace, quoted and translated by WILLIAMS, *Roman Homosexuality*, 43).

[16] Seneca, *Contr.* 2.1.6; Martial 2.47; Plutarch, *Amat.* 751a–b.

The man who seduces other men's wives is generally seen as corrupt and unrestrained. And the very worst example of deficient self-restraint (*akrasia*) is the man who becomes involved in incestuous relationships with his sisters, or even with his own mother. Such behaviour is emblematic of utter corruption and typical for tyrants or decadent barbarians. A man who has the power to do whatever he wants, but lacks the necessary power over himself, will inevitably indulge in all possible kinds of humiliating effeminacy.[17]

For Greeks and Romans, sex is not a private sector of life.[18] A man's sexual behaviour is seen as a symptom of his character. Dominance and self-restraint are the main criteria, not only of masculine sexual behaviour, but also of masculinity, overall. If a man is known to behave properly in his erotic relations, he can be expected to act like a man in other respects too. And unmanly sexual behaviour is seen as a serious character flaw, which casts doubt upon a man's ability to provide leadership and proper judgement. Therefore, sexual slander is very common in polemic and political agitation.[19] The speeches of Cicero and Suetonius' biographies of the emperors are filled with allegations of sexual irregularities – senators and emperors are accused of seducing married women and citizen youths, forcing their own wives or other men's wives into prostitution, depilating their body hair, indulging in incest, and submitting to male lovers. These allegations are certainly not all true – some may not even be meant to be taken seriously – but they illustrate the high cultural and political value of masculinity. A masculine man can be trusted, but an effeminate man is necessarily immoral.

'Others' are often stereotyped as effeminate and sexually deviant. Greeks frown upon the strange sexual practices of barbarians, while Romans blame the Greeks for introducing effeminate behaviours.[20] Another example of this phenomenon is the Jewish stereotype of the lascivious and deviant gentiles. Jewish writers often contrast the chastity and high morals of the Jews to the effeminacy and promiscuity of the gentiles. But this might be evidence of the participation of Jews in Graeco-Roman culture rather than of their separation therefrom – they presuppose the same basic

---

[17] WILLIAMS, *Roman Homosexuality*, 138–142.

[18] HALPERIN, *One Hundred Years of Homosexuality*, 31–33.

[19] EDWARDS, *Politics of Immorality*. Cf. Jennifer WRIGHT KNUST, *Abandoned to Lust: Sexual Slander and Ancient Christianity* (New York: Columbia University Press, 2006).

[20] EDWARDS, *Politics of Immorality*, 92–97; Emma DENCH, 'Austerity, Excess, Success, and Failure in Hellenistic and Early Imperial Italy', in *Parchments of Gender: Deciphering the Bodies of Antiquity* (ed. Maria Wyke; Oxford: Clarendon, 1998), 121–146. Juvenal, *Sat.* 8.113–115, points out 'perfumed Corinth' as a place for 'smooth-skinned young men with depilated legs'.

values of masculinity and effeminacy, and use the same patterns of sexual rhetoric.[21] The values of Jewish moralists are not so different from the values of Greek and Roman moralists. A Graeco-Roman Jew, like Paul, would share the fundamental protocols of masculine sexual behaviour with his gentile neighbours.

Penetrated by *Porneia* (1 Cor 5:1–13)

In 1 Cor 5:1, Paul starts to use his metaphorical stick in order to chastise his arrogant children in Corinth (cf. 4:21). He has heard (*akouetai*) that there is *porneia* among them of a kind that not even gentiles would tolerate. According to Paul, someone is living with his father's wife, which is clearly an outrage. Most commentators of this passage focus on reconstructing the circumstances of this incestuous relationship, and on clarifying Jewish and gentile attitudes to this kind of incest. But Paul is not interested in details and circumstances. The mere rumour of incest is enough for him to take action. As we have noted above, ancient sexual protocols are concerned about appearance and reputation. What seems to be going on is more important than what is actually happening. Like Caesar's wife, the Corinthians must be above suspicion.[22]

Clearly, Paul thinks that his information is correct and that the incestuous man must be expelled from the community. But the thrust of Paul's argument is not directed against that immoral man. His scandalous behaviour merely serves as an example. The focus of Paul's attention is a comparison between how the Corinthians are handling the situation, and how Paul himself is handling it. '*You* have *porneia* among you', Paul says. '*You* are arrogant, instead of mourning and removing this man from among you. But *I*, on the other hand, have already pronounced judgement on him'. *Hymeis pefysiōmenoi* in 5:2 is contrasted with *egō kekrika* in 5:3 (note the emphatic use of the pronouns and that both verbs are in the perfect tense). Thus Paul displays his own firm leadership, in contrast to the failure of the Corinthian leaders. Despite his physical absence, Paul is the one who can

---

[21] Michael L. SATLOW, 'Rhetoric and Assumptions: Romans and Rabbis on Sex', in *Jews in a Graeco-Roman World* (ed. Martin Goodman; Oxford: Clarendon, 1998), 135–144.

[22] The proverbial saying about Caesar's wife is originally from Plutarch's account of a certain famous incident. The young man Clodius dressed up as a woman to enter Caesar's house at a religious ceremony for women only. He was caught in the act and charged with sacrilege. Caesar did not believe the rumours that his wife Pompeia had a relationship with Clodius, but divorced her anyway, as Caesar's wife must be above suspicion (Plutarch, *Caes.* 9–10)

exercise authority and discipline. He has access to the power of the Lord Jesus, and he is the one who can protect the vulnerable community from the threat of *porneia*.

What, then, is *porneia*? And why is it so dangerous? It is of course well known that the general Greek meaning of *porneia* is prostitution, while the word in Jewish usage is a designation for unlawful sexual relations with some smack of gentile idolatry and depravity.[23] But beyond that, it is diffi cult to make a more precise definition of what Paul refers to as *porneia*. Would all extra-marital sex count as *porneia*?[24] Would even some (non-incestuous) marital unions be included in his definition?[25] Some types of sexual behaviour between husband and wife?[26] Paul does not say, so we do not know. But the exact definition might be beside the point. More important for understanding Paul's rhetoric are the overtones and connotations associated with *porneia*. *Porneia* is 'bad sex' – sexual activities that are impure, rebellious, and humiliating. And, I would argue, a man who involves himself in *porneia* compromises his masculinity. In the LXX, the words *porneia* and *(ek)porneuein* are mainly used for either the activity of female prostitutes, or metaphorically for Israel's disloyalty to God.[27] The prophets repeatedly use the image of Israel as a whore, e.g. in Hosea and in Ezek 16 and 23. Therefore, when men engage in *porneia*, they act like whores. Even if a *pornos*, in Jewish usage, is not actually a male prostitute, he still acts like a prostitute. He is a sexual sell-out. The male body of a *pornos* is defiled by female sin and weakness. Through his lack of self-restraint, he breaks the second protocol of masculine sexual behaviour. The only occurrences of the word *pornos* in the LXX are in Sir 23:16–18, where the expression *anthrōpos pornos* is used for a man who is obsessed with sex. He burns with desire, and as a consequence he will be burned himself.

---

[23] See e.g. LSJ; and F. HAUCK and S. SCHULZ, *'porneia'*, in *TDNT* 6:579–595.

[24] Bruce MALINA, 'Does Porneia Mean Fornication?', *NovT* 14 (1972): 10–17, argues that 'pre-betrothal, pre-marital, non-commercial sexual intercourse between man and woman' does not fall under the condemnation of *porneia* (17).

[25] Kathy L. GACA, *The Making of Fornication: Eros, Ethos, and Political Reform in Greek Philosophy and Early Christianity* (Berkeley: University of California Press, 2003), 151, claims that Paul's concept of *porneia* includes all sexual activities within all marriages that are not 'in the Lord'.

[26] E.g. oral sex was generally considered impure in the ancient world (WINKLER, *Constraints of Desire*, 38). A man could be ridiculed for performing *cunnilingus* on his wife, as that was seen as a sign of submission on his part. See Holt N. PARKER, 'The Teratogenic Grid', in *Roman Sexualities* (ed. Hallett and Skinner), 47–65. *Barn.* 10.8 categorically prohibits oral sex.

[27] GACA, *Making of Fornication*, 165–170.

An interesting parallel to Paul's attack on the *pornos* in the Corinthian *ekklēsia*, is Aeschines attack on Timarchus.[28] Aeschines claims that Timarchus is a *pornos*, and therefore unfit to speak in the *ekklēsia* of Athens. A young man in Athens could have honourable erotic relationships to citizen men. But according to Aeschines, Timarchus is far from honourable. He is a simple prostitute, a *pornos*, for at least three reasons: he has received money for his sexual services, his partners are dubious and immoral men of low status, and he has found pleasure in being sexually submissive.[29] Timarchus has allegedly shown all kinds of excess and lack of self-restraint, such as drinking, gambling, and consorting with harlots. Aeschines concludes that Timarchus is 'a creature with the body of a man defiled with the sins of a woman'.[30] The presence of his un-disciplined, emasculated body would defile the pure and noble Athenian *ekklēsia*.

There are of course many differences between the context and worldview of Paul and that of Aeschines. They would differ on many important points when it comes to religious belief and acceptable sexual behaviour. And the *ekklēsiai* they are addressing are quite different with respect to status, size, and constituency. Even so, there are also striking similarities between their arguments. A man who can be labelled a *pornos* is morally and bodily corrupt. His flesh is ruined and beyond restoration. He can be expected to be involved in all kinds of excessive behaviour, such as those which Paul exemplifies in his catalogues of vices (1 Cor 5:10–11, 6:9–10). The *pornos* defiles the community through his mere presence, and he must therefore be expelled. If he was tolerated in the *ekklēsia*, the whole community would suffer.

Gentile Effeminacy (1 Cor 6:9–11)

Just as the Greeks considered barbarians effeminate, and the Romans questioned the masculinity of the Greeks, so the Jews often stereotyped gentiles as effeminate. For example, the books of Judith and *4 Maccabees* both demonstrate the inferiority of elite, gentile men (Holofernes, Antiochus Epiphanes) compared to Jewish women and youths (Judith, the seven martyrs and their mother) with respect to courage, self-restraint, and masculin-

---

[28] The Athenian politician Aeschines's speech against his rival Timarchus was launched in 345 B.C.

[29] Aeschines, *Tim.* 40–42, 54, 70.

[30] Aeschines, *Tim.* 185.

ity.[31] Gentile effeminacy is often connected with sexual licentiousness, as e.g. in the Wisdom of Solomon, where idolatry is the explicit origin of *porneia* (14:12). Gentile idolatry leads to all kinds of evil and excessive behaviour, and different kinds of sexual excess and deviance are prominent among these vices (Wis 14:22–28).

This theme is famously developed by Paul in Rom 1:18–32. The outline is the same as in Wis 14 – idolatry leads to vices and lack of self-restraint. But Paul emphasizes the sexual effeminacy of the gentiles even more strongly. Gentile men do not even try to control their women in order to prevent their shameful and 'unnatural' behaviour, but are preoccupied with desire for each other instead. Paul is not explicit about what the men do, but in the light of the Graeco-Roman sexual protocols, his strong expressions about 'humiliation of their bodies' (1:24) and 'receiving in themselves the proper punishment for their error' (1:27) can only mean that the men are penetrated by each other. In other words, Paul portrays gentile men, including the highest ranking and most respected citizens of the empire, as *cinaedi*. They actually desire to be penetrated, which makes them the lowest and most despicable of men.[32]

This stereotype of gentile effeminacy is deployed by Paul in 1 Cor 5–6 as well. First, the incestuous *porneia* that they tolerate is of a kind that is 'not even among the gentiles' (5:1). No verb is supplied, so exegetes discuss whether Paul means that it is not *tolerated* among the gentiles, or that it does not *exist* among the gentiles. This discussion has little relevance for Paul's point, which is to shame the Corinthians by comparing them to the gentiles.[33] A little later, Paul warns the Corinthians not to let themselves be infiltrated by gentile effeminacy (5:9–13). The boundary between those who are outside and those who are inside must be clear and sharp. Typical outsiders, i.e. gentiles, are characterised as *pornoi*, and as committing other excessive vices in the same vein. Effeminate male bodies belong outside the community. Another case of boundary blurring is the prosecution of brothers in front of unrighteous, gentile judges (6:1). Useful judges must of course be just and righteous, so the Corinthians' choice of un-

---

[31] Stephen D. MOORE and Janice Capel ANDERSON, 'Taking it Like a Man: Masculinity in 4 Maccabees', *JBL* 117 (1998), 249–273.

[32] Cf. Philo's 'disease of effeminacy' (*thēleia nosos*), which is caused by gentile men who desire and penetrate gentile boys (*Contempl.* 60).

[33] Of course, many of Paul's addressees in Corinth are actually gentiles, in the sense of non-Jews. But Paul makes it clear that Christ-believing non-Jews are supposed not to be gentiles, in the sense of archetypal sinners. Cf. Mikael WINNINGE, *Sinners and the Righteous: A Comparative Study of the Psalms of Solomon and Paul's Letters* (ConBNT 26; Stockholm: Almqvist & Wiksell International, 1995), 260–262, for this slip between different meanings of the word gentiles in this text.

righteous judges exposes their own lack of proper judgement. They actually behave as badly as their gentile judges when brothers prosecute and defraud each other. Again, Paul has already shown his ability both to judge the community and to protect it from unrighteousness and effeminacy.

And then, in 6:9–11, Paul makes his most comprehensive repudiation of gentile vice. The Corinthians are dangerously close to crossing the boundary and indulge in unrighteous behaviour (6:8). Therefore Paul must warn them not to be led astray and he does so by providing the whole list of examples of gentile unrighteousness (6:9–10). The list begins with the most typical of gentile vices – *porneia* and idolatry. Then comes three other sexual vices (or at least possibly sexual), and finally five further examples of excessive and unrestrained behaviour. These ten items on the list do not describe ten different kinds of people who engage in ten different vices. All these vices are different aspects of the same gentile depravity and the man, who commits one of them, can be expected to indulge in all ten.[34] The emphasis on sexual vices can be explained partly by Paul's focus on sexual behaviour in 1 Cor 5–7, and partly by his 'sexualized' view of gentile corruption. Just as in Romans 1:24–27, Paul here portrays stereotypical gentile men as sexually effeminate. As *pornoi* and *moichoi* (adulterers), they indulge in sex with the wrong women. As we have seen, this is an offence against the second protocol of masculine sexual behaviour. Their lack of self-restraint is manifested in illicit sexual relations.

Further, the gentiles are also *malakoi* and *arsenokoitai*.[35] When used derogatory of a man, the word *malakos*, means 'effeminate'. This effeminacy is primarily a gender deviance, a failure of masculine gender performance, which can be manifested in many different kinds of womanish behaviour. One example is sexual submissiveness. Sexual deviance, in the sense of a man who lets himself be penetrated by other men, is thus one possible connotation of *malakos*. Unfortunately, we do not know the exact meaning of the word *arsenokoitēs*. It probably refers to some kind of degrading homoerotic activity, but we cannot be more precise than that, since we have too little evidence of the use of this word. As noted earlier, the ordinary Greek, non-Jewish, meaning of *pornos* is a male prostitute, a man

---

[34] As I have argued elsewhere. See Fredrik IVARSSON, 'Vice Lists and Deviant Masculinity: The Rhetorical Function of 1 Corinthians 5:10–11 and 6:9–10', in *Mapping Gender in Ancient Religious Discourses* (ed. Todd Penner and Caroline Vander Stichele; Biblical Interpretation Series 84; Leiden: Brill, 2007), 163–184.

[35] The meanings of these words are contested. See e.g. Dale MARTIN, '*Arsenokoitēs* and *Malakos*: Meanings and Consequences', in *Biblical Ethics and Homosexuality: Listening to Scripture* (ed. R. L. Brawley; Louisville: Westminster John Knox, 1996), 117–136, for an introduction to this polemic. I agree with Martin on the meaning of *malakos*, but I am not quite convinced by his reading of *arsenokoitēs*.

who sells his body to other men. Thus, all in all, Paul probably character-
ises the gentiles as offenders against the first protocol of masculine sexual
behaviour as well. The combined force of *pornoi*, *malakoi*, and *arsenokoitai* suggests that gentile men are the worst kind of sexual effeminates, who
indulge in womanish submissive behaviour.

Paul draws this gloomy picture of gentile effeminacy in order to warn
the Corinthians of the consequences of their lack of discipline. These corrupt creatures will certainly not inherit the kingdom of God (6:9). Some of
the Corinthians have been part of this gentile depravity, but they have been
purified in Christ and in the spirit of God (6:11). Thus, in contrast to Paul,
they have an effeminate past, into which they might slip back. Their present, unstable masculine status depends on whether or not they manage to
stay in contact with Christ and the spirit, under Paul's surveillance.

To Sin Against the Body (1 Cor 6:12–20)

'I will not be dominated by anything', Paul boldly claims (6:12). This is
the first protocol of masculinity. To be truly masculine means not to be
submissive to anything or to anyone (*hypo tinos* could mean both). But
Paul immediately modifies this absolute statement by saying that the body
belongs to the Lord. The Corinthians – as well as Paul, we might presume
– do not belong to themselves. They are bought at a price, and must therefore be loyal to their master (6:19–20). This metaphor of slavery might be
provocative for free men.[36] However, for mortals, submission to divine
power is a matter of necessity, and it therefore does not imply any actual
curtailment of a man's masculinity. Even the emperor must obey the gods.
And Paul describes this bodily belonging to Christ as the source of divine
power. Christ's body was humiliated on the cross, but he has been raised
and glorified by God's power (6:14). The risen Christ subjugates all powers and rules over the whole universe (15:24–28). By belonging to Christ
and by being members of his spiritual and powerful body, the bodies of the
believers are made holy and spiritual. If they stay pure and righteous, they
will also be raised by God's power. Belonging to Christ is thus the source
of true masculinity. In stark contrast to the effeminate gentiles, Paul and
other Christ-believers will not be dominated by anything, as long as they
preserve their bodily integrity as members of Christ.

---

[36] As Halvor MOXNES has pointed out. See 'Asceticism and Christian Identity in Antiquity: A Dialogue with Foucault and Paul', *JSNT* 26 (2003), 3–29.

However, a masculine body can easily be emasculated. Paul claims that a man who is united to a whore becomes one body with her (6:16).[37] This is doubly offensive according to ancient standards of masculinity. First, by opposing membership in Christ to membership in a whore, Paul implies that a man who unites with a whore belongs to her and is ruled by her, just as he would otherwise belong to and be ruled by Christ. In Graeco-Roman culture, men would normally be considered dominant in relationship to prostitutes, as long as they do not exhibit any submissive behaviour. To penetrate a prostitute is a masculine thing to do. But Paul claims the opposite: A man who unites with a prostitute will immediately lose control and be dominated by her. Paul's proof of this is a quotation from Scripture: 'The two shall be one flesh' (Gen 2:24).[38] Secondly, by contrasting 'flesh', as the result of union with a whore, to 'spirit', as the result of union with Christ, Paul alludes to the destructive effect of *porneia*.[39] To become one body with a whore does not only mean to be dominated by her. It also means that the man's body becomes like hers – soft, corrupt, and receptive to penetration. He does not only become like a woman, but like a sinful and despicable woman.[40] *Porneia* emasculates and destroys the male body.

This is probably the reason why Paul considers *porneia* worse and qualitatively different compared to all other sins. 'Every sin that a man (*anthrōpos*) commits is outside the body, but the man who commits *porneia* sins against his own body' (6:18). This very expression is another point of similarity between Paul and Aeschines. Aeschines repeatedly states that Timarchus has sinned against his own body (*eis to sōma to heautou hēmartēken*).[41] By being submissive to and having sex with the

---

[37] A 'whore', *pornē*, in the biblical sense, is not necessarily a prostitute, but any gentile woman that entices God-fearing men to break the law and the covenant (GACA, *Making of Fornication*, 165–170).

[38] Gen 2:24 refers to the relationship between a man and his wife, which makes the relevance of this verse to the relationship between a man and a whore far from obvious. Maybe Paul also alludes to Sir 19:2–3, where the man who unites with whores (*ho kollōmenos pornais*) is threatened with death and destruction.

[39] Cf. 1 Cor 5:5, where Paul also contrasts the flesh and the spirit. The flesh of the *pornos* must be destroyed in order to save his spirit.

[40] The misogyny of this passage is often underestimated.

[41] Aeschines, *Tim.* 39; cf. 22, 94, 159, and 195. Actually, the first historical evidence for this Greek expression is in Aeschines, and the second in Paul. See Renate KIRCHHOFF, *Die Sünde gegen den eigenen Leib: Studien zu* pornē *und* porneia *in 1 Kor 6,12–20 und dem sozio-kulturellen Kontext der paulinischen Adressaten* (SUNT 18; Göttingen: Vandenhoeck und Ruprecht, 1994), 180. The reason why this connection tends to be neglected might be that Timarchus' transgression is 'homosexual', while Paul writes about 'heterosexual' offences. That difference might be more important to modern than to ancient readers.

wrong partners, Timarchus has defiled and emasculated his own body. Therefore, he cannot speak in front of the *ekklēsia* like other Athenian men. Likewise, Paul seems to mean that every man who commits *porneia* has defiled and emasculated his body, just like the incestuous man in 5:1–5, and he has thereby disqualified himself from membership in the *ekklēsia* of God in Corinth.

Marriage as Bondage (1 Cor 7:1–40)

It is often supposed that Paul changes his subject in 7:1 from sexual misconduct to marriage by referring to the Corinthian letter ('concerning the matters about which you wrote'). However, the theme is still male sexual behaviour – 'it is well for a man not to touch a woman'. Having exposed the vulnerability of the Corinthian men to *porneia*, and having warned them of the dire consequences, Paul now turns to the alternatives: Sexual abstinence or sex with their wives. According to Paul, abstinence is the best option, but for those who lack the necessary self-restraint, sex within marriage is acceptable.[42] Not to 'touch' a woman at all is preferable, but since they obviously have problems in the community with men who touch all the wrong women (*dia tas porneias*), 'each man should have his own woman' (7:2). In this context, Paul's emphasis seems to be on everyone having *his own* woman. They should not have someone else's woman, like the man referred to in 5:1 (note the similar constructions of *gynaika echein* in 5:1 and 7:2).

Further, 'each woman should have her own man'. For the first time in 1 Corinthians 5–7, Paul here says something about the behaviour of the women. This is not simply an exhortation to mutual fidelity between husband and wife. Marriages were not equal and symmetrical relationships in the ancient world.[43] And Paul is not a social revolutionary, trying to introduce this anachronistic view of marriage to the Corinthians. In 1 Corin-

---

[42] Many commentators claim that Paul actually argues the opposite. Allegedly, some women in Corinth have opted for abstinence, which forces Paul to argue for the legitimacy of married life. This reading, which seems to be appealing to both evangelicals and feminists, makes Paul a defender of modern 'family values', and grants the presence of influential women theologians in the early Christian communities. But this mirror reading of Paul requires a rather speculative hypothesis about ascetic women, which in turn is based on this very same passage. Therefore, I prefer to read Paul as actually meaning what he is repeatedly asserting, namely that abstinence is preferable to marriage (7:1, 7, 8, 26, 28, 32, 34, 38, 40).

[43] See WILLIAMS, *Roman Homosexuality*, 47–56, for the asymmetrical expectations on husbands and wives.

thians 11:3–16 and 14:34–35, Paul makes it very clear that he has a traditional view of the hierarchy between man and wife, and of their different
social roles. In ancient discourse, reference to the modest or outrageous
behaviour of someone's wife, is often meant as praise or criticism of her
husband.[44] It was taken for granted that a woman must be sexually faithful
to her husband, and that a man's honour was dependant on the chastity and
reputation of his wife (remember Caesar's wife and the gentile women in
Rom 1:26). Therefore, Paul's remark about female fidelity may not be as
innocent as it might look to modern eyes. When Paul says that 'each
woman should have her own man', he implies that it might not be so.
Could the Corinthian women be having extra-marital affairs, too? That
would be even more obviously outrageous than the men's behaviour. Does
Paul refer to the woman who is involved with the son of her husband
(5:1)? Or does Paul imply that the other Corinthian men could also be
shamed by the loose behaviour of their wives? Is he saying that their lack
of discipline and self-control might make them lose control over their
women?

Paul goes on to stress the equal standing of husband and wife. In a context in which hierarchy is seen as 'natural', equality would be offensive
and demeaning for the superior part. Thus, the sting of Paul's argument is
directed towards the married men. Paul instructs them that husband and
wife must fulfil their sexual duties to each other (7:3). As if the man would
have any such duties to his wife, and as if his wife could deny him his
rights. Already, the masculinity of married men starts to crumble under the
weight of Paul's rhetoric. 'For the wife does not have authority over her
own body, but the husband does' (7:4). Yes, everyone would agree about
that. However, this truism is immediately followed by Paul's deathblow to
married masculinity: 'likewise the husband does not have authority over
his own body, but the wife does'. Such enormity. Paul seems to say that
married men live in sexual submission to their wives. The first protocol of
masculinity, dominance, is thus incompatible with married life.[45]

---

[44] WINKLER, *Constraints of Desire*, 6, famously notes that 'most of men's observations and moral judgements about women and sex and so forth have minimal descriptive
validity and are best understood as coffeehouse talk, addressed to men themselves'.

[45] I am not aware of any other ancient evidence for the view that a married man concedes the authority over his own body to his wife. Musonius Rufus says that husband and
wife should have everything in common, including their bodies. See Cora E. LUTZ, 'Musonius Rufus: "The Roman Socrates",' in *Yale Classical Studies* 10 (ed. Alfred R. Bellinger; New Haven: Yale University Press, 1947), 3–147, here 94.2–11. But this is far from
saying that a married man does not have authority over his own body. The agitated reaction of some men in another context comes to mind: 'If such is the case of a man with his
wife, it is better not to marry' (Matt 19:10).

So how can Paul defend this obscene statement? His earlier quote from Gen 2:24, that 'the two shall be one flesh', echoes in the background (6:16). Does Paul mean that a married man is dominated by his wife in the same way as he would be dominated by a whore if he united with her? Paul does not quite say that. He gives another reason for male submission, which is dependent on the defective character of the Corinthian men rather than on the ontological nature of marriage. Because of their *akrasia*, their lack of self-control, they must not be separated from their wives for too long (7:5). The married men are as vulnerable to passions and temptations as their wives. Therefore, the same strict regulations must be enforced for the men as for the women, in order to protect them from themselves. The Corinthian men are as weak as women.

Therefore, Paul's instructions about the sexual relationship between husband and wife are not necessarily meant for universal application. Paul says this as a 'concession' (7:6) to weak men who cannot maintain authority over their own bodies. Marital sexual indulgence is conceded, not commanded. Stronger men do not need to cling anxiously to their wives. Indeed, Paul wishes that all men were like himself (7:7), i.e. capable of sexual abstinence. *Paul* would not let himself be dominated by anyone (6:12 – note that he uses the same word, *exousiazein*, for the married men's submission as for his own non-submission). Paul's body is dominated by himself (9:27), not by some woman. 'But each has a particular gift from God', Paul graciously concedes. 'The one is like this, the other like that' (7:7). Some men are strong, some men are weak. And every man must accommodate to his own level of self-restraint. A man has to do what a man has to do.

Thus, Paul's instructions about sex and marriage are quite humiliating for the Corinthian men. They are morally weak like women, not self-restrained like Paul. Therefore, they must follow the same rules for sexual conduct as women do. Having established his own masculinity and the relative effeminacy of the Corinthians, Paul goes on to give advice about family matters. He orders his household like a just and authoritative *paterfamilias* (cf. 4:14–21). The preferred conduct is to imitate Paul and to remain unmarried (7:8), but for those who are incapable of that level of self-restraint, marriage is allowed. 'For it is better to marry than to be aflame with passion' (7:9; cf. 7:36–38). Marriage is just like slavery – uncomfortable, but possible to endure. Therefore, everyone should remain in the condition in which he was called (7:20). Slaves should remain slaves, and married men should stay married. For the slave is a freedman in the Lord (7:22), and those who have wives should be as though they had none (7:29). Marriage is bondage (cf. 7:32–35), but Christ can set every man free.

Conclusions

Reading 1 Cor 5–7 in the light of Graeco-Roman protocols of masculinity and masculine sexual behaviour provides us with new perspectives on several notoriously problematic passages. The result is a coherent reading of Paul's line of argument, focusing on the threat of effeminacy. Paul argues that the Corinthian community is vulnerable to gentile effeminacy. Therefore, the Corinthian men must heed Paul's instructions and protect the integrity of their bodies and of their body politic. They must expel a certain *pornos* from the community, they must not submit to gentile judges, and they must stay away from 'whores'. Their shortcomings in discipline and self-restraint forces Paul to recommend some special measures – they must accept the relative humiliation of being sexually submissive to their wives, in order to avoid the absolute humiliation of *porneia*.

Paul stands out in his own discourse as the only example of a truly masculine man. The gentiles are his opposite – they are all effeminates, who live in *porneia* and utter depravity. The Corinthian men are somewhere in between. They are weak and vulnerable, and must be protected by their spiritual father. If they submit to Paul's discipline and imitate him, they can presumably grow up into mature men. It is tempting to see Paul's assault on gentile effeminacy and on Corinthian semi-effeminacy in 1 Cor 5–7 as a defence of his own contested masculinity. Paul might have difficulties in upholding the dominating ideal of manhood. He cannot protect his own body from beatings, and his physical presence is weak and servile (1 Cor 2:3; 4:10–13; cf. 2 Cor 10:10; 11:21–27; Gal 4:13–14). Therefore, Paul emphasizes self-restraint and sexual integrity as the defining factors of true masculinity. The male body is not emasculated by beatings, but by *porneia*.

New Testament scholarship on 1 Cor 5–7 is often flawed by the neglect of available research on ancient constructions of gender and sexuality. The import of modern constructions, such as heterosexuality and gender equality, into the reading of Paul, will necessarily prevent us from making plausible interpretations of the historical meaning of his rhetoric of sex and gender. Obviously, this is not only a matter of historical accuracy or scientific pedantry. To situate Paul firmly in his cultural context creates a healthy friction between the biblical texts and their modern interpretation. Paul might be a truly masculine man – but he is not a modern man.

Masculine or Feminine? Male Virgins in *Joseph and Aseneth* and The Book of Revelation

Hanna Stenström

In this essay, I will draw attention to some aspects of how gender is used in two texts that can be read as witnesses to strategies of identification in the Hellenistic world.

The first is *Joseph and Aseneth*, an early Jewish text,[1] most probably written in the century before, or the century following, the beginning of the Common Era, perhaps in Egypt.[2] This text is concerned with ethnic-cultic-religious identity and the relations between a Jewish community and Gentiles.[3] The other text is an early Christian text that was most probably written in the 90s CE, Revelation, a text in which the identity of the community, or communities, which are its original audience – most probably, small apocalyptic group(s) in Asia Minor – is a prominent theme.[4]

---

[1] It has been discussed whether *Jos. Asen.* is Jewish or Christian. Today, it is generally accepted as Jewish. See e.g. Randall CHESNUTT, "Joseph and Aseneth", *ABD*, III: 969–971, here 969, John J. COLLINS, *Between Athens and Jerusalem: Jewish Identity in the Hellenistic Diaspora*. Second Edition. (Grand Rapids: Eerdmans, 2000), 103–105, Angela STANDHARTINGER, *Das Frauenbild im Judentum der Hellenistischen Zeit. Ein Beitrag anhand von 'Joseph und Aseneth'* (AGJU XXVI; Leiden: Brill, 1995), 5–6. The majority of scholars date *Jos. Asen.* between 100 BCE and 135 CE. See e.g. Christoph BURCHARD, "Joseph and Aseneth", (English translation with introduction) in *The Old Testament Pseudiepigrapha vol 2* (ed. James H. Charlesworth; London: Darton, Longman & Todd, 1985), 177–247, here 187; CHESNUTT, "Joseph and Aseneth", III: 970.

[2] So e.g. CHESNUTT, "Joseph and Aseneth", III: 970. STANDHARTINGER, *Frauenbild* 19–20 argues that it must suffice to claim that *Jos. Asen.* was written in the Greek-speaking Jewish diaspora close to the beginning of the CE. See also COLLINS, *Athens and Jerusalem*, 105–106, 108–110. For a dissenting voice, claiming that it cannot be ruled out that *Jos. Asen.* is Christian, written later than 200 CE and not in Egypt, see Ross Shepard KRAEMER, *When Aseneth Met Joseph: A Late Antique Tale of the Biblical Patriarch and his Egyptian Wife, Reconsidered* (New York: Oxford University Press, 1998), 5–6, 225–293.

[3] On *Jos. Asen.* and Jewish identity see COLLINS, *Athens and Jerusalem*, 231, 236–237, cf. CHESNUTT, "Joseph and Aseneth", III: 970.

[4] For such a reading of Revelation see Hanna STENSTRÖM, *The Book of Revelation: A Vision of the Ultimate Liberation or the Ultimate Backlash? A study of 20th Century in-*

The aspect of gender, to which I draw attention, is the use of *parthenos*[5] with reference to men, in *Jos. Asen.* B4:7/Ph 4:9, B8:1/Ph8:1[6] and Rev 14:4.[7]

I will structure my presentation as follows: After a short presentation of the aim of the essay, I will present the basic assumptions behind the formulation of the aim and behind my way of accomplishing the task. More specifically, I will first substantiate the claim that *Jos. Asen.* and Revelation can be read as texts concerned with constructions of identity, and then turn to the understanding of gender, especially masculinity, that are fundamental to my reading of these texts. After the general issues of gender, I turn to the possible meanings of *parthenos*, and to male *parthenoi* in general. With those basic assumptions made clear, I will turn to the texts, first to *Jos. Asen.* and then to Revelation. Given the limited space of this essay, my study is necessarily tentative and sketchy.

The Aim of the Essay

My aim is to show how *parthenos* is used in *Joseph and Aseneth* and in Rev 14:4 as part of constructions of identity, individual and collective.

In both cases, characters in the text are described as men and as *parthenos/parthenoi*. A first step in the analysis is to look at these *parthenoi* as characters in the text. Since *parthenos* is not normally used with

---

terpretations of Rev 14:1–5, with special emphasis on feminist exegesis (Ph.D. diss, Uppsala University, 1999), 66–97.

[5] I use *parthenos, parthenia*, not "virgin, virginity", to make clear that *parthenos* does not necessarily have the same meaning as "virgin" in contemporary English. If I use "virgin, virginity", I refer to persons, male or female, who have never had sexual intercourse.

[6] The text-critical issues concerning *Jos. Asen.* are complex. Two recensions are used in contemporary scholarship, a longer one (accepted by the majority of scholars), Christoph BURCHARD, *Joseph und Aseneth: Kritisch Herausgaben von Christoph Burchard* (PVTG Vol 5, Leiden: Brill, 2003), and a shorter one, Marc PHILONENKO, *Joseph et Aséneth: Introduction, texte critique, traduction et notes par Marc Philonenko* (StPB 13; Leiden: Brill, 1968). For my purpose, it is not necessary to decide for one or the other, and I will give references to both, with B and Ph before the chapter and verse. See also BURCHARD, "Joseph and Aseneth", in Charlesworth *Pseudepigrapha*, 178–181, COLLINS, *Athens and Jerusalem*, 103–104.

[7] The use of *parthenos* with reference to men in Rev 14:4 is a well-known *crux interpretum*. See e.g. STENSTRÖM, *Liberation or Backlash?*, 120–149; David E. AUNE, *Revelation 6–16* (WBC 52B; Nashville: Thomas Nelson Publishers, 1998), 811 for surveys of the discussion. See also BURCHARD, "Joseph and Aseneth" in Charlesworth, *Pseudepigrapha*, 406, note n to *Jos. Asen.* 4.

reference to men, I will investigate the relationship between the characters who are described both as man/men and as *parthenos/parthenoi*. Is there a tension between being a man and being a *parthenos*? Are they actually described as feminine? Is this maybe a case of gender-bending, where men are turned into women? Or does being a *parthenos* – being a man interplay in a construction of a certain kind of masculinity, and perhaps even reinforce one another? How can the masculinity of Joseph and the 144,000 be related to the dominant discourses of masculinity in their contexts, or to specifically Jewish or Christian masculinities known from the formative period of these traditions?[8]

A second step is to ask whether the meanings produced in this interplay between being a man – being a *parthenos* can be used in a transferred sense, not only as a description of a literary character (who may function as an example to be followed by the individual members of the audience), but also as elements in the construction of a collective identity.

Basic Assumptions

Joseph and Aseneth *and Revelation as Texts that Construct Identity*

I assume that *Jos. Asen.* and Revelation can be read as texts that construct an identity for their (implied) original audiences.

In the case of Revelation, this reading presents itself easily. In a recent article on the 144,000 male *parthenoi* in Rev 14:4, for example, Lynn R. Huber assumes that Revelation "calls its audience to create a communal identity within a context of Roman religious, social, and political dominance..."[9] Revelation presents a number of images to its audience, including the image of 144,000 male *parthenoi*, with which they can imagine their identity.[10] In the discussion of Rev 14:4, I will also show the function of the passage in Revelation as a whole, to substantiate the claim that Rev

---

[8] For Early Christian and Jewish masculinities see Daniel BOYARIN, "Homotopia: The *Feminized* Jewish Man and the Lives of Women in Late Antiquity", *Differences* (2:1995), 41–81, Gillian CLARK, "The Old Adam: The Fathers and the Unmaking of Masculinity," in *Thinking Men: Masculinity and its Self-Representation in the Classical Tradition* (eds. Lin Foxhall and John Salmon; London: Routledge, 1998).

[9] Lynn R. HUBER, "Sexually Explicit? Re-reading Revelation's 144,000 Virgins as a Response to Roman Discourses", *Journal of Masculinity, Men and Sprituality* vol 2, No 1 (2008), 3–28, here 3, online www.jmmsweb.org. Cited 2007-12-28. Huber gives references to other works arguing along the same line.

[10] HUBER, "Sexually Explicit?", 3.

14:1–5 can be used as a key to the understanding of Christian identity in Revelation.

In *Jos. Asen.*, *parthenos* is an important characteristic of its male chief character and hero, Joseph. However, an understanding of Joseph as not only a literary character and a role model for the reader to follow, but also as a symbol of the Jewish community may seem farfetched, and therefore also the use of *parthenos* as a description of collective identity.

I take my point of departure in Collins' statement that "Joseph has an obvious representative role as the embodiment of the true (Jewish) religion".[11] Thus, I find that it is at least *possible* to understand Joseph's interactions with Aseneth, the Egyptian, not only as the interaction between literary characters but also, at another level, as the interaction between Jews and Gentiles, with Joseph as a personification of the Jewish community. Then, it is worth asking what the characteristics of Joseph, including being *parthenos*, might mean if they are understood in a transferred sense with reference to the Jewish community.

Assumptions on Gender

One of the tools available when constructing identities for individuals and collectives in the Hellenistic world was gender. One reason for such uses of gender is that understandings of gender belong to the "assumed, unspoken values of society."[12] As has been shown by feminist and gender studies during the last three to four decades, gendered words and concepts can be charged with meanings far beyond the biological. As I will show, *parthenos* is one example of a basically gendered concept, which refers to biological facts, but which is given social significance, and which then takes on new meanings far beyond the biological ones.

Therefore, analyses of texts with gender as an analytical tool lead to deeper understandings, not only of the actual persons involved (i.e. whether they are men or women) or of aspects of identity obviously related to gender (e.g. understandings of the ideal husband and the ideal wife) but also of other aspects of identity.

This is obviously the case in Revelation. Even a cursory reading makes evident that certain understandings of gender and sexuality are presupposed in the rhetorics of the text. The dichotomy between a Good and a Bad Woman – between a Woman who is concerned about shame, and a

---

[11] COLLINS, *Athens and Jerusalem*, 236.

[12] I owe the formulation to Halvor MOXNES, "Conventional Values in the Hellenistic World: Masculinity" in *Conventional Values of the Hellenistic Greeks* (eds. Per Bilde *et al.*; Studies in Hellenistic Civilization VIII; Aarhus: Aarhus University Press, 1997), 263–284, here 263. The understanding is basic in gender studies generally.

shameless Woman,[13] between ideal femininity and non-ideal femininity, between a Bride and a Whore – are used as a means to speak about the world of the audience as a world in which God fights against Evil and to exhort the audience to make their own choices in a world within which no-one can be neutral.[14]

The use of gendered symbolism is not as evident in *Jos. Asen.*, but feminist studies have shown that conventional constructions of gender are utilized and that the work reflects a hierarchy in which women are subordinated to men, slaves to owners, human beings to angels and angels to God.[15] Thus, *Jos. Asen.* is suitable for an analysis with gender as an analytical tool.[16]

A context for this essay is the phenomenon of gender-bending in early Christianity.[17] Gender-bending is present in the idea that women must become men in order to reach spiritual perfection.[18] The question is whether

---

[13] About honour-and-shame, see e.g. Bruce MALINA, *The New Testament World: Insights from Cultural Anthropology*. Rev. ed. (Louisville: WJKP, 1993) 28–62, MOXNES, "Honor and Shame", *BTB* 23:4, 167–176, 1993.

[14] For gender analysis of Revelation, see Tina PIPPIN, *Death and Desire: The Rhetoric of Gender in the Apocalypse* (Literary Currents in Biblical Interpretation; Louisville: WJKP, 1992); Caroline VANDER STICHELE, "Just a Whore: The Annihilation of Babylon According to Revelation to Revelation 17:16", *lectio.difficilior*, 1, 2000, n. p. http://www.lectio.unibe.ch, cited 17 November 2007; Jorunn ØKLAND, "Sex, gender and ancient greek: a case-study in theoretical misfit", *ST* 57 (2003), 124–162; Jorunn ØKLAND , "Why Can't the Heavenly Miss Jerusalem Just Shut Up?" in *Her Master's Tools? Feminist and Postcolonial Engagements of Historical-Critical Discourse* (eds. Caroline Vander Stichele and Todd Penner, Global Perspectives on Biblical Scholarship 9, Atlanta: Society of Biblical Literature, 2005), 311–332; STENSTRÖM, *Liberation or Backlash?*, 83–97; Hanna STENSTRÖM, "New Voices in Biblical Exegesis – New Views on the Formation of the Church" in *The Formation of the Early Church* (ed. Jostein Ådna, Tübingen: Mohr Siebeck, 2005), 72–90, here 88–89.

[15] Ross Shepard KRAEMER, "The Book of Aseneth" in *Searching the Scriptures. Vol 2: A Feminist Commentary* (ed. Elisabeth Schüssler Fiorenza; London: SCM Press, 1995), 859–888, here 885.

[16] KRAEMER, *Aseneth* 191–221. There are two major studies of gender in *Jos. Asen.*, STANDHARTINGER, *Frauenbild* and KRAEMER, *Aseneth*. See also Angela STANDHART-INGER, "Joseph and Aseneth. Vollkommenen Braut oder himmlische Prophetin" in *Kompendium Feministische Bibelauslegung. 2 Auflage* (ed. Luise Schottroff and Marie-Theres Wacker; Gütersloh: Chr.Kaiser/Gütersloher Verlagshaus, 1999), 459–464, KRAE-MER, "Book of Aseneth". The main focus for both is the image of Aseneth.

[17] See e.g. Elizabeth A. CLARK, *Reading Renunciation: Asceticism and Scripture in Early Christianity* (Princeton: Princeton University Press, 1999), 138–141, 197, 201.

[18] See e.g. Kerstin ASPEGREN, *The Male Woman: A Feminine Ideal in the Early Church* (ed. René Kieffer, AUU, Uppsala Women Studies. A: Women in Religion 4; Uppsala: Uppsala University, 1990).

the use of a normally feminine word, *parthenos*, with reference to men is a case of gender-bending, in the opposite direction.

A pre-supposition for gender-bending is a certain understanding of gender.[19] To describe it, I borrow words from Virginia Burrus:[20]

There is by now widespread scholarly agreement that gender in antiquity was mapped not as a binary of two fixed and "opposite" sexes (as is typical of our own modern western culture) but rather as a dynamic spectrum or gradient of relative masculinities. On the positively valorized end of the spectrum were "true men," fully masculine; on the negatively valorized end, "true women," lacking masculinity. For men, the challenge was to establish virility and to avoid sliding down the slippery slope of feminization. [...] Women were, in turn, expected to conform to their essentially feminine nature and a drift toward the masculine pole was deemed highly suspect...

With such an understanding of gender, it is possible for females to become male (and vice versa). Masculinity is not something that a person "has" or "is" as a biological fact. Rather, a person's masculinity is always under threat and must be guarded. Masculinity is continuously constructed by defending one's honour, shunning everything weak and feminine, behaving in a way that befits a man, and by being in competition with other men.[21]

Although there is not one monolithic discourse of masculinity in antiquity, a central and common trait in the discourses is "mastery".[22] It may be

---

[19] For the original work on the one-sex-model see Thomas LAQUEUR , *Making Sex: Body and Gender from the Greeks to Freud*, (Cambridge: Harvard University Press, 1990)

[20] Virginia BURRUS, "Mapping as Metamorphosis: Initial Reflections on Gender and Ancient Religious Discourses" in in *Mapping Gender in Ancient Religious Discourse* (ed. Todd Penner and Caroline Vander Stichele, Biblical Interpretation Series volume 84; Leiden: Brill, 2007), 1–10, here 4–5.

[21] So, e.g. Fredrik IVARSSON, "Vice Lists and Deviant Masculinity: The Rhetorical Function of 1 Corinthians 5:10–11 and 6:9–10" in Penner and Vander Stichele (eds.) *Mapping*, 163–184, here 166. In addition to works quoted, my presentation of masculinity is dependent of: Stephen D. MOORE and Janice Capel ANDERSON., eds. *New Testament Masculinities* (Atlanta: Society of Biblical Literature, 2003), FOXHALL and SALMON (eds.), *Thinking Men*, Craig A. WILLIAMS, *Roman Homosexuality. Ideologies of Masculinity in Classical Antiquity* (Ideologies of Desire; New York: Oxford University Press, 1999).

[22] See e.g. Page DUBOIS, "Ancient Masculinities" in Moore and Anderson, *Masculinities*, 319–323, here 321.

mastery of oneself[23] or of others, [24] the mastery of the soldier or of the elite male participating in public life.[25]

Before relating *Jos. Asen.* and Revelation to discourses of masculinity, it is necessary to ask if the discourses are relevant. Apart from the "popular discourse" that will be presented below, the masculinity that can be reconstructed through texts from Antiquity is an ideal for society's elite.[26] Therefore, it must be asked whether such an elite ideal is relevant for *Jos. Asen,* and for Revelation. It is also necessary to reflect on the issues of dating, since discourses of masculinity may change over time, as will be shown.

It has been argued that *Jos. Asen.* was written for (perhaps also by) persons of a relatively high social status, although not at the very top of society. Therefore an elite ideal may be relevant.[27] The issue of Revelation is more difficult: it was most probably written in a small group that deliberately took on an identity as a counter-culture to the rest of society, and it is also extremely difficult to know anything about the social status of its members. However, we may at least assume that a popular discourse of masculinity – which will be described below – is relevant for Revelation, and that the author and audience shared the understanding of gender in general, including an understanding of masculinity as "mastery".[28]

When it comes to changes over time, it is safe to relate Revelation to discourses current in the Roman Empire at the end of the first century CE. *Jos. Asen.* is more difficult, since the proposed dating of the text vary from about 100 BCE to about 100 CE. I will begin in the text itself by looking at the masculinity that emerges in the description of Joseph, and then I will relate it to the understandings of masculinity described below.

Masculinity studies have shown that the time of the late Roman Republic and the early Empire was a time of change in understandings of mascu-

---

[23] IVARSSON, "Vice Lists", 166.

[24] IVARSSON, "Vice Lists", 166, defines others as "non-men (women, slaves, children, barbarians)".

[25] See Karen BASSI, "The Semantics of Manliness in Ancient Greece" in *Andreia: Studies in Manliness and Courage in Classical Antiquity* (eds. Ralph M.Rosen and Ineke Sluiter, Mnemosyne: bibliotheca classica Batava. Supplementum 238, Leiden: Brill, 2003), 25–58, esp. 25–26 for the development from a period when being a man meant facing death on the battlefield to a time when *andreia* referred to "a defining ethical characteristic of the fifth-century *polis.*" (26).

[26] See e.g. Lin FOXHALL, "Introduction" in *When Men were Men: Masculinity, Power and Identity in Classical Antiquity* (eds. Lin Foxhall and John Salmon: London: Routledge, 1998), 1–9, here 4.

[27] So BURCHARD, "Joseph and Aseneth" in Charlesworth, *Pseudepigrapha*, 188, 193.

[28] FOXHALL, "Introduction", 4, argues that that gender roles have been "replicated in ... social locations beyond those in which they were founded and remained most potent."

linity, a time for struggles and negotiations.[29] It has been shown,[30] that this was the result of an encounter between a Roman understanding of masculinity, based on martial prowess, and a Greek understanding, according to which ethical issues were central: to be really masculine was to be able to practice virtues, such as self-control.[31]

Moxnes argues – in a study of two Greek authors from the early imperial period, Dio Chrysostom and Plutarch (both late 1st and early 2nd Century CE) – that changes in the understanding of masculinity in the Hellenistic world can also be related to the changed status of the *polis*, i.e. to their loss of political autonomy in the Roman Empire.[32] The ideals of masculinity had to change when the citizens (read: adult free men) of the cities no longer related to one another in agonistic competition (which was central to masculinity) but related instead to external powers. The ideal masculinity that emerged in this process was the masculinity of the responsible citizen, who exercised public virtues: peaceful qualities and acts such as self-mastery, the administration of public affairs and participation in judicial decisions.

Thus, masculinity becomes a moral quality. In antiquity, there is a connection between masculinity and virtue as well as between the lack of masculinity and vice.[33]

Huber shows that there were two dominant discourses of masculinity in the Roman Empire.[34] In both, it was a contradiction in terms to be both a man and a virgin.

First, the family laws of Augustus were supported by a discourse of masculinity in which the very essence of masculinity was to be married and to beget children[35]. This discourse became an important part of imperial rhetorics, and was so still in the time of Domitian. The imperial rhetoric of the ideal family gave rise to an ethical ideal for the upper-classes.[36]

---

[29] So e.g. Myles MCDONNELL, "Roman Men and Greek Virtue", in Rosen and Sluiter (eds.), *Andreia*, 235–261, see esp. 235–236, MOXNES, "Masculinity".

[30] MCDONNELL, "Roman Men", 235–236.

[31] On masculinity in Greek sources, see Karen BASSI, "Semantics of Manliness" in Rosen and Sluiter (eds.), *Andreia*, 25–58, see esp. 25–26, for the development from a period when being a man meant facing death on the battlefield to a time when *andreia* referred to "a defining ethical characteristic of the fifth-century *polis*." (26).

[32] MOXNES, "Masculinity".

[33] See e.g. IVARSSON, "Vice Lists", 166; BASSI, "Semantics of Manliness".

[34] HUBER, "Sexually Explicit?", 13–14, briefly presents medical and philosophical discourses, in which masculine self-mastery is realized as sexual moderation and virginity is understood as good for health, even for men.

[35] HUBER, "Sexually Explicit?", 9–11.

[36] HUBER, "Sexually Explicit?", 10.

There was also a popular discourse of masculinity, of which sexual domination and power was the central element.[37] These two discourses are certainly not mutually exclusive – sexual domination may lead to the begetting of children – but the emphasis is different.[38] In the popular discourse, the emphasis was on mastery as sexual domination of others, on a real man as a sexually active being, who penetrates others sexually and who does not yield himself to sexual penetration.

The Meanings of Parthenos

Jos. Asen. B4:7/Ph 4:9, B8:1/Ph8:1 and Rev14:4 are almost generally accepted as the earliest known examples of the use of *parthenos* with reference to men.[39]

If we regard a *parthenos* as a female person with an intact hymen, it is impossible to use the term with reference to men.[40] In the honour-and-shame culture of the Mediterranean world, the values of honour and shame were intimately connected with gender and sexuality. A central element of masculinity was to preserve and to defend one's own honour and the honour of the family; a central element of femininity was to show concern for

---

[37] HUBER, "Sexually Explicit?", 11–13, with references. The popular understanding is reconstructed through works by "poets, playwrights, humorists" and through material culture such as findings of decorations and pictures found in Pompeii and Herculaneum (12).

[38] HUBER, "Sexually Explicit?", 11.

[39] This is recurrent in scholarly works on Revelation and *Jos. Asen.* See, for example, Christoph BURCHARD, "The Importance of *Joseph and Aseneth* for the Study of the New Testament: a General Survey and a Fresh Look at the Lord's Supper", *NTS* 33, (1987), 102–134, here 102–103, and the survey in STENSTRÖM, *Liberation or Backlash?*, 71. Sometimes 1 Cor 7:25–26 is added, see e.g. ØKLAND, "Sex, gender", 132, for arguments against see e.g. AUNE, *Revelation*, 811. The reference to a man in *Jos. Asen.* is indisputable. *Jos. Asen.* B4:7/Ph 4:9: *Iōsēph anēr theosebēs ... kai parthenos*; *Jos. Asen.* B8:1: *autos parthenos estin*; *Jos. Asen.* Ph8:1: *autos parthenos esti*. It is possible to translate Revelation 14:4 as including both women and men, but the description of the 144,000 in opposition to women (*meta gynaikōn ouk emolynthēsan*) makes this improbable, as is argued in ØKLAND, "Sex, gender", 132–138; STENSTRÖM, *Liberation or Backlash?*, 71–72; STENSTRÖM, "New Voices", 87. See also AUNE, *Revelation* 811–812 for examples of the use of *parthenos* and *parthenikos* with reference to unmarried men, and of *parthenikos* (and the Latin word *virgineum*) with reference to men who had been married only once. For surveys of later texts where *parthenos* and related words are used with reference to men, see Chrys C. CARAGOUNIS, *The Development of Greek and the New Testament: Morphology, Syntax, Phonology and Textual Transmission* (Tübingen: Mohr Siebeck, 2004), 307 n. 247.

[40] BURCHARD, "Importance", 128, n. 5, p. 103, asks if the formulation *parthenos hōs sy* might indicate that *parthenos* "is still so fundamentally feminine that its use for males is a comparison rather than a predication."

shame. Women showed concern for shame by adhering to the rules of sexual exclusivity, i.e. to remain a virgin while unmarried and to remain faithful to her husband when married. This exclusivity was symbolised by the hymen, which thus became much more of a cultural and social than a biological phenomenon. Masculine honour was not bound up with sexual exclusivity.[41]

To illustrate the impossibility of using *parthenos* with reference to men, scholars[42] often quote a work by Achilles Tatius (2nd century CE) in which a character asks whether there is such a thing as *parthenia* among men, *ei tis esti kai en andrasi parthenia*. (*Leucippe et Clitophon* 5.20).

Parthenos and *parthenia* have a number of meanings, in addition to a concrete female body with an unbroken hymen, sexual unapproachability and chastity.[43] Within the ancient Jewish purity system, the female reproductive body – with all its bodily fluids – was interpreted as impure, while the virginal female body could be interpreted as less impure. Therefore, the virginal female body can inspire meanings such as self-containment.[44] The intact female body of the virgin is a vivid image of integrity. Thus, *parthenos* includes a number of elements and possible meanings. None of the elements are indispensable and none of them can determine or condition the use of the term. The meaning of *parthenos* is therefore not dependent on the hymen element. Some meanings of the word can be transferred to men.[45]

Still, the tensions between the dominant discourses of masculinity in the historical contexts in which *Jos. Asen.* and Revelation were written, and the use of *parthenos* with reference to a man remain. Either, those who identify as male *parthenoi* must accept that they risk sliding down the slippery slope towards femininity, or they must reformulate their understand-

---

[41] See e.g. MALINA, *New Testament World*, 28–62; MOXNES, "Honor and Shame"; MOXNES, "Masculinity", 264.

[42] See BURCHARD, "Joseph and Aseneth", in Charlesworth, *Pseudepigrapha*, 206, note to *Jos. Asen.* 4:7; PHILONENKO, *Joseph et Aséneth*, 144; CLARK, "Old Adam", 180; C. H. LINDIJER, "Die Jungfrauen in der Offenbarung des Johannes XIV 4" in *Studies in John Presented to Professor Dr. J. N. Sevenster on the occasion of his seventieth birthday* (NovTSup XXIV; Leiden: Brill, 1970), 128; AUNE, *Revelation*, 811; HUBER "Sexually Explicit? ", 6.

[43] ØKLAND , "Sex, gender", 132. See also HUBER, "Sexually Explicit?", 5, where it is claimed that the reference is rather to an unmarried woman than to an intact hymen: "Virginity was so closely connected to the social role of the unmarried woman, that the term did not always refer specifically to anatomical virginity." Huber gives references for further reading.

[44] ØKLAND, "Sex, gender", 136. On virginity as purity in non-Jewish sources see HUBER, "Sexually Explicit?", 5–6.

[45] ØKLAND, "Sex, gender", 132.

ing of masculinity. The question is whether we can find any of these alternatives in *Jos. Asen.* and in Revelation.

To show that and how masculinity could be redefined, we may cast a short glance at some later texts.[46]

In works on masculinities in patristic and rabbinic texts,[47] Daniel Boyarin argues that the masculinities of the early Jews and Christians were different from the masculinity of the Gentiles. Jewish men were regarded as feminized, and accepted this, while Christian ascetic men renounced ordinary masculinity.[48]

In a similar vein, Gillian Clark claims with references to patristic texts, that there were tensions in the masculinity of male ascetics. To renounce marriage meant to renounce both the sexual domination over non-men and the role as the head of the household which were central in discourses on masculinity.[49] Ascetic men may have renounced their public roles as well, and thereby also have made themselves less masculine.[50] Thus, redefinitions of masculinity became necessary in ascetic discourses.[51] One way to combine virginity and masculinity was to enact mastery as mastery over one's body, one's desires and urges, and over hostile spirits.[52]

---

[46] I do not claim that the later texts were influenced by Revelation and *Jos. Asen.* I look at the later texts to gain some knowledge of what was possible. However, there is an ascetic reception of Rev 14:4, see e.g. Methodius of Olympus, *Symposium*, Discourse 1, Chapter 5:25–27; CLARK *Renunciation*, 139, 218–219. See BURCHARD, "Importance", 103; KRAEMER, *Aseneth*, 6, about the lack of references to *Jos. Asen.* in later works.

[47] BOYARIN, "Homotopia", Daniel BOYARIN, *Dying for God: Martyrdom and the Making of Christianity and Judaism* (Figurae. Reading Medieval Culture; Stanford: Stanford University Press, 1999), 67–92. See esp. 69, 73–75, 78–79. See also BURCHARD, "Joseph and Aseneth" in Charlesworth, *Pseudepigrapha*, 406, note n to *Jos. Asen.* 4: the use of *parthenos* with reference to a man might have been both a Jewish and a Christian phenomenon.

[48] Boyarin understands what these Jews and Christians did as "acts of resistance against the Roman culture of male power wielding," "resistance to a culture that equated power and dominance with maleness and maleness with the 'husband's natural position' in coitus." BOYARIN, "Homotopia", 42. See also BOYARIN, *Dying*, 79–81.

[49] CLARK, "Old Adam", 179.

[50] Virginia BURRUS, *The Making of a Heretic. Gender, Authority and the Priscillianist Controversy*, (Berkeley: University of California Press, 1995), 14.

[51] CLARK, "Old Adam", see esp. 178–180 on "virgin men".

[52] CLARK, "Old Adam", 179–181.

Joseph as *Parthenos*

The Story

Joseph and Aseneth takes Genesis 41:45 as its point of departure: Pharaoh gave to Joseph Aseneth, daughter of an Egyptian Priest, for a wife. (See also Gen 41:50–52; 46:20.) Obviously, when Gen 41:45 was written, this was not a problem. In Hellenistic times, when biblical texts used "foreign women" as symbols of the forces that would lead people away from the One God, and when intermarriage was a burning issue, Gen 41:45 became a problem.[53]

Part One, *Jos. Asen.* B1:1–21:19/Ph1:1–21:8, speaks about the relation between Joseph (a Jew) and Aseneth (an Egyptian), two virgins who refuse to mix with foreigners.

Chs. 1–2 introduce the characters and the milieu. The events take place in the first of the seven good years, when Joseph is sent by Pharaoh to travel around Egypt to collect grain. (Gen 41, esp, 41:46b–49). Aseneth lives in a tower, despises men and is devoted to the Egyptian gods. Ross Kraemer shows, that Aseneth is an Other, both as a Woman and as a Foreigner. She, like the Egyptian women who try to seduce Joseph, is a foreign Woman (cf. e.g. Ezra 9; Prov 5).[54] Joseph is extremely handsome – a number of Egyptian women have made a pass at him – and he is a virgin.

In ch. 3, Joseph announces a visit to Pentephres. Although he arrives in ch. 5, he is introduced in ch. 4, where Pentephres tells Aseneth that he wants her to marry Joseph. Aseneth refuses to marry a foreigner of low social standing, who is known to be sleeping with his master's wife (Gen 39:6b–20). However, when Aseneth sees Joseph (ch. 6), she starts trembling with fear, and breaks out in a monologue about her fear and awe, and about his splendour: he resembles Helios, the Sun God, himself. In ch. 7, after receiving assurances that she will not molest him – she is a man-hating virgin, so it must be safe! – Joseph agrees to meet her (ch. 8).[55] Gradually, their love grows. After Aseneth has left her Egyptian Gods, turned to the God of Israel and been accepted as a member of His People,[56] it becomes possible for them to marry.[57]

---

[53] See.e.g. Hedvig LARSSON, *Jews and Gentiles in early Jewish Novels*, (Ph. D. diss, Uppsala University, 2006), 261.

[54] KRAEMER, *Aseneth*, 193–196. See also LARSSON, *Jews and Gentiles*, 30–35, 261–310 for an analysis of *Jos. Asen.*, as a work where a Jewish view of "the Other," i.e. the Gentile, becomes visible.

[55] The plot in chs 1–8 is the same in both versions, B and Ph.

[56] Aseneth's conversion is often understood as *a*, not to say *the*, central theme of the story: e.g. BURCHARD, "Importance", 107–108; BURCHARD, "Joseph and Aseneth", in

In Part Two, *Jos. Asen.* B22:1–29:9/Ph22:1–29:11, Pharaoh's first-born son tries to kidnap Aseneth to have her as his own wife, but fails. After a series of thrilling events, with Joseph's brothers involved on both sides, Aseneth is saved while Pharaoh's son dies, and so does Pharaoh (from grief, it seems), leaving the kingship of Egypt to Joseph. Joseph becomes like a father to Pharaoh's youngest son and eventually, after 48 years, he hands over the kingship to him..

Joseph as a Man – Joseph as a Parthenos

Joseph is called a *parthenos* in two texts, in which Aseneth's father tries to convince Aseneth to marry him:

B4:7 – *Iōsēph anēr theosebēs kai sōphrōn kai parthenos hōs sy sēmeron kai estin Iōsēph anēr dynatos en sophia kai epistēmē ... B8:1 – parthenos estin hōs sy sēmeron kai misei pasan gynaika allotrian* [58]

Kraemer shows how Joseph "exemplifies virtuous masculinity"[59] when described as as *anēr dynatos en sophia kai epistēmē* ... and as *sōphrōn*, "one of the cardinal virtues of the male Greek philosopher."[60] He gives us an example of two elements of masculinity: control, including self-control, and virtue. Thus, that Joseph has successfully defended himself against Egyptian women can be understood as the ultimate proof and consequence of his masculinity. At the same time, this description of Joseph makes him a model of exemplary Jewish piety: he has resisted the "Foreign Woman" (cf. e.g. Ezra 9; Prov 5),[61] an image of all that leads away from God. Kraemer does not discuss the possible tensions between being masculine and being a *parthenos*.

Since *parthenos* is mentioned as parallel to the other virtues, it may be understood as another way of saying that Joseph is virtuous. Meanings of virginity as "self-containment" and "integrity" are activated.

Charlesworth, *Pseudepigrapha*, 189–195; CHESNUTT, "Joseph and Aseneth" III: 970, COLLINS, *Athens and Jerusalem*, 230–239. A central text is *Jos. Asen.* B15:7/Ph15:6, B16:6 and B19:5 (B16:16 and B19:5 have no counterparts in Ph).

[57] In Philonenko's version, this part of the story ends with the birth of their sons. In Burchard's version, a long prayer by Aseneth, 21:10–21, follows the birth of the sons.

[58] The wordings are in both cases the same in Ph4:9; 8:1 (Ph8:1 has *esti*).

[59] KRAEMER, *Aseneth*, 195.

[60] KRAEMER, *Aseneth*, 195 points to the fact that *dynatos* is also an attribute of God in *Jos. Asen.* B8:10/Ph8:10.

[61] *Jos. Asen.* B8:4–7/Ph8:4–7 emphasises this theme.

As Helen North shows,[62] *sōphrosynē* is a virtue that carries different meanings when used with reference to men and to women.[63] The meanings of *sōphrosynē* as a feminine virtue remain the same throughout antiquity – "chastity, modesty, obedience, inconspicuous behaviour"[64]– while the meanings of *sōphrosynē* in relation to masculinity change. During certain periods, it was questioned whether *sōphrosynē* could be used as a designation for a really masculine man. There was a tension between *sōphrosynē* and a heroic masculinity.[65] Gradually, meanings of *sōphrosynē* were developed that were connected with ideal masculinity.[66]

North also shows how Joseph became a primary example of the virtue *sōphrōn, sōphrosynē* in Philo, *De Iosepho*.[67] In this work, Joseph is an example of the "effects of sophrosyne on affairs of the state."[68] Although Philo's picture of Joseph as a type of the *bios politikos* is much more systematic and sophisticated than *Jos. Asen.*, both of them emphasize the same virtue, and speak of Joseph as a good citizen, who eventually becomes a good ruler. This is an example of the masculinity of the responsible citizen.

Finally, as Hedvig Larsson shows, the son of Pharaoh shows himself unable to control his desires, in contrast to the always well-controlled Joseph.[69] Thus, the son of Pharaoh is actually, in contrast to Joseph, lacking in masculinity.

The Male and the Female Parthenos in Joseph and Aseneth

While calling a man a *parthenos* is unusual, the virginity of the female protagonist is a conventional element in ancient romances.[70] Aseneth's virginity also serves the purpose of ensuring that their children are Joseph's off-

---

[62] Helen NORTH, *Sophrosyne: Self-Knowledge and Self-Restraint in Greek Literature* (Cornell Studies in Classical Philology volume XXXV, Itacha, New York: Cornell University Press, 1966).

[63] KRAEMER, *Aseneth*, 195 mentions that *sōphrōn* was a cardinal virtue of the Greek philosopher; while *sōphrosynē* used about women primarily meant "chastity".

[64] NORTH, *Sophrosyne*, 1.

[65] See e.g. NORTH, *Sophrosyne*, ix.

[66] In the *Testament of Joseph*, Joseph is a model of *sōphrosynē*. It is difficult to decide whether *T. Jos.* is relevant here, since the text in its present form may be Christian and its date is not sure. However, it can be argued that *T. 12 Patr.* has its origins in Hellenistic Judaism and bears witness of its ethics. See COLLINS, *Athens and Jerusalem*, 174–183.

[67] NORTH, *Sophrosyne*, 327. NORTH, *Sophrosyne*, 312–379 discusses *sōphrosynē* in the LXX, New Testament and patristic writings.

[68] NORTH, *Sophrosyne*, 327.

[69] LARSSON, *Jews and Gentiles*, 277.

[70] So e.g. KRAEMER, "Book of Aseneth", 863.

spring.[71] Kraemer argues that it also shows the difference between Aseneth and other "foreign women", exemplified by all the women in Egypt, who try to lay hold on Joseph in order to have sex with him (*Jos. Asen.* B7:3/Ph7:3). Aseneth is not like other Egyptian women, but similar to the daughters of the Hebrews (B1:5/Ph1:7–8).[72] Her virginity may also be "consistent with the emphasis on sexual purity required for various magical and mystical experiences in numerous ancient sources"[73] that is, the kind of experiences Aseneth will have in the story. (*Jos. Asen.* B14–17/Ph14–17)

Joseph's virginity is both part of and an expression of his fidelity to (what the author considers) the True God, and a consequence of his masculine virtues. Therefore, his virginity is something positive: it is a way of speaking about the positive aspects of integrity, pride and faithfulness. Aseneth's virginity, on the other hand, is of no real help to her as long as her house is full of Egyptian idols. Outside of the covenant with (what the author considers) the True God, her virginity shows the negative aspects of integrity and faithfulness:[74] it is connected with her pride, and pride is not characteristic of ideal femininity.

It is thereby made clear that *Jos. Asen.* does not advocate renunciation of sexuality as a value in itself.[75] Eventually, the goal of life is not to keep one's virginity, but to find the way to the True God and to live one's life – as husband, wife, father, mother and (in case of the man) as a responsible citizen – in fidelity to the covenant with Him.[76]

Kraemer shows how Joseph is described as a contrast to Aseneth, in a way that uses gender stereotypes. He is wise and exercises self-control. She is foolish, miserable and ignorant.[77] Not only is Aseneth feminine; in her initial state she exemplifies the "most negative aspects of ancient constructions of the feminine."[78] The worst of femininity is thus contrasted with all the good that is real masculinity.[79]

---

[71] KRAEMER, "Book of Aseneth", 863.

[72] KRAEMER, "Book of Aseneth", 864.

[73] KRAEMER, "Book of Aseneth", 864.

[74] Cf. BURCHARD, "Importance", 128 n. 5.

[75] Cf. BURCHARD, "Importance", 128 n. 5, KRAEMER, *Aseneth*, 204–205

[76] Cf. KRAEMER, *Aseneth*, 204–205.

[77] KRAEMER, *Aseneth*, 195.

[78] KRAEMER, *Aseneth*, 195.

[79] KRAEMER, *Aseneth*, 195, shows that after her conversion, Aseneth is transformed into an epitome of the good woman.

Conclusions

First, the use of *parthenos* with reference to a man can be understood within the logic of the actual story. When the sexual assaults of foreign women are a prominent theme, the virginity of the hero shows clearly that it is he, actually, who is the hero.

The use of *parthenos* with reference to a man in *Jos. Asen.* was probably born in the intersection between texts which say that Foreign Women must be avoided and an ideal of masculinity shared by Jews and Gentiles in the Hellenistic world. It is obvious that *Jos. Asen.* is not a text in which life-long virginity is an ideal. By managing to keep his virginity in spite of the efforts of all the women of Egypt Joseph shows that he is a virtuous man, a really masculine man, and a really pious Jew, who moves on to a proper marriage with a proper woman. The description of Joseph as husband and father owes, of course, much to the ideals of Jewish culture, but, if *Jos. Asen.* was written during the 1st Century CE, it can also be understood in line with that Roman discourse of masculinity according to which being married, begetting children and being the head of the household were central characteristics of a really masculine man.

Although there are tendencies towards a different masculinity – the virginal Joseph does not conform to discourses of masculinity based on sexual domination – the story basically affirms the dominant discourses of masculinity. After the phase in Joseph's life when he shows his masculinity through mastery of his own desires and by not yielding to the attacks of women, he continues in the central masculine roles as the father of a house and as husband, i.e. as sexually dominant within the relationship with a non-man. He is active in public life and takes up power and responsibility in the city as behoves a real man, i.e. he is an example of the masculinity of the responsible citizen. Thus, there are no lasting or deeper tensions in his masculinity.

Although it is impossible to imagine the original audience of *Jos. Asen.* as a company of would-be rulers over all Egypt, it is easy to imagine them as persons who, like Joseph, marry, raise children, relate to the Gentiles of the neighbourhood and, if they are men, take responsibility for their community. Joseph is an example of piety and masculinity who should be followed by the individual (male) members of the audience. There is no conflict between faithfully following the laws of the God of Israel and being a Real Man in the sense given to that expression by non-Jews. *Jos. Asen.*

may reflect the ethics of a community, which regards a strict sexual ethics as a central element of a life lived in accordance with God's will.[80]

Jos. Asen. also deals with collective identity, i.e. with the identity of the Jewish community. The story treats themes, such as intermarriage and conversion, that are intimately connected with the identity of the community and its relationships to others. The story can therefore also be read as a story about Us *vs* Them, the Others.[81] Joseph shows how distance can be kept to the Others.[82] Still, this difference is not an ontological one, and it is therefore a difference that it is possible to overcome. Christoph Burchard emphasises how *Jos. Asen.* is not about an absolute dualism. Although the non-Jews are far from God, it is possible for each and every one of them to choose conversion, as Aseneth did, and thus to become members of the People of God.[83]

As mentioned, it is possible to understand Joseph as a personification of the Jewish community in a Hellenistic city.[84] It is worth asking whether Joseph, who guards his individual body against the Egyptian women, is an image of how the social body of the community guards itself against the dominant culture (Cf. *Jos. Asen.* B8:4–7/Ph.8:4–7).[85] This may be reinforced through *parthenos*: the intact body of the female virgin inspires meanings such as integrity and unbroken boundaries that are transferred to a man and then to the social body of the text's original audience. At the same time, Joseph is also a model to be followed for a community that accepts proselytes, under certain conditions and after proper procedures. *Jos. Asen.*, then, is a story that describes, or perhaps even produces, a collective identity.

This social body is aware that it is in central aspects different from the Gentiles, but it also shares central cultural values with the Gentiles and it is really good at keeping them.

---

[80] Here, we may have traces of a masculinity closer to the minority discourses of philosophers than to the popular discourses of masculinity as sexual domination.

[81] LARSSON, *Jews and Gentiles*.

[82] BURCHARD, "Joseph and Aseneth", in Charlesworth, *Pseudepigrapha*, 191.

[83] Cf. BURCHARD, "Joseph and Aseneth", in Charlesworth, *Pseudepigrapha*, 194; BURCHARD, "Importance", 108–109.

[84] Cf. COLLINS, *Athens and Jerusalem*, 236: "Joseph has an obvious representative role as the embodiment of the true (Jewish) religion."

[85] For the concepts "individual body – social body" see e.g MALINA, *New Testament World*, 157.

The Male *Parthenoi* in Revelation

A Move to a Different World

When we turn to Revelation, we enter a totally different world. In *Jos. Asen.*, the distance between the People of God and the Gentiles can be overcome by humans who decide to change their way of life and worship.[86] In the world of *Jos. Asen.* we are among well-to-do people who marry, have children and participate in the civic life of their societies. *Jos. Asen.* is certainly not an apocalyptic text.[87]

When we move to Revelation, we move to an apocalyptic text and an apocalyptic world, where dualisms are clear-cut and the entire cosmos is split between Us and Them, the Elect and the Condemned. The final struggle between God and the Forces of Evil is moving towards its climax. There is no place here for a peaceful life with family, politics and all the other small and great events of ordinary life. So, what does it mean to describe literary characters as men and as *parthenoi* when creating such a world?[88]

Rev 14:1–5 within Revelation as a Whole

The rhetorical and mythopoetical language of Revelation is a language in which every element evokes many meanings, even logically contradictory meanings, which interplay with one another, and which reach their audience at levels deeper than the rational mind.[89] With Elisabeth Schüssler Fiorenza, I read Revelation as a poetic work, which invites its audience to participate in its imagined world, and as a rhetorical work that aims at changing the audience's attitudes and motivations.[90]

---

[86] Cf. BURCHARD, "Joseph and Aseneth", in Charlesworth, *Pseudepigrapha*, 194, BURCHARD, "Importance", 108–109.

[87] Cf. BURCHARD, "Joseph and Aseneth", in Charlesworth, *Pseudepigrapha*, 194, BURCHARD, "Importance", 108–109.

[88] There are so many understandings of the structure of Revelation, the place of 14:1–5 in that structure and of the images in 14:1–5, that a survey of all possible readings and a full argumentation to support my readings would take all the space I have here and more. For surveys of possible interpretations and my arguments see. STENSTRÖM, *Liberation or Backlash?*, 66–97. See also AUNE, *Revelation*, 794–796, 803–823.

[89] So e.g. Elisabeth SCHÜSSLER FIORENZA, *The Book of Revelation: Justice and Judgment* (Philadelphia: Fortress Press, 1985), 183–186; cf. HUBER, "Sexually Explicit?", 7–8 on reading the metaphorical language of Revelation.

[90] SCHÜSSLER FIORENZA, *Justice and Judgment*, 187.

Taking Rev 14:1–5 as a key text for the constructions of Christian identity[91] in Revelation is motivated by the central place of this passage in the
structure of the Book; it is a central text in the central section of Revelation (Rev 12–14).

In Rev 14:1–5, the 144,000 followers of the Lamb are envisioned as a
contrast to the followers of the Beast in Rev 13.[92] 14:1–5 makes clear to
the audience that they have to decide: either "worship the anti-divine
forces embodied by Rome" or "worship God and follow the Lamb."[93] In
other words, Rev 14:1–5 is a text about Us in contrast to Them, the Others
– and thereby a text about Christian identity.[94]

Rev 14:1–5 uses the purity language that is basic in the construction of
the world in Revelation.[95] It is a well-integrated part of the rhetorics in
Revelation and of the feminine and sexual imagery.[96] The fundamental
dualism between the Evil Empire of the world that is, and the New World
that is to come, is described in Revelation with the dichotomy of Whore
and Bride. The Whore and the Bride have their allies among humans, who
resemble them. Those who have sided with Evil, the Others, are *pornoi,* as
the Evil Empire is a *pornē.* Therefore, it is fully logical that the Good ones,
the We, are *parthenoi.*

---

[91] I understand "the 144,000" as a description of all Christians, not as an elite within
the Christian communities, (i.e. not as, for example, ascetics in contrast to ordinary married persons). The number "144,000", 12x12,000, suggests that they are described as the
People of God, True Israel, and thereby as all Christians. Those "all Christians" were in
fact most probably a small group within the Christian communities in Asia Minor who
regarded themselves as the only true Christians (or whatever name they used for themselves) in a world of apostates, as is evidenced by Rev 2–3. With such a self-
understanding, it is possible to describe all Christians with images of total commitment
and very radical demands. See STENSTRÖM, *Liberation or Backlash?,* 70; HUBER "Sexually Explicit?", 4 (who assumes that the 144,000 is the New Israel, with references), 27
note 6–8 to 45.

[92] For a careful analysis of Rev 14:1–5 in the context of Revelation as a whole, see
SCHÜSSLER FIORENZA, *Justice and Judgment,* 188–192.

[93] SCHÜSSLER FIORENZA, *Justice and Judgment,* 191.

[94] This approach must be possible to combine with the approach formulated in HU-
BER, "Sexually Explicit?", 3: the audience is provided with "a series of images with
which to imagine its identity, including that of a multitude of male virgins." See also
HUBER, "Sexually Explicit?, 4–5, for a reading of Rev 14:1–5 that I am willing to make
my own.

[95] STENSTRÖM, *Liberation or Backlash?,* 83–88, 95–97; HUBER, "Sexually Explicit?",
17.

[96] For a more detailed presentation see STENSTRÖM, *Liberation or Backlash?,* 88–97. I
acknowledge my general indebtedness to other studies of the rhetoric of gender in Revelation, especially PIPPIN, *Death and Desire.*

The uses of *pornoi* and *parthenoi* lead to associations to those biblical texts in which lack of fidelity to the covenant with God is described as adultery or promiscuity, although usually with a woman as subject, since sexual exclusivity was required of women.[97] Negative meanings of femininity are thus transferred to the Others. In addition, since they are *deiloi* (Rev 21:8), the *pornoi* can be understood as lacking in masculine virtues.[98]

No treatment of Rev 14:1–5 is really complete without some comments on Rev 7:1–8 and 7:9–17. That 14:1–5 is the second vision of the 144,000 strengthens the impression that they are an important element in Revelation as a whole, and a more developed analysis must read the two visions together in order to show how they complement one another. However, there is no space here for such an analysis. It must just suffice to say that I understand Rev 7:1–8, 7:9–17 and 14:1–5 as three complementary visions[99] "with which the audience can imagine its identity."[100]

The 144,000 as Masculine and as Parthenoi

The 144,000 are described as a company of men. The masculine grammatical form may be understood as inclusive of women and men, but the contrast with "women" in Rev 14:4 makes this understanding improbable.[101] This suggests that the construction of Christian identity in Revelation is androcentric.[102]

The self-control exercised by the 144,000 and their refusal to be dominated by those threatening women makes them masculine. At the same time, being *parthenos* is not compatible with being masculine in the dominant discourses of masculinity in the Roman Empire at the end of the 1st Century CE.

Thus, there are tensions in the description of the 144,000, which can be described as a tension between the 144,000 as active (read: masculine) –

---

[97] For a discussion of this reading see HUBER, "Sexually Explicit?", 6–8.

[98] Chris FRILINGOS, "Sexing the Lamb", in Moore and Anderson, *New Testament Masculinities*, 297–317, here 307.

[99] Thus, all three visions refer to the same group, "the Christians" to use our terminology, not to two or three different groups. For a survey of the discussion of the relation between the three texts with references see e,g. AUNE, *Revelation*, 440–447, 796, for my own arguments for reading them as sketched above and references to other scholars see STENSTRÖM, *Liberation or Backlash?*, 81–82. See also HUBER, "Sexually Explicit?", 27, note 7 to p. 5.

[100] HUBER, "Sexually Explicit?", 3.

[101] So e.g. ØKLAND, "Sex, gender", 132–138; STENSTRÖM, *Liberation or Backlash?*, 71–72; STENSTRÖM, "New Voices", 87.

[102] So e.g. HUBER, "Sexually Explicit?", 16.

they actively follow the Lamb (14:4b) – and passive (read: feminine):[103] they are bought (14:3c, 4c), they are described as sacrificial animals (14:5b).[104] However, it is possible to argue that positive meanings of femininity are also activated. Meanings of *parthenos* as self-containment and integrity fit in a context in which the 144,000 are described with imagery that speaks of utmost commitment; they carry the name of the Lamb and his Father on their foreheads to show to whom they belong (14:1), they follow the Lamb wherever he goes (14:4b), they have not lied (14:5), they are blameless (14:5).

Therefore, we do not find a clear case of gender-bending, with males turned female, although there are tendencies in that direction. Some recent works draw attention to the masculinity of the 144,000.[105] Three main alternatives have emerged.

The first alternative emphasizes the masculinity of the 144,000. It takes into account that they are described as *parthenoi*, but it does not explore the possible tensions between being a man – being a *parthenos*.

This alternative can be found in works by Moore and Frilingos.[106] When reading Revelation as a text about the Messianic War, Moore comments on the 144,000. He assumes (the traditional exegetical hypothesis) that the description of the 144,000 as *parthenoi* is an exaggerated version of the claim that soldiers in the Holy War should abstain temporarily from sexual

---

[103] ØKLAND, "Miss Jerusalem", 331–332: "Knowing that femininity is usually lurking somewhere just under the surface of the term παρθένος, the use of this term on men is a bit queer ... these 144,000 are not their own ... They are described as firstfruits and as blameless, like appropriate but powerless victims bought for animal sacrifice in the heavenly Temple. In this way, then, their masculinity does not imply any kind of control over the discourse."

[104] For this interpretation of *amōmoi* see e.g. AUNE, *Revelation*, 823. Even *aparchē* in 14:4c can be interpreted as sacrificial language, although this is contested. For surveys of different possible interpretations of *aparchē* with references see e.g. STENSTRÖM, *Liberation or Backlash?*, 75; AUNE, *Revelation*, 814–818.

[105] For a survey of feminist exegesis of Revelation see Hanna STENSTRÖM, "Feminists in Search for a Usable Future: Feminist Reception of the Book of Revelation" (forthcoming 2008 in William John Lyons and Jorunn Økland (eds.), *The Way the World Ends? The Apocalypse of John in Culture and Ideology* (The Bible in the Modern World 18; Sheffield: Sheffield Phoenix Press).

[106] See FRILINGOS, "Sexing", 307, for a reference to Stephen D. MOORE, "Revolting Revelations" in *The Personal Voice in Biblical Interpretation* (ed. Ingrid Rosa Kitzberger; London: Routledge, 1998), 183–199, esp. 193, where we find the same reading of Revelation 14:1–5 as the one mentioned in note 110. See also Chris FRILINGOS, "Wearing it Well: Gender at Work in the Shadow of the Empire" in: Penner and Vander Stichele (eds.), *Mapping*, 333–349, for a reading of Revelation concerned with masculinity that is not immediately relevant for my article.

relations.[107] The Holy War is "conducted by exclusively male subjects (note the notorious 14:4) and is constitutive of the masculinity of those subjects, since it is ultimately directed against the feminine (note again, the no less infamous 17:3–6)."[108]

Thus, Moore argues that the 144,000 represent an archaic masculinity, the masculinity of the soldier. Since being *parthenoi* is an integral part of being soldiers in the Holy War, it rather reinforces their masculinity.[109]

In "Sexing the Lamb" Frilingos argues, that the influence of certain Roman understandings of masculinity connected with "(s)toicizing ethics,"[110] in which self-control is central, was strong in the understanding of both the saved and the condemned in Revelation.[111] This is evident in 14:4: the 144,000 have not lost their self-control and they have not defiled themselves with women.

The second alternative explores the relationship between the 144,000 being men and being *parthenoi*, emphasising the instability of their masculinity, and their feminine traits. This alternative is represented by Pippin,[112] Økland[113] and by my own earlier works.[114]

Huber also makes the ambiguity of the gender of the 144,000 clear: although they are described as *parthenoi*, a word that normally refers to young women and girls, they are not "womanish" in the sense of "soft, weak": rather, they are strong and steadfast in times of turmoil, and maybe also during persecution (Rev 1:9; 2:2–3; 13:10; 14:12).[115]

To give justice to this ambiguity, Huber formulates a third alternative: the 144,000 male *parthenoi* represent an alternative masculinity, along the lines sketched by Boyarin, for later Christian ascetics. As part of the anti-imperial rhetoric in Revelation, they reject the dominant imperial dis-

---

[107] On this interpretation with references see STENSTRÖM, *Liberation or Backlash?*, 73.

[108] Stephen D. MOORE, *God's Beauty Parlour and Other Queer Spaces in and Around the Bible* (Conversions; Stanford: Stanford University Press, 2001), 186 and n 18, p. 270.

[109] Another possible understanding of Rev 14:4a is that it is an exaggeration of the rules for temporary sexual abstention of Priests in the Temple in Jerusalem. The 144,000 are here still in a masculine role, and the tensions in their identity are reinforced; they are both priests and sacrifices. Some scholars combine a "priestly" interpretation with an understanding of the 144,000 as soldiers. See STENSTRÖM, *Liberation or Backlash?*, 73, for a short survey of works proposing such interpretations.

[110] FRILINGOS, "Sexing", 298

[111] FRILINGOS, "Sexing", 298–99.

[112] Tina PIPPIN, *Apocalyptic Bodies: The Biblical End of the World in Text and Image* (London: Routledge, 1999), 117–25, esp. 121.

[113] ØKLAND, "Miss Jerusalem", 331–332.

[114] STENSTRÖM, *Liberation or Backlash?*, 65–97; STENSTRÖM, "New Voices", 88–89.

[115] HUBER, "Sexually Explicit?", 17–18.

courses of masculinity, especially the masculinity of the father and the husband.[116] Thus, Huber's reading has the advantage of integrating gender analysis with analysis of the anti-imperial rhetoric of Revelation.

In my opinion, the second and the third alternative are the most interesting, since they take the possible tensions between being masculine and being *parthenos* seriously.

Conclusions

While the masculinity of a man described as a *parthenos* in *Jos. Asen.* is in line with commonly assumed values of its time and culture, the masculinity of the 144,000 is more complex.

It is possible to argue, with Moore, that they are masculine, and that their masculinity is the archaic masculinity of the soldier. However far Revelation is from the masculinity of good citizens and philosophers, it is also possible to argue that the 144,000 are masculine in terms of self-control: they have not yielded to their own desires, nor to the attacks by women.[117] They are not dominated by others (except by God). They are virtuous in contrast to the condemned.

But this is not the whole story. It is difficult to imagine that the original audience did not see a tension between being *parthenos* – being masculine, since this is a contradiction in terms in the dominant discourses of masculinity. Furthermore, the passivity of the 144,000 is a feminine, not a masculine, characteristic. Thus, their masculine traits are in tension with feminine traits, expressed by imagery that evades all attempts to pinpoint its precise meanings.

In my opinion, there are (at least) two ways to handle the complex mix of femininity and masculinity.

First, the reader can stay in the world of the text and understand the 144,000 as characters in the story, who can be described as if they were persons. In such a reading, the 144,000 are really masculine in relation to other humans and to everyone and everything that is against God. They become who they are through keeping themselves away from and undefiled by women. They are the soldiers who fight the Holy War.

At the same time, they also relate to God. In relation to God, they are passive *parthenoi,* who relate to God as an ideal woman to her male head. They are examples to be followed, whatever this might mean in practice.

Secondly, we may read Rev 14:1–5 as an example of the imagery of Revelation. The audience is challenged to choose between the Beast and

---

[116] HUBER, "Sexually Explicit?", 4, 8, 15–21.

[117] Here, I and HUBER, "Sexually Explicit?", 18, have reached the same conclusion independently of one another.

the Lamb. To follow the Lamb is made attractive by the use of imagery through which many possible meanings are opened and interact with one another, including a play with images that can be described as feminine, as representations of an archaic masculinity and as representions of an alternative masculinity.

To summarise: I do not make a definitive choice of one understanding of the 144,000 as men and as *parthenoi* in Rev 14:4 rather than of another; it is the many possible meanings that are the strength of the text.[118]

It is not easy to imagine what concrete practices would have followed when an audience understood its identity, as a collective and maybe even as individuals, through the images in Rev 14:1–5. Asceticism is a possibility, but we cannot know for sure.[119] The 144,000 *parthenoi,* who successfully guard the boundaries of their bodies, may be understood as images of a group that guards of the boundaries of its social body, the community, but we cannot know for sure what this meant in practice.

Final Reflections

Scholarship on *Joseph and Aseneth* and Revelation has often seen the use of *parthenos* with reference to men as an oddity that is difficult to interpret meaningfully. I hope that I have shown how contemporary gender studies, which focus mainly on masculinity, contributes to such interpretations, and show that this unusual use of *parthenos* can actually be a useful tool in the construction of early Jewish and early Christian identity.

---

[118] Cf. HUBER, "Sexually Explicit?", 9.
[119] Cf. HUBER, "Sexually Explicit?", 16.

Parousia as Medicine: A Postcolonial Perspective on Mark and Christian Identity Construction

Hans Leander

In 1896, during the hey-days of Western colonialism, a commentary on the Gospel of Mark (hereafter abbreviated Mk) was published. The author was Ezra P. Gould, a well respected American exegete. According to the reviewer, the commentary met the need in the English-speaking world of a "thorough, scholarly, up-to-date" commentary. Gould's commentary "surpasses all others".[1] Commenting on the pericope about Jesus' entering Jerusalem on a colt (Mark 11:1–11), Gould states that although Jesus hereby claims to be a king, it does not change the direction of his "merely spiritual work". Admitting an ostensible inconsistency, Gould claims that the key is to be found in "the splendid self-consistency of Jesus' procedure, and in its absolute inconsistency with worldly ideas and policies." Jesus would use "absolutely only spiritual means". Hence, the kingship of Jesus "did not interfere with the state".[2]

A little more than one hundred years later, in 2001, another work on Mk was published, written by Richard A. Horsley, American exegete as well. Horsley reads the same pericope about Jesus entry into the ruling city and its temple and finds that the "Hosanna"-cries are recitations of the Hallel psalms (Pss 113–118), that alludes strongly to the exodus. Consequently, he finds that Mk here presents Jesus as confronting the "Roman-sponsored Jerusalem rulers in a way reminiscent of the exodus" – exodus being a memory of "liberation from oppressive foreign rule".[3]

While Gould interprets the Markan Jesus as not challenging Roman colonialism at all, Horsley makes the opposite interpretation. Two biblical interpreters with much in common – working in highly respected universities, historical-critically oriented, living privileged lives in the centre of global empires – are nevertheless in total disagreement about how Mk re-

---

[1] Clyde Weber VOTAW, review of Ezra P. Gould, A Critical and Exegetical Commentary on the Gospel According to St. Mark, BW 8 (1896)

[2] Ezra P. GOULD, *A Critical and Exegetical Commentary on the Gospel According to St. Mark* (Edinburgh: T&T Clark, 1969), 206, 284.

[3] Richard A. HORSLEY, *Hearing the Whole Story: The Politics of Plot in Mark's Gospel* (Louisville: Westminster John Knox Press, 2001), 109–110.

lates to the colonizing power of its time. Is the Markan Jesus then either a pro- or anti-colonial character? Or are there other possibilities? Such questions – crucial for understanding early Christian identity – point to a number of interrelated developments within biblical studies in the last hundred years, such as the social context turn[4] and the growing awareness of the importance of the reader's location[5] in all textual interpretation. Most of all, however, it actualizes a growing interest among biblical scholars for the relationship between the New Testament and its Roman imperial context.

Since the work of Adolf Deissmann[6] in the beginning of the 20th century, the subject of the New Testament and the Roman Empire has been largely neglected. Scholars have focused instead on the relationship between Christianity and its parent, Judaism. Recent years, however, have seen renewed interest in the subject, signified among other things by a whole issue of the *Journal for the Study of the New Testament* being devoted to the imperial culture and the New Testament. In the introduction, David G. Horrell draws two conclusions from the articles in the issue: 1) The Roman imperial culture is without doubt an important part of the reality, in which the first Christians lived. It is necessary to study this culture in order to understand the texts. 2) The New Testament alludes in different ways to Roman imperial ideology. However, this does not necessarily mean that all texts should be read straightforwardly as "anti-imperial". Surely there are such rival elements, yet "the various ways in which this material echoes, parallels, or opposes Roman claims, combine to require rather more nuanced and subtle analyses".[7] And as argued by a growing

---

[4] "The social context turn" is one of several terms that could be used to describe an interest among biblical scholars for the social and cultural contexts of Jesus and the New Testament writings. See for instance Bengt HOLMBERG, *Sociology and the New Testament: An Appraisal* (Minneapolis: Fortress Press, 1990); John Hall ELLIOTT, *What is Social-Scientific Criticism?* (Minneapolis: Fortress Press, 1993); Wolfgang STEGEMANN, Bruce J. MALINA and Gerd THEISSEN, *The Social Setting of Jesus and the Gospels* (Minneapolis, MN: Fortress Press, 2002).

[5] The hermeneutical development from Schleiermacher, Gadamer, and Ricoeur to the poststructuralists, can be seen as a shift of focus from the author to the reader. For biblical interpretation, that highlights the importance of the social location of the interpreter, see for instance Fernando F. SEGOVIA and Mary Ann TOLBERT, *Reading from this Place* (2 vols.; Minneapolis: Fortress Press, 1995).

[6] Adolf DEISSMANN, *Light from the Ancient East; the New Testament Illustrated by Recently Discovered Texts of the Graeco-Roman World* (New York: Baker Book House, 1978).

[7] David G. HORRELL, "Introduction," *JSNT* 27 (2005), 255.

number of biblical scholars, such analyses are significantly enhanced and deepened by the perspective offered by postcolonial criticism.[8] Since this is a relatively new and emerging area of literary and cultural study, I will give a short introduction to postcolonial criticism, including its contribution to the understanding of identity formation. I will then analyze, from a postcolonial perspective, how Mk relates to the colonizing power at the time. After a brief look at the Markan beginning (1.1), the main part of this article will be devoted to an analysis of a saying by the Markan Jesus in which he foretells his return in glory (8:31), the so called parousia.

A Postcolonial Perspective on Biblical Interpretation

As Anna Runesson has argued, "the postcolonial world" is a better term than "the global village" by which to describe our present time, since the latter tends to hide the power relations, which stems from the Western colonial enterprises, and which still affect us in many ways.[9] Runesson also clarifies the term "postcolonial" in important ways. First, since colonialism goes a long way back in history, the term is not limited to the present situation. She defines colonization as the creation of power relations, in which one or several nations constitute the centre and the others are periphery. For my purposes, it is important to note that, with this definition, the Roman Empire was a colonial power that included vast geographical areas from 100 BCE until 500 CE Secondly, Runesson clarifies that "post" does not simply mean "after" in the sense that the colonial era is over. Rather, a postcolonial situation is always constituted by a relation to colonialism and its long lasting effects, including neocolonization. It consists of the conse-

---

[8] Some of the most important are Laura E. DONALDSON, ed., *Postcolonialism and Scriptural Reading* (Semeia 75; Atlanta: Society of Biblical Literature, 1996); Musa W. DUBE, *Postcolonial Feminist Interpretation of the Bible* (St. Louis: Chalice, 2000); Fernando F. SEGOVIA and Stephen D. MOORE, eds., *Postcolonial Biblical Criticism: Interdisciplinary Intersections* (The Bible and Postcolonialism; Edinburgh: T&T Clark, 2005); R. S. SUGIRTHARAJAH, ed., *The Postcolonial Biblical Reader* (Oxford: Blackwell, 2006); Kwok PUI-LAN, *Postcolonial Imagination and Feminist Theology* (London: SCM Press, 2005); Stephen D. MOORE, *Empire and Apocalypse: Postcolonialism and the New Testament* (Sheffield: Sheffield Phoenix Press, 2006).

[9] Anna RUNESSON, "Kontextuell exegetik i en postkolonial värld: Bibeltolkning i dagens Indien," in *Varför ser ni mot himlen? Utmaningar från den kontextuella teologin* (ed. Runesson and Sjöholm; Stockholm: Verbum; Institutet för kontextuell teologi, 2006), 122–149, 123–124.

quences of, and the reactions against, the colonization.[10] Therefore, the postcolonial condition occurs both during and after the colonization. Another term for the postcolonial condition is "postcoloniality"[11]. This is not to be confused with the more narrow term "postcolonial criticism" or "postcolonialism"[12], which refers to the academic field that has developed in the aftermath of the Western colonization and decolonization.

Although Runesson's map of the postcolonial research field helps to clarify the usage of terms, it leaves out the extensive debates that are characteristic of the postcolonial field. For instance, some would argue that postcolonialism is a kind of neocolonialism, where the so called Third World supplies raw material that is refined by French philosophy into luxury products in the First World, in order to be re-exported as theory to the Third World.[13] Obviously, postcolonialism is a highly contested interdisciplinary field of research and my presentation here does not attempt to be all-embracing.[14]

One of the foundational texts for postcolonial criticism is Edward Said's *Orientalism* from 1978, in which he explored the knowledge about the "Orient" that was produced in Europe, and how that knowledge functioned as an ideological accompaniment of the Western colonial enterprises. Rather than describing non-Western cultures as such, Said showed how these cultures were presented in the West, especially in the human disciplines such as history, philology, anthropology, philosophy, archaeology, and literature. This academic research constituted, together with key literal and cultural texts, certain ways of seeing and thinking – i.e. a discourse – that made the European colonization of the Near East possible. By this discourse, he argued, the West constructed the Orient as something essentially different and imbued it with degrading notions, thereby creating an image of "the Other". By this discourse, Western identity was formed in contrast to that of the Orientals.

---

[10] RUNESSON, "Kontextuell exegetik," 125. Cf Ania LOOMBA, *Kolonialism/Postkolonialism: en introduktion till ett forskningsfält* (trans. Söderlind; Stockholm: Tankekraft, 2006), 23–37.

[11] Cf. the term "postmodernity".

[12] The term "postcolonialism" might imply a kind of unified ideology and is therefore avoided by some critics. I use it here as a synonym to "postcolonial criticism" or "postcolonial theory".

[13] Aijaz AHMAD, *In Theory: Classes, Nations, Literatures* (London: Verso, 1994). Cf. Bart J. MOORE-GILBERT, *Postcolonial Theory: Contexts, Practices, Politics* (London: Verso, 1997), 17–19.

[14] There are many good introductions, such as LOOMBA, *Kolonialism/Postkolonialism*; Leela GANDHI, *Postcolonial Theory: A Critical Introduction* (Edinburgh: Edinburgh University Press, 1998); MOORE-GILBERT, *Postcolonial Theory*.

For a Biblical scholar, Said's mention of the historical-critical revolution in biblical research is particularly interesting. According to Said, historical-critical pioneers, such as Bishop Robert Lowth, Johann Gottfried Eichhorn, Johann Gottfried von Herder, and Johann David Michaelis, stood for one of the most important impulses to the study of the Orient during the eighteenth century.[15] These scholars are often seen as liberators of biblical research from narrow Church doctrine towards a neutral and scientific study of the origin and meaning of the biblical text.[16] However, as postcolonial critics typically argue, the liberation was far from unambiguous. The historical-critical studies of the biblical texts became part of the wider discourse of orientalizing the East. This thread is picked up by Kwok Pui-lan. Working with the binary opposition between "native" and "master" she shows how the quest for the historical Jesus was an important part of the construction of the Christian European identity as rational and historical, compared to the myth-believing "natives". Here, "natives" could mean people in the European colonies as well as people in Palestine at the time of Jesus. So the historical critical method, she maintains, was in fact embedded in the "cultural space and political configurations" of the nineteenth century and closely connected to European colonialism.[17]

Said calls this way of relating texts to their contemporary discourses *contrapuntal reading* and explains it as an analysis "of intertwined and overlapping histories".[18] In biblical studies, this is often done in the sense that biblical texts are placed in their historical social contexts. What Said and Pui-lan shows is, however, that biblical interpreters and *their* texts are also part of a particular social location and of particular discourses. Therefore, postcolonial biblical criticism often implies an interest in the reception of biblical texts – particularly in the relationship of this reception to colonial enterprises.

In line with this, it is interesting to look briefly again at Gould's interpretation of the Markan Jesus, who, he claimed, was absolutely inconsis-

---

[15] Edward W. SAID, *Orientalism* (New York: Pantheon Books, 1978), 17.

[16] Samuel BYRSKOG, "Nya testamentets forskningshistoria," in *Jesus och de första kristna: Inledning till Nya testamentet* (ed. Mitternacht and Runesson; Stockholm: Verbum, 2007), 34–35.

[17] Kwok PUI-LAN uses the Foucaultian "episteme" to designate this cultural space, see her article "Jesus/the Native: Biblical Studies from a Postcolonial Perspective," in *Teaching the Bible: The Discourses and Politics of Biblical Pedagogy* (ed. Tolbert and Segovia; Maryknoll: Orbis, 1998), 80.

[18] Edward W. SAID, *Culture and Imperialism* (London: Chatto & Windus, 1993), 18. The term "contrapuntal" is an adjective of the noun "counterpoint" that is used in music theory for the art of writing or playing a melody or melodies in conjunction with another, according to fixed rules. PUI-LAN calls it "parallel processing", in "Jesus/the Native," 80–81.

tent with worldly ideas and policies. Jesus used "absolutely only spiritual means" and did not interfere at all with the colonizing power. Anyone acquainted with social-scientific approaches to biblical studies would probably disagree with the application of the spiritual-worldly binary to a text from antiquity. As has been shown, such a division is modern and does not correspond to the society in which Mk was written.[19] Moreover, Gould's interpretation can also be read contrapuntally (with Said) to the European colonizing discourse, especially to Christian mission. By reading missionary magazines from this time, one finds that the binary opposition between spiritual and worldly was part of an identity construction, by which many churches took part in the colonial enterprises.[20] The same binary perspective therefore affected, not only how Mk was read, but also how Christian identity was constructed in the Western empire. Paradoxically, the allegedly scientific and unbiased interest of biblical scholars in the ancient and "original" context was highly selective and bore the stamp of the researchers' location and identity.

So, when postcolonialism is applied to biblical studies, a criticism is delivered against the historical-critical paradigm. One point of critique concerns the exclusive priority given to the meaning of the biblical text in its original setting. Some scholars therefore draw the problematic conclusion that the historical situation more or less needs to be left out. Even when avoiding such extremes, a postcolonial perspective still implies studying the text in different settings, not only the ancient one, and to analyze how it has been part of, as well as resisted, colonial discourses. Further, postcolonial criticism invites us to examine how the Bible is read as both part of and resistance against today's (mostly U.S.) discourses of domination. Another point of the criticism concerns the claims of neutrality and objectivity that comes with the historical-critical paradigm. These claims, the postcolonial critics argue, should be understood as expressions of Western hegemony.[21]

Said's seminal project initiated a wide debate and critique.[22] Among other things, Said was criticized for being one-sided in his description of

---

[19] See for instance Bruce J. MALINA, *The Social Gospel of Jesus: The Kingdom of God in Mediterranean Perspective* (Minneapolis: Fortress Press, 2001).

[20] H. W. TOTTIE, "De kristnas förpligtelser i fråga om missionsarbetet ibland hedningarne (2 Mos. 17:8–13)," *Missions-Tidning* 10 (1885).

[21] This is argued persuasively by Anna RUNESSON, "Exegesis in the Making: The Theoretical Location and Contribution of Postcolonial New Testament Studies" (Licentiate Thesis, Lund University, 2007).

[22] For a good review of the critique against Orientalism, see LOOMBA, *Kolonialism/ Postkolonialism*, 63–64. See also Edward W. SAID, Anne BEEZER and Peter OSBORNE, "Efter Orientalism: Edward Said intervjuad av Anne Beezer och Peter Osborne," in *Glo-

the colonizing enterprise unilaterally as an expression of the dominant's will to power, thereby ignoring the self-representations of the colonized. The debate after Said therefore brought forth an intense interest in the relationship between the master and the native, the colonizer and the colonized, and it has generated a number of concepts that are of great interest for the interpretation of the New Testament and the understanding of early Christian identity.[23] Here I will briefly introduce some postcolonial concepts developed by Gayatri Spivak and Homi Bhabha.[24]

Anyone acquainted with the writings of Derrida will recognize his thoughts as an important background for both Spivak and Bhabha. Not least Derrida's deconstructive reading of texts, his demonstrations of the impossibility of establishing stable meanings, and his fascination with the ambiguous have had a strong impact on many postcolonial scholars. As an example, in his famous essay "Plato's Pharmacy", Derrida examines a passage of the Phaedrus, in which the god Theuth offers king Thamus the gift of writing – as a medicine for wisdom and memory. But the king rejects it as poison and claims that it will bring false wisdom and no real memory. Derrida's essay then discusses the confusion that stems from the ambiguous Greek word *pharmakon*, which can mean both "medicine" and "poison".[25] This metaphor of medicine and poison has become a frequently used symbol of the ambiguity of the postcolonial situation, and in particular of the experience that resistance tends to turn into repression.

Spivak's seminal essay "Can the subaltern speak?"[26] highlights her constant struggle to look for the marginalized, to ask whose voices are heard and whose are silent. She has contributed in a critical appreciation to the subaltern studies of the collective by historians, who wanted to rewrite the

---

baliseringens kulturer: den postkoloniala paradoxen, rasismen och det mångkulturella samhället (ed. Eriksson, Eriksson Baaz, and Thörn; Nora: Nya Doxa, 1999).

[23] The underlying assumption is that the master-native relationship has many similarities in Roman and European colonization. For a justification to apply postcolonial criticism to the study of the New Testament, see Fernando F. SEGOVIA, "Biblical Criticism and Postcolonial Studies: Toward a Postcolonial Optic," in *Postcolonial Biblical Reader* (ed. Sugirtharajah; Oxford: Blackwell, 2006) and Fernando F. SEGOVIA, "Mapping the Postcolonial Optic in Biblical Criticism: Meaning and Scope," in *Postcolonial Biblical Criticism: Interdisciplinary Intersections* (ed. Moore and Segovia; The Bible and Postcolonialism; Edinburgh: T&T Clark, 2005).

[24] Said, Spivak and Bhabha are often referred to as the "postcolonial troika".

[25] Jacques DERRIDA, *Dissemination* (Chicago: Univ. of Chicago Press, 1981).

[26] Gayatri Chakravorty SPIVAK, "Can the Subaltern Speak?," in *Marxism and the Interpretation of Culture* (ed. Nelson and Grossberg; Communications and Culture; Houndmills: Macmillan Education, 1988). To summarize Spivak's work is a difficult task. Her style is often described as "fractured", "rough" and "unfinished", see MOORE-GILBERT, *Postcolonial Theory*, 74.

history of colonial India from below.[27] Related to this is her concept *cata-chresis*, with which she has become associated.[28] Originally it was a Greek term from the field of rhetoric, where it denotes "the misapplication of a word".[29] In Spivak's writing, however, catachresis assumes the extended meaning of a concept-metaphor without an adequate referent. This enables her to understand the postcolonial relationship to Western ideas in a new and challenging way. Concepts, such as nationhood, constitutionality, citizenship, and democracy are all coded within the legacy of imperialism, and hence they lack adequate referents in a decolonized context. As Spivak argues, they are "reclaimed, indeed claimed, as concept-metaphors for which no historically adequate referent may be advanced from postcolonial space".[30] For Spivak then, catachresis marks a local, linguistic tact, performed in the (post)colonial margins, that involves twisting particular ideas or rhetorical practices out of their place within a colonial discourse and using them to open up new arenas of meaning, quite different from their conventionally understood meanings and functions.[31]

Coming from more of a psychoanalytic perspective, Homi Bhabha has developed concepts with a similar meaning by which to understand the elusive relationship between the colonizer and the colonized. Bhabha's work builds to a large extent on Fanon, whose psychological descriptions of this relationship constitute one of Bhabha's main sources for claiming that the process of colonization was far from a unilateral enterprise, in which one part simply exercised power over the other.

One of his concepts, hybridity, is developed from Fanon's claim that anti-colonial conditions are fundamentally unstable: The struggle against foreign domination, he claimed, "brings about essential mutations in the consciousness of the colonized".[32] As a telling and uncanny image, this mutation was picked up by Bhabha in the discourse on hybridity that has

---

[27] Gayatri Chakravorty SPIVAK, "Subaltern Studies: Deconstructing Historiography," in *The Spivak Reader: Selected works of Gayatri Chakravorty Spivak* (ed. Landry and MacLean; New York: Routledge, 1985).

[28] Cf Amitava KUMAR, "Catachresis is Her Middle Name: The Cautionary Claims of Gayatri C. Spivak," *CS* 11 (1997).

[29] Christopher BALDICK, "Catachresis", in *The Concise Oxford Dictionary of Literary Terms: Oxford Reference Online*, (Oxford University Press, 1996). Catachresis in its ordinary sense is a way to understand the development and change of language. For instance, the word "table legs" was from the beginning a catachresis (tables don't have legs) but is now a correct usage.

[30] Gayatri Chakravorty SPIVAK, "Poststructuralism, Marginality, Post-coloniality and Value," in *Literary Theory Today* (ed. Collier and Geyer-Ryan; Cambridge: Polity, 1990), 225.

[31] Cf. MOORE-GILBERT, *Postcolonial Theory*, 84.

[32] Frantz FANON, *A Dying Colonialism* (New York: Grove Press, 1965), 69.

gained prominence, not least in the discussions about postmodern identities.[33]

Related to hybridity is the concept of colonial ambivalence. When looking for traces of hybridity, Bhabha teaches us that we should look for tendencies towards identity shifts and dislocations, especially in settings of cultural crashes and conflicts. To analyze such relationships, Bhabha studies both literary works, such as *Heart of Darkness* and more interestingly, the reports from Christian missionaries. In these he finds "neither an untroubled, innocent dream of England nor a /.../ nightmare of India [or] Africa". And consequently he argues that "the colonial presence is always ambivalent, split between its appearance as original and authoritative and its articulation as repetition and difference".[34]

Closely related to this relationship of ambivalence and hybridity is the concept of mimicry.[35] The colonizers teach the colonized to behave according to the colonizer's "universal" culture. However, the imitation of the colonizers is never perfect. It is *"almost the same, but not quite"*.[36] Mimicry, in Bhabha's understanding, involves a constant slipping over into mockery. Rather than seeing this in a negative way as a sign of dependence, as Fanon did, Bhabha sees it as a type of ironic resistance. Mimicry destabilizes the colonial discourse, since it threatens the borderlines on which it rests. The power to discriminate is impossible without upholding certain borders. Hence, "mimicry is at once resemblance and menace" and "the effect of mimicry on the authority of colonial discourse is profound and disturbing".[37]

The colonial processes of ambivalence, hybridity and mimicry are interrelated and Bhabha connects the three concepts through the image of an interstitial "third space".[38] On the border between the colonizers and the colonized there are, because of these processes of simultaneous attraction and repulsion, constant dislocations of the given identity positions, which result in a space where new identities are negotiated. Characteristic of

---

[33] Homi BHABHA and Jonathan RUTHERFORD, "The Third Space: Interview with Homi Bhabha," in *Identity: Community, Culture, Difference* (ed. Rutherford; London: Lawrence & Wishart, 1990).

[34] Homi BHABHA, *The Location of Culture* (London: Routledge, 2004), 153.

[35] Bhabha imports this concept from Jacques Lacan, a French Freudian psychoanalyst with an interdisciplinary orientation. He illustrated his concept of psychic mimicry by comparing to biological defences of insects (i.e. a moth that has the same color as a wasp), Jacques LACAN and Jacques-Alain MILLER, *The Four Fundamental Concepts of Psycho-Analysis* (London: Hogarth, 1977), 98–100.

[36] BHABHA, *Location of Culture*, 122 (Bhabha's italics).

[37] BHABHA, *Location of Culture*, 123.

[38] BHABHA and RUTHERFORD, "Third Space".

Bhabha's thinking, this radically undermines any notions of identities or cultures as fixed and stable. The dialectical scheme of thesis, anti-thesis and synthesis inevitably comes to mind, but there are important differences. Whereas the dialectical scheme rests on the notion of original entities that collide (thesis and anti-theses), Bhabha refuses to admit of any such essentialist or original understanding of cultures. Rather, he understands all cultures as de-centred structures and involved in a constant process of hybridization. Therefore, the third space is not the same as a Hegelian synthesis, although there are similarities. In the third space, Bhabha argues, new representations can be formed that are not the linear result of previous historical categories, but rather "a new area of negotiation of meaning", that "displaces the histories that constitute it, and sets up new structures of authority, new political initiatives".[39]

Bhabha's understanding of identity resonates closely with discourse theory, according to which a subject acquires its identity by identifying with a subject position, conveyed by a discourse.[40] The subject's constant quest for identity positions is explained in terms of Lacan's psychoanalytical theory, as a combination of recognition and alienation. Moreover, there is usually more than one discourse present, which creates a competition or a combination of different subject positions. Hence, according to discourse theory, the subject becomes fragmented and overdetermined, which means that a given identity is contingent – "possible but not necessary".[41]

For my purposes, it is important to note that this understanding also includes formation of collective identities.[42] Of particular interest is the significance of representation in the development of a group identity. The existence of a particular group is not given beforehand, but rather as a result of its representation. A representation should therefore not be understood as the expression of an already existing group, but rather as constituting a particular group and its identity. With this discursive understanding of how a group identity is formed, Mk can be read as a text that *forms*, not just reflects, early Christian identity. As I now begin to read Mk in its colonial setting, I will try to locate its identity position in relation to the colonizing discourse.

---

[39] Bhabha and Rutherford, "Third Space," 211.
[40] Marianne WINTHER JÖRGENSEN and Louise PHILLIPS, *Diskursanalys som teori och metod* (Lund: Studentlitteratur, 2000), 48–51.
[41] WINTHER JÖRGENSEN and PHILLIPS, *Diskursanalys*, 51.
[42] WINTHER JÖRGENSEN and PHILLIPS, *Diskursanalys*, 51–54.

Mark and Colonialism: The Beginning as Mimicry

When it comes to Mk and how it relates to the Roman Empire, there are quite a few scholars who have addressed this issue, of which only a few have used an articulated postcolonial perspective.[43] Whereas previous works have tended to force the Markan story into the simple categories of either pro- or anti-Roman, the postcolonial perspective invites us to move beyond such binaries and rather to look for traces of ambiguity and hybridity. In order to see whether this perspective is at all applicable to Mk, I will do a brief postcolonial reading on the beginning of Mk, i.e. of the so-called Markan incipit.[44]

Mk begins with the pregnant phrase "The beginning of the gospel of Jesus Christ, the Son of God". Most probably, this should be read as an "in-

---

[43] The readings can be divided into four categories: 1) Mk as a pro-colonial gospel. This was first argued by Samuel George Frederick BRANDON, *Jesus and the Zealots: A Study of Political Factor in Primitive Christianity* (New York: Charles Scribner's Sons, 1967) who called Mk a "Roman apology", and later Hendrika Nicoline ROSKAM, *The Purpose of the Gospel of Mark in its Historical and Social Context* (Leiden; Boston: Brill, 2004). According to these readings, the purpose of Mk is to minimize Roman hostility and hence Jesus is dissociated from the Jewish nationalists and presented as cooperative towards the Roman government in Judea. 2) Mark as an anti-colonial gospel. There are several scholars that belong to this group: Fernando BELO, *A Materialist Reading of the Gospel of Mark* (Maryknoll, New York: Orbis Books, 1981); Ched MYERS, *Binding the Strong Man: A Political Reading of Mark's Story of Jesus* (Maryknoll: Orbis Books, 1988); Herman C. WAETJEN, *A Reordering of Power: A Sociopolitical Reading of Mark's Gospel* (Minneapolis: Fortress Press, 1989) and HORSLEY, *Hearing*. These scholars are generally oriented towards liberation theology and they read Mk as standing in clear opposition to the Roman empire. 3) Mark as a reproduction of colonial ideology. This category is represented by Tat-siong Benny LIEW, *Politics of Parousia: Reading Mark Inter(con)textually* (Leiden; Boston: Brill, 1999), who reads Mk and particularly the Markan parousia as a duplication of imperial ideology. See below. 4) Mark as a postcolonial gospel. Here, the focus is on the ambivalence, which is typical for the relationship between the colonizer and the colonized, see Simon SAMUEL, *A Postcolonial Reading of Mark's Story of Jesus* (London: T&T Clark, 2007) and Stephen D. MOORE, "Mark and Empire: 'Zealot' and 'Postcolonial' Readings," in *The Postcolonial Biblical Reader* (ed. Sugirtharajah; Malden, MA: Blackwell, 2006).

[44] This has been done by other scholars to whom I am indebted for this part. Especially valuable is the article by Simon SAMUEL, "The Beginning of Mark: A Colonial/Postcolonial Conundrum," *Biblical Interpretation* 10 (2002), 405–419. See also Craig A. EVANS, "Mark's Incipit and the Priene Calendar Inscription: From Jewish Gospel to Greco-Roman Gospel," *JGRCJ* 1 (2000) who finds that Mk is mimicking the language of the imperial cult while he proclaims to the Jewish people, at the same time, the fulfilment of their fondest hopes.

cipit", a brief phrase or a title that introduces the story.[45] Its meaning is crucial for the understanding of Mk as a whole, and if this phrase bears postcolonial traits, it is likely that the same could be said of Mk as a whole. All the words in the phrase are loaded with complex and diverse meaning. With the exception of "Jesus Christ" they all resemble both local Jewish and colonial Greco-Roman discourses.

"The beginning" (*archē*) has a wide range of meaning and could also signify "power" or "empire".[46] The analysis the *archē* (empire) of Rome, shows that its expansion, and especially its military victories, are often described as "gospel" (*euangelion*). In particular we can assume that the *euangelion* on peoples' mind at the time that Mk was written[47] was the ascension of Vespasian as emperor and the beginning of the Flavian dynasty. The Romans had been fighting two wars simultaneously – against the Batavian rebellion in the north and the Jewish war in the east – and the situation following Nero's death in 68 was therefore instable. The resolution of the crisis was manifested by Vespasian's victory in Jerusalem. After this victory, Josephus tells us, "every city kept festivals, and celebrated sacrifices and oblations for such good news (*euangelia*)".[48]

Stemming from the reign of Augustus, the emperor was often called "the Son of God" (*Theou huios*)[49] and was worshiped as such in the imperial cult. As shown by scholars of ancient history, the imperial cult was an integral part of Roman religion.[50] It had a remarkable ability to synthesize itself with local traditions in various subtle ways and thus to make the colonial religion permeate ordinary peoples' lives to a great extent. In this way, a religio-political discourse with a supernatural character, which defined and upheld the Roman Empire, was established. In many places of

---

[45] For an introduction to the different kinds of narrative beginnings and their importance in ancient literature, see Dennis E. SMITH, "Narrative Beginnings in Ancient Literature and Theory," *Semeia* 52 (1990), 4. See also Leander E. KECK, "Introduction to Mark's Gospel," *NTS* 12 (1966).

[46] Henry George LIDDELL and Robert SCOTT, *A Greek-English Lexicon: With a Supplement* (Oxford: Clarendon Press, 1968), 252.

[47] Like most Markan scholars, I assume Mk was written around year 70 CE.

[48] Josephus, *B.J.* 4.618, 656–657.

[49] Wilhelmus DITTENBERGER, ed., *Orientis Graeci Inscriptiones Selectae: Supplementum Sylloges Inscriptionum Graecarum* (2; Lipsiae, 1903–1905), inscr 328, 532, 659. See also Tae Hun KIM, "The Anarthrous yios theou in Mark 15,39 and the Roman Imperial Cult," *Biblica* 79 (1998) which gives many references to the use, mainly for Augustus, of the title Son of God in both Latin and Greek.

[50] James B. RIVES, *Religion in the Roman Empire* (Malden, MA: Blackwell Pub., 2007). Simon R. F. PRICE, *Rituals and Power: The Roman Imperial Cult in Asia Minor* (Cambridge: Cambridge U.P., 1984).

the empire, this discourse became a hegemony – the Pax Romana – that was upheld without the use of force.

From a Jewish point of view, the incipit brings to mind many different associations, of which the most important ones are: "In the beginning", when "God created the heavens and the earth" (Gen 1:1), Zion as a "herald of good news", of redemption from the Babylonian colonial captivity (Isa 40:9; 41:27; 52:1–7), the complex notion of the Messiah (*Christos*, anointed one), which included the tradition of the Israelite monarchy (1 Sam 2:10 etc), a "king to come" (Jer 23:5–6; Ezek 34:23–24), the son of David, who will destroy the unrighteous rulers (the Romans) by supernatural powers (*Psalms of Solomon* 17:21–33; *4 Ezra* 12:33).

Hence, when Mk begins in this way, the reader/hearer[51] recognizes these words as part both of the Roman colonial discourse and as the discourse of local Jewish traditions. And supposing familiarity with the subsequent story, the reader/hearer will be somewhat perplexed to hear in what way these terms are used. This is not an *euangelion* of a new Roman emperor, nor is it an *euangelion* of an anti-Roman national Davidic monarchy. Rather, it is an *euangelion* of a popular Galilean leader, entitled the Son of God, who gathers large crowds of people by his proclamation of the kingdom of God and by his work of healing and teaching in the eastern outskirts of the empire, and whose followers are mostly poor and lacking in social status. Further, this Son of God is crucified by a Roman governor for being "the King of the Jews", and then brought alive again.

The ambiguous way in which these colonial Roman and local Jewish concepts are used implies at the same time resemblance and menace, reminding of Bhabha's mimicry, as a repetition but with a difference. This strengthens the suggestion made above that a postcolonial perspective is relevant for the reading of Mk. As part of the ambivalence created by these terms, a third space is created, from which a new identity position potentially arises. This is a new *archē* (beginning/power), which is not derived from a previous Hegelian antagonism between thesis and anti-thesis, but which is rather the result of both mimicry and mockery at once. Consequently, the exact meaning of these loaded terms, and the identity position that they imply, is not fixed but rather fluid and vague, and something that awaits definition through the unfolding of the story. From this short analysis of the Markan beginning, it seems safe to say that the relationship between Mk and the colonizing power is characterized by subtlety and ambivalence, which are precisely those traits for which Bhabha urges us to

---

[51] Considering that very few people could read, many scholars argue that Mk was listened to rather than read, see Jonathan A. DRAPER, *Orality, Literacy, and Colonialism in Antiquity* (Leiden; Boston: Brill, 2004).

look. There are therefore reasons to read Mk as postcolonial literature, i.e. as a representation of a hybrid identity with similarities to the postcolonial literature of our time.[52] The suggestion to use postcolonialism when reading Mk therefore proves to be increasingly useful.

There is however another aspect of the story of Mk as a whole, which complicates the analysis. Judging from the above, the allusions to colonialist discourse ought to be read as mimicry in Bhabha's sense, which implies a distortion and even a parody of the colonial discourse, and therefore also a kind of resistance and counterculture. One key question concerns how this countercultural strand in Mk relates to the image of Jesus, who will return in power and glory, i.e. to images of what is often referred to as the parousia. Does not the Markan Jesus appear here as an authority figure with striking similarities to the Emperor himself? Does not Mk here slip over from an ambivalent mimicry to a traditional anti-colonial discourse that more or less reproduces the ideology of colonization? And does this not diminish the countercultural strand beyond recognition? Is this not another example of resistance that turns into repression, and an example of when medicine becomes a poison? Tat-siong Benny Liew is a postcolonial biblical scholar, who raises these crucial questions.[53]

Politics of Parousia

Liew urges us, rightly in my view, to look for Roman imperial ideology in Mk. As I have shown above, imperial discourse is certainly echoed in Mk.[54] The question is how it should be interpreted and what it means for early Christian identity. Although Liew certainly found anti-colonial elements in Mk, he still sees the Markan parousia as thwarting these aspects.[55] In the final analysis, Liew claims, Jesus is actually portrayed as an authority figure with absolute tyrannical power. Hence, "Mark's politics of parousia" is a duplication of "the authoritarian, exclusionary, and coercive politics of his [Roman] colonizers".[56]

---

[52] Cf. SAMUEL, *Postcolonial Mark.*

[53] LIEW, *Politics of Parousia.*

[54] Here I take ideology as a synonym for discourse, which is somewhat risky, cf. Beverly J. STRATTON, "Ideology," in *Handbook of Postmodern Biblical Interpretation* (ed. Adam; St. Louis, Mo: Chalice Press, 2000). However, I use "discourse" in a Foucaultian sense and it seems that Liew uses "ideology" in a similar way.

[55] LIEW, *Politics of Parousia*, 103. He refers specifically to Mark 8:39–9:1; 12:9; 12:36; 13:26; 14:61-62.

[56] LIEW, *Politics of Parousia*, 149.

In his recent postcolonial reading of Mk, Simon Samuel criticizes Liew for "idealizing" Mk as a colonial duplication.[57] According to Samuel, "Liew does not sufficiently exhibit the complex portraiture of Jesus in Mark" and he misuses Bhabha's concept of mimicry, which he takes to mean simply reproduction or duplication, thereby disregarding that mimicry also includes mockery, menace, and subversion (see above).[58] Although this is an important point, Samuel still avoids discussing the problems of colonial duplication in the parousia.[59] "If 'might is right' for the Markan Jesus, how can he possibly be crucified on a Roman cross?", Samuel rhetorically asks himself.[60] But according to Liew, the cross is only a means to an end, and the end is unlimited (eschatological) authority. Hence, Samuel tends to overlook the issue that Liew is raising about the apocalyptic image of Jesus returning in power.

Considering the Constantinian turn in the 4th century and how the Gospels in the 19th century became the kernel of an imperial religion, Liew's claim is not as improbable as it might first seem. As a parallel, Liew compares how Foucault handles the problem of Marx and the Gulag.[61] Foucault does not look for the wrong interpretation of Marx. Rather, he looks at Marx's texts from the perspective of the Gulag, and asks what in Marx made the Gulag possible. Similarly, Liew argues, we should not ask how the Gospels were interpreted wrongly, but rather what in the Gospels made Western imperialism possible. This is certainly an essential ingredient in postcolonial biblical criticism, and Liew has initiated an important discussion. But a postcolonial reading also involves other important ingredients, one of which is to read the Gospels as postcolonial responses to the colonizing enterprise of its time.[62] Liew seems to limit himself to the first part and the way in which he does so is questionable. How did Mk make Western imperialism possible? Since that is a crucial issue for Liew (and for me

---

[57] SAMUEL, *Postcolonial Mark*, 79–81, 84–85. See also MOORE, "Mark and Empire," who finds the Markan parousia to be a much milder and more muted affair than Liew claims.

[58] SAMUEL, *Postcolonial Mark*, 84–85. Cf. LIEW, *Politics of Parousia*, 93.

[59] When discussing the Markan parousia Samuel does not consider the possibility of a duplication of the Roman ideology, but looks only at how it relates to Jewish traditions of the parousia, see SAMUEL, *Postcolonial Mark*, 134–135.

[60] SAMUEL, *Postcolonial Mark*, 85.

[61] Tat-siong Benny LIEW, "Tyranny, Boundary and Might: Colonial Mimicry in Mark's Gospel," in *The Postcolonial Biblical Reader* (ed. Sugirtharajah; Oxford: Blackwell, 2006),206–207.

[62] Liew does not call his reading "postcolonial", but rather "inter(con)textual". Still he often alludes to postcolonial studies and particularly refers to Bhabha. His work on Mark has later been published in The Postcolonial Biblical Reader and it is therefore adequate to discuss whether his work is representative of postcolonial biblical criticism.

as well), it is somewhat surprising that he doesn't show how Mk was actually read in the colonizing enterprise, neither by the Roman, the Western-
ers nor by any others. He has no interest in the reception history of Mk,
and he makes no contrapuntal reading of Markan interpretation. Rather, he
reads Mk more or less directly in relation to today's egalitarian standards
and not surprisingly he finds many problems with, for example, patriarchy
and images of tyrannical power, all adding up to a "might is right" ideology in Mk. This is not to say that Liew is completely wrong in his claims.
Surely Mk has been part of colonial discourses, and still can be. But Liew
avoids showing how that happened or is happening.

Further, and related to this, since Liew's reading is rhetorical rather than
historical, he is not so interested in locating Mk in its ancient colonial setting.[63] This is regrettable, since this is the location within which we are
most likely to find the postcolonial ambivalence. And needless to say, the
historical setting is indispensable for the determination of the position of
early Christian identity. Therefore, being challenged but not persuaded by
Liew, I will present a reading that seeks to take seriously the issues that he
raises.

Although Mk never uses the word parousia, it is implied in several passages.[64] The word parousia was used in the Greco-Roman world as a term
for the official visit of an emperor, or some other high ranking official, to a
provincial city.[65] Hence, these sayings in Mk allude to the colonial discourse. The question is (again) how it alludes, whether it is an outright duplication – as Liew argues – or a representation of a more of an ambivalent
position. A full treatment of the Markan parousia extends beyond the scope
of this article and here I will limit myself to the first of the passages:

Whoever is ashamed of me and of my words in this unfaithful and sinful generation, of
him will the Son of Man also be ashamed when he comes in the glory of his Father with
the holy angels." (8:39)[66]

This particular saying by the Markan Jesus is located at the beginning of
the story's main turning point (8:27–10:52), where the reader's/hearer's

---

[63] LIEW, *Politics of Parousia*, 64.

[64] Particularly 13:24–27 and 14:61–62. See also 9:42–50. The word "parousia" is used
in the Gospel of Matthew, creating the fixed formula "the coming of the Son of Man", *hē
parousia tou huiou tou anthrōpou* (Matt 24:27, 37 and 39).

[65] W RADL, "Parousia," *EDNT* 3:43–44. See also Deissmann, *Light from the Ancient
East*, 368–373. G. H. R. HORSLEY, *New Documents Illustrating Early Christianity: A Re-
view of Greek Inscriptions and Papyri Published in 1976* (Sydney: Macquarie University
Press, 1981), 46.

[66] My translation.

understanding of Jesus is challenged in important ways.[67] In the first part of the story, Jesus and the disciples have been travelling between the villages of Galilee, proclaiming the kingdom of God, driving out demons, curing illnesses, teaching and feeding people, thereby generating support from large portions of the population, and also provoking the local leadership. Read with the exorcism of the Gerasene demoniac (5:1–20) as an interpretative key,[68] the direction of this first part of Mk is anti-colonial. Jesus is presented as a prophet, who renews and vitalizes a society that suffers from possession by legions of unclean colonizers and a collaborative local leadership.

The turning point in the story begins when Jesus and the disciples are on their way to Caesarea Philippi, talking about who Jesus actually is. In response to Peter's confession that Jesus is "the Christ" (8:29), the suffering-death theme (8:31) is explicitly introduced for the first time. A conflict then arises between Jesus and the disciples, which signals a tension with the previous anti-colonial section.[69] Quite tellingly, this is also where most anti-colonial interpreters of Mk run into problems. And when Mk doesn't seem to deliver the unambiguous anti-colonial story they expect to find, they argue for the presence of some kind of second layer in Mk, "a post-paschal discourse" (Belo) or "a messianic script" (Horsley), which in their view corrupts the original story.[70] But since I read Mark as a representation of Christian identity, speculations about a lost purely anti-colonial layer will not be helpful. Rather, I take the story as it is and read the contradictions and tensions as subtle signs of colonial ambivalence, significant for early Christian identity.[71]

At this point in the story, Peter takes Jesus aside and questions his teaching about suffering and death. This is not very surprising, considering the previous anti-colonial portrait of Jesus. For Mk however, this seems to be a crucial issue and Jesus openly challenges Peter: "If anyone would

---

[67] Most Markan scholars agree that 8:27 is a turning point, see e.g. Lars HARTMAN, *Markusevangeliet 8:27–16:20* (Stockholm: EFS-förlaget, 2005), 597–599.

[68] "Legion" is the name of the unclean spirits that were driven out. This exorcism alludes heavily to the Roman military presence in the land. See Anna RUNESSON, "'Legion heter jag, för vi är många': En postkolonial läsning av Mark 5:1–20", in *Jesus och de första kristna: Inledning till Nya testamentet* (ed. Mitternacht and Runesson; Stockholm: Verbum, 2007). See also MOORE, "Mark and Empire".

[69] The suffering-death theme could actually be said to begin partially in the story about the beheading of John (Mark 6:14–29).

[70] HORSLEY, *Hearing*; BELO, *Materialist*, 238–240.

[71] As Joanna Dewey argues, Mark survived as a Gospel partly because it was regarded as a good story. This is another reason for taking Mk as it is and analyse it as a representation of Christian identity. See Joanna DEWEY, "The Survival of Mark's Gospel: A Good Story?" *JBL* 123 (2004).

come after me, let him deny himself and take up his cross and follow me"
(8:34). For the Markan readers, following Jesus implied a constant risk of
being prosecuted and sentenced to death. "Take up one's cross" is therefore a saying that represents a particular socio-religious practice. Since it is
introduced in tension to the previous anti-colonial section, does this mean
that it bears a pro-colonial message? Judging from the legendary vision of
Constantine, in which he saw the sign of the cross together with the words
in hoc signo vinces (in this sign conquer), one might actually argue that
this is the case. Considering that the cross today is the Christian symbol
par excellance, the question is delicate. Read in its narrative and historical
context, however, the cross in Mk has a highly ambiguous and complex
meaning and can hardly be seen as an unequivocal symbol of winning
power, or of triumph.

For the Markan readers/hearers, the cross was a Roman penalty for in-
surgency, a symbol of imperial control – the bottom line of the power of
the empire. Considered atrocious and cruel, most "cultured" Roman writers
refrained from saying much about it. Nevertheless, it was a widely spread
punishment, that aimed at upholding Roman order by deterrence.[72] And its
most deterring effect was not the killing or the physical pain, but the humiliation and shame implied.[73] In order to increase the deterring effect
crosses were often set up along the busiest roads.

To talk of "the cross" as something to "take up" voluntarily is therefore
awkward and provocative. In Mk, the phrase has both a literal and metaphorical meaning.[74] Literally, to "take up one's cross" refers to the condemned person, who had to carry the crossbeam to the place of execution.
Metaphorically, it becomes an image for the Markan readers of being faithful to Jesus despite the risk of persecution. Compared to Luke, Mk has a
more literal meaning.[75] But there is no reason to choose between the metaphorical and the literal meanings. Rather, the literal meaning adds weight
to the metaphor. Therefore, Mk can be understood as transforming a means
of deterrence into a metaphor of faithfulness.

To use the cross in this literal and metaphorical way, is not an invitation
to suffering in general (as is often claimed), but could rather be understood
as a catachresis in Spivak's sense. The cross was one of the colonizers'
most terrifying means of deterrence and in Mk it is twisted out of its colo-

---

[72] Gerald G. O'COLLINS, "Crucifixion," *ABD* 1:1207–1208.

[73] Martin HENGEL, *Crucifixion in the Ancient World and the Folly of the Message of
the Cross* (London: SCM, 1977), 87–88.

[74] The Gospel of Luke emphasizes the metaphorical meaning by adding "daily" (Luke
9:23). Cf. Adela Yarbro COLLINS, *Mark: A Commentary* (ed. Attridge; Minneapolis: Fortress Press, 2007), 407–408.

[75] O'COLLINS, "Crucifixion," 1208–1209.

nial discourse and used as an image for the life in a community of Jesus believers, which often implied the renunciation of one's kinship group.[76] Used in this way, "the cross" opens up a new arena of negotiations of meaning, in which a new identity position is formulated, which is neither pro- nor anti-colonial, but rather transformative, and in this sense counter-cultural.[77]

The catachrestic invitation to take up the cross, naturally raised the objection to which Peter gave voice (8:32), i.e. the fear of being ashamed. Considering that the shame was inferred by both Roman and Jewish discourses (Deut 21:23), it was probably a quite serious objection. In order to rhetorically counter such an objection, and to wrench out the imperative from its colonial discourse, Mk introduces the notion of the parousia. He lets Jesus foretell his coming in power (cited above): "Whoever is ashamed of me…" (8:38). For Liew, this means that those who "'ousted' Jesus will [at the parousia], in turn, be completely 'ousted'" and therefore the Markan parousia is only a replacement of one empire by another.[78] But Liew overlooks the tactical-rhetorical purpose of the saying, indicated in the narrative in its historical context, which is to maintain the catachrestical usage of the cross and the implied social practice and identity position, formulated in the margins of an empire.

But to what does this rhetorical tactic actually add up? In the parousia Jesus is undeniably depicted as an authority figure with boundless colonial power. The announcement has the form of a threat (or promise) of a future coming in glory of a Son of Man, an image which draws decisively on Jewish apocalyptic discourse (Dan 7, *1 Enoch* 37–71, and *4 Ezra* 13). In order better to understand this particular rhetoric in Mk, and its implication for the Markan construction of identity, an excursus on apocalyptic literature and its relationship to colonialism is needed.

Excursus: Apocalyptic Literature and Colonialism

Apocalyptic literature is generally described in dictionaries as having been developed during postexilic Judaism from prophetic traditions, but also as

---

[76] BRANDON, *Jesus and the Zealots*, 57, suggests that "taking up one's cross" may have been a Zealot expression taken up by the Jesus followers. If correct, it might signal a second level of catachresis, since Mk uses the phrase similarly and yet differently as compared to the Zealot discourse.

[77] For a recent reading of Mk 8:34 in support of a (feminist) countercultural practice, see Joanna DEWEY, "'Let Them Renounce Themselves and Take up Their Cross': A Feminist Reading of Mark 8:34 in Mark's Social and Narrative World," *BTB* 34 (2004). See also MYERS, *Binding*, 245–247.

[78] LIEW, *Politics of Parousia*, 103.

influenced by the wisdom tradition and by Persian, Egyptian, and Hellenistic traditions. It is often assumed that the background is some kind of difficulties or crisis, and it is generally agreed that the bulk of Jewish apocalyptic literature was produced between 200 BCE and 100 CE. These centuries were plagued by colonialism, which is shown not least by the major anticolonial crises: the Maccabean revolt (167–164 BCE), the first (66–70 CE) and second (132–135 CE) Jewish-Roman wars, of which the second is also known as the Bar Kokhba rebellion. It seems reasonable, therefore, to state that the development of apocalyptic literature was connected to these colonial relationships.[79]

As Liew argues, apocalyptic literature has developed from a mixture of sources, including the different colonizers. By incorporating these traditions into their work, Liew claims, the apocalyptic writers became protesters against colonialism. For example, the Book of Daniel, written at the turbulent time of Antiochus Epiphanes and the Maccabean revolt, presents the history of succeeding empires as battles between supernatural powers. In this way, Daniel incorporates non-Jewish literary and conceptual features and uses them to affirm Yahweh's control of the world, to ascertain the destruction of the gentile kingdoms, and to give support to those who struggled to remain faithful to Yahweh in the face of persecution.[80]

However, Liew fails to acknowledge that these anti-colonial protests (and the support of the faithful) were accompanied by dreams of a new empire, an everlasting dominion over all peoples, nations, and languages (Dan 7:14, 27). Is this not a duplication of imperial ideology? Considering Liew's eagerness to find such duplication in Mk, his exclusion of that possibility here is somewhat surprising. In order to understand what kind of protest these apocalyptic writers represent, we need to look more closely at the character of apocalyptic writings.

Generally, apocalyptic writings are characterized by a dualistic world view. The present age was perceived as ruled by evil powers, whose reign

---

[79] Paul D. HANSON, "Apocalypses and Apocalypticism: the Genre," *ABD* 1:279–280. He mentions that the book of Daniel and Revelation was related to Antiochus IV and Rome respectively. In the first (1915) edition of the International Standard Bible Encyclopaedia, this connection is spelled out more clearly: "Apocalypse could only have been possible under the domination of the great empires." J. E. H. THOMSON, "Apocalyptic Literature," n. p. ISBE electronic resource from Dr. Stanley Morris, IBT, 1997. And Thomson continues to argue that whereas prophetic literature lacks an imperial outlook, "in the Apocalypses the imperial outlook is prominent". It is not clear why this discussion of the social setting of apocalyptic literature was removed in the revised edition (1979) of the ISBE and why it is absent in dictionaries such as D. C. ALLISON, "Apocalyptic," *DJG*:17–20.

[80] LIEW, *Politics of Parousia*, 57–58.

would last until the day of the Lord, when God would intervene to save the elect, judge the wicked and inaugurate the future good age. Through this discourse, existence was interpreted in a way which made it possible to have faith in spite of the trials and sufferings inflicted by the colonizers. Apocalyptic writings could be understood as a kind of coded and elusive form of speech, which constructed a counter-hegemonic identity. However, this kind of anti-colonial resistance typically remained inside the mind of the subordinate people. No matter how violent the fantasies and how seething the outrage, its very secrecy of the apocalyptic work prevented it from challenging the dominating power – unless there was an outburst of violent rebellion. In terms of social practice, apocalyptic literature often implied one of two possibilities: most often it implied an adaptation vis-à-vis the colonizers. On rare occasions, however, the internal resistance exploded in violent revolts and open defiance.[81]

To conclude this excursus, it seems that apocalyptic writings can be seen as responses to subjection under colonial domination; responses that are characterized by a counter-hegemonic mirroring of the colonizing ideology. I will now proceed with the analysis of the Markan parousia – first its relation to apocalyptic discourse and secondly, where this places Mk and its identity position in relation to the Roman Empire.

The Markan Parousia as Rhetorical Medicine

Although not apocalyptic in a strict sense, there are features and ideas in Mk that allude to typical apocalyptic beliefs: the struggle between Jesus and Satan (1:13; 3:26–27; 4:15; 8:33), Jesus' proclamation of the closeness of the kingdom of God (1:15), the closeness of end time (13:7–8), and the coming of the Son of Man in power and glory (8:38; 13:26; 14:62).[82] These allusions, however, are not made without important twists and modifications. The most significant aspect is, probably, the blurring of the clear-cut apocalyptic boundary between the present evil age and the coming good age. This boundary is made permeable by sayings about the kingdom of God that, according to the Markan Jesus, is at hand (1:15), can be

---

[81] Although the evidence is scarce regarding the social settings of apocalyptic writings, these claims seem quite safe. Social passivity and determinism is generally agreed to be part of the apocalyptic discourse. In terms of violent resistance, HANSON, "Apocalypses," 280, claims that it is clear that the "Animal Apocalypse" and the "Apocalypse of the Week" in *1 Enoch* 93 and 91:12–17 are connected to the Maccabean revolt.

[82] For a similar argumentation, see Vernon K. ROBBINS, "The Intertexture of Apocalyptic Discourse in the Gospel of Mark," in *The Intertexture of Apocalyptic Discourse in the New Testament* (ed. Watson; Society of Biblical Literature, 14; Leiden: Brill, 2002).

likened to a growing seed (4:1–20; 30–34), should be received like a child receives (10:13–16), and is near at hand when people learn the most important commandment: to love God and neighbour (12:28–34). Hence, Mk stands in an ambiguous relationship to the apocalyptic discourse. He repeats some of its concepts but shifts their meaning. The blurring of the apocalyptic curtain displaces the focus from a distant other-worldly redeemer to the kingdom as a seed, which is already growing in the present.

If we go back to the harsh saying about the Markan parousia, in which Jesus says: "whoever is ashamed of me /.../ of him will the Son of Man also be ashamed..." (8:39), we should ask: To whom is this parousia-threat directed? It is not, as in the Book of Daniel, a threat against the colonizers. Nor is it a threat against the opponents of Jesus (the collaborative local leadership). Rather, in Mk, the threat is directed to the (anti-colonial) disciples, in particular to Peter, who was reluctant to take up the cross. And supposing the readers/hearers identified themselves as disciples, it is also directed at them. Therefore, the Markan parousia not only blurs the eschatological curtain, but transforms the metaphor of the Son of Man from an anti-colonial avenger into a rhetorical figure, who subverts the expected anti-colonial agenda. Rather than being an essential part of an anti-colonial identity construction, the Markan Son of Man helps forming a new kind of identity, characterized by the catachrestical usage of the cross, which goes beyond the dichotomic positions pro- and anti-colonial.

Still, the Son of Man in Mk is an authority figure and taken away from his historical context he can be seen as representing a colonizing ideology, especially if Mk is transferred from the colonial margins to its centre and made part of the colonizers' identity – as indeed happened later. However, in the first century, when Mk was written in the Roman Empire it helped to form a new group identity, and at that time the Markan parousia had a much more ambivalent meaning. Considering the massive obstacles implied in a minority identity position characterized by the taking up of the cross, the parousia became a part, or even a necessary ingredient, in the formation of a catachrestic and hybrid identity.

The catachrestic use of the cross, with its associated implied socio-religious practice and hybrid identification was not an easy way, especially considering the shame. But rather than simply duplicating the shame and mirroring it back as a retribution against the colonizers (as Liew claims that Mk is doing), the Markan Jesus uses the Son of Man as a rhetorical medicine for the disciples. The disciples' fear of shame by identification with someone who died on the colonizers' cross is neutralized by the fear of being shamed by the crucified and risen Son of Man. So the Markan parousia can be understood as a medicine against the colonial terror of shaming, a medicine that makes possible the formation of a new identity.

This identity is formulated in a terrain of local Jewish and imperial Roman discourses. In Mk, these discourses are not only present, but also reformulated, intertwined and twisted in a way that creates a (third) social space, in which a new subject position can be negotiated, one which does not really fit any of the previous positions. Consequently, early Christian identity, as represented by Mk, affected the discursive landscape significantly by creating displacements and destabilizations in the Roman hegemony. Compared to an anti-colonial position, Mk is less confrontational. Nevertheless, because of its ambivalence and mimicry, Mk might have represented an even greater problem for the Pax Romana.

Christian identity as articulated by Mk could potentially undermine the colonizing hegemony. One part of this articulation includes the rhetorical medicine of the Son of Man, who will come in clouds with power and glory. Crucial for such an interpretation of the parousia is its location on the margins of an empire, and its character of having been formulated by a differing minority community. When Christianity later became an imperial religion, and the parousia was formulated from a dominant position, it could easily become oppressive. Interpreting the Markan parousia as medicine in this way has the advantage of also implying a warning – and taken as such, Liew's reading is a significant contribution: as with all medicine, if taken excessively, or in a wrong way, it can become a poison.

Mission of Christ and Local Communities in Acts

Christina Petterson

Introduction

The Book of Acts has many potential postcolonial readings. Thus the figure of Paul and his appeals to the imperial centre and the Emperor could be
one interesting approach, and the distribution of space in the roles of Jerusalem, Rome and the missionary field within the narrative of Acts could be
another. I have chosen the issue of representation, which is also a central
issue in postcolonial interpretation. I am particularly interested in the representation of the local, indigenous communities encountered during the
missionary journeys in Acts. How are they portrayed, how do they respond
to the missionaries and how are we, as readers, encouraged to understand
their response? In addressing these kinds of questions, I will select three
narratives and follow in the footsteps of the missionaries to Samaria, Lystra and Ephesus.

The first step will be to consider the situation from the missionaries'
point of view or rather, from the perspective of Luke's master narrative.[1]
Then I wish to place these readings in conversation with some of the information on Inuits from a family of Danish missionaries, namely Hans
Egede and his son Paul, who were both missionaries in Greenland in the
late 18th century, and Paul's brother Niels, who was a shopkeeper.[2] Finally, I will attempt to read 'against' the narrative and try to understand
what the situation must have looked like from the local perspective. This is
"the perspective of the Canaanite."[3] As theologians, we have been trained

---

[1] The Book of Acts has been used as a missionary book, or as the Comaroffs put it, a
holy narrative in South Africa, J. & J. COMAROFF, *Of Revelation and Revolution. Vol. 1:
Christianity, Colonialism and Consciousness in South Africa* (Chicago and London: The
University of Chicago Press, 1991), 231.

[2] Hans Egede came to Greenland in 1721. In 1905 Greenland ceased to be a mission
field and received the status of a church under the Diocese of Copenhagen.

[3] In her introduction to the first Semeia volume on postcolonial biblical criticism,
Laura Donaldson speaks of the possibilities in this reading strategy: '...[T]he defamil-
iarization of the Exodus story through the witness of its Canaanite victims functions as a
microcosm of the impact postcolonialism should have on biblical studies and readers.
They could no longer ignore either the existence of the colonized within the texts of the

to follow the sympathies of the apostolic narrative, which could be characterized as "the perspective of the Israelites." The time has perhaps come to ask some different questions, and to wonder what sort of man Publius on Malta is. What is a man with a Roman name doing there, and how did he become the leading man on Malta? Where did his money and property come from, what sort of power did he have, how and over whom did he use it (Acts 28:7–9)? These questions are not answered, or even posited in the narrative. They simply do not interest the author. What interests the author is that Paul and his fellows found favor with the most important person on Malta, which is meant to prove the validity and the appeal of the mission. But does that mean that these questions should not interest us?

Postcolonial Biblical Studies: Pitfalls

Within the last decades, postcolonial studies have carried out much hard work by cataloguing the literature, art and cultural practices of colonial discourse. In spite of the usefulness of the uncovering of these practices and their consequences, postcolonialism is not without its problems. As Anne McClintock has shown in "The Angel of Progress: Pitfalls of the term 'Postcolonialism,'"[4] the term postcolonialism gives the impression of a 'historical rupture,' which fails to highlight or to expose the continuities and discontinuities of power within empires and the newer forms of imperialism. Implicit in this problem is a second one, namely that of geographical one-sidedness: the use of the term seems, more often than not, to be connected with the British Empire and so the cataloguing mentioned above is usually carried within the parameters of that selfsame empire.

Finally, it seems that the use of the term has become increasingly *understood* and *used* as a literary theory. A reason for this could be the increasing dominance of textual analysis and the broadening of literary texts 'to stand in for social processes' – a focus, which then, inadvertently downplays, or practically eliminates material reality.[5] The Comaroffs also name their unease at literary approaches to colonialism because this '... occludes practices and institutional forms, material conditions and the

---

Bible or promote reading practices which erase their existence.' Laura DONALDSON, "Postcolonialism and Biblical Reading: An Introduction," *Semeia* 75 (1996): 1–14, 12.

[4] Anne MCCLINTOCK, "The Angel of Progress: Pitfalls of the Term 'Postcolonialism'", in *Colonial discourse / postcolonial theory*, (edited by F. Barker, P. Hulme and M. Iversen; Manchester & New York: Manchester University Press), 253–266.

[5] Ania LOOMBA, *Colonialism/Postcolonialism*, (2nd ed.; London & New York: Routledge, 2005), 83

realpolitik of everyday life.'[6] Regarding this particular issue, postcolonial biblical studies are no exception. The use in biblical studies of postcolonial theory is limited to textual analysis because of the relatively limited knowledge of the material reality of the world of the biblical texts.[7] However, if we insist on asking questions regarding 'practices and institutional forms, material conditions and the realpolitik of everyday life', which the narrative avoids asking, not to mention answering, then maybe we can reinstate some of the lost political impetus into postcolonial biblical interpretation. Another problem, which rests with the biblical aspect in postcolonial biblical studies, is the nature of the material at hand, namely its function as Scripture. This is not a problem that applies to, for example, English literature, and thus is left for theologians to wrestle with. It has been recognized among biblical scholars inspired by liberation theology that biblical studies from the period of emerging colonialism shares in the complicity of Western literature with Eurocentrism and subjugation.[8] The problem arises with the status of the biblical texts as sacred literature. Are the colonial interpretations of the Bible an imposition of foreign matters upon the biblical texts, or are the colonial interpretations too close for comfort? The need to face this uncomfortable possibility can be diverted through several means, all of which deploy more or less the same argument: This was not – for various reasons (such as the goodness of God, the Roman social order, the Jewish sects and so on) – the intention of the text. Thus, by keeping the text within its 'original' first century context, we can discern its 'original' intention, which can then be used to avoid confrontation with issues such as slavery, anti-Judaism, colonialism and misogyny. If the history of interpretation is brought into consideration at all, then this is seen as a distortion or as an anachronistic interpretation of an original intention, made morally palatable by historical circumstances and social contexts.

---

[6] John and Jean COMAROFF, *Of Revelation and Revolution. Vol. 2: The Dialectics of Modernity on a South African Frontier* (Chicago & London: University of Chicago Press, 1997), 410

[7] Jorunn ØKLAND's paper from the *Archaeology of Religion in the Roman World* session at the SBL 2005 Annual meeting, "Anything to Offer? A Gendered, Viewer-response Approach to Corinthian Votive Offerings and Their Donators" makes extensive use of archaeological findings from the Roman layers of the Demeter and Kore sanctuary and discusses the use of archaeological findings as cultural texts.

[8] Richard HORSLEY, "Subverting Disciplines. The Possibilities and Limitations of Postcolonial Theory for New Testament Studies," in *Toward a New Heaven and a New Earth. Essays in Honor of Elisabeth Schüssler Fiorenza* (ed. F. F. Segovia; Maryknoll, New York: Orbis Books) 90–105, p. 91.

The same underlying apologetics may be seen in the veritable explosion of literature on the Roman Empire in contemporary biblical studies.[9] But neither should this trend be confused with postcolonial biblical theory. Yes, postcolonial theory looks at empire, but critically. The historical focus in studies on the Roman Empire, automatically posits an opposition to empire in the New Testament, presumably in order indirectly to subvert contemporary *abuses* of the Bible in modern imperial politics. There is a fixed meaning of the text, which is counter-imperial, and thus is being distorted by, for example the current US administration. However, the agenda of historical empire studies is hardly ever voiced, but is presented as objective neutral exegesis. This runs almost contrary to the programme, if one may speak of a postcolonial biblical programme, of postcolonial biblical studies. These historical empire studies are signs of postcolonial issues that have been domesticated and contained within mainstream biblical studies, predominantly carried out be white, male scholars.

The postcolonial feminist scholar, Musa W. Dube, claims that biblical studies becomes a colonizing body of knowledge when biblical scholars only focus on the ancient world, and thus do not look at the role which the biblical texts play in contemporary power structures and politics.[10] She calls for an investigation into how the Bible has been, and still is, used to suppress; and then into how to facilitate liberating readings. Dube's unraveling and disclosing of western scholarship as a self-serving colonial discourse is greatly inspired by Edward Said[11] and Valentin Mudimbe[12] and their unpacking of the construction of the Orient/Africa by the West through the *representation* of the Orient/Africa in literature and academia.

Said is one of the key figures in the development of postcolonial *theory*, which may be characterized as the theoretical outcome of postcolonial *criticism*,[13] which rose among Marxist political activists, such as Franz Fanon in opposition to the French colonization of Algeria, and became theorized with intellectuals from (former) colonized countries. The godhead of post-

---

[9] See Stephen D. MOORE, *Empire and Apocalypse. Postcolonialism and the New Testament* (*The Bible in the Modern World*, 12; Sheffield Phoenix Press 2006), 3–23 for a comprehensive overview of various approaches that deal with empire and the New Testament.

[10] Musa W. DUBE, "Savior of the World but not of this World: A Post-Colonial Reading of Spatial Construction in John," in *The Postcolonial Bible* (ed. R. S. Sugirtharajah; Sheffield: Sheffield Academic Press), 118–135, 131.

[11] Edward SAID, *Orientalism* (London: Penguin Books, 2003 [1978]).

[12] Valentin MUDIMBE, *The Invention of Africa: Gnosis, Philosophy and the Order of Knowledge* (London: James Currey, 1988).

[13] Bart MOORE-GILBERT, *Postcolonial Theory: Contexts, Practices, Politics* (London: Verso, 1997).

head of postcolonial theory is Homi Bhabha, Gayatri Spivak and Edward Said, all of whom were heavily influenced by poststructuralist currents (especially Derrida, Foucault and Lacan), Marxist theory (excluding Bhabha) and their own 'diaspora'-identities (Bhabha and Spivak from India, Said from Palestine). While Bhabha and Spivak focus on present issues and identity formations, Said's most influential postcolonial studies have been historical, or archaeological in the Foucauldian sense. In spite of the differences in their methodological approaches, all three point to the instability of identity formations and to the constant struggle for hegemony or unity, a point taken from Gramsci. This instability is an aspect which is important to remember when dealing with postcolonial biblical interpretation, since it flies in the face of any notion of original or true meaning.

The Abuse of Acts in Colonialism:
R. S. Sugirtharajah and Postcolonial Biblical Interpretation

When dealing with postcolonial biblical criticism, it is impossible to ignore the name of R. S. Sugirtharajah. Apart from being the series editor of Sheffield Academic Press' (now taken over by T & T Clark International) groundbreaking series The Bible and Postcolonialism, featuring 6 volumes on the subject, and of which he has edited two, he is also the author of a number of books on postcolonialism,[14] as well as the editor of Blackwell's comprehensive Postcolonial Biblical Reader.[15] There is however something ironic in one scholar dominating the field to this extent, especially when bearing in mind that the field in question is postcolonialism. Ironies aside, it means that Sugirtharajah's definition of postcolonialism will be the one that people chiefly know and use. For this reason it is somewhat unfortunate that his exegetical work is very apologetic, and thus closes down a number of possible interpretations and explorations from the outset.

In his article "A Postcolonial Exploration of Collusion and Construction in Biblical Interpretation", Sugirtharajah sets out, among a number of things, to unveil the construction of a missionary journey structure in Acts

---

[14] R. S. SUGIRTHARAJAH, *Postcolonial Criticism and Biblical Interpretation* (Oxford: Oxford University Press, 2002); *Postcolonial Reconfigurations: An alternative Way of Reading the Bible and Doing Theology* (St. Louis, Missouri: Chalice Press, 2003); *The Bible and Empire: Postcolonial Explorations* (Cambridge: Cambridge University Press, 2005).

[15] R. S. SUGIRTHARAJAH, ed. *The Postcolonial Biblical Reader* (Oxford: Blackwell Publishing, 2006).

which took place during the colonial period.[16] He argues that this pattern, along with the concoction of Jerusalem as the missionary headquarter, is an imposition on the text, 'made to serve the political and commercial interests of the West'.[17] Sugirtharajah insists that this distortion of the text has constructed a false situation, according to which the West is installed as the centre of salvation and thus the rest of the world as the submissive recipient of the gospel message. He suggests that the commentators of the mercantile period were reading the events of their own time into the apostolic period (if so, this would neither be the first nor the last time). Sugirtharajah seems to have a notion of what the text means on its own terms, which collides with the imperialist abuse of later periods. In light of my comments above, I find it extremely important to acknowledge Sugirtharajah's emphasis on the historical conditions concerning the interest in missionary headquarters and missionary patterns, while I find his insistence that this interest is a distortion and an imposition on the text less useful.

With this in mind, the time has come to enter the world of Acts. First Samaria, then Lystra and finally Ephesus.

The Gospel in Samaria (Acts 8:5–25)

When Philip arrives in Samaria as a result of the persecution in Jerusalem he immediately begins to preach and heal and cause great happiness (8:5–8). But, we are suddenly told, he is not alone. There is another man, Simon, who had enamored everyone by his magic and pretences at greatness (vv. 9–11). However, when Philip arrives, they believe him and are baptized. So too is Simon, who stays close to Philip and who is time and again astonished at the signs and wonders Philip performs (12–13). The chief apostles from Jerusalem come down and seal the matter by granting the Holy Spirit to the baptized (14–17). Simon attempts to buy this skill of bestowing the Spirit, is cursed for his approach, and encouraged to repent, which he does (18–24). The apostles return to Jerusalem and preach in many Samaritan villages on the way (25).

The emphasis in this story is less on the Samaritans than on Simon. The issue becomes a contest over spiritual powers, where one is false and fake and the other is from God. The dispute comes to a head when Simon, wishing to buy the power of bestowing the Holy Spirit, is cursed by Peter. As

---

[16] R. S. SUGIRTHARAJAH, "A Postcolonial Exploration of Collusion and Construction in Biblical Interpretation," in *The Postcolonial Bible* (ed. R. S. Sugirtharajah; Sheffield: Sheffield Academic Press, 1998), 91–116, 100.

[17] SUGIRTHARAJAH, "Collusion and Construction," 107.

Barrett notes, Luke is sensitive to money matters in general, and the attempt to make profit out of the supernatural arouses his indignation.[18] Tannehill also mentions the use of money to vilify the objectives of undesirables, a factor which we will discuss in more detail in the case of Demetrius, the silver worker.[19] But as all the commentaries make clear, Simon should be viewed as a charlatan, who makes money by trickery. The apostles and Luke are perceptive enough to see this, but not the people on the missionary field, the Samaritans.

The Samaritans

The Samaritans are, as mentioned, the underemphasized people of the story. Not only are they underemphasized by the text itself, but commentators have followed the lead. Thus Robert Tannehill does not mention them apart from noting that they are the target of this mission.[20] Scott Spencer brings them a little more to life by suggesting that the reputation of the apostles and of Simon among the Samaritans may be influenced by the conflict between the two powers.[21] Haenchen is more interested in whether the Samaritans in the text were 'Jewish-Samaritans' with their centre in Shechem or pagans living in Sebaste.[22] Dunn's view of the Samaritans is based on his unfavorable view of Philip. He sees no articulated difference between Simon's deeds and Philip's, but argues that the difference is revealed through the notion of 'the gift of God'.[23] This in turn has a bearing on his understanding of the Samaritans, whose response to Philip is the same as their response was to Simon. Dunn suggests that the 'unusual formulation' *they believed Philip* (ἐπίστευσαν τῷ Φιλίππῳ) may be a signal from Luke that 'all was not right with the Samaritans' response'.[24] In Dunn's interpretation, the Samaritans do not respond in the appropriate manner to Philip's preaching, despite that it was 'wholly in accord with the gospel'.[25]

The Samaritans are thus represented as spellbound by a charlatan and they believe his claims to be someone important (*tina megan*) and that he

---

[18] C. K. BARRETT, *A Critical and Exegetical Commentary on the Acts of the Apostles* (Edinburgh: T & T Clark, 1994), 413.

[19] Robert TANNEHILL, *The Narrative Unity of Luke-Acts. A Literary Interpretation* (Fortress Press: Minneapolis, 1990), 106, n. 6.

[20] TANNEHILL, *Narrative Unity*. See also Barrett, *Critical Commentary*.

[21] F. S. SPENCER, *Acts* (Sheffield: Sheffield Academic Press, 1997), 88.

[22] Ernst HAENCHEN, *Die Apostelgeschichte* (Göttingen: Vandenhoeck & Ruprecht, 1977), 297.

[23] James DUNN, *The Acts of the Apostles* (Petersburough: Epworth Press 1996), 112.

[24] DUNN, *Acts*, 110.

[25] DUNN, *Acts*, 110.

is the power (*dynamis*) of God. When Philip comes, they believe in him instead. When the apostles descend from Jerusalem, the Samaritans disappear. Or rather, they are still there, as the grammatical object in the pericope, but they seem to be of no interest to the author, once their indecisiveness has been cemented.

This contest over spiritual powers has been the 'plight' of many missionaries within the local communities that they encountered. The spiritual powers may lie within the community itself or belong to a competing missionary. In the first case, the local people are often dubbed as superstitious (as we shall see in Lystra) and unable to see through the shenanigans of their deceiver, while the second situation has them acting like lemmings, merely following along because of some superficial attraction, without thinking. This is how the Samaritans are depicted, how Paul portrays the Galatians, and how, to a certain extent, the Inuits of Greenland were portrayed by the Egedes in their struggles with the Moravian Brethren over potential Inuit converts. The following description of the situation is written more than a century after the events, but still clearly conveys the hierarchies of representation:[26]

> It is significant for Zinzendorf's demands to the catechumens, that they only needed 'a notion' of the Christian enlightenment, which was seen as necessary for them to be presented for baptism; in this is expressed his lack of insight into the significance of a clear and definite form of faith, *most necessary for children, which the Greenlanders were.* As for the content, then one cannot be astonished that it, according to Zinzendorf's dogmatic outlook became so, as it is observed from his Instruction and Heathen-catechism; it has recently been shown what corrupt fruit was produced in Greenland. How much higher does not Egede stand on this point with his insistence on the articles of faith as foundation for the education of the catechumens? Even if he did go too far in his demands for their Christian knowledge, the content of his teaching possessed the true apostolic influence, which is a praise that one could hardly with any truth bestow on Zinzendorf and his missionaries in Greenland.

The quote shows that the issues concerned the missionaries and their disagreements about doctrine and to how best to teach and convert the Inuit, who then become 'talked about'; as though they were a houseplant that one could not decide where to place. So, although the topic is the mission to the Inuit, they are not really present in the text. The same may be said about the Samaritans in Acts 8.

---

[26] H. M. FENGER, *Hans Egede og den grønlandske missions historie 1721–60 efter trykte og utrykte kilder* (København: G. E. C. Gad, 1879), 210. My translation and my italics

However, following Justin, some see Simon as a Samaritan.[27] In this case, we are in the first situation mentioned above, and the Samaritans, as the Lycaonians after them, can be seen as utterly deceived by one of their own. As Philip and Paul struggled against local superstition in Samaria, also Hans Egede and his sons Paul and Niels constantly battled against crude and glaringly deceptive superstition.

And even though these angekut[28] are crude liars, and the result often reveals their power-lessness and deceit, the other stupid and foolish people believe them and hold them in great esteem and do not dare to transgress whatever is commanded them in name of Tornarsuk for fear of what evils might befall them.[29]

But I have said, to his son, as well as to others, that he and all other angekut were great liars and deceivers, and those who believed them, were great fools.[30]

So the Greenlanders are stupid and gullible,[31] ignorant of their own misery, childish and foolish,[32] but also wild[33] and superficial, hypocritical and their grasp of Christianity may be likened to that of parrots, mimicking the speaker without understanding.[34]

With this insertion of Greenlandic missionary narrative, I wish to present the reader with a more contemporary master narrative in order to guide the reading of the following pericopes. I want to emphasize that cultural stereotypes are a product of a somewhat inflated western feeling of superiority,[35] which will become even more apparent in the study of the following pericope and of its commentators, who have readily followed the ideology of the Lucan narrative. The representation of the Greenlanders will bring us to the image of the 'natives' in Lystra, to which we now turn.

---

[27] Hans-J. KLAUCK, *Magic and Paganism in Early Christianity* (Edinburgh: T & T Clark, 2000), 14 and SPENCER, *Acts*, 86.

[28] Angagoq, an Inuit shaman, here in plural.

[29] Hans EGEDE, *Det gamle Grønlands ny perlustration* (København: C. A. Reitzel 1941 [1741]), 394, my translation.

[30] Paul & Niels EGEDE, *Continuation af Hans Egedes relationer fra Grønland*, København: C. A. Reitzel, 1939), 43.

[31] EGEDE, *Perlustration*, 394.

[32] EGEDE, *Perlustration*, 399.

[33] EGEDE & EGEDE, *Continuation*, 27.

[34] EGEDE & EGEDE, *Continuation*, 243.

[35] I have previously discussed missionary Paul Egede's self-representation as the apostle Paul in his introduction to the first Greenlandic bible translation, which he (with the help of others) completed in 1766. See, Christina PETTERSON, "Kap farvel til Umanarssuaq," *DTT* 1 (2007), 103–115.

The Mission to the First Gentiles (Acts 14:8–20)

After narrowly avoiding getting stoned in Iconium, Paul and Barnabas escaped to Lycaonia, to the cities of Lystra and Derbe, and their surroundings, where they preached the gospel (14:5–7). The events in Lystra are set in motion when Paul heals a man who had been lame from birth (8–10). This generates an ecstatic atmosphere, where the crowd, yelling in Lycaonian, thinks that Barnabas and Paul are Zeus and Hermes in the flesh, and the priest at the temple initiates a sacrifice (11–13). The two apostles rend their garments and, by means of a short sermon on the nature of God over against the empty gods of the Lycaonians, manage to dissuade the crowds from the sacrifice (14–18). However, Paul is stoned by the crowds, after they were persuaded by incoming Jews. They leave him for dead outside the city, but he rises and returns to the town, only to move on to Derbe (19–20).

In 'Cultural Divides and Dual Realities,' Amy L. Wordelman points to the cultural bias in scholarship on Acts 14. Dean Bechard notes that this event has been overshadowed by the later trip to Athens, and Paul's speech on the Areopagus in Acts 17:14–34. The main reason for this focus is apparently the wish to connect the mission to the Gentiles closer to the Greco-Roman culture and less so to the primitive savages of Lycaonia. But as Bechard then argues, this is the first narration of Paul's meeting with an exclusively Gentile audience and thus it must have some significance of its own, rather than only serving as a mere foreshadowing of the 'real thing' in Athens.

I will take as my point of departure Bechard's[36] and Wordelman's[37] analyses of this pericope, in order to look at how they construct the Lycaonians in conscious opposition to earlier scholars, particularly of the German tradition.

To begin with, a brief comparison of this event with the trip to Samaria, where Simon who was the main focus, shows that the depiction of this crowd is much more detailed than that of the crowd in Samaria, and therefore this text calls for further scrutiny. I would like to discuss two issues: The first one is the reference to the Lycaonian language. Then I will broa-

---

[36] Dean BECHARD, *Paul outside the Walls. A Study of Luke's Socio-Geographical Universalism in Acts 14,8–20* (Roma: Editrice Pontificio Istituto Biblico, 2000).

[37] Amy L. WORDELMAN, "Cultural Divides and Dual Realities: A Graeco-Roman context for Acts 14," in *Contextualizing Acts: Lucan Narrative and Graeco-Roman discourse* (ed. T. Penner and C. Vander Stichele; Atlanta: Society of Biblical Literature 2003), 205–232.

broaden the subject and look at the healing itself, as well as at the reaction and compare it with the reaction of the crowd in Athens.

Luke the Ethnographer

It was Cadbury, who first called attention to the fact that Luke – on several occasions – is very explicit about which language is being spoken (ch. 2; 21:37; 21:40; 26:14). Whereas Dibelius denied that the geographical references had any literary significance, apart from naturally Athens, Bechard (following Cadbury) wishes to draw attention to precisely the geographical and 'ethnographical' references, especially those in Acts 14, which have been overlooked for so long. He wishes to present Luke as a kind of ethnographer, along the lines of Strabo (late 1st century BCE), since they both show an excessive interest in languages, ethnicity and customs of ethnic groups.[38] Let us for a moment forget that ethnography is a discipline which arose in the heyday of colonialism and, as such, has a colonial history of its own. Bechard's main argument, that the Lycaonian pericope is as significant in Luke's narrative as the pericope in Athens, will be discussed in the next section. To support this thesis, he draws on Luke's interest in languages and ancient mythographic traditions and points to Luke's mention of precisely these local insignia in order to highlight the significance of the Lycaonian pericope within the narrative.[39] Luke highlights that Paul is accomplished in both Greek and Aramaic in order to establish Paul's identity as 'a legitimate Ῥωμαῖος from Tarsus *and* as a recognizable Ἰουδαῖος in good standing.'[40] Similarly, Luke emphasizes the local dialect in Lystra to portray 'the Lycaonians as primitive rustics, whose physical and cultural isolation allowed them to preserve an ancient language fully unintelligible to the wider Greek world.' It may be noted that while the prior focus on the Athens pericope is presumably founded on cultural bias,[41] Bechard hardly overcomes this bias by giving priority to the episode in Lystra, but reinforces it, to the extreme, one might add.[42]

I agree with Bechard that Luke's mention of various languages is significant within Luke's world view. This is suggested from the outset at the Pentecost event in Jerusalem, which is seen as a reversal of the confusion of languages at Babel.[43] So what is the universal language, into which all

---

[38] BECHARD, *Paul outside the Walls*, 343–345.
[39] BECHARD, *Paul outside the Walls*, 149.
[40] BECHARD, *Paul outside the Walls*, 343.
[41] BECHARD, *Paul outside the Walls*, 413.
[42] This is also a point of criticism in Amy WORDELMAN's article, "Cultural Divides," 321, n. 53.
[43] BECHARD, *Paul outside the Walls*, 223–24.

differences are absorbed? Which language does the Spirit speak? Well, taking into account that the *lingua franca* of Acts is Greek, which again provides the narrative with the linguistic unity, and which could be seen as a signal of the coming unity under God, Greek would be a good choice. It is the Greek of the text that gives the Pentecost narrative – and for that matter the episode in Lystra – its coherence. Furthermore, we may recall Cadbury's insight, that Luke avoids Semitic words either by translating them into Greek or by eliminating them.[44] Thus the universal scope of Acts and the local communities, which the missionaries target, may be symbolized by Luke's use of languages. The episode in Lystra is translated for us by Luke, even though we are told that the spoken language is Lycaonian. Thus, at the moment of narration in Greek, the Lycaonian culture is hellenized, subsumed under the Greco-Roman imperial umbrella and represented to us on these terms.[45]

Paul and the Gentiles

Bechard notes that the encounters in Lystra and in Athens are, apart from the defense speeches in chs. 24 and 26, the only depictions of Paul actually fulfilling his divinely appointed task of mission to the Gentiles. This calls for a comparative analysis of the two episodes.[46] The issues that Bechard compares are social setting, social identity and reaction.[47] The social setting in Athens is the *agora*, which not only emphasizes the urban setting, but also alludes to Socrates. In Lystra, we are placed, after much discussion of the meaning of ἐπὶ τοὺς πυλῶνας, in front of the gates to the temple-shrine, a cultic setting, which will be used to explain the reaction of the local people.

   With regard to the social identity of the people who are mentioned in the episodes, he calls attention to the ethnic diversity in Athens, the affiliations to the philosophical schools, as well as specifically naming Dionysius the Aeropagite and the woman, Damaris (17:34). By contrast, the people mentioned in Lystra are a crowd (ὄχλος), who are characterized as speaking Lycaonian. We also meet a priest, as well as the unnamed man, who

---

[44] See BECHARD, *Paul outside the Walls*, 148, n. 13.

[45] Virginia Burrus has some interesting observations on language and heteroglossia in her contribution to *A Postcolonial Commentary on the New Testament Writings*, which came more or less on this article's deadline. Thus there has not been time to engage with her arguments, unfortunately. See Virginia BURRUS, "The Gospel of Luke and The Acts of the Apostles," in *A Postcolonial Commentary on the New Testament Writings*, (ed. F. F. Segovia and R. S. Sugirtharajah; *The Bible and Postcolonialism* 13; London: T & T Clark, 2007), 133–155.

[46] BECHARD, *Paul outside the Walls*, 355.

[47] BECHARD, *Paul outside the Walls*, 408–419.

was cured. Finally there is the reaction of the crowds, which according to Bechard, shows the clearest indication of the contrasting cultural set-tings.[48] In Athens, Paul's 'kerygmatic preaching' is answered with skepticism, characterized by urbanity, sophistication and the learned status of the interlocutors. In Lycaonia, the reaction is an 'overreaction of a wildly enthusiastic and seemingly uncritical throng of worshippers'.[49]

Although Bechard spends the next couple of pages depicting Paul as the incarnation of a literary topos of the authentic sage in Lycaonia, he nevertheless does not discuss *what* it is that the Athenians and the Lycaonians react against. In Lystra, it is a healing of a lame man, while in Athens it is Paul's speech, which Bechard characterizes as 'kerygmatic preaching'.[50] This difference in Paul's performance is picked up by Amy L. Wordelman,[51] who analyses the missionary activities of the apostles, and argues that a cultural map in three spheres can be produced by such a reading.[52] The first sphere is a limited barbarian sphere, represented by the island of Malta. The second sphere includes the eastern empire from Macedonia, through Asia Minor (where we find Lycaonia) and on to the road to Gaza. Finally, the last sphere encompasses the home territories of Greece and Rome. The key to reading the map is the way in which the apostles' supernatural miracles and preaching are distributed. In the first sphere, she notes that miraculous deeds are mentioned, although without any spoken message. No words are exchanged between the missionaries and the savages (οἱ βάρβαροι). In the next sphere, we find a combination of miraculous deeds and preaching, while in the third sphere, the miraculous deeds dis-

---

[48] BECHARD, *Paul outside the Walls*, 415.

[49] BECHARD, *Paul outside the Walls*, 417.

[50] I cannot help but wonder whether Bechard wishes to highlight the pericope and to bring out the differences in order intentionally to expose, not only an extreme cultural bias, but a specifically Protestant cultural bias against the cultic oriented Lycaonians.

[51] WORDELMAN, "Cultural Divides," 217.

[52] There are several analyses which use mapping as an approach to interpreting Acts. Drawing on insights from cognitive geography, Loveday Alexander uses the concept of mental, or cognitive, maps to illustrate Luke's frame of reference and worldview. In other words, a mental map is Luke's implied map of the world, which is presupposed in his narrative. See Loveday ALEXANDER, "Narrative Maps: Reflections on the Toponomy of Acts," reprinted in Loveday Alexander, *Acts in its Ancient Literary Context* (London: T & T Clark 2005), 97–131, 98. Vernon K. Robbins uses mapping in order to understand the particular places in which power is enacted within the narrative of Luke-Acts. His approach is informed by human geography, which is a discipline drawing on social and historical geography. See Vernon K ROBBINS, "Luke-Acts: A Mixed Population seeks a Home in the Roman Empire," in *Images of Empire* (ed. L. Alexander; JSOTSup 122; Sheffield: Sheffield Academic Press, 1991), 202–221, 211. (Society of Biblical Literature 2003), 205–232. Wordelman's cultural map may thus be determined as Luke's implied understanding of culture mapped out through Paul's travels.

appear altogether. So in the Greek territories and in Rome, Paul only speaks. 'Paul's power and persuasiveness arise solely from his words'.[53]

Wordelman sees this difference between the East (the first and the second sphere) and 'home' as providing the author with a way of addressing Greek mythological issues away from home, so to speak.[54] In this way, Wordelman places the events in Lystra within the second sphere. She thus avoids attributing superstition to the Lycaonians alone, but understands it as a part of a 'larger phenomenon of marvels and wondrous deeds.' She then proceeds to situate the Lycaonian experience within a Greco-Roman mythological context, by connecting it to the Lycaon tale.[55] This makes a difference to the understanding of the Lycaonian narrative, because the episode then addresses dominant religious and philosophical beliefs, and not 'insignificant and backward local traditions' as previously thought.[56]

Wordelman's article is intended to address prejudices and 'deep-seated assumptions about cultural differences' and the episode in Lystra shows how Orientalism shaped historical-critical interpretation.[57] I fail to see, however, why her portrayal of the Lycaonians is much better than the portrayals by previous scholarship, just because she situates it within a Greco-Roman mythological tradition. Rather than being characterized as credulous (Renan), primitively superstitious (Conybeare and Howson), naturally simpleminded and fickle (Ramsay), the 'new' cultural context which Wordelman provides characterizes the Lycaonians as wolf-like (deceitful and cunning) and bloodthirsty.[58] This she does in order to handle the tension that she has located in Greek culture between the traditional mythology and the theology argued by philosophy. The author of Acts separates the competing interpretations geographically, and thus uses the Lycaonians to address matters of mythology, without having to situate this in the cultural centers of Greece and Rome.[59] However hard she attempts to get around this problem, the Lycaonian narrative still becomes a way of characterizing the periphery as that which the center is not. And this is (one of) Said's point(s) in *Orientalism*. Wordelman assumes that by situating the narrative within the mythology of the Greco-Roman tradition, the cultural stereotyping vanishes, or at least it loses its orientalist flavor. I do not see how it makes any difference.

---

[53] Wordelman, "Cultural Divides," 218.

[54] Wordelman, "Cultural Divides," 219.

[55] Where Zeus turns king Lycaon into a wolf as a punishment for serving him human flesh.

[56] WORDELMAN, "Cultural Divides," 226.

[57] WORDELMAN, "Cultural Divides," 232.

[58] WORDELMAN, "Cultural Divides," 227.

[59] WORDELMAN, "Cultural Divides," 222.

Does not the problem lie at the level of representation within the text itself, and is it then not exacerbated by the interpretations? If we agree with Bechard that Paul's mission among the Gentiles is only narrated in Lystra and Athens, then the cultural differences are obvious; and as the history of interpreting the two pericopes have shown, the narrative seems to cater primarily for an intellectually sophisticated audience, who would rather identify with the Athenians than with the Lycaonians. As a thought experiment, let us imagine that the Lycaonians are like the Maoris of Aoteaora, New Zealand, i.e. a proud warrior people, who have held on to their language and their religious traditions in the face of British colonization. Continuing along this speculative line, what could the Jews from Antioch and Iconium have said to generate such a furious response? Taking our thought experiment further, let us assume that the Jews had the gift of prophecy and imagine that they conveyed to the Lycaonians the events that would take place in the following 500 years in order to get rid of Paul and Barnabas as quickly as possible. What if they said: 'These men are trying to eradicate your ancient cultural heritage, and will try to enslave you as the Persians, the Greeks and the Romans have tried before. Finally, after 500 years, they will take away your power to enact and enforce all legal provisions and place them in the hands of a praetorial governor with legal foundation in a document, Novellae 25 named 'On the Praetor of Lycaonia.' The military will force you to progress from a barbaric anarchy to a civilized society'?[60] How may we then imagine the Lycaonians' response?

The Silversmiths' Struggle in Ephesus

The connection between money and Satan is a recurring theme in Luke's narrative. This connection is first voiced by Peter in the story of Ananias and Sapphira (Acts 5:3). It appears subsequently in the story of Simon and his attempt to purchase the gift of bestowing the spirit (8:18–19), and then again in the account of the slave-girl with the prophetic but unclean spirit which provides a valuable income for her masters (16:16). Finally we meet Demetrius, the silversmith, who makes money from the Artemis cult (19:24).

In his analysis of economic and social relations in Luke, Halvor Moxnes has described how accusations of avarice and greed are well-known ways

---

[60] The source for all this information on the history of the Lycaonians is BECHARD, *Paul outside the Walls*, ch. 5: Greco-Roman sources of Luke's Imago Mundi, esp. pp. 235–279.

of criticizing opponents.[61] In Luke's gospel, the accusation is directed towards the Pharisees within Luke's overall social and economic project of re-distribution of wealth. In Acts, the accusation functions more as 'a description of negative personal characteristics' or as a code, which then serves to mark those so described as opponents of the apostles.[62] The examples given are Simon Magus and the silversmiths of Artemis in Ephesus.[63]

Staying within the notion of economy, we must appreciate that the situation of the silversmiths is highly one-dimensional and selectively narrated for the overriding theological purpose of Acts. We do not get the larger picture that may have made the reaction of the silversmiths understandable. Instead, the report of riot is governed by the narrator's comment in verse 24, where we are told that Demetrius brought no little business to the craftsmen and thus 'reveals' his self-interested motives.[64] So, keeping Moxnes' analysis in mind, we are here supplied with the code that should automatically make us think: oh oh, opponent, beware! And this is presumably where our senses should be most alert. But what do the commentators say?

Dunn points out that Luke cleverly makes Demetrius attest to the success of Christianity, as well as expressing the Jewish/Christian objections against the contemporary religions, namely that gods made with hands are not gods.[65] In addition, Demetrius is stapled as a familiar figure 'to any visitor to religious shrines over the centuries'.[66] This has a slightly derogatory tone, as though Demetrius were a souvenir peddler. Johannes Munck mentions that miniature terracotta temples have been found at excavations in Ephesus, but none made of silver.[67] According to Paul Trebilco, a number of terracotta and marble miniatures have been discovered.[68] Furthermore an inscription that reads 'To Artemis he gave a shrine as a vow'[69] may support the argument that the shrines themselves were votive offerings. Finally, the value of silver makes it unlikely that any such items

---

[61] Halvor MOXNES, *The Economy of the Kingdom. Social Conflict and Economic Relations in Luke's Gospel* (Philadelphia: Fortress Press, 1988), 160.

[62] MOXNES, *Economy*, 161.

[63] MOXNES, *Economy*, 161, note 12.

[64] TANNEHILL, *Narrative Unity*, 243.

[65] DUNN, *Acts*, 263.

[66] DUNN, *Acts*, 262.

[67] Johannes MUNCK, *The Acts of the Apostles* (New York: Doubleday, 1978), 194.

[68] Paul TREBILCO, "Asia" in The book of Acts in its Graeco-Roman Setting (ed. David W. J. Gill and Conrad Gempf; volume 2 of *The Book of Acts in Its First Century Setting*, ed. Bruce W. Winter; Grand Rapids: Eerdmans 1993), 291–363, 336.

[69] TREBILCO, "Asia", 337. The inscription is bilingual: *[Di]anae aidicolam votum dedit / *Ἀρτάμιτι εὐχὰν ναίσκον ἀπέδωκε.

should have been preserved.[70] However, since silver was a precious metal, how likely is it that the non-elite could afford such offerings? Would not the terracotta votives have outnumbered the silver ones by far? And how large an income could Demetrius have hoarded if the elite population of Ephesus matched that of the Mediterranean world in general, which was between 2 % and 5 % of the total population?[71] And if they were votive offerings, Demetrius would be far from a greedy souvenir monger, but connected to the temple, making and selling votives to worshippers.[72]

Tannehill[73] sees commerce, narrow patriotism and religion intermingle, which paint an unsympathetic picture of the silversmiths.[74] He points to the fact that Demetrius' perception of Paul as a threat is in fact accurate, to judge from Paul's teachings in Athens (Acts 17:24–25:29).[75] Spencer notes that Demetrius' accusations are left unanswered, because they endorse the viewpoint of the narrative. However, Spencer maintains that the narrator cannot support the actions of the crowds, and in order to show his disapproval of their behavior he uses 'confusion' (19:29) to denote lack of coherence and purpose.[76]

To move on from the viewpoint of Dunn, Tannehill and Spencer, that Demetrius expresses the viewpoint of the narrator, even though he is an opponent, then how does this function within Acts as a whole? Why is Demetrius used as a mouthpiece?

Interestingly, the only institution which receives a full-blown criticism in Acts is the temple in Jerusalem. Apart from Stephen's attack on the shrine in chapter 7, the narrative is somewhat vague in its criticism of other cultic shrines. In Lystra, it was not the shrine itself that was the rea-

---

[70] TREBILCO, "Asia", 337.

[71] MOXNES, *Economy*, 164.

[72] Codex Bezae does not mention that the shrines were made from silver. It just has *naoi*. See STRELAN, *Paul, Artemis and the Jews in Ephesos* (BZNW 80; Berlin & New York: Walter de Gruyter, 1996), 135, n. 14.

[73] TANNEHILL, *Narrative Unity*, 243.

[74] Strelan mentions scholars (Kistemaker and Pereira) who see Demetrius as only pretending to be pious, while he really only thinks of money, STRELAN, *Paul, Artemis and the Jews*, 136. As he points out, this is a misunderstood separation of issues that were (and are) intimately intertwined. Tannehill's characterization of the pericope also seems to presuppose a separation between commerce, patriotism, religion, which then are mingled. A similar separation seems to govern Trebilco's introduction to the section on Artemis in Ephesus, 'It was the cult of the Ephesian Artemis, which, more than anything else, made Ephesus a centre of religious life during our period. But the influence of the cult of Artemis extended beyond the religious sphere to the civic, economic, and cultural life of the city'. See TREBILCO, "Asia", 316.

[75] TANNEHILL, *Narrative Unity*, 243.

[76] SPENCER, *Acts*, 188.

son for Paul's speech. In Athens, it is an altar with the inscription 'To an unknown god' that sets him off on another doctrinal outburst. The narrative does not attack any specific institution, nor any specific divinity *except* here in Ephesus, where it does so indirectly, or through one of the cult's own worshippers. And the perceived accuracy of the criticism is discursively corroborated by Paul's former doctrinal speeches. But why Artemis? Going back to the economic perspective, an outline of the role of the Artemis temple within Ephesian society could be helpful in addressing these questions. Apart from all the various social and cultic functions that were connected to the temple, the Artemis temple in Ephesus was the financial and banking pillar of Asia.[77] Apparently, Artemis had one of the largest financial estates in Asia.[78] The assets came from revenue from property, such as vineyards, quarries, pastures and sacred herds. Money was loaned and mortgages taken,[79] and it was managed by employed money keepers and a *gerousia* of 400 members, who controlled the funds.[80]

Luke does not mention the wealth of the Artemis-estate, but through the figure of Demetrius, who links the Artemis-temple and silver, a connection is made between the temple and more than enough money. Could the critique of Demetrius be a way of criticizing the wealth of the Artemis estate indirectly? Politically speaking, the author of Acts would have been somewhat unwise to criticize directly one of the largest cult figures in Asia, but here it is done with genius. The end-result is, however, that Luke leaves the impression of the silversmiths of Ephesus as money-hungry souvenir mongers, who whip up an ignorant crowd into a frenzy.

The Power to Represent

Does Acts give us fair representations of the local communities discussed above? What image did the Samaritans, the Lycaonians and the Ephesians have of themselves, and to what extent does this corroborate the representations we find in the narrative in Acts? Naturally we cannot answer these questions, but at least we can question the accuracy of the cultural stereotypes, which Acts presents.

---

[77] STRELAN, *Paul, Artemis and the Jews*, 76. In this sense the Artemis temple does not differ from the temple in Jerusalem, which had the same functions.

[78] TREBILCO, "Asia", 325.

[79] STRELAN, *Paul, Artemis and the Jews*, 77; Trebilco, "Asia", 325.

[80] STRELAN, *Paul, Artemis and the Jews*, 77.

Last year saw the arrival of a documentary on Greenland by the award-winning Danish film-maker Anne Wivel: 'Menneskenes land. Min film om Grønland' (The Land of People. My Film about Greenland). While the film was highly acknowledged in Denmark and won an award for the best documentary, the feelings in Greenland were mixed. Some did not appreciate the way that the Greenlandic people were represented in the movie, and could not recognize themselves, their culture or their society. They felt that some (negative) issues had been magnified and others (more positive) eclipsed. Kirsten Thisted has pointed to the stereotyping of Greenlanders in Danish fiction through the centuries, where they represent the uncivilized savages, dressed in fur, gnawing on raw seal and killing polar bears with their bare hands. It is an image that prevails, and which she characterizes as 'arctic orientalism'.[81] To this, we could add the image of a society and a people harrowed by the abuse of children, alcohol and drugs, which is what one walks away with from Anne Wivel's portrait. These are very powerful representations, especially when the people reading or watching them have limited or no knowledge of the other sides of the stories.[82]

In a similar fashion, Luke has the power to represent the local communities in Samaria and Asia Minor. Set within an agenda of universalism, the local populations are denigrated as superstitious, fickle and wild. But this denigration is not limited to Acts, to the 18th century, or to the Orient. It is present in theology, as a western discipline, and more specifically for our purposes, in the commentaries on the biblical texts. The cultural stereotypes are thus perpetuated within the discipline. This is where postcolonialism can be of great value. Therefore I will discuss the merits of postcolonial biblical criticism within a broader theological agenda in my conclusion.

Conclusion

Following in the footsteps of feminism and liberation theology, postcolonial biblical interpretation presents theology with yet another substantial

---

[81] Kirsten THISTED, "Danske Grønlandsfiktioner: Om billedet af Grønland i dansk litteratur," *Kosmorama* 232, *Film fra Nord* (2003), 32–67, 33.

[82] THISTED "The Power to represent: Intertextuality and Discourse in Smilla's Sense of Snow" in *Narrating the Arctic: A Cultural History of Nordic Scientific Practices* (ed. M. Bravo and S. Sörlin: Canton: Science History Publications, 2001), 311–342, p. 329. I discuss the representations of women in the film Menneskenes Land and in Hosea. See Christina PETTERSON, "Profeten Hoseas møder Anne Wivel: Nationer, allegorier og kvinder", *Grønlandsk kultur- og Samfundsforskning*, 2006–2007, Ilisimatusarfik/Forlaget Atuagkat, 2008, 201–216.

challenge. At its best, postcolonial criticism can set the agenda for theology and thus reinstate critical biblical studies at the centre of theological reflection.

Postcolonial biblical analysis can roughly be divided into two different ways of reading. One is informed by liberation theology and/or historical apologetics, and is thus concerned with the liberating potential of the text (what it could or should mean). The other is focused on oppression, from the point of view of the text's history of effects[83] and is concerned with the use of the Bible in colonialism, and the way in which the text can underpin a colonial agenda. In effect, one does not exclude the other, but if we were to use postcolonial biblical interpretation within a larger theological framework, I would find it necessary for one to prefigure the other. In other words, there should first be *a recognition* of the negative use of the text and then a focus on its liberating potential. The first task is critical, the second is theological.

Postcolonialism's poststructuralist heritage, with its emphasis on instability, discourse and deferral of meaning implies that a reading which claims to be postcolonial, should not be apologetic, that is, blaming the problematic use of the text on a false interpretation and then proceeding to uncover what the text actually means (as in liberation theological approaches to the biblical texts, represented by Horsley,[84] Schottroff[85] and Rowland[86]). In this article, I have only taken the first step in an attempt to unveil our own disciplinary assumptions and cultural bias in the interpretations of three pericopes in Acts. The next step would push the readings further and discuss these issues within a broader theological scope; a move to include the various contexts, which theology has taken place within and influenced. Theology, as a particular worldview, is a historical manifestation with profound material and cultural consequences. It has developed in interaction with its political and social contexts. As such, the political and social contexts, which inform various theological traditions, should also be included in a postcolonial liberationist approach. Returning to the biblical

---

[83] History of effects as discussed by Ulrich LUZ in *Matthew in History: Interpretations, Influence, and Effects* (Minneapolis: Fortress Press, 1994), 23–38.

[84] Richard HORSLEY, "Subverting Disciplines: The Possibilities and Limitations of Postcolonial Theory for New Testament Studies", in *Toward a New Heaven and a New Earth. Essays in Honor of Elisabeth Schüssler Fiorenza* (ed. Fernando. F. Segovia; Maryknoll: Orbis Books, 2003), and *Jesus and Empire: The Kingdom of God and the New World Disorder* (Minneapolis: Fortress Press, 2003).

[85] Luise SCHOTTROFF, *The Parables of Jesus.* Translated by L. M. Maloney. (Minneapolis: Fortress Press, 2006).

[86] Christopher ROWLAND and Judith KOVACS, *Revelation: The Apocalypse of Jesus Christ* (Blackwell Bible Commentaries; Oxford: Blackwell Publishing, 2004).

text, which is what we, as exegetes, are trained to analyze, we can begin by recognizing that the text can mean (and indeed has meant) many things, but if we *want* to be open-minded towards difference and sensitive towards oppression, then what *should* it mean? And how can we develop a theology that contains and pays attention to these sensibilities?[87]

[87] I would like to thank the participants in the Postcolonial Hermeneutics seminar group at the Nordic Conference 2007 (Lone Fatum, Kåre Fuglseth, Ingeborg A. K. Kvammen, Hans Leander, Lennart Thörn, Håkan Ulfgard, and Walter Übelacker) for helpful comments and suggestions for improvements. I would especially like to thank Lone Fatum for inviting me and Hans Leander to a provocative and engaging response.

Perpetua and Felicitas –
Reinterpreting Empire, Family and Gender

Anna Rebecca Solevåg

The Martyrdom of Perpetua and Felicitas (hereafter referred to as the *Passio*)[1] tells the story of the martyrdom deaths of six Christians, two of whom are women. In the narrative the women, Perpetua and Felicitas, are at the center of attention. Perpetua has a baby with her in prison, while Felicitas is pregnant and gives birth a few days before the fight in the arena. In this essay, I will look at the different roles that the two women play, and show how Perpetua goes through a transformation, in which her social status is reinterpreted. I will argue that the conflict between the Christians and the Roman authorities can be seen in three different areas: There is conflict over the understanding of *empire*, including reverence for the emperor, respect for the law and acknowledgement of authority and power. There is conflict over *family* – especially over the role of the *paterfamilias* and the meaning of motherhood. Finally there is conflict over the meaning of *gender*, both concerning the female body and concerning perceived male and female virtues.

What is a martyrdom story and what does it do? Elizabeth Castelli sees the martyrdom narratives as an attempt "to subvert the meanings imposed by the physical arrangements of the arena."[2] Judith Perkins understands the martyrdom stories as part of a discursive construction of the Christians as sufferers: "Contemporaries knew so well that Christians suffered and died not because they witnessed multitudes swept up and executed, but

I am grateful to Carolyn Osiek, Turid Karlsen Seim and Marianne Bjelland Kartzow for reading my manuscript and giving valuable feedback. I would also like to thank the participants in the "Gender seminar" at the Nordic NT Conference for fruitful discussions and helpful suggestions.

[1] "Passio Sanctarum Perpetuae et Felicitatis" in Herbert MUSURILLO, *The Acts of the Christian Martyrs* (Oxford: Clarendon Press, 1972), 106–131. All citations in Latin and English are from Musurillo.

[2] Elizabeth A. CASTELLI, *Martyrdom and Memory: Early Christian Culture Making* (New York: Columbia University Press, 2004), 120.

rather because this was how Christians represented themselves."[3] I agree with Castelli and Perkins that the martyrdom texts are conscious efforts to subvert meaning and to create a specific Christian understanding of society and of the self. The *Passio* partakes in this Christian discourse by reinterpreting the concepts of empire, family and gender. In this Christian narrative, the Roman Empire is superseded in power by God's kingdom, and the Roman family is replaced by the Christian family, in which God is the father. Finally, the female body is perceived as capable of transformation into maleness when a woman takes on male virtues and characteristics, such as courage, authority and the ability to initiate action.

A Carefully Composed Narrative

In the main part of the *Passio* Perpetua narrates in the first person the story of her imprisonment and trial together with her Christian companions. She tells about their experiences while in prison and she also recounts four visions that she has had during this period. The visions are full of images about heaven and predict her outcome – death and a glorious afterlife. This "diary" is framed by an introduction and conclusion by an anonymous editor. In the introduction, the editor argues that accounts of martyrdom are witnesses to God's mercy and should be written down and read aloud in order to glorify God (1.5). Following the "diary," the editor has added a vision by Saturus, apparently a lead figure in the group of martyrs. This vision is also narrated in the first person and supposedly written down during imprisonment (14.1). Then follows an account of how Felicitas gave birth in prison two days before the games, how the prisoners spent their penultimate day in prison and how they fought in the arena on their "day of victory" (*dies victoriae illorum*, 18.1).

I regard this text as one coherent whole and do not judge the "diary" part to be historical material written by Perpetua.[4] Concerning time and

---

[3] Judith PERKINS, *The Suffering Self: Pain and Narrative Representation in the Early Christian Era* (London: Routledge, 1995), 23.

[4] I agree with Ross Kraemer and Shira Lander that what we have in the text "is a 'representation' whose correspondence to actual persons and events cannot be determined." Ross S. KRAEMER and Shira L. LANDER, "Perpetua and Felicitas," in *The Early Christian World*, ed. Philip F. Esler (London and New York: Routledge, 2000), 1058. Similarly, Lone Fatum calls the *Passio* "en raffineret komposition" (a refined composition), Lone FATUM, "Lidelsens politik: Fra Paulus til Perpetua," in *Lidelsens former og figurer*, ed. Bodil Ejrnæs and Lone Fatum (København: Museum Tusculanums Forlag, 2002), 230. Judith Perkins contends that the *Passio*'s focus on maternity is a further argument for scepticism towards its historical veracity: "Their depictions are so rhetorically pertinent

provenance of its composition, I follow the consensus: within the reign of Septimius Severus[5] in the vicinity of Carthage in North Africa.[6]

In addition to the redactional layers, the narrative tells a story on two levels – that of the ordinary world and that of the visionary world. For lack of better terms, I will call these levels historical and cosmic. At the historical level, it is the account of Perpetua's and her group's purportedly historical imprisonment, trial and execution. At the cosmic level, it is the story about the visions, which both predict and interpret events at the historical level. Even though the text's account of the events is an interpretation, it stays within the boundaries of plausibility at the historical level. There is no account of wonders or of a supernatural involvement that defies the laws of nature.[7] It is my opinion that these narrative restrictions are resolved by the use of visions which shed light and interpret the events, and which add another layer that underscores the idea that there are cosmic forces involved. The cosmic level reinforces the interpretation that is already taking place at the historical level.[8]

Together, these layers, levels and redactions function as a story that conveys a meaningful recollection of the experience of persecution and execution: "Reports of martyrdom provided key documents for reformulat-

---

to the discourse of the period in Carthage as evidenced by Tertullian as to make one suspect the women's authenticity as real persons." Judith PERKINS, "The Rhetoric of the Maternal Body in the Passion of Perpetua," in *Mapping Gender in Ancient Religious Discourses*, ed. Todd Penner and Caroline Vander Stichele (Leiden: Brill, 2007), 316. Many scholars consider the diary to be written by Perpetua: Jakob BALLING, Ulla Morre BIDSTRUP, and Torben BRAMMING, *De unge skal se syner: Perpetuamartyriet oversat og kommenteret* (Århus: Aarhus Universitetsforlag, 1997), 55–56; Margaret R. MILES, *Carnal Knowing: Female Nakedness and Religious Meaning in the Christian West* (Boston: Beacon Press, 1989), 61–62. See also Jennifer A. GLANCY, *Slavery in Early Christianity* (Oxford: Oxford University Press, 2002), 17.

[5] KRAEMER and LANDER, "Perpetua and Felicitas," 1051–1052. Since the text seems to be known by Tertullian when he writes *De Anima,* it is probably not later than 211 CE. See Jacqueline AMAT, *Passion de Perpetué et de Felicité suivi des actes* (Paris: Cerf, 1996), 20; BALLING, BIDSTRUP, and BRAMMING, *De unge skal se syner*, 57.

[6] KRAEMER and LANDER, "Perpetua and Felicitas," 1051; Amat, *Passion*, 22–23.

[7] This is different from the canonical gospels and Acts, as well as the Apocryphal Acts. See J. K. ELLIOTT and Montague Rhodes JAMES, *The Apocryphal New Testament: A Collection of Apocryphal Christian Literature in an English Translation* (Oxford: Clarendon Press, 1993).

[8] According to Elizabeth Castelli, the addition of a cosmic layer typifies the Christian interpretation of martyrdoms: "the Christian theory of martyrdom qua sacrifice detached the experience of persecution from the historical context and resituated it in a cosmic realm, rendering it meaningful only in a divine register." CASTELLI, *Martyrdom and Memory*, 56.

ing and resituating what might look like shaming, humiliating and public
executions into public enactments of Christians' positions and beliefs."[9]

Intersecting Power Structures

There is a growing understanding within feminist scholarship that power
structures are multidimensional and intersectional. Also within New Testament and early Christian studies, this awareness makes its claims.[10] It
seems that these intersecting structures of domination and subordination
play an important role in the *Passio*. Empire, family and gender can be
seen as power structures, which work together in different ways. In the
Roman Empire, the image of the Emperor as *Pater Patriae*, Father of the
Fatherland, rested on the metaphor of fatherhood.[11] The head of the Roman
family, the *paterfamilias*, exercised power over his family, *patria potestas*,
in the same way that the emperor exercised power over his citizens and
other underlings. Both institutions were in turn shaped by the society's
perception of masculinity – i.e. of what behavior was expected of a man.

One way to describe how gender was thought of in antiquity is to apply
a "one-sex model" where men and women were "arrayed according to their
degree of metaphysical perfection, their vital heat, along an axis whose te-
los was male."[12] The *Passio* provides an example of a woman who moves

---

[9] PERKINS, "The Rhetoric of the Maternal Body in the Passion of Perpetua," 323.

[10] See e.g. Caroline VANDER STICHELE and Todd PENNER, eds., *Her Master's Tools.
Feminist and Postcolonial Engagements of Historical-Critical Discourse*, vol. 9, Global
Perspectives on Biblical Scholarship (Atlanta: Society of Biblical Literature, 2005);
Elisabeth SCHÜSSLER FIORENZA, *Rhetoric and Ethic: The Politics of Biblical Studies*
(Minneapolis: Augsburg Fortress, 1999), ix. Schüssler Fiorenza argues that "domination
is not simply a matter of patriarchal, gender-based dualism but of more comprehensive,
interlocking, hierarchically ordered structures of domination, evident in a variety of op-
pressions, such as racism, poverty, heterosexism, and colonialism." Marianne BJELLAND
KARTZOW, "Gossip and Gender: Othering of Speech in the Pastoral Epistles" (University
of Oslo, Faculty of Theology, 2007). For the combination of feminist and postcolonial
perspectives, see also Christina Petterson's essay in this volume.

[11] Eva Maria LASSEN, "The Roman family: Ideal and Metaphor," ed. Halvor Moxnes,
Constructing Early Christian families: Family as Social Reality and Metaphor (London:
Routledge, 1997), 112.

[12] Thomas LAQUEUR, *Making Sex: Body and Gender from the Greeks to Freud* (Cambridge, Massachusetts and London, England: Harvard Universty Press, 1992), 5–6. See
also John J. WINKLER, *The Constraints of Desire: The Anthropology of Sex and Gender
in Ancient Greece* (New York: Routledge, 1990). Fredrik Ivarsson describes the following protocols as "the ground rules of Greco-Roman masculinity": 1) Having mastery over
non-men and controlling one's passions and desires, 2) Masculinity is a construction,
manliness is achieved through competition with other men, 3) Manliness is a moral qual-

in the approved direction on this continuum, from female to male. But it was also possible to move in the opposite direction. Men, who spent too much time with women, could lose the hardness that defined their more perfect bodies and become effeminate.[13]

Perpetua and Felicitas share the title of this story,[14] and they are the only named women therein.[15] Perpetua is, however, the single protagonist, and the focus is on her experiences and visions most of the time. She clearly goes through a transformation, in which her relationships to empire, family and her own gender are given a new meaning. Felicitas does not experience the same transformation but plays a different role in this narrative – a role that might be harder to discern. "Why does Felicitas vanish when Perpetua writes?" asks John W. Marshall, referring to the fact that Felicitas is never mentioned in the "diary" part of the *Passio*.[16] He points to the colonial setting of this narrative as an explanation of its treatment of gender and class.[17] I see a similar treatment of Felicitas as 'other' throughout the narrative.[18] The birth-giving scene is a case in point, and I will come back to that. Is Perpetua present when Felicitas gives birth? She is not mentioned; neither are her co-martyrs. We only learn that the Christian comrades pour forth prayers for her delivery prior to the fact (15.4). I will argue in this paper that the difference in social position between the free, respectably married Perpetua and the pregnant slave, Felicitas, is a key to understanding the way in which these two women are presented and used symbolically in the narrative. In the following I will explore the three areas of empire, family and gender and show how Per-

---

ity (cf. *virtus, andreia*), and is a positive value, even when applied to a woman. See Fredrik IVARSSON, "Vice Lists and Deviant Masculinity: The Rhetorical Function of 1 Corinthians 5:10–11 and 6:9–10," in Penner and Stichele, *Mapping Gender*, 165–166.

[13] LAQUEUR, Making Sex: Body and Gender, 7.

[14] At least in the modern editions, this is so. When it comes to the ancient manuscripts, the situation is less clear. Most title pages are missing, but in the extant ones, the male martyrs are mentioned first. Jan N. BREMMER, "The Motivation of Martyrs. Perpetua and the Palestinians," in *Religion im kulturellen Diskurs. Festschrift für Hans G. Kippenberg zu seinem 65. Geburtstag*, ed. Brigitte Luchesi and Kocku von Stuckrad (Berlin/ New York: de Gruyter, 2004), 542.

[15] There are a few other minor female characters: Perpetua's mother is present in one of the prison scenes (3.8), her aunt and her mother are mentioned by her father (5.2), Felicitas' baby is a girl, and this baby is taken away and raised by a Christian "sister" (15.7).

[16] John W. MARSHALL, "Postcolonialism and the Practice of History," in Stichele and Penner, *Her Master's Tools?*, ed. , 101.

[17] MARSHALL, "Postcolonialism," 103.

[18] Lone Fatum also notes the difference between Perpetua as the protagonist and Felicitas as merely a figure in the narrative and shows how their difference in status is used to enhance Perpetua's spiritual development. FATUM, "Lidelsens politik," 230.

petua's transformation can be understood as a reinterpretation of these three categories.

Reinterpreting Empire

In the Roman legal system, punishments were "simultaneously bodily, material and social."[19] Loss of status was an intrinsic part: "The person who entered the arena as a combatant or condemned had already crossed over a symbolic line, his or her status radically diminished and his or her very claim to membership in human society denied."[20] By defying the Roman law and refusing to sacrifice to the Emperor, the catechumens in the *Passio* show their allegiance to Christ, and not to the Emperor. Because of their Christian confession, they had been sentenced to death by Hilarianus, the procurator. From a Roman perspective, Perpetua's imprisonment would seem to be a shift downwards in status – from a woman of respectable family to a condemned criminal. In the Christian interpretation of the *Passio,* however, the shift is seen as a witness to her allegiance to a higher authority than that of the Emperor. Perpetua is not ashamed to be marched through town on the way to the stadium. Rather, stares down everyone by her gaze (18.2).

Although they are criminals, convicted and at the end spectacularly executed, the text presents the martyrs as the real winners. They are also portrayed as active, and as more powerful than the authorities. This is seen especially in the many references to God as the one who decides and in the portrayal of Perpetua as someone who speaks out against the authorities. I will elaborate on these two points in the following.

First, in the *Passio* it is not the Roman Emperor, but God who has the ultimate power. It is God's decision that the martyrs should die. The Holy Spirit's advice, following their baptism, that they should ask for nothing but for the perseverance of the flesh (*sufferentia carnis,* 3.5), shows that God knows what will happen. Perpetua even tries to persuade her father about this faith during one of his visits: "*non in nostra esse potestate constitutos, sed in Dei*" (5.6). Power over the events is transferred from the Roman authorities to God, and the entire ordeal is raised to a cosmic level.[21]

The visions underscore this belief in God's control of the events and elaborate on the meaning of the actions at the cosmic level. Perpetua's first

---

[19] CASTELLI, *Martyrdom and Memory*, 40.
[20] CASTELLI, *Martyrdom and Memory*, 41, 108.
[21] CASTELLI, *Martyrdom and Memory*, 56.

vision is of God's answer to her request to know about what will happen to them. Afterwards she realizes that they will die – she should not have any hopes in this age (*nullam iam spem in saeculo*, 4.10). But even if the visions do not give them any hope for this life, they certainly do for the life to come. All the visions have an element of the transfer of a person into God's realm. In Perpetua's first vision and in Saturus' vision, Perpetua and Saturus enter heaven together, Dinocrates receives healing and comfort through the second and third visions; and Perpetua enters the Gate of Life in the fourth. Thus, not only do the visions predict the outcome, but they also make martyrdom the *desired* outcome by drawing up vivid images of the prize, the heavenly reward, that awaits them.

Secondly, Perpetua speaks out against the Roman authorities and forces them to change their decisions on several occasions. Action and initiative seem to reside with the imprisoned Christians and not with the Roman authorities. Perpetua confesses in front of the tribunal (6.4), she protests against ill treatment in the prison (16.2–4) and again at the theatre, when they are forced to wear Roman religious clothing (18.6–7). In this last incident, Perpetua even claims that they have come to the theatre of their own free will (*ad hoc sponte pervenimus*, 18.5). It seems that her authority exceeds that of the Roman authorities. Ultimately, she takes charge of her own death and steers the sword of the trembling gladiator to her neck (21.9). Here, too, the text portrays Perpetua as more powerful than the representative of the Roman Empire, and as active in her own execution because she herself desires it (*non potuisset occidi ... nisi ipsa voluisset*, 21.10).

Again, the visions support this understanding of authority and action on behalf of the martyrs. Through courage and action, Perpetua steps on the dragon's head (first vision) and on the Egyptian's head (fourth vision) and she wins the victory. Similarly, through her fervent, authoritative prayer Dinocrates gains health and happiness. Even Perpetua's ability to receive the visions is a matter of authority. Her relationship with the Lord is such that she can demand a vision and receive it (*Et postulavi, et ostensum est mihi hoc*, 4.2).

Empire and family are brought together in the references to the day of the martyrs' fight: Caesar Geta's birthday (7.9). Geta was the son of the Emperor Septimius and still a child at the alleged time of the martyrdom events. Fighting on Caesar Geta's birthday seems to become an irony in this text, where the martyrs are portrayed as the children of an even more powerful king than Caesar. When Perpetua speaks out against the harsh treatment in prison, she says mockingly "we are Caesar's" (*Caesaris scilicet*, 16.3). But they are someone else's children, as Perpetua has confessed, both to her father and at the tribunal – "*Christiana sum*" (3.2; 6.4). Their day of death becomes their birthday, too – it is the day on which they are born into eternal life.[22]

The hierarchical ordering of society was a fundamental aspect of the Roman Empire. Distinctions between those who were members of the elite and those who were not permeated all social interaction.[23] The very different symbolic roles that Perpetua and Felicitas play in the text can be explained by the differences in their social status. Perpetua's loss of status must be negotiated and reinterpreted. But Felicitas is already at the bottom of the social ladder, so there is no position for the text to negotiate or to defend. According to Jennifer Glancy, one of the most important characteristics of the slave was its "open" body. Slaves' bodies were targets for physical violence and sexual exploitation.[24] They were outside the honor/shame-game but not outside the system. Unable to guard their bodies from insult or injury, they were always in a state of dishonor.[25]

Perpetua has visions, and she assumes an active role as confessor and public speaker. By use of the visions she comes out as powerful vis-à-vis the empire. But her transformation is not paralleled by any change on Felicitas' part. Is Perpetua's power accentuated by Felicitas' submissive and stable role? Felicitas has no visions, and she does not exercise authority or leadership.[26] I agree with Lone Fatum that the unchanging figure of Felicitas puts Perpetua's identity-transformation into relief.[27]

It is only ultimately, at the brink of death, that Perpetua and Felicitas join hands. For a brief moment, they seem to be standing side by side as equals, both dressed in the same fashion, sharing their suffering in the arena (20.6). But even in death, Perpetua supersedes Felicitas by taking an active role in her own execution, guiding the sword to her throat. Perpetua

---

[22] The martyrs' day of death as their "dies natalis" was a common feature in Christian martyrdom discourse. See BALLING, BIDSTRUP, and BRAMMING, *De unge skal se syner*, 78. The *Passio* was read as a commemoration on the anniversary for their alleged day of death, March 7. There might even be a hint at this in the introduction (1.6). See AMAT, *Passion*, 19, 79–81.

[23] Jerome Neyrey describes a social pyramid with rulers and / or aristocratic families on top, followed by those who serve them – soldiers, priests, scribes, imperial slaves, and the like. Then came merchants, peasants and landless peasants, and at the bottom "the unclean, degraded, and expendables" – beggars, thieves and prostitutes. Jerome H. NEYREY, "Jesus, Gender and the Gospel of Matthew," in *New Testament Masculinities*, ed. Stephen D. Moore and Janice Capel Anderson (Atlanta, GA: Society of Biblical Literature, 2003), 52.

[24] GLANCY, *Slavery*, 12.

[25] GLANCY, *Slavery*, 28.

[26] KRAEMER and LANDER, "Perpetua and Felicitas," 1060.

[27] FATUM, "Lidelsens politik," 230.

emerges as actively choosing death, while Felicitas succumbs to violence and penetration by the sword without resistance.

Reinterpreting Family

It is only Perpetua's family that plays a role in the narrative, and early on her father is a very important figure.[28] The father shows a strange mixture of tender affection and violent, almost crazy, behavior. He visits her several times in prison, begging her to change her mind for the sake of her family (3.1; 5.1–5; 6.2; 9.2–3). The focus is on Perpetua's shift in family allegiance from her Roman family to God's family. Both the father and the procurator appeal to Perpetua's duties as a daughter and a mother in order to persuade her to sacrifice. The father refers to his own grey hair and invokes the whole family, including her brothers, her mother and her aunts (5.2–5). Finally he appeals to her by mentioning her son, who cannot live if she dies (5.3). In this passage he starts out by calling her his daughter and ends up calling her a lady (*non filiam nominabat, sed dominam*, 5.5). He also wonders if he is worthy to be called her father (*si dignis sum a te pater vocari*, 5.2), and his attempts at persuasion are called diabolical arguments (*argumentis diaboli*, 3.3). Through their three encounters, we perceive the gradual mutual alienation of father and daughter. Underneath the whole argument lies his fear of being shamed because of his daughter's misbehavior, i.e. the "reproach of men" (*in dedecus hominum*, 5.2).[29]

Perpetua renounces her father, and her son is taken away from her. The introduction tells us that she is married (*matronalita nupter*, 2.2), but the husband is never mentioned by name or discussed.[30] From a Roman perspective, she exhibits a shameful disrespect for her father, who represents

---

[28] Jan Bremmer notes that the martyrdom sources usually lack information about the martyrs' social context: family relations, occupation etc. BREMMER, "The Motivation of Martyrs," 547.

[29] According to Fredrik Ivarsson's protocols of masculinity, the father is portrayed as far from an ideal man. He cannot control his daughter nor does he have mastery over his own feelings. IVARSSON, "Vice Lists and Deviant Masculinity," 165–166. See also note 12 in this essay. Elizabeth Castelli describes the father actions as feminizing. Elizabeth A. CASTELLI, "'I Will Make Mary Male'," in *Body Guards*, ed. Julia Epstein and Kristina Straub (New York: Routledge, 1991), 38.

[30] Carolyn Osiek argues for the possibility that her husband is one of her co-martyrs, Saturus. Carolyn OSIEK, "Perpetua's Husband," *Journal of Early Christian Studies* 10, no. 2 (2002). Lone Fatum sees the absence of a named husband as a necessity, since Perpetua is transformed from matron to virgin hero in the narrative. It is the father-daughter relationship, not the husband-wife, that is in focus in the text. See FATUM, "Lidelsens politik," 232.

the *paterfamilias* institution. She also shows neglect of the *matrona*'s duty as a mother and wife, when she turns her back to her father and her baby. Her transformation in social status is certainly a shift downwards, but the text reinterprets Perpetua's actions as testimony to her allegiance to a new family. In the eyes of the Christian narrator, she is not only a daughter but also still a matron. She is described as the wife of Christ (*matrona Christi*, 18.2). She is also God's favorite (*Dei delicata*, 18.2), just as she had been her earthly father's favorite over her brothers (5.2). In this interpretation, Perpetua is still submissive to her true *paterfamilias* – God – even if she renounces her Roman *paterfamilias*. In the eyes of Christian readers, she can still be seen as a respectable matron.[31]

In the visions, God is cast in fatherly imagery. In the first vision, God is a shepherd, with grey hair like her father's, who welcomes her to heaven and calls her child (*bene venisti, tegnon*, 4.9) In Saturus' vision, God is an old man with white hair. Angels lift them up to kiss him, and he caresses their faces (12.2–5). Also in the arena vision, Perpetua is called a daughter and given a blessing by a heavenly figure (*filia, pax tecum*, 10.13). This imagery stands out as a contrast to Perpetua's earthly father and his erratic behavior. The fatherly God of the visions is tender and loving.

There is also a conflict about the understanding of motherhood in the *Passio*. In the figure of Perpetua, the true meaning of motherhood is reinterpreted, while the discourse of motherhood and family is upheld. For instance, Perpetua's maternal concern is extended beyond care for her own baby when she prays for her dead brother. In two visions, Perpetua sees him in the afterlife, and he earns a better outcome through Perpetua's intercessory prayer. Perpetua also shows motherly concern for her Christian "siblings" when she encourages them by her visions and her actions. As mentioned earlier, images of God as a parent are abundant in the visions. Once, she is encouraged by heavenly beings to go and play (*ite et ludite*, 12.6). She is also fed baby food by the divine shepherd, who gives her curdled milk. Just as Perpetua, as a mother, nursed her baby until it was taken away from her, she is herself the child and God is the parent (mother?), feeding (or nursing?) her (4.9) in her visions.

According to Carolyn Osiek and Margaret Y. MacDonald, Perpetua exhibits the qualities of the ideal Roman matron and mother. She shows concern for her baby and wishes to nurse him herself, and she tries desperately to preserve her modesty during her arena fight, when she binds her hair and pulls the tunic over her thighs.[32] Although both Perpetua and Felicitas

---

[31] I thus disagree with Lone Fatum that Perpetua is portrayed as a virgin hero.

[32] Carolyn OSIEK and Margaret Y. MACDONALD, *A Woman's Place: House Churches in Earliest Christianity* (Minneapolis: Fortress Press, 2006), 46–48.

have to give up their children, it is understood that they are received into good and caring hands – Perpetua's boy is taken care of by her family, Felicitas' girl by a Christian sister (6.8; 15.7). Osiek and MacDonald point out that the happy outcome for the babies helps to resolve the tension between motherhood and martyrdom. [33]

There is no mention of Felicitas' family relations in the *Passio*. As a slave, she would not have had any acknowledged family. She becomes a mother while she is in prison, but this baby is immediately taken away from her. Who is the father of her baby? The text gives no answer. As a slave, she would have been available for her owner's sexual exploitation. There was also a close connection between slavery and prostitution in antiquity. [34] If the father was a fellow slave, he could not claim paternity of the child. Under Roman law, only a free man could acknowledge a child as his own. [35] As I see it, what characterizes Felicitas most is that she is alone. Perpetua is constantly interacting, both in the visions and at the historical level, and with people of her Christian family as well as with her Roman family. Felicitas takes center stage only once – when she gives birth. Here she is portrayed with no helpers. Her Christian friends have only helped by bringing on the contractions through their prayers. Except for the prison guard, who chastises her, no one seems to be with her while she struggles in labor. Felicitas' answer to the guard underscores her loneliness: in childbearing she has to suffer alone, but in martyrdom Christ will suffer in her (*modo ego patior quod patior...* 15.6).

Felicitas' answer makes a connection between childbirth and martyrdom. Later in the narrative, Felicitas' labor pains are explicitly likened to the pains of martyrdom: "glad that she had safely given birth, so that now she could fight the beasts, going from one bloodbath to another, from the midwife to the gladiator, ready to wash after childbirth in a second baptism" (18.3). Here a midwife is introduced, though none is mentioned in the actual birth scene.

Marshall pointed out that Felicitas is absent when Perpetua writes, but Perpetua is also absent from the childbirth scene. Osiek and MacDonald believe that "in reality, Felicitas was probably assisted in labor by her companions." [36] I am doubtful with regard to what we can know about the reality behind the text. But why is she not present in the text? The text does not seem to be interested in the relationship between the two women. Perpetua's interactions are with men, both in the visions and at the histori-

---

[33] OSIEK and MACDONALD, *A Woman's Place*, 47.
[34] GLANCY, *Slavery*, 51.
[35] GLANCY, *Slavery*, 26.
[36] OSIEK and MACDONALD, *A Woman's Place*, 60.

cal level. These interactions are part of her transformation into the masculine category.

I understand the childbearing scene as a way to show extreme suffering.
Felicitas can be portrayed as someone struggling alone in labor, because of
her low social status. Similarly, she is portrayed with breasts dripping
when she enters the arena. Her suffering and painful state is not negotiated.
Motherhood includes extreme suffering, just as martyrdom does, and the
body of the female slave is evidently a useful "site" to extrapolate this suffering. This is very different from the way in which the figure of Perpetua
is explained and "rescued" from the dishonorable things that happen to her
at every stage – through interpretation.[37]

Reinterpreting Gender

I have shown how the *Passio* negotiates Perpetua's potential loss of status
by reinterpreting the meanings of emperor/empire and of family. The third
area of negotiation and reinterpretation is Perpetua's gender. Through the
story, she achieves prized male characteristics and virtues, such as courage
and heroic action. I have already mentioned her authority vis-à-vis the
Roman authorities, and even vis-à-vis God in requesting the visions. She
dares to speak in defiance of her enemies, but she also speaks words of
comfort to her Christian family. Just as she has strengthened her group by
her visions, so she encourages her fellow believers by her final words:
"Stand firm in the faith and love one another, and do not be weakened by
what we have gone through" (*In fide state et invice omnes diligite, et pas-
sionibus nostris ne scandalizemini*, 20.10). Further, when they march into
the arena, she stares down everyone with her gaze (18.2), as a man might
do.[38] She has the wits to reach out and help Felicitas in the midst of their
fight with a wild cow (20.6), just like a brave soldier during a battle. Her
final act of courage is when she assists the gladiator in her own execution
(21.9) thus performing the role of gladiator herself.[39]

In her fourth vision, Perpetua even becomes male physically when she
enters the arena. She discovers this when her clothes are stripped off before the fight, and assistants rub her body with oil (*et expoliata sum et fac-*

---

[37] I see a similar use of the figure of a slave girl in Blandina in "The Letter of the
Churches of Lyons and Vienne." Blandina goes through terrible tortures, while we hear
nothing of the tortures of her mistress, who is also among the imprisoned Christians.
MUSURILLO, *The Acts of the Christian Martyrs*, 67.

[38] BREMMER, "The Motivation of Martyrs," 543.

[39] Following Fredrik Ivarsson's protocols of masculinity, Perpetua gains the top score.
IVARSSON, "Vice Lists and Deviant Masculinity," 165–166.

facta sum masculus, 10.7). One might assume that her "discovery" relies on bodily signs, but the text gives no details about what they might be (a male torso? male genitals?). As a courageous man, she wins a fistfight with the gladiator (10.1–15). But even if Perpetua has a male body in her vision, in the actual arena fight, the two women's female characteristics are highlighted. Here, too, they are stripped naked. But when the crowd is shocked by their nakedness, they are clad in tunics (20.1–3). During the attack by a mad heifer, Perpetua's tunic is torn and her hair comes unbound (20.4–5). What the spectators see in the stadium is thus not heroic action against an animal or a gladiator, as the vision predicted, but a woman struggling to preserve her modesty by tying her hair and pulling at her frayed tunic to cover her thighs. While loose hair is referred to in the text as a sign of mourning, in antiquity it was also a sign of sexual availability.[40] Ultimately, the vision predicted victory, including her reception of the golden branch and entrance through the Gate of Life. In the arena, this turns out to be death by the sword, a death by "penetration" that has sexual overtones. The matron's body turns out to be as vulnerable as that of the slave.

But even this ultimate loss of honor and status has been negotiated and reinterpreted in the *Passio*. The visions have prepared the reader to see Perpetua as something other than a shamefully suffering woman. What the Roman spectators might see as shameful nakedness is, in this Christian interpretation, understood as a woman achieving the male virtues of courage, self-mastery and heroic action. She is a woman who is "really" (at the cosmic level) a man.

As mentioned above, the only women named in this story are Perpetua and Felicitas. Felicitas does not exist at the cosmic level: in the visions there are no other female characters apart from Perpetua. The men seem to be her spiritual guides, not vice versa. In the first vision, Saturus climbs the ladder first (4.5) and in the fourth vision, Pomponius leads her to the arena and promises her that he will fight alongside her (10.4). In Saturus' vision, Perpetua and Saturus are side by side all the time, and they speak together when chastising the clergy (13.1–6). The elders, who prostrate themselves, do so in front of this male-female couple, not in front of Perpetua alone. It seems that the visions equip Perpetua at the cosmic level with the male counterpart that she lacks at the historical level of the narrative. Is this a way to reduce the troubling implications of a woman, who speaks in public and who is the leader of her group of martyrs? To a certain extent, Saturus functions as a counterpart to Perpetua at the historical level also, though he is a less important figure than Perpetua herself. Both he and Perpetua have visions. Also, in the arena account he is at one gate

---

[40] MILES, *Carnal Knowing*, 49–50.

comforting a surviving member of the Christian community while Perpetua is doing the same at another gate at the same time (20.10; 21.1–4).[41]

Felicitas has not gone through the same gender transformation but, as a slave, she has no honor to safeguard. The difference in their physical appearance when they enter the arena also highlights the difference in social status. Perpetua is described as beautiful and young, while Felicitas bears all the signs of a post-partum woman. While Perpetua painlessly stopped lactating when she was in prison (6.8), Felicitas' breasts are still dripping with milk as she stands in the arena.[42] Felicitas is still at the same level of female embodiment as Perpetua was at the beginning of the story. Here, at the end, Perpetua has overcome that. She has become male, and she stands in contrast to the lactating slave woman.

Early in the story, the catechumens are baptized, and the Holy Spirit warns Perpetua to ask for nothing from "the water" but for the perseverance of the flesh (*et mihi Spiritus dictavit non aliud petendum ab aqua nisi sufferentiam carnis*, 3.5). Does *sufferentia carnis* have a special meaning to women, who are thought to be bodily weaker? Does it mean suffering bodily pain or avoiding bodily (female) weakness? It seems to me that the two women's *sufferentia carnis* are very different. While Perpetua symbolically eclipses her female weaknesses and becomes male, Felicitas' *sufferentia carnis* is childbearing and embodiment of female suffering.

In the narrative, there are many references to the ritual of baptism.[43] Martyrdom is explicitly likened to a second baptism (*baptismo secundo*, 18.3). Thus the nakedness of two women in the arena could play on the fact that, in the ritual of baptism, the catechumens were stripped naked before they entered the water.[44] But why is it only the two women who appear naked? None of their male co-martyrs are undressed and there does not seem to be any interest in their bodies. Perpetua is described as "young and delicate" and Felicitas has "milk dripping from her breasts" (*puellam delicatam ... stillantibus mammis*, 20.2). "Involuntary nakedness is a regu-

---

[41] Osiek also notes this, but sees it in relation to the theory that they were married. OSIEK, "Perpetua's Husband," 290.

[42] I disagree with Jennifer Glancy's statement that the arena scene is an instance where, "the capacity to produce milk dissolved differences between an elite woman and a humble slave woman." GLANCY, *Slavery*, 17.

[43] They are baptized early during their imprisonment (3.5). In the first vision, Perpetua receives milk from the heavenly shepherd (4.9). The water in the Dinocrates visions (7.7; 8.3–4), the kiss of peace in Saturus' (12.6) and the cries from the mob in the arena ("*salvum lotum*," 21.2) also give associations to baptism.

[44] MILES, *Carnal Knowing*, 33. In the vision Perpetua is rubbed down with oil. This echoes the ritual of anointing the newly baptized with oil after immersion in the water.

lar feature in the accounts of female martyrs," Margaret Miles points out.[45]
She sees this as a sign of the male authors' confusion between "respect and
esteem for woman martyrs" and "textual interest in their bodies or concern
to establish the inferiority of their sex."[46]

The text evokes vivid images of a spectacle that Christians were advised
not to attend.[47] The *Passio* itself is negative to several varieties of Roman
spectacle. In Saturus' vision, quarrelling Christians are likened to people
arguing at the races (13.6). The crowd at the arena is charged with participation in the crime committed, since they watch it with their eyes (*oculos
suos comites homicidii*, 21.7). It is even suggested that those who watch
are enemies of the martyrs, and that they will be recognized as such on the
day of judgement (17.1–3). The Christian reader can allow her/himself to
gaze at the women's naked bodies, and later, at Perpetua when she is penetrated by the sword, because the visions provide another layer of interpretation, as a veil, so to speak. The reader has already been encouraged to see
her as a man, fighting an honorable fistfight, rather than as a naked woman
attacked by a cow.

Conclusions

As I see it, the *Passio* reinterprets but also re-establishes social status, by
subverting the meanings of empire, family and gender. Even if the text
rejects the conventional understanding of what allegiance to the emperor,
respect for the *paterfamilias,* and even what being male means, it still up-
holds these categories as something positive. This narrative attempt to
formulate a useful and meaningful memory of the events of persecution
and execution ended by the reproduction of society's patriarchal norms
within the Christian community. It is only that the roles are recast. God is
now starring in the roles of emperor and father, and the exceptional hero-
ine, Perpetua, is cast in the role of a courageous male. The *Passio* attempts,
not to subvert any categories, but to subvert the meaning of the still respected categories of emperor/empire, father/family and masculinity. Thus,
I do not perceive Perpetua's "becoming male" as a sign of her spiritual
progress. Rather, it is an interpretation of what would seem – to the Roman
spectator – like a loss of status and honor as being instead, a positive trans-

---

[45] MILES, *Carnal Knowing*, 54.

[46] MILES, *Carnal Knowing*, 57. Elisabeth Castelli also notes an ambivalence in the
Christian narrator, "at once repelled and drawn to the sight." CASTELLI, *Martyrdom and
Memory*, 123.

[47] CASTELLI, *Martyrdom and Memory*, 106.

formation. Felicitas role is to serve as a backdrop for Perpetua's transformations. There are sufficient likenesses – they are "co-martyr(s), co-mother(s) and co-namesake(s)"[48] – to enhance the differences in their sufferings. Despite these differences, they receive the same reward – their salvation is the same. They walk in different ways to the same goal, and those ways are allotted them according to their social status, not according to their gender.

In *A Woman's Place*, Osiek and MacDonald want to remind us that there is "a world of women of which the texts remain silent – a world of sisterhood" where distinctions of class broke down.[49] The *Passio*, with a title that couples the names of a Roman matron and a slave woman, might seem like a promising place to look for this world of sisterhood. But, in my view, it cannot be detected in this text.

The martyrdom stories created a usable memory of the experience of suffering, and the stories were shaped so that the readers could find examples of how to live their own lives as Christians.[50] The *Passio* does not empower women to assume leadership roles in the church, despite the fact that a woman is the leader of these martyrs. It does not challenge the inferiority of the slave girl to the Roman matron, despite the fact that a slave girl is prominent in the story. Neither does it question the male characteristics of the divine, despite the nurturing and childbearing images that are incorporated. Through the focus on these two women, the allegiance to the Christian king/emperor and *paterfamilias* – God – is repeated, and support for male church leadership is strengthened.

---

[48] MARSHALL, "Postcolonialism and the Practice of History," 93.
[49] OSIEK and MACDONALD, *A Woman's Place*, 19.
[50] CASTELLI, *Martyrdom and Memory*, 69.

Contributors

Samuel Byrskog, Professor, Lund University, Sweden
Per Jarle Bekken, Associate professor, Oslo University College, Norway
Tobias Hägerland, Ph.D. candidate, Göteborg University, Sweden

Judith M. Lieu, Lady Margaret's Professor of Divinity, Cambridge University, Great Britain
Lauri Thurén, Professor, Joensuu University, Finland
Thomas Kazen, Associate professor, Stockholm School of Theology, Sweden
Raimo Hakola, Ph.D., Postdoctoral researcher, Helsinki University, Finland
Rikard Roitto, Ph.D. candidate, Linköping University, Sweden

Halvor Moxnes, Professor, Oslo University, Norway
Fredrik Ivarsson, Lic.theol., Ph.D. candidate, Göteborg University, Sweden
Hanna Stenström, Ph.D., Researcher at the Church of Sweden Research Unit, Uppsala, Sweden

Hans Leander, Ph.D. candidate, Göteborg University, Sweden
Christina Petterson, Ph.D. candidate, Macquarie University, Sydney, Australia
Anna Rebecca Solevåg, Ph.D. candidate, Oslo University, Norway

Editors

Bengt Holmberg, Professor emeritus, Lund University, Sweden
Mikael Winninge, Associate professor, Umeå University, Sweden

Bibliography

Abrahams, Israel. *Studies in Pharisaism and the Gospels*. 2nd Series. Cambridge: Cambridge University Press, 1924. Repr. Eugene, Oregon: Wipf & Stock, 2004.

Abrams, D. "Social Identity, Social Cognition and the Self." Pages 197–229 in *Social Identity and Social Cognition*. Edited by D. Abrams and M. A. Hogg. Oxford: Blackwell, 1999.

Achilles Tatius. *Leucippe and Clitophon*. With an English translation by S. Gaselee. Loeb Classical Library; Cambridge: Harvard University Press, 1917, reprint 1961.

Ahmad, Aijaz. *In Theory: Classes, Nations, Literatures*. London: Verso, 1994.

Allen, Graham. *Intertextuality*. London: Routledge, 2000.

Allison, Dale C. Jr. *Jesus of Nazareth: Millenarian Prophet*. Minneapolis: Fortress Press, 1998.

Amat, Jacqueline. *Passion de Perpetué et de Felicité suivi des actes*. Paris: Cerf, 1996.

Anderson, A. A. *Psalms (73–150)*. New Century Bible; London: Marshall, Morgan and Scott, 1972.

Anderson, Janice Capel, see Moore, Stephen D. (1998).

Arnold, Russell C. D. *The Social Role of Liturgy in the Religion of the Qumran Community*. Studies on the Texts of the Desert of Judah 60. Leiden: Brill, 2006.

Aspegren, Kerstin. *The Male Woman: A Feminine Ideal in the Early Church*. Edited by René Kieffer. Acta Universitatis Upsaliensis, Uppsala Women's Studies, A. Women in Religion 4, Uppsala: Uppsala University, 1990.

Asting, Ragnar. *Die Verkündigung des Wortes im Urchristentum, dargestellt an den Begriffen „Wort Gottes", „Evangelium" und „Zeugnis"*. Stuttgart: Kohlhammer, 1939.

Attridge, Harold W. "Argumentation in John 5," Pages 188–199 in *Rhetorical Argumentation in Biblical Texts: Essays from the Lund 2000 Conference*. Edited by A. Eriksson, T. H. Olbricht, and W. Übelacker. Emory Studies in Early Christianity, vol. 8; Harrisburg, Penn.: Trinity Press International, 2002.

Attridge, Harold W. "Genre Bending in the Fourth Gospel." *Journal of Biblical Literature* 121 (2002): 3–21.

Aubin, Melissa. "'She is the Beginning of All Ways of Perversity:' Femininity and Metaphor in 4Q184." *Women in Judaism: A Multidisciplinary Journal* (2001). Cited 27 August 2007. https://jps.library.utoronto.ca/index.php/wjudaism/article/view/182/257.

Aune, David E. *Prophecy in Early Christianity and the Ancient Mediterranean World*. Grand Rapids: Eerdmans, 1983.

Aune, David E. *Revelation 6–16*; Word Biblical Commentary 52B, Nashville: Thomas Nelson Publishers, 1998.

Balch, David L. *Let Wives be Submissive. The Domestic Code in 1 Peter*. Society of Biblical Literature Monograph Series 26. Chico, CA.: Scholars Press, 1981.

Baldick, Christopher. "Catachresis." In *The Concise Oxford Dictionary of Literary Terms*. Oxford University Press, 1996. *Oxford Reference Online*. Oxford University Press. No pages. Accessed 20 April 2008. www.oxfordreference.com/views/ BOOK_SEARCH.html?book=t56&subject=s13.

Balling, Jakob, Ulla Morre Bidstrup, and Torben Bramming. *De unge skal se syner. Perpetuamartyriet oversat og kommenteret.* Århus: Aarhus Universitetsforlag, 1997.

Balz, Horst Robert and Gerhard Schneider. *Exegetical Dictionary of the New Testament.* Vol. 3 Grand Rapids: T&T Clark, 1993.

Barclay, John M. G. "Mirror-Reading a Polemical Letter: Galatians as a Test Case." *Journal for the Study of the New Testament* 31 (1987): 73–93.

Barrett, Charles Kingsley. *The Gospel according to St John: An Introduction with Commentary and Notes on the Greek Text.* 2. ed.; London: SPCK, 1978.

Barrett, C. K. *A Critical and Exegetical Commentary on The Acts of the Apostles.* The International Critical Commentary on the Holy Scriptures of the Old and the New Testaments. 2 vols. Edinburgh: T&T Clark, 1994.

Barth, Markus and Helmut Blanke. *Colossians.* Anchor Bible 34B. New York: Doubleday, 1994.

Bassi, Karen. "The Semantics of Manliness in Ancient Greece." Pages 325–258 in *Andreia. Studies in Manliness and Courage in Classical Antiquity.* Edited by Ralph M. Rosen and Ineke Sluiter. Mnemosyne: Bibliotheca Classica Batava. Supplementum 238, Leiden: Brill, 2003.

Bauckham, Richard. *Jude, 2 Peter.* Word Biblical Commentary 50. Waco: Word, 1983.

Bauckham, Richard. "Historiographical Characteristics of the Gospel of John." *New Testament Studies* 53 (2007): 17–36.

Baumgarten, Joseph M. *Qumran Cave 4.XVIII: The Damascus Document (4Q266–273).* Discoveries in the Judaean Desert XVIII. Oxford: Clarendon Press, 1996.

Baynes, Leslie. "Philo, Personification, and the Transformation of Grammatical Gender." *Studia Philonica Annual* 14 (2002): 31–47.

Bechard, Dean Philip. *Paul outside the Walls: A Study of Luke's Socio-Geographical Universalism in Acts 14:8–20.* Analecta Biblica 143. Roma: Editrice Pontificio Istituto Biblico, 2000.

Bekken, Per Jarle. *The Word is Near You: A Study of Deuteronomy 30:12–14 in Paul's Letter to the Romans in a Jewish Context.* BZNW 144; Berlin/New York: Walter de Gruyter, 2007.

Belo, Fernando. *A Materialist Reading of the Gospel of Mark.* Maryknoll: Orbis Books, 1981.

Berger, Klaus. "Die impliziten Gegner. Zur Methode des Erschliessens von 'Gegnern' in neutestamentlichen Texte." Pages 372–400 in *Kirche.* Edited by D. Lührmann and G. Strecker. Tübingen: Mohr, 1980.

Berman, T. R., see Schank, R. C.

Betz, Hans Dieter. *Galatians: A Commentary on Paul's Letter to the Churches in Galatia.* Hermeneia. Philadelphia: Fortress Press, 1979.

Beutler, Johannes. *Martyria: Traditionsgeschichtliche Untersuchungen zum Zeugnisthema bei Johannes.* Frankfurter Theologische Studien 10; Frankfurt am Main: Verlag Josef Knecht, 1972.

Beutler, Johannes. "Literarische Gattungen im Johannesevangelium: Ein Forschungsbericht 1919–1980." *Aufstieg und Niedergang der römischen Welt* 2.25.3 (1985), 2506–2568.

Bhabha, Homi and Jonathan Rutherford. "The Third Space: Interview with Homi Bhabha." Pages 207–221 in Jonathan Rutherford, ed. *Identity: Community, Culture, Difference.* London: Lawrence & Wishart, 1990.

Bhabha, Homi K. *The Location of Culture.* London: Routledge, 2004.

Bhabha, Homi K. "Of Mimicry and Man: The Ambivalence of Colonial Discourse." Pages 121–131 in H. K. Bhabha, *The Location of Culture.*

Bhabha, Homi K. "Signs Taken for Wonders: Questions of Ambivalence and Authority under a Tree outside Delhi, May 1817." Pages 145–174 in H. K. Bhabha, *The Location of Culture*.

Bjelland Kartzow, Marianne. *Gossip and Gender: Othering of Speech in the Pastoral Epistles*. Thesis for the degree of Dr.Theol., Faculty of Theology, University of Oslo, 2007.

Black, Matthew. "The Messianism of the Parables of Enoch: Their Date and Contribution to Christological Origins". Pages 145–168 in *The Messiah: Developments in Earliest Judaism and Christianity*. Edited by J. H. Charlesworth. The First Princeton Symposium on Judaism and Christian Origins. Minneapolis: Fortress Press, 1992.

Black, Steve. "The Construction of Christian Identity through Stereotyping of the Pharisees in the Gospel of Matthew." A Paper Presented at the SBL Annual Meeting in Washington, DC, November 2006.

Blank, Josef. *Krisis: Untersuchungen zur johanneischen Christologie und Eschatologie*. Freiburg: Lambertus Verlag, 1964.

Blinzler, Joseph. *"Eisin eunouchoi," Zeitschrift für neutestamentliche Wissenschaft* 48 (1957): 254–270.

Bloch, M. *How We Think They Think: Anthropological Approaches to Cognition, Memory, and Literacy*. Boulder; Oxford: Westview, 1998.

Block, Daniel I. "The Prophet of the Spirit: The Use of *rwḥ* in the Book of Ezekiel." *Journal of the Evangelical Theological Society* 32 (1989): 27–49.

Bloomfield, Morton W. "A Grammatical Approach to Personification Theory." *Modern Philology* 60 (1963): 161–171.

Boccaccini, Gabriele. *Beyond the Essene Hypothesis: The Parting of the Ways between Qumran and Enochic Judaism*. Grand Rapids: Eerdmans, 1998.

Boccaccini, Gabriele, ed. *Enoch and the Messiah Son of Man: Revisiting the Book of Parables*. Grand Rapids: Eerdmans, 2007.

Boccaccini, Gabriele. "Finding a Place for the Parables of Enoch within Second Temple Jewish Literature". Pages 263–289 in Boccaccini, *Enoch and the Messiah Son of Man*.

Boccaccini, Gabriele. "The Enoch Seminar at Camaldoli: Re-entering the Parables of Enoch in the Study of Second Temple Judaism and Christian Origins." Pages 11–16 in Boccaccini, *Enoch and the Messiah Son of Man*.

Borgen, Peder. *Bread from Heaven*. Novum Testamentum Supplements 10; Leiden: Brill, 1965. Reprint 1981.

Borgen, Peder. "Review of J. Beutler, *Martyria: Traditionsgeschichtliche Untersuchungen zum Zeugnisthema bei Johannes*." *Biblica* 55 (1974): 582–583.

Borgen, Peder. *Philo, John and Paul: New Perspectives on Judaism and Early Christianity*. Brown Judaic Studies 131; Atlanta, Ga.: Scholars Press, 1987.

Borgen, Peder. *Early Christianity and Hellenistic Judaism*. Edinburgh: T&T Clark, 1996.

Borgen, Peder. *Philo of Alexandria: An Exegete for His Time*. Novum Testamentum Supplements 86; Leiden: Brill, 1997.

Borgen, Peder. "The Gospel of John and Philo of Alexandria." Pages 45–76 in *Light in a Spotless Mirror: Reflections on Wisdom Traditions in Judaism and Early Christianity*. Edited by J. H. Charlesworth and M. A. Daise; Harrisburg/London/New York: Trinity Press International. A Continuum imprint, 2003.

Boring, M. Eugene. *Sayings of the Risen Jesus: Christian Prophecy in the Synoptic Tradition*. Society for New Testament Studies Monograph Series 46. Cambridge: Cambridge University Press, 1982.

Boring, M. Eugene. "Mark 1:1–15 and the Beginning of the Gospel." *Semeia* 52 (1990): 43–81.

Bornkamm, Günther. "The Heresy of Colossians." Pages 123–145 in *Conflict at Colossae*. Edited by F. O. Francis and W. A. Meeks. Missoula: Scholars Press, 1975.

Borsch, Frederick H. *The Son of Man in Myth and History*. New Testament Library. London: SCM, 1967.

Boyarin Daniel. "Homotopia: The Feminized Jewish Man and the Lives of Women in Late Antiquity." *Differences* 2 (1995): 41–81.

Boyarin Daniel. *Dying for God. Martyrdom and the Making of Christianity and Judaism*. Figurae. Reading Medieval Culture, Stanford: Stanford University Press, 1999.

Brandon, Samuel George Frederick. *Jesus and the Zealots: A Study of Political Factor in Primitive Christianity*. Manchester: Manchester University Press, 1967.

Bremmer, Jan N. "The Motivation of Martyrs. Perpetua and the Palestinians." Pages 535–554 in *Religion im kulturellen Diskurs. Festschrift für Hans G. Kippenberg zu seinem 65. Geburtstag*. Edited by Brigitte Luchesi and Kocku von Stuckrad. Berlin/New York: Walter de Gruyter, 2004.

Brower, A. M. and J. L. Nye. *What's Social about Social Cognition? Research on Socially Shared Cognition in Small Groups*. Thousand Oaks: Sage Publications, 1996.

Brown, Peter. *Body and Society. Men, Women and Sexual Renunciation in Early Christianity*. New York: Columbia University Press, 1988.

Bühlmann, Walter and K. Scherer. *Stilfiguren der Bibel: Ein kleines Nachschlagewerk*. Biblische Beiträge 10. Fribourg: Schweizerisches Katholisches Bibelwerk, 1973.

Bultmann, Rudolf. *Der Stil der paulinischen Predigt und die kynisch-stoische Diatribe*. Göttingen: Vandenhoeck, 1910.

Bultmann, Rudolf. *The Gospel of John: A Commentary*. Translated by G. R. Beasley-Murray. Oxford: Basil Blackwell, 1971.

Burchard, Christoph. "Joseph and Aseneth" (English translation with introduction). Pages 177–247 in *The Old Testament Pseudepigrapha, vol. 2*, edited by James H. Charlesworth. London: Darton, Longman & Todd, 1985.

Burchard, Christoph. "The Importance of *Joseph and Aseneth* for the Study of the New Testament: a General Survey and a Fresh Look at the Lord's Supper." *New Testament Studies* 33 (1987): 102–134.

Burkert, Walter. "Hesiod in Context: Abstractions and Divinities in an Aegean-Eastern Koiné." Pages 3–20 in Stafford and Herrin, *Personification*.

Burkett, Delbert. *The Son of Man Debate: A History and Evaluation*. Society for the Study of the New Testament Monograph Series, 107. Cambridge: University Press, 1999.

Burrus, Virginia. *The Making of a Heretic. Gender, Authority, and the Priscillianist Controversy*. Berkeley: University of California Press, 1995.

Burrus, Virginia. "Mapping as Metamorphosis: Initial Reflections on Gender and Ancient Religious Discourses." Pages 1–10 in Penner and Stichele, *Mapping Gender*.

Burton, Diana. "The Gender of Death." Pages 45–68 in Stafford and Herrin, *Personification*.

Byrskog, Samuel. "Nya testamentets forskningshistoria." Pages 33–41 in Mitternacht and Runesson, *Jesus och de första kristna*.

Byrskog, Samuel. *Romarbrevet 1–8*. Kommentar till Nya testamentet 6a; Stockholm: EFS-förlaget, 2006.

Byrskog, Samuel. "A New Quest for the Sitz im Leben: Social Memory, the Jesus Tradition and the Gospel of Matthew." *New Testament Studies* 52 (2006): 319–336.

Byrskog, Samuel. "Anthropologie als Heilsgeschichte. Römerbrief 7,14–20." Pages 245–252 in *Verantwortete Exegese: Hermeneutische Zugänge – Exegetische Studien – Systematische Reflexionen – Ökumenische Perspektiven – Praktische Konkretionen. FS*

Franz Georg Untergassmair. Edited by Gerhard Hotze and Egon Spiegel; Vechtaer Beiträge zur Theologie 13; Berlin: LIT-Verlag, 2006.

Byrskog, Samuel. "A Century with the Sitz im Leben: From Form-Critical Setting to Gospel Community and Beyond." *Zeitschrift für neutestamentliche Wissenschaft* 98 (2007): 1–27.

Byrskog, Samuel. "The Apostolate in the Early Church: From Luke-Acts to the Pauline Tradition." In *The Chosen Lady: Scandinavian Essays on Emerging Institutions of the Church*. Edited by S.-O. Back and T. Holmén. New York: T&T Clark, forthcoming.

Campbell, Barth. "Flesh and Spirit in 1 Cor 5:5: An Exercise in Rhetorical Criticism of the NT." *Journal of the Evangelical Theological Society* 36 (1993): 331–342.

Caragounis, Chrys C. *The Development of Greek and the New Testament: Morphology, Syntax, Phonology and Textual Transmission*. Wissenschaftliche Untersuchungen zum Neuen Testament 167; Tübingen: Mohr Siebeck, 2004.

Carter, Warren. "Matthew's Gospel: Jewish Christianity, Christian Judaism, or Neither?" Pages 155–179 in *Jewish Christianity Reconsidered: Rethinking Ancient Groups and Texts*. Edited by Matt Jackson-McCabe. Minneapolis: Fortress Press, 2007.

Casey, Maurice. *Son of Man: The Interpretation and Influence of Daniel 7*. London: SPCK, 1979.

Casey, Maurice. *The Solution to the 'Son of Man' Problem*. LNTS 343. London: T&T Clark, 2007.

Castelli, Elizabeth A. "'I Will Make Mary Male'." Pages 29–49 in *Body Guards*. Edited by Julia Epstein and Kristina Straub. New York: Routledge, 1991.

Castelli, Elizabeth A. *Martyrdom and Memory. Early Christian Culture Making*. New York: Columbia University Press, 2004.

Chazon, Esther G. "Liturgical Communion with the Angels at Qumran." Pages 95–105 in *Sapiential, Liturgical and Poetical Texts from Qumran: Proceedings of the Third Meeting of the International Organization for Qumran Studies, Oslo, 1998*. Edited by D. K. Falk, F. García Martínez, and E. M. Schuller. Studies on the Texts of the Desert of Judah 35. Leiden: Brill, 2000.

Chesnutt, Randall. "Joseph and Aseneth." Pages 969–971 in vol. 3 of *Anchor Bible Dictionary*. Edited by David Noel Freedman *et al.*, 6 volumes, New York: Doubleday, 1992.

Chialà, Sabino. "The Son of Man: The Evolution of an Expression". Pages 153–178 in Boccaccini, *Enoch and the Messiah Son of Man*.

Cicero, Marcus Tullius. *On the Orator*. Books 1–2. 1942. Translated by E. W. Sutton and H. Rackham. Loeb Classical Library. Cambridge: Harvard University Press.

Cicero, Marcus Tullius. *Rhetorical Treatises. Rhetorica ad Herennium*. 1954. Translated by H. Caplan. Loeb Classical Library. Cambridge: Harvard University Press.

Cinnirella, M. "Towards a European Identity? Interactions between the National and European Social Identities Manifested by University Students in Britain and Italy." *British Journal of Social Psychology* 36 (1997): 19–31.

Clark, Elizabeth A. *Reading Renunciation: Asceticism and Scripture in Early Christianity*. Princeton: Princeton University Press, 1999.

Clark, Elizabeth A. *History, Theory, Text: Historians and the Linguistic Turn*. Cambridge: Harvard University Press, 2004.

Clark, Gillian. "The Old Adam: the Fathers and the Unmaking of Masculinity." Pages 170–182 in *Thinking Men: Masculinity and its Self-Representation in the Classical Tradition*. Edited by Lin Foxhall and John Salmon. London: Routledge, 1998.

Cohen, Shaye J. D. "The Rabbi in Second Century Jewish Society." Pages 922–990 in *The Cambridge History of Judaism, Volume Three: The Early Roman Period*. Edited by W. Horbury, W. D. Davies and J. Sturdy. Cambridge: Cambridge University Press, 1999.

Collins, Adela Yarbro. "The Function of 'Excommunication' in Paul." *Harvard Theological Review* 73 (1980): 251–263.

Collins, Adela Yarbro. *Mark: A Commentary*. Edited by Harold W Attridge. Hermeneia. Minneapolis: Fortress Press, 2007.

Collins, John J. "Pseudepigraphy and Group Formation in Second Temple Judaism". Pages 43–58 in *Pseudepigraphic Perspectives: The Apocrypha and Pseudepigrapha in Light of the Dead Sea Scrolls. Proceedings of the International Symposium of the Orion Center for the Study of the Dead Sea Scrolls and Associated Literature, 12–14 January, 1997*. Edited by E. G. Chazon and M. Stone. Leiden: Brill, 1999.

Collins, John J. "The Heavenly Representative: The 'Son of Man' in the Similitudes of Enoch". Pages 111–133 in *Ideal Figures in Ancient Judaism: Profiles and Paradigms*. Edited by G. W. E. Nickelsburg and J. J. Collins. Society of Biblical Literature Septuagint and Cognate Studies, 12. Chico: Scholars, 1980.

Collins, John J. *Daniel: A Commentary on the Book of Daniel*. Hermeneia. Minneapolis: Fortress Press, 1993.

Collins, John J. *The Scepter and the Star: The Messiahs of the Dead Sea Scrolls and Other Ancient Literature*. New York: Doubleday, 1995.

Collins, John J. *Between Athens and Jerusalem. Jewish Identity in the Hellenistic Diaspora*. Second Edition. Grand Rapids: Eerdmans, 2000.

Collins, John J. "Enoch and the Son of Man: A Response to Sabino Chialà and Helge Kvanvig". Pages 216–227 in Boccaccini, *Enoch and the Messiah Son of Man*.

Comaroff, Jean and John. *Of Revelation and Revolution. Vol. 1: Christianity, Colonialism and Consciousness in South Africa*. Chicago and London: The University of Chicago Press, 1991.

Comaroff, Jean and John. *Of Revelation and Revolution. Vol. 2: The Dialectics of Modernity on a South African Frontier*. Chicago and London: The University of Chicago Press, 1997.

Cooper, Joel and Jeff Stone. "Cognitive Dissonance and the Social Group." Pages 227–244 in *Attitudes, Behavior and Social Context*. Edited by D. J. Terry and M. A. Hogg. Applied Social Research. Mahwah, New Jersey: Lawrence Erlbaum Associates, 2000.

Coppens, Joseph. *La relève apocalyptique du messianisme royal, vol. 3. Le fils de l'homme néotestamentaire*. Bibliotheca ephemeridum theologicarum lovaniensium 55. Leuven: Peeters, 1981.

Crownfield, Frederic C. "The Singular Problem of the Dual Galatians." *Journal of Biblical Literature* 64 (1945): 491–500.

Cullmann, Oscar. *The Christology of the New Testament*. 2nd edn. London: SCM, 1963 [German original 1957].

Dahl, Nils Alstrup. "The Johannine Church and History." Pages 124–142 in *Current Issues in New Testament Interpretation: FS O. A. Piper*. Edited by W. Klassen and G. F. Snyder. New York: Harper, 1962.

Davie, D. "Personification." *Essays in Criticism* 31 (1981): 91–104.

Davies, W. D. *The Setting of the Sermon on the Mount*. Cambridge: Cambridge University Press, 1964.

Decety, J. and J. A. Sommerwille. "Shared Representations between Self and Other: A Social Cognitive Neuroscience View." *Trends in Cognitive Science* 7 (2003): 527–533.

Deines, Roland. *Die Pharisäer: Ihr Verständnis im Spiegel der christlichen und jüdischen Forschung seit Wellhausen und Graetz.* Wissenschaftliche Untersuchungen zum Neuen Testament 101. Tübingen: Mohr Siebeck, 1997.

Deissmann, Adolf. *Licht vom Osten: Das Neue Testament und die neuentdeckten Texte der hellenistisch-römischen Welt.* 4th ed. Tübingen: Mohr Siebeck, 1923.

Deissmann, Adolf. *Light from the Ancient East; the New Testament Illustrated by Recently Discovered Texts of the Graeco-Roman World.* New York: Baker Book House, 1978, [German original 1908].

Dench, Emma. "Austerity, Excess, Success, and Failure in Hellenistic and Early Imperial Italy," Pages 121–146 in *Parchments of Gender: Deciphering the Bodies of Antiquity.* Edited by Maria Wyke. Oxford: Clarendon, 1998.

Derrett, J. Duncan M. "The Reprobate's Peace: 4QD^a (4Q266) (18 v 14–16)." Pages 245–249 in *Legal Texts and Legal Issues: Proceedings of the Second Meeting of the International Organization for Qumran Studies, Cambridge, 1995.* Edited by M. Bernstein, F. García Martínez, and J. Kampen. Studies on the Texts of the Desert of Judah 23. Leiden: Brill, 1997.

Derrida, Jacques. *Dissemination.* Chicago: Univ. of Chicago Press, 1981.

Dewey, Joanna. "'Let Them Renounce Themselves and Take up Their Cross': a Feminist Reading of Mark 8:34 in Mark's Social and Narrative World." *Biblical Theology Bulletin* 34 (2004): 98–104.

Dewey, Joanna. "The Survival of Mark's Gospel: A Good Story?" *Journal of Biblical Literature*, 123 (2004): 495–507.

Dibelius, Martin and Conzelman, Hans. *The Pastoral Epistles.* Translated by P. Buttolph and A. Yarbro. Hermeneia. Minneapolis: Fortress Press, 1989.

Dibelius, Martin. "The Isis Initiation in Apuleius and Related Initiatory Rites." Pages 61–121 in Francis and Meeks, *Conflict at Colossae.*

Dittenberger, Wilhelmus, ed. *Orientis Graeci Inscriptiones Selectae: Supplementum Sylloges Inscriptionum Graecarum* 2; Lipsiae, 1903–1905.

Dixon, Suzanne. 'Sex and the Married Woman in Ancient Rome', Pages 111–129 in *Early Christian Families in Context: An Interdisciplinary Dialogue.* Edited by David L. Balch and Carolyn Osiek. Grand Rapids: Eerdmans, 2003.

Donaldson, Laura E. "Postcolonialism and Biblical Reading: An Introduction." *Semeia* 75 (1996): 1–14.

Donaldson, Laura E. and R. S. Sugirtharajah. *Postcolonialism and Scriptural Reading.* Semeia 75; Atlanta: Scholars Press, 1996.

Douglas, Mary. *Purity and Danger.* London: Routledge & Kegan Paul, 1966.

Douglas, Mary. *Natural Symbols.* New York: Pantheon, 1970.

Draper, Jonathan A. *Orality, Literacy, and Colonialism in Antiquity.* Leiden; Boston: Brill, 2004.

Du Toit, Andrie. "Vilification as a Pragmatic Device in Early Christian Epistolography." *Biblica* 75 (1994): 403–412.

Dube, Musa W. "Savior of the World but not of this World: A Post-Colonial Reading of Spatial Construction in John." Pages 118–135 in *The Postcolonial Bible.* Edited by R. S. Sugirtharajah. Sheffield: Sheffield Academic Press, 1998.

DuBois, Page. "Ancient Masculinities." Pages 319–323 in Moore and Anderson, *New Testament Masculinities.*

Dunn, James D. G. *The Acts of the Apostles.* Petersburough: Epworth Press, 1996.

Dunn, James D. G. *The Theology of Paul the Apostle*. Grand Rapids: Eerdmans, 1998.
Dunn, James D. G. *Jesus Remembered*. Christianity in the Making, 1. Grand Rapids: Eerdmans, 2003.
Dupont, Jacques. "Le logion des douze trônes (Mt 19,28; Lc 22,28–30)." *Biblica* 45 (1964): 355–392.

Edwards, Catharine. *The Politics of Immorality in Ancient Rome*. Cambridge: Cambridge University Press, 1993.
Egede, Hans. *Det gamle Grønlands ny perlustration. Meddelser om Grønland* LIV. Edited by Louis Bobé. København: C. A. Reitzel, 1941.
Egede, Paul, and Egede, Niels. *Continuation af Hans Egedes relationer fra Grønland. Meddelelser om Grønland* 120. Edited by H. Ostermann. København: C. A. Reitzel, 1939.
Eilberg-Schwartz, H. "The Problem of the Body for the People of the Book." Pages 17–46 in *People of the Body: Jews and Judaism from an Embodied Perspective*. Edited by H. Eilberg-Schwartz. Albany, NY: SUNY, 1992.
Elliott, J. K., and Montague Rhodes James. *The Apocryphal New Testament. A Collection of Apocryphal Christian Literature in an English Translation*. Oxford: Clarendon Press, 1993.
Elliott, John H. *1 Peter*. Anchor Bible 37B. New York: Doubleday, 2000.
Esler, Philip. *Galatians*. London and New York: Routledge, 1998.
Esler, Philip F. *Conflict and Identity in Romans: The Social Setting of Paul's Letter*. Minneapolis: Fortress Press, 2003.
Evans, Craig A. "Mark's Incipit and the Priene Calendar Inscription: From Jewish Gospel to Greco-Roman Gospel." *Journal of Greco-Roman Christianity and Judaism* 1 (2000): 67–81.

Fanon, Frantz. *A Dying Colonialism*. New York: Grove Press, 1965.
Fatum, Lone. "Image of God and Glory of Man: Women in the Pauline Congregations." Pages 56–137 in *The Image of God and Gender Models: In Judaeo-Christian Tradition*. Edited by K. E. Børresen. Oslo: Solum Forlag, 1991.
Fatum, Lone. "Lidelsens politik. Fra Paulus til Perpetua." Pages 216–240 in *Lidelsens former og figurer*. Edited by Bodil Ejrnæs and Lone Fatum. København: Museum Tusculanums Forlag, 2002.
Fauconnier, G., see Turner, M.
Fee, Gordon D. *1 and 2 Timothy, Titus*. New International Biblical Commentary on the New Testament. Grand Rapids: Eerdmans, 1988.
Fenger, H. M. *Hans Egede og den grønlandske missions historie 1721–60 efter trykte og utrykte kilder*. København: G. E. C. Gad, 1879.
Festinger, Leon. *The Theory of Cognitive Dissonance*. Stanford, CA: Stanford University Press, 1957.
Fiske, S. T. and S. E. Taylor. *Social Cognition*. Topics in Social Psychology. New York: Random House, 1984.
Fitzmyer, Joseph A. "A Feature of Qumrân Angelology and the Angels of 1 Cor. XI.10." *New Testament Studies* 4 (1957): 48–58.
Fitzmyer, Joseph A. *Romans*. Anchor Bible 33. New York: Doubleday, 1993.
Fontaine, Carole R. *Smooth Words: Wisdom, Proverbs and Performance in Biblical Wisdom*. Journal for the Study of the Old Testament: Supplement Series 356. Sheffield Academic Press, 2002.

Forkman, Göran. *The Limits of the Religious Community: Expulsion from the Religious Community within the Qumran Sect, within Rabbinic Judaism, and within Primitive Christianity.* Coniectanea Biblica: New Testament Series 5. Lund: Gleerup, 1972.

Foucault, Michel. *The History of Sexuality.* Translated by R. Hurley. 3 vols. New York: Pantheon, 1978–1986.

Foucault, Michel, *The Use of Pleasure.* New York: Vintage, 1985.

Foxhall, Lin and John Salmon, eds. *Thinking Men: Masculinity and its Self-Representation in the Classical Tradition.* London: Routledge, 1998.

Foxhall, Lin. "Introduction." Pages 1–9 in *When Men were Men: Masculinity, Power and Identity in Classical Antiquity.* Edited by Lin Foxhall and John Salmon, London: Routledge, 1998.

Francis, Fred O. "Humility and Angelic Worship in Col 2:18." Pages 163–185 in Francis and Meeks, *Conflict at Colossae.*

Francis, Fred O. and Wayne A. Meeks. *Conflict at Colossae.* Missoula: Scholars Press, 1975.

Frennesson, Björn. *"In a Common Rejoicing": Liturgical Communion with Angels in Qumran.* Acta Universitatis Upsaliensis, Studia Semitica Upsaliensia 14. Uppsala: Uppsala University, 1999.

Frilingos, Chris. "Sexing the Lamb." Pages 297–317 in Moore and Anderson, *New Testament Masculinities.*

Frilingos, Chris. "Wearing it Well: Gender at Work in the Shadow of the Empire." Pages 333–349 in Penner and Stichele, *Mapping Gender.*

Frymer-Kensky, T. *In the Wake of the Godesses: Women, Culture, and the Biblical Transformation of Pagan Myth.* New York: The Free Press/ Macmillan, 1992.

Funk, Robert W. "The Apostolic Presence: Paul." Pages 81–102 in *Parables and Presence: Forms of the New Testament Tradition.* Philadelphia: Fortress Press, 1982. Repr. from pages 249–268 in *Christian History and Interpretation: Studies Presented to John Knox.* Edited by W. R. Farmer, C. F. D. Moule, and R. R. Niebuhr. Cambridge: Cambridge University Press, 1967.

Furnish, Victor Paul. *II Corinthians: A New Translation with Introduction and Commentary.* Anchor Bible 32A. New York: Doubleday, 1984.

Gaca, Kathy L. *The Making of Fornication: Eros, Ethos, and Political Reform in Greek Philosophy and Early Christianity.* Berkeley: University of California Press, 2003.

Gaddis, J. L. *The Landscape of History: How Historians Map the Past.* Oxford: Oxford University Press, 2002.

Gandhi, Leela. *Postcolonial Theory: A Critical Introduction.* Edinburgh: Edinburgh University Press, 1998.

García Martínez, Florentino. "La reprensión fraterna en Qumrán y Mt 18,15–17." *Filología Neotestamentaria* 2 (1989): 23–40.

García Martínez, Florentino, and Eibert J. C. Tigchelaar. *The Dead Sea Scrolls Study Edition.* Paperback ed. 2 vols. Leiden: Brill, 2000.

Garland, David E. *The Intention of Matthew 23.* Novum Testamentum Supplements 52. Leiden: Brill, 1979.

Gärtner, Bertil. *The Temple and the Community in Qumran and the New Testament: A Comparative Study in the Temple Symbolism of the Qumran Texts and the New Testament.* Society for New Testament Studies Monograph Series 1. Cambridge: Cambridge University Press, 1965.

Gaston, Lloyd. *No Stone on Another: Studies in the Significance of the Fall of Jerusalem in the Synoptic Gospels.* Novum Testamentum Supplements 23. Leiden: Brill, 1970.

Georgi, Dieter. *Die Geschichte der Kollekte des Paulus für Jerusalem.* Hamburg: Reich, 1965.

Glancy, Jennifer A. *Slavery in Early Christianity.* Oxford: Oxford University Press, 2002.

Gould, Ezra P. *A Critical and Exegetical Commentary on the Gospel according to St. Mark.* The International Critical Commentary on the Holy Scriptures of the Old and New Testaments; Edinburgh: T & T Clark, 1969, [1896].

Goulder, Michael. "The Pastor's Wolves: Jewish Christian Visionaries behind the Pastoral Epistles." *Novum Testamentum* 38 (1996): 242–256.

Grabbe, Lester L. "The Social Setting of Early Jewish Apocalypticism." *Journal for the Study of the Pseudepigrapha* 4 (1989): 27–47.

Grabbe, Lester L. "The Parables of Enoch in Second Temple Jewish Society." Pages 386–402 in Boccaccini, *Enoch and the Messiah Son of Man.*

Graesser, A. C., *et al.* "How Does the Mind Construct and Represent Stories?" Pages 229–262 in *Narrative Impact: Social and Cognitive Foundations.* Edited by J. J. Strange, *et al.* Mahwah: Lawrence Erlbaum, 2002.

Grappe, Christian. "Le logion des douze trônes: Eclairages intertestamentaires." Pages 204–212 in *Le Trône de Dieu.* Edited by M. Philonenko. Wissenschaftliche Untersuchungen zum Neuen Testament 69; Tübingen: Mohr Siebeck, 1993.

Green, Joel B., Scot McKnight, and I. Howard Marshall, eds. *Dictionary of Jesus and the Gospels.* Downers Grove; Leicester: InterVarsity Press, 1992.

Green, William Scott. "Heresy, Apostasy in Judaism." Pages 366–380 in *The Encyclopaedia of Judaism* Vol I. Edited by J. Neusner, A. J. Avery-Peck & W. S. Green. Leiden: Brill, 2000.

Grudem, Wayne A. *The Gift of Prophecy in 1 Corinthians.* Washington: University Press of America, 1982.

Haapa, Esko. *Kirkolliset kirjeet.* Suomalainen Uuden testamentin selitys 9. Helsinki: Kirjapaja, 1978.

Haenchen, Ernst. *Die Apostelgeschichte.* Kritisch-exegetischer Kommentar über das Neue Testament. Göttingen: Vandenhoeck & Ruprecht, 1977.

Hägerland, Tobias. "The Power of Prophecy: A Septuagintal Echo in John 20:19–23." *Catholic Biblical Quarterly.* Forthcoming.

Hagner, D. W. "Matthew: Apostate, Reformer, Revolutionary?," *New Testament Studies* 49 (2003): 193–209.

Hakola, Raimo and Adele Reinhartz. "John's Pharisees." Pages 131–147 in Neusner and Chilton, *In Quest of the Historical Pharisees.*

Hakola, Raimo. *Identity Matters: John, the Jews and Jewishness* Novum Testamentum Supplements 118; Leiden/Boston: Brill, 2005.

Hakola, Raimo. "Social Identities and Group Phenomena in the Second Temple Period." Pages 259–276 in *Explaining Early Judaism and Christianity: Contributions from Cognitive and Social Science.* Edited by P. Luomanen, I. Pyysiäinen and R. Uro. Biblical Interpretation Series 89. Leiden: Brill, 2007.

Hallett, Judith P., and Marilyn B. Skinner, eds. *Roman Sexualities.* Princeton: Princeton University Press, 1997.

Halperin, David M. *One Hundred Years of Homosexuality: And Other Essays on Greek Love.* New York: Routledge, 1990.

Halperin, David M., John J. Winkler, and Froma I. Zeitlin, eds. *Before Sexuality: The Construction of Erotic Experience in the Ancient World.* Princeton: Princeton University Press, 1990.

Hanson, K. C. "How Honorable! How Shameful! A Cultural Analysis of Matthew's Makarisms and Reproaches." *Semeia* 68 (1994): 81–111.

Hanson, Paul D. "Apocalypses and Apocalypticism: The Genre, and Introductory Overview." Pages 279–282 in Gary A. Herion, David Noel Freedman, and Astrid B. Beck, eds. *The Anchor Bible Dictionary* 1; New York: Doubleday, 1992.

Hare, Douglas R. A. "How Jewish is the Gospel of Matthew," *Catholic Biblical Quarterly* 62 (2000): 264–277.

Harrill, Albert J. *Slaves in the New Testament*. Minneapolis: Fortress Press, 2006.

Harris, Gerald. "The Beginnings of Church Discipline: 1 Corinthians 5." *New Testament Studies* 37 (1991): 1–21.

Harris, S. L. *Understanding the Bible*. Boston: McGraw-Hill, 2006.

Hartin, Patrick J. "The Woes against the Pharisees (Matthew 23,1–39): The Reception and Development of Q 11,39–52 within the Matthean Community." Pages 265–283 in *From Quest to Q: Festschrift James M. Robinson*. Edited by J. M. Asgeirsson, K. de Troyer and M. W. Meyer. Bibliotheca ephemeridum theologicarum lovaniensium 146. Leuven; Leuven University Press, 2000.

Hartman, Lars. *Kolosserbrevet*. Kommentar till Nya Testamentet 12. Uppsala: EFS, 1985.

Hartman, Lars. "Johannine Jesus-Belief and Monotheism." Pages 85–99 in *Aspects on the Johannine Literature: Papers presented at a conference of Scandinavian New Testament exegetes at Uppsala, June 16–19, 1986*. Edited by L. Hartman and B. Olsson. Coniectanea Biblica. New Testament Series 18; Uppsala: Almqvist & Wiksell International, 1987.

Hartman, Lars. *Markusevangeliet 8:27–16:20*. Kommentar till Nya testamentet, 2B; Stockholm: EFS-förlaget, 2005.

Hatina, Thomas. "Intertextuality and Historical Criticism: Is There a Relationship?" *Biblical Interpretation* 7 (1999): 28–43.

Hauck, F., and S. Schulz. "*Porneia*." Pages 579–595 in vol. 6 of *Theological Dictionary of the New Testament*. Edited by G. Kittel and G. Friedrich, transl. by G. W. Bromiley. 10 volumes. Grand Rapids, 1964–1976.

Hay, David. "Philo's References to Other Allegorists." *Studia Philonica* 6 (1979–1980): 41–75.

Hay, David. *Both Literal and Allegorica: Studies in Philo of Alexandria's Questions and Answers on Genesis and Exodus*. Brown Judaic Studies 232; Atlanta: Scholars Press, 1991.

Hays, Richard B. *Echoes of Scripture in the Letters of Paul*. New Haven: Yale University Press, 1989.

Hays, Richard B. *The Conversion of the Imagination: Paul as Interpreter of Israel's Scripture*. Grand Rapids: Eerdmans, 2005.

Hengel, Martin. *Crucifixion in the Ancient World and the Folly of the Message of the Cross*. London: SCM, 1977.

Hengel, Martin and Anna Maria Schwemer. *Paul between Damascus and Antioch*. Louisville: John Knox, 1997.

Henze, Matthias. "Enoch's Dream Visions and the Visions of Daniel Reexamined." Pages 17–22 in *Enoch and Qumran Origins: New Light on a Forgotten Connection*. Edited by G. Boccaccini. Grand Rapids: Eerdmans, 2005.

Heschel, Susannah. "The German Theological Tradition." Pages 353–373 in Neusner and Chilton, *In Quest of the Historical Pharisees*.

Hezser, Catherine. *The Social Structure of the Rabbinic Movement in Roman Palestine*. Texte und Studien zum antiken Judentum 66. Tübingen: Mohr Siebeck, 1997.

Hirsch, Emanuel. "Zwei Fragen zu Galater 6." *Zeitschrift für die neutestamentliche Wissenschaft* 29 (1930): 192–197.

Hogg, Michael A. "Social Categorization, Depersonalization and Group Behavior." Pages 56–85 in *Blackwell Handbook of Social Psychology: Group Processes*. Edited by Michael A. Hogg and R. Scott Tindale. Oxford: Blackwell, 2001.

Hogg, M. A. and D. Abrams. *Social Identifications: A Social Psychology of Intergroup Relations and Group Processes*. London: Routledge, 1988.

Hollander, John. *The Figure of Echo: A Mode of Allusion in Milton and After*. Berkeley: University of California Press, 1981.

Holmberg, Bengt. *Paul and Power: The Structure of Authority in the Primitive Church as Reflected in the Pauline Epistles*. Coniectanea biblica: New Testament Series 11. Lund: Gleerup, 1978.

Holtz, Traugott. *Der erste Brief an die Thessaloniker*. Evangelisch-katholischer Kommentar zum Neuen Testament, 13. Zürich/Neukirchen-Vluyn: Benziger/Neukirchener Verlag, 1986.

Holyoak, K. J., *et al.* "Introduction: The Place of Analogy in Cognition." Pages 1–19 in *The Analogical Mind: Perspectives from Cognitive Science*. Edited by D. Gentner, *et al.* Cambridge: MIT Press, 2001.

Hooker, Morna D. "Adam in Romans 1." *New Testament Studies* 6 (1959–60): 297–306.

Hooker, Morna D. "A Further Note on Romans 1." *New Testament Studies* 13 (1966–67): 181–183.

Hooker, Morna D. "Were there False Teachers in Colossae?" Pages 315–331 in *Christ and Spirit in the New Testament*. Edited by B. Lindars and S. S. Smalley. Cambridge: Cambridge University Press, 1973.

Horbury, William. "Extirpation and Excommunication." *Vetus Testamentum* 35 (1985): 13–38.

Horrell, David G. "Introduction." *Journal for the Study of the New Testament* 27 (2005): 251–255.

Horsley, G. H. R. *New Documents Illustrating Early Christianity, Vol 1: A Review of Greek Inscriptions and Papyri Published in 1976*. Sydney: Macquarie University Press, 1981.

Horsley, Richard A. *Hearing the Whole Story: The Politics of Plot in Mark's Gospel*. Louisville: Westminster John Knox Press, 2001.

Horsley, Richard. *Jesus and Empire. The Kingdom of God and the New World Disorder*. Minneapolis: Fortress Press, 2003.

Horsley, Richard. "Subverting Disciplines. The Possibilities and Limitations of Post-colonial Theory for New Testament Studies." Pages 90–105 in *Toward a New Heaven and a New Earth. Essays in Honor of Elisabeth Schüssler Fiorenza*. Edited by F. F. Segovia. Maryknoll, New York: Orbis Books, 2003.

Hourihane, Colum, ed. *Virtue and Vice: The Personifications in the Index of Christian Art*. Princeton: Princeton University Press, 2000.

Howard, George. *Paul's Crisis in Galatia*. Society for New Testament Studies Monograph Series 35. Cambridge: Cambridge University Press, 1979.

Huber, Lynn R. "Sexually Explicit? Re-reading Revelation's 144,000 Virgins as a Response to Roman Discourses." *Journal of Masculinity, Men and Spirituality* 2 (2008): 3–28. Online www.jmmsweb.org. Cited 28 December 2007.

Hübner, Hans. "Intertextualität – die hermeneutische Strategie des Paulus." *Theologische Literaturzeitung* 116 (1991): 881–898.

Humphrey, Edith M. *The Ladies and the Cities: Transformation and Apocalyptic Identity in Joseph and Aseneth, 4 Ezra, the Apocalypse and The Shepherd of Hermas*. Journal for the Study of the Pseudepigrapha: Supplement Series 17. Sheffield: Sheffield Academic, 1995.

Ivarsson, Fredrik. "Vice Lists and Deviant Masculinity: The Rhetorical Function of 1 Corinthians 5:10–11 and 6:9–10." Pages 162–184 in Penner and Stichele, *Mapping Gender*.

Järvinen, Aarto. "The Son of Man and his Followers." Pages 180–222 in *Characteriza-tion in the Gospels: Reconceiving Narrative Criticism*. Edited by D. Rhoads and K. Syreeni. Journal for the Study of New Testament: Supplement Series 184. Sheffield: Academic Press, 1999.

Järvinen, Aarto. "Jesus as Community Symbol in Q." Pages 515–521 in Lindemann, *The Sayings Source Q and the Historical Jesus*.

Jastrow, Marcus. *A Dictionary of the Targumim, the Talmud Babli and Yerushalmi, and the Midrashic Literature*. New York: Judaica Press, 1996.

Jervell, Jacob. *Imago Dei: Gen 1,26f. im Spätjudentum, in der Gnosis und in den paulini-schen Briefen*. Forschungen zur Religion und Literatur des Alten und Neuen Testa-ments 58; Göttingen: Vandenhoeck & Ruprecht, 1960.

Jewett, Robert. "The Agitators and the Galatian Congregation." *New Testament Studies* 17 (1979): 198–212.

Jewett, Robert. *Romans*: A Commentary. Hermeneia; Minneapolis: Fortress Press, 2007.

Johnson, Luke Timothy. "The New Testament's Anti-Jewish Slander and the Conven-tions of Ancient Polemic." *Journal of Biblical Literature* 108 (1989): 419–441.

Johnson, M. D. The Life of Adam and Eve. Pages 249–295 in vol. 2 of *Old Testament Pseudepigrapha*. Edited by James H. Charlesworth. 2 vols. New York, 1983.

Jokiranta, Jutta M. *Identity on a Continuum: Constructing and Expressing Sectarian So-cial Identity in Qumran Serakhim and Pesharim*. Ph.D. Diss., University of Helsinki, 2005.

Jonge, H. J. de. "The Sayings on Confessing and Denying Jesus in Q 12:8–9 and Mark 8:38." Pages 105–121 in *Sayings of Jesus: Canonical and Non-Canonical: Essays in Honour of Tjitze Baarda*. Edited by W. L. Petersen, J. S. Vos and H. J. de Jonge. Novum Testamentum Supplements 89. Leiden: Brill, 1997.

Joseph et Aséneth. Introduction, texte critique, traduction et notes par Marc Philonenko. Studia Post-Biblica 13; Leiden: Brill, 1968.

Joseph und Aseneth. Kritisch herausgegeben von Christoph Burchard. Pseudepigrapha Veteris Testamenti Graece 5. Leiden: Brill, 2003.

Kärkkäinen, Veli-Matti. *Christology: A Global Introduction*. Grand Rapids: Baker, 2003.

Karris, Robert J. "Background and Significance of the Polemic of the Pastoral Epistles," *Journal of Biblical Literature* 92 (1973): 549–564.

Käsemann, Ernst. "Sätze heiligen Rechtes im Neuen Testament." *New Testament Studies* 1 (1955): 248–260.

Kazen, Thomas. "Son of Man as Kingdom Imagery: Jesus between Corporate Symbol and Individual Redeemer Figure." Pages 87–108 in *Jesus from Judaism to Christiani-ty: Continuum Approaches to the Historical Jesus*. Edited by T. Holmén. ESCO; LNTS (Journal for the Study of New Testament: Supplement Series) 352. London: T&T Clark, 2007.

Kazen, Thomas. "The Coming Son of Man Revisited." *Journal for the Study of the His-torical Jesus* 5 (2007): 157–176.

Keck, Leander E. "Introduction to Mark's Gospel." *New Testament Studies* 12 (1966): 352–370.

Kelly, John N. D. *A Commentary on the Pastoral Epistles, 1 Timothy, 2 Timothy, Titus.* Black's New Testament Commentaries. London: Black, 1983.

Kim, Seyoon, *Paul and the New Perspective: Second Thoughts on the Origin of Paul's Gospel.* Grand Rapids: Eerdmans, 2002.

Kim, Tae Hun. "The Anarthrous yios theou in Mark 15,39 and the Roman Imperial Cult." *Biblica* 79 (1998): 221–241.

Kirchhoff, Renate. *Die Sünde gegen den eigenen Leib: Studien zu* pornē *und* porneia *in 1 Kor 6,12–20 und dem Sozio-kulturellen Kontext der paulinischen Adressaten.* Studien zur Umwelt des Neuen Testaments 18. Göttingen: Vandenhoeck und Ruprecht, 1994.

Klauck, Hans-Josef. *Magic and Paganism in Early Christianity.* Translated by B. McNeil. Edinburgh: T&T Clark, 2000.

Kloppenborg, John S. *The Formation of Q: Trajectories in Ancient Wisdom Collections.* Studies in Antiquity and Christianity. Philadelphia: Fortress Press, 1987.

Kloppenborg Verbin, John S. *Excavating Q: The History and Setting of the Sayings Gospel.* Edinburgh: T&T Clark, 2000.

Knust, Jennifer Wright. *Abandoned to Lust: Sexual Slander and Ancient Christianity.* New York: Columbia University Press, 2006.

Koester, Helmut. "Häretiker im Urchristentum." Pages 17–21 in vol. 3 of *Religion in Geschichte und Gegenwart.* Edited by K. Galling. 7 vols. 3d ed. Tübingen, 1957–1965.

Koester, Helmut. *Introduction to the New Testament. Vol 2. History and Literature of Early Christianity.* New York: de Gruyter, 1982.

Kovacs, Judith, and Christopher Rowland. *Revelation. The Apocalypse of Jesus Christ.* Blackwell Bible Commentaries; Oxford: Blackwell Publishing, 2004.

Kraemer, R. S. *Her Share of the Blessings: Women's Religions among Pagans, Jews, and Christians in the Greco-Roman World.* New York: Oxford Univ. Press, 1992.

Kraemer, Ross Shepard. "The Book of Aseneth." Pages 859–888 in *Searching the Scriptures. Volume Two: A Feminist Commentary.* Edited by Elisabeth Schüssler Fiorenza. London: SCM Press, 1995.

Kraemer, Ross Shepard. *When Aseneth Met Joseph. A Late Antique Tale of the Biblical Patriarch and his Egyptian Wife, Reconsidered.* New York: Oxford University Press, 1998.

Kraemer, Ross S., and Shira L. Lander. "Perpetua and Felicitas." Pages 1048–1068 in *The Early Christian World,* edited by Philip F. Esler. London and New York: Routledge, 2000.

Kreplin, Matthias. *Das Selbstverständnis Jesu: Hermeneutische und christologische Reflexion. Historisch-kritische Analyse.* Wissenschaftliche Untersuchungen zum Neuen Testament 2:141. Tübingen: Mohr Siebeck, 2001.

Kristeva, Julia. *Desire in Language: A Semiotic Approach to Literature and Art.* Edited by Leon S. Roudiez. New York: Columbia University Press, 1980.

Kuefler, Mathew. *The Manly Eunuch: Masculinity, Gender Ambiguity and Christian Ideology in Late Antiquity.* Chicago: Chicago University Press, 2001.

Kuhn, Heinz-Wolfgang. "The Impact of the Qumran Scrolls on the Understanding of Paul." Pages 327–339 in *The Dead Sea Scrolls: Forty Years of Research.* Edited by D. Dimant and U. Rappaport. Studies on the Texts of the Desert of Judah 10. Leiden: Brill, 1992.

Kuhn, Heinz-Wolfgang. "A Legal Issue in 1 Corinthians 5 and in Qumran." Pages 489–499 in *Legal Texts and Legal Issues: Proceedings of the Second Meeting of the*

International Organization for Qumran Studies, Cambridge, 1995. Edited by M. Bernstein, F. García Martínez, and J. Kampen. Studies on the Texts of the Desert of Judah 23. Leiden: Brill, 1997.

Kumar, Amitava. "Catachresis is Her Middle Name: The Cautionary Claims of Gayatri C. Spivak." *Cultural Studies* 11 (1997): 176–179.

Lacan, Jacques and Jacques-Alain Miller. *The Four Fundamental Concepts of Psycho-Analysis.* The International Psycho-Analytical Library, 106; London, New York: Hogarth; Norton, 1977.

LaFleur, William R. "The Body." Pages 36–54 in *Critical Terms for Religious Studies* . Edited by Mark C. Taylor. Chicago: Chicago University Press, 1998.

Lakoff, G. and M. Johnson. *Philosophy in the Flesh: The Embodied Mind and Its Challenge to Western Thought.* New York: Basic Books, 1999.

Laqueur, Thomas. *Making Sex: Body and Gender from the Greeks to Freud.* Cambridge: Harvard University Press, 1990.

Larsson, Hedvig. *Jews and Gentiles in Early Jewish Novels.* Ph.D. diss., Uppsala University, 2006.

Lassen, Eva Maria. "The Roman Family: Ideal and Metaphor." Pages 103–120 in *Constructing Early Christian Families: Family as Social Reality and Metaphor.* Edited by Halvor Moxnes. London: Routledge, 1997.

Lausberg, Heinrich. *Handbuch der literarischen Rhetorik,* 2d ed. München: Hueber, 1973.

Lawrence, L. J. *An Ethnography of the Gospel of Matthew: A Critical Assessment of the Use of the Honour and Shame Model in New Testament Studies.* Tübingen: Mohr Siebeck, 2003.

Levison, John. *Portraits of Adam in Early Judaism: From Sirach to 2 Baruch.* Journal for the Study of the Pseudepigrapha: Supplement Series 1; Sheffield: JSOT Press, 1988.

Levison, John. "Adam and Eve in Romans 1.18–25 and the Greek Life of Adam and Eve." *New Testament Studies* 50 (2004): 519–534.

Lichtenberger, Hermann. *Das Ich Adams und das Ich der Menschheit: Studien zum Menschenbild in Römer 7.* Wissenschaftliche Untersuchungen zum Neuen Testament 164; Tübingen: Mohr Siebeck, 2004.

Liddell, Henry George and Robert Scott. *A Greek-English Lexicon: A New Edition.* Oxford: Clarendon Press; Reprint, 1958.

Lieu, Judith. "Temple and Synagogue in John." *New Testament Studies* 45 (1999): 51–69.

Lieu, Judith M. "The Synagogue and the Separation of the Christians." Pages 189–207 in *The Ancient Synagogue from its Origins until 200 C.E.* Edited by B. Olsson and M. Zetterholm. ConBNT 39. Stockholm: Almqvist & Wiksell, 2003.

Lieu, J. *Christian Identity in the Jewish and Graeco-Roman World.* Oxford: Oxford University Press, 2004.

Liew, Tat-Siong Benny. *Politics of Parousia: reading Mark Inter(con)textually.* Biblical Interpretation series 42; Leiden; Boston: Brill, 1999.

Liew, Tat-Siong Benny. "Tyranny, Boundary and Might: Colonial Mimicry in Mark's Gospel." Pages 206–223 in Sugirtharajah, *Postcolonial Biblical Reader.*

Lincoln, Andrew T. *Truth on Trial: The Lawsuit Motif in John's Gospel.* Peabody: Hendrickson Publishers, 2000.

Lindars, Barnabas. *The Gospel of John.* London: Oliphants, 1972.

Lindemann, Andreas, ed. *The Sayings Source Q and the Historical Jesus.* Bibliotheca ephemeridum theologicarum lovaniensium 158. Leuven: Peeters, 2001.

Lindijer, C.H. "Die Jungfrauen in der Offenbarung des Johannes XIV 4." Pages 125–142 in *Studies in John Presented to Professor Dr. J. N. Sevenster on the Occasion of his Seventieth Birthday*. Novum Testamentum Supplements 24; Leiden: Brill, 1970.

Lohse, Eduard. *Die Briefe an die Kolosser und an Philemon*. Kritisch-exegetischer Kommentar über das Neue Testament 9:2. Göttingen: Vandenhoeck & Ruprecht, 1986.

Longenecker, Rickhard. *Galatians*. Word Biblical Commentary 41. Waco: Word, 1990.

Loomba, Ania. *Colonialism/Postcolonialism*. 2nd ed. London and New York: Routledge, 2005.

Loomba, Ania. *Kolonialism/Postkolonialism: En introduktion till ett forskningsfält*. Translated by Oskar Söderlind. Stockholm: Tankekraft, 2006, [English original 1998].

L'Orange, H. P. *Mot Middelalder*. Oslo: Dreyer, 1963.

Luomanen, Petri. *Entering the Kingdom of Heaven: A Study on the Structure of Matthew's View of Salvation*. Wissenschaftliche Untersuchungen zum Neuen Testament, 2. Series 101. Tübingen: Mohr Siebeck, 1998.

Luomanen, Petri. "The 'Sociology of Sectarianism' in Matthew: Modeling the Genesis of Early Jewish and Christian Communities." Pages 107–130 in *Fair Play: Diversity and Conflicts in Early Christianity. Essays in Honour of Heikki Räisänen*. Ed. by I. Dunderberg, C. Tuckett and K. Syreeni. Novum Testamentum Supplements 103. Leiden: Brill, 2002.

Luomanen, Petri, Ilkka Pyysiäinen and Risto Uro, Risto, eds. *Explaining Early Judaism and Christianity: Contributions from Cognitive and Social Science*. Biblical Interpretation. Leiden: E. J. Brill, 2007.

Lütgert, Wilhelm. *Gesetz und Geist, eine Untersuchung zur Vorgeschichte des Galaterbriefes*. Beiträge zur Förderung christlicher Theologie 22.6. Gütersloh: Bertelsman, 1919.

Lutz, Cora E. "Musonius Rufus: The Roman Socrates." Pages 3–147 in *Yale Classical Studies* 10. Edited by ed. Alfred R. Bellinger; New Haven: Yale University Press, 1947.

Luz Ulrich. *Matthew 1–7: A Continental Commentary*. Translated by W. C. Linss. Minneapolis: Fortress Press, 1989.

Luz, Ulrich. *Matthew 21–28: A Commentary*. Translated by. W. C. Linss. Hermeneia. Minneapolis: Fortress Press, 2005.

Lyonnet, Stanislas S. J. "Paul's Adversaries in Colossae," in Francis and Meeks. *Conflict at Colossae*.

Lyons, George. *Pauline Autobiography: Toward a New Understanding*. Atlanta: Scholars Press, 1985.

MacDonald, Margaret Y. "Slavery, Sexuality and House Churches: A Reassessment of Colossians 3.18–4.1 in Light of New Research on the Roman Family," *New Testament Studies* 53 (2007): 94–113.

Maier, H. O. *The Social Setting of the Ministry as Reflected in the Writings of Hermas, Clement and Ignatius*. Dissertations Series 1. Ontario: Wilfrid Laurier UP, 1991.

Malina, Bruce. "Does Porneia Mean Fornication?" *Novum Testamentum* 14 (1972): 10–17.

Malina, Bruce J. and Jerome H. Neyrey. *Calling Jesus Names: The Social Value of Labels in Matthew*. Foundations and Facets: Social Facets; Sonoma: Polebridge, 1988.

Malina, B. J. and J. H. Neyrey. *Portraits of Paul: An Archaeology of Ancient Personality*. Louisville: Westminster/John Knox Press, 1996.

Malina, B. J. *The New Testament World: Insights from Cultural Anthropology*. Louisville: Westminster/John Knox Press, 2001.

Malina, Bruce J. *The Social Gospel of Jesus: The Kingdom of God in Mediterranean Perspective*. Minneapolis: Fortress Press, 2001.

Manson, T. W. *The Teaching of Jesus: Studies of Its Form and Content*. Cambridge: Cambridge University Press, 1931.

Manson, T. W. *Studies in the Gospels and Epistles*. Edited by M. Black. Manchester: Manchester University Press, 1962.

Marshall, Ian H. *A Critical and Exegetical Commentary on the Pastoral Epistles* in collaboration with Philip H. Towner. International Critical Commentary. Edinburgh: T&T Clark, 1999.

Marshall, John W. "Postcolonialism and the Practice of History." Pages 93–108 in Stichele and Penner, *Her Master's Tools?*

Martin, Dale B. *Slavery as Salvation. The Metaphor of Slavery in Pauline Christianity*. New Haven: Yale University Press, 1990.

Martin, Dale B. *The Corinthian Body*. New Haven: Yale University Press, 1995.

Martin, Dale. "*Arsenokoitēs* and *Malakos*: Meanings and Consequences." Pages 117–136 in *Biblical Ethics and Homosexuality: Listening to Scripture*. Edited by R. L. Brawley. Louisville: Westminster John Knox, 1996.

Martin, Joseph. *Antike Rhetorik: Technik und Methode*. Handbuch der Altertumswissenschaft 2.3. München: Beck, 1974.

Mason, Steve. "Pharisaic Dominance before 70 CE and the Gospels' Hypocrisy Charge (Matt 23:2–3)." *Harvard Theological Review* 83 (1990): 363–381.

Matz, David C. and Wendy Wood. "Cognitive Dissonance in Groups: The Consequences of Disagreement." *Journal of Personality and Social Psychology* 88 (2005): 22–37.

May, Alistair Scott. *'The Body for the Lord': Sex and Identity in 1 Corinthians 5–7*. Journal for the Study of the New Testament: Supplement Series 278. London: T&T Clark International, 2004.

McCarty, W. *Humanities Computing*. Basingstoke: Palgrave Macmillan, 2005.

McClintock, Anne. "The Angel of Progress: Pitfalls of the Term 'Postcolonialism'." Pages 253–266 in *Colonial Discourse/Postcolonial Theory*. Edited by F. Barker, P. Hulme and M. Iversen. Manchester & New York: Manchester University Press, 1992.

McDonnell, Myles. "Roman Men and Greek Virtue." Pages 235–261 in *Andreia. Studies in Manliness and Courage in Classical Antiquity*. Edited by Ralph M. Rosen and Ineke Sluiter. Mnemosyne: Bibliotheca classica Batava. Supplementum 238. Leiden: Brill, 2003.

McKimmie, Blake M., Deborah J. Terry, Michael Hogg, Antony S. R. Manstead, Russell Spears and Bertjan Doosje. "I'm a Hypocrite, but So Is Everyone Else: Group Support and the Reduction of Cognitive Dissonance." *Group Dynamics: Theory, Research, and Practice* 7 (2003): 214–224.

Meeks, Wayne A. "The Man from Heaven in Johannine Sectarianism." *Journal of Biblical Literature* 91 (1972): 44–72.

Meeks, W. A. *The First Urban Christians: The Social World of the Apostle Paul*. New Haven: Yale University Press, 1983.

Meeks, Wayne A. *The Moral World of the First Christians*. Philadelphia: Westminster-John Knox Press, 1986.

Merklein, Helmut. "Der Theologe als Prophet: Zur Funktion prophetischen Redens im theologischen Diskurs des Paulus." *New Testament Studies* 38 (1992): 402–429.

Méthode d'Olympe. *Le Banquet* (Methodius Olympos, *Symposion*). Introduction et texte critique par Herbert Musurillo; traduction et notes par Victor-Henry Debidour. Paris: Cerf, 1963.

Miles, Margaret R. *Carnal Knowing: Female Nakedness and Religious Meaning in the Christian West*. Boston: Beacon Press, 1989.

Minear, Paul S. "Christ and the Congregation: 1 Corinthians 5–6." *Review and Expositor* 80 (1983): 341–350.

Mitternacht, Dieter. *Forum für Sprachlose, ein kommunikationspsychologische und epistolär-rhetorische Untersuchung des Galaterbriefes*. Coniectanea Biblica New Testament Series 30. Stockholm: Almqvist & Wiksell International, 1999.

Mitternacht, Dieter, and Anders Runesson, eds. *Jesus och de första kristna: Inledning till Nya testamentet*. Stockholm: Verbum, 2007.

Mlicki, P. P. and N. Ellemers. "Being Different or Being Better? National Stereotypes and Identifications of Polish and Dutch Students." *European Journal of Social Psychology* 26 (1996): 97–115.

Moore, Stephen D. *God's Gym: Divine Male Bodies of the Bible*. New York: Routledge, 1996.

Moore Stephen, D. "Revolting Revelations." Pages 183–199 in *The Personal Voice in Biblical Interpretation*. Edited by Ingrid Rosa Kitzberger. London: Routledge, 1998.

Moore Stephen, D. *God's Beauty Parlour and Other Queer Spaces in and around the Bible*. Conversions; Stanford: Stanford University Press, 2001.

Moore, Stephen D. and Janice C. Anderson, eds. *New Testament Masculinities*. Semeia Studies 45. Atlanta, Society of Biblical Literature, 2003.

Moore, Stephen D. "Mark and Empire: 'Zealot' and 'Postcolonial' Readings." Pages 193–205 in Sugirtharajah, *The Postcolonial Biblical Reader*.

Moore, Stephen D. *Empire and Apocalypse: Postcolonialism and the New Testament*. Bible in the Modern World; 12; Sheffield: Sheffield Phoenix Press, 2006.

Moore, Stephen D., and Janice Capel Anderson. "Taking it Like a Man: Masculinity in 4 Maccabees." *Journal of Biblical Literature* 117 (1998): 249–273.

Moore-Gilbert, Bart. *Postcolonial Theory: Contexts, Practices, Politics*. London: Verso, 1997.

Morales, F. J., *et al.* "Discrimination and Beliefs on Discrimination in Individualists and Collectivists." Pages 199–210 in *Social Identity: International Perspectives*. Edited by S. Worchel, *et al.* London: SAGE, 1998.

Moule, C. F. D. *The Phenomenon of the New Testament: An Inquiry into the Implications of Certain Features of the New Testament*. Studies in Biblical Theology 2:1. London: SCM, 1967.

Moxnes, Halvor, "Kropp som symbol: Bruk av sosialantropologi i studiet av Det nye testamente," *Norsk Teologisk Tidskrift* 84 (1983): 197–217.

Moxnes, Halvor. *The Economy of the Kingdom. Social Conflict and Economic Relations in Luke's Gospel*. Philadelphia: Fortress Press, 1988.

Moxnes, Halvor. "Honor and Shame." *Biblical Theology Bulletin* 23 (1993): 167–176.

Moxnes, Halvor. "Conventional Values in the Hellenistic World: Masculinity." Pages 263–284 in *Conventional Values of the Hellenistic Greeks*. Studies in Hellenistic Civilization 8. Edited by Per Bilde *et al.* Aarhus; Aarhus University Press, 1997.

Moxnes, Halvor. "Asceticism and Christian Identity in Antiquity: A Dialogue with Foucault and Paul," *Journal for the Study of the New Testament* 26 (2003): 3–29.

Moxnes, Halvor. *Putting Jesus in His Place. A Radical Vision of Household and Kingdom*. Louisville: Westminster-John Knox Press, 2003.

Mudimbe, Vincent Y. *The Invention of Africa: Gnosis, Philosophy and the Order of Knowledge*. African Systems of Thought. London: James Currey, 1988.

Müller, Mogens. *Der Ausdruck "Menschensohn" in den Evangelien: Voraussetzungen und Bedeutung*. Acta Theologica Danica, 17. Leiden: Brill, 1984.

Müller, Ulrich B. *Prophetie und Predigt im Neuen Testament: Formgeschichtliche Untersuchungen zur urchristlichen Prophetie*. Gütersloh: Mohn, 1975.

Munck, Johannes. *The Acts of the Apostles*. The Anchor Bible 31. New York: Doubleday & Company Inc. [1967], 1978.

Murphy-O'Connor, Jerome. "I Corinthians, v, 3–5." *Revue biblique* 84 (1977): 239–245.

Mussner, Franz. *Der Galaterbrief*. Herders theologischer Kommentar zum Neuen Testament 9. Freiburg: Herder, 1974.

Musurillo, Herbert. *The Acts of the Christian Martyrs*. Oxford: Clarendon Press, 1972.

Myers, Ched. *Binding the Strong Man: A Political Reading of Mark's Story of Jesus*. Maryknoll: Orbis Books, 1988.

Nanos, Mark, ed. *The Galatians Debate: Contemporary Issues in Rhetorical and Historical Interpretation*. Peabody: Hendrickson, 2002.

Nanos, Mark. "The Local Contexts of the Galatians: Toward Resolving A Catch-22." June 2003, 1–17. Online: http://marknanos.com/ GalatiansLocalContext-6-03.pdf. Accessed 19 October 2007.

Neusner, Jacob. *Judaism: The Evidence of the Mishnah*. Chicago: Chicago University Press, 1981.

Neusner, Jacob. *The Mishnah: Social Perspectives*. Handbuch der Orientalistik, Section One, Vol. 46. Leiden: Brill, 1999.

Neusner, Jacob, and Bruce Chilton, *In Quest of the Historical Pharisees*. Waco, Texas: Baylor University Press, 2007.

Neusner, Jacob. "The Anglo-American Theological Tradition to 1970." Pages 375–394 in Neusner and Chilton, *In Quest of the Historical Pharisees*.

Neyrey, Jerome N. *Paul in Other Words: A Cultural Reading of his Letters*. Louisville: Westminster-John Knox Press, 1990.

Neyrey, Jerome H. *2 Peter, Jude: A New Translation with Introduction and Commentary*. New York: Doubleday, 1993.

Neyrey, Jerome H. "Jesus, Gender and the Gospel of Matthew." Pages 43–66 in Moore and Anderson, *New Testament Masculinities*.

Nikiprowetzky, Valentin. *Le commentaire de l'Écriture chez Philon de'Alexandrie: son caractère et sa portée; observations philologiques*. Arbeiten zur Literatur und Geschichte des hellenistischen Judentums 11; Leiden: Brill, 1977.

North, Helen. *Sophrosyne. Self-Knowledge and Self-Restraint in Greek Literature*. Cornell Studies in Classical Philology 35. Ithaca: Cornell University Press, 1966.

Nugent, S. Georgia. "Virtus or Virago? The Female Personifications of Prudentius' Psychomachia." Pages 13–28 in Hourihane, *Virtue and Vice*.

Oakes, Penelope J. "The Categorization Process: Cognition of the Group in the Social Psychology of Stereotyping." Pages 28–47 in *Social Identity Theory: Constructive and Critical Advances*. Edited by D. Abrams and M. A. Hogg. London: Harvester Wheatsheaf, 1990.

Oakes, Penelope J., S. Alexander Haslam and Katherine J. Reynolds. "Social Categorization and Social Context: Is Stereotype Change a Matter of Information or of Meaning?" Pages 55–79 in *Social Identity and Social Cognition*. Edited by D. M. Abrams and M. A: Hogg; Oxford: Blackwell, 1999.

O'Banion, John D. "Narration and Argumentation: Quintilian on *Narratio* as the Heart of Rhetorical Thinking." *Rhetorica* 5 (1987): 325–351.

O'Brien, Peter T. *Colossians, Philemon.* Word Biblical Commentary 44. Waco: Word, 1982.

O'Collins, Gerald G. "Crucifixion." Pages 1207–1210 in vol. 1 of *Anchor Bible Dictionary.* Edited by Gary A. Herion, David Noel Freedman, and Astrid B. Beck. 6 vols. New York: Doubleday, 1992.

Økland, Jorunn. "Sex, Gender and Ancient Greek: A Case-Study in Theoretical Misfit." *Studia Theologica* 57 (2003): 124–162.

Økland, Jorunn. *Women in Their Place: Paul and the Corinthian Discourse of Gender and Sanctuary Space.* Journal for the Study of the New Testament: Supplement Series 269. London: T&T Clark, 2004.

Økland, Jorunn. "Why Can't the Heavenly Miss Jerusalem Just Shut Up?" Pages 211–232 in *Her Master's Tools? Feminist and Postcolonial Engagements of Historical-Critical Discourse.* Edited by Caroline Vander Stichele and Todd Penner. Global Perspectives on Biblical Scholarship 9. Atlanta: Society of Biblical Literature, 2005.

Økland, Jorunn. "Anything to Offer? A Gendered, Viewer-Response Approach to Corinthian Votive Offerings and Their Donators." Paper presented at the annual meeting of SBL, Philadelphia, November 19th, 2005.

Olson, Daniel C. "An Overlooked Patristic Allusion to the Parables of Enoch?" Pages 492–496 in Boccaccini, *Enoch and the Messiah Son of Man.*

Olsson, Birger. "'All My Teaching Was Done in Synagogues ...' (John 18,20)." Pages 203–224 in *Theology and Christology in the Fourth Gospel: Essays by the Members of the SNTS Johannine Writings Seminar.* Edited by G. Van Belle, J. G. Van der Watt, and P. Maritz; Bibliotheca Ephemeridum Theologicarum Lovaniensium 184. Leuven: Leuven University Press, 2003.

Osiek, C. and D. L. Balch. *Families in the New Testament World: Households and House Churches.* Family, Religion, and Culture. Louisville: Westminster John Knox Press, 1997.

Osiek, Carolyn. *The Shepherd of Hermas.* Hermeneia. Minneapolis: Fortress Press, 1999.

Osiek, Carolyn. "Perpetua's Husband." *Journal of Early Christian Studies* 10 (2002): 287–290.

Osiek, Carolyn, and Margaret Y. MacDonald. *A Woman's Place: House Churches in Earliest Christianity.* Minneapolis: Fortress Press, 2006.

Overman, J. Andrew. *Matthew's Gospel and Formative Judaism: The Social World of the Matthean Community.* Minneapolis: Fortress Press, 1990.

Paez, D., *et al.* "Constructing Social Identity: The Role of Status, Collective Values, Collective Self-Esteem, Perception and Social Behaviour." Pages 211–229 in *Social Identity: International Perspectives.* Edited by S. Worchel, *et al.* London: SAGE, 1998.

Pancaro, Severino. *The Law in the Fourth Gospel: the Torah and the Gospel, Moses and Jesus, Judaism and Christianity according to John.* Novum Testamentum Supplements 13; Leiden: Brill, 1975.

Pannenberg, Wolfhart. *Systematische Theologie. vol. 2.* Göttingen: Vandenhoeck & Ruprecht, 1991.

Parker, Holt N. "The Teratogenic Grid." Pages 47–65 in *Roman Sexualities.* Edited by Judith P. Hallett and Marilyn B. Skinner. Princeton: Princeton University Press, 1997.

Paxson, James J. *The Poetics of Personification.* Literature, Culture, Theory 6. Cambridge: Cambridge University Press, 1994.

Paxson, James J. "Personification's Gender." *Rhetorica* 16 (1998): 149–179.
Penner, Todd, and Caroline Vander Stichele, eds. *Mapping Gender in Ancient Religious Discourses.* Leiden: Brill, 2007.
Perelman, Chaim and Olbrechts-Tyteca, Lucie. *The New Rhetoric: A Treatise on Argumentation.* Trans. by J. Wilkinson and P. Weaver. Notre Dame: University of Notre Dame, 1969.
Perkins, Judith. *The Suffering Self: Pain and Narrative Representation in the Early Christian Era.* London: Routledge, 1995.
Perkins, Judith. "The Rhetoric of the Maternal Body in the Passion of Perpetua." Pages 313-332 in Penner and Stichele, *Mapping Gender.*
Petterson, Christina, "Kap farvel til Umanarssuaq." *Dansk Teologisk Tidsskrift* 1 (2007): 103–115.
Petterson, Christina, "Profeten Hoseas møder Anne Wivel: Nationer, allegorier og kvinder." in *Grønlandsk kultur- og Samfundsforskning* 2007, Ilisimatusarfik/Forlaget Atuagkat; in print.
Philo, *De Iosepho.* Pages 138–271 in *Philo in 10 volumes, vol VI.* With an English translation by F. H.Colson. Loeb Classical Library. Cambridge: Harvard University Press, 1935, reprint 1959.
Pickup, Martin. "Matthew's and Mark's Pharisees." Pages 67–112 in Neusner and Chilton, *In Quest of the Historical Pharisees.*
Pietersen, Lloyd. "Despicable Deviants: Labelling Theory and the Polemic of the Pastorals." *Sociology of Religion 58* (1997): 343–352.
Pietersen, Lloyd, *The Polemic of the Pastorals: A Sociological Examination of the Development of Pauline Christianity.* Journal for the Study of the New Testament: Supplement Series 264. London, New York: T&T Clark, 2004.
Pippin, Tina. *Death and Desire: The Rhetoric of Gender in the Apocalypse.* Literary Currents in Biblical Interpretation. Louisville: Westminster/John Knox Press, 1992.
Pippin, Tina. *Apocalyptic Bodies: The Biblical End of the World in Text and Image.* London: Routledge, 1999.
Poschmann, Bernhard. *Paenitentia secunda: Die kirchliche Buße im ältesten Christentum bis Cyprian und Origenes: Eine dogmengeschichtliche Untersuchung.* Theophaneia 1. Bonn: Hanstein, 1940.
Powell, Mark Allan. "Do and Keep What Moses Says (Matthew 23:2–7)." *Journal of Biblical Literature* 114 (1995): 419–435.
Preiss, Théo. *Life in Christ.* StBth 13; London: SCM. Translation of *La Vie en Christ.* Neuchâtel-Paris, 1951.
Price, Simon R. F. *Rituals and Power: The Roman Imperial Cult in Asia Minor.* Cambridge: Cambridge U.P., 1984.
Pui-lan, Kwok. "Jesus/The Native: Biblical Studies from a Postcolonial Perspective." Pages 69–85 in Fernando F. Segovia and Mary Ann Tolbert, eds. *Teaching the Bible: The Discourses and Politics of Biblical Pedagogy.* Maryknoll: Orbis Books, 1998.
Pui-lan, Kwok. *Postcolonial Imagination and Feminist Theology.* London: SCM, 2005.
Pyysiäinen, I. *How Religion Works: Towards a New Cognitive Science of Religion.* Leiden; Boston: Brill, 2003.

Quintilian. *The Orator's Education. Books 3–5.* Edited and translated by D. A. Russell. Loeb Classical Library. Cambridge: Harvard University Press, 2001.

Rabbinowitz, Noel S. "Matthew 23:2–4: Does Jesus Recognize the Authority of the Pharisees and Does He Endorse Their *Halakhah*?" *Journal of the Eavngelical Theological Society* 46 (2003): 423–447.

Radl, W. "Parousia." Pages 43–44 in *Exegetical Dictionary of the New Testament*. Edited by H. Balz and G. Schneider. English translation. Grand Rapids, 1990–1993.

Reicher, S. D. *et al.* "A Social Identity Model of Deindividuation Phenomena." *European Review of Social Psychology* 6 (1995): 161–198.

Richlin, Amy. *The Garden of Priapus: Sexuality and Aggression in Roman Humor.* New Haven: Yale University Press, 1983.

Richlin, Amy ."Towards a History of Body History." Pages 16–35 in *Inventing Ancient Culture.* Edited by Mark Golden and Peter Toohey. London: Routledge, 1997.

Rives, James B. *Religion in the Roman Empire.* Blackwell Ancient Religions; Malden: Blackwell, 2007.

Robbins, Vernon K. *The Tapestry of Early Christian Discourse: Rhetoric, Society, and Ideology.* London; New York: Routledge, 1996.

Robbins, Vernon K. "The Intertexture of Apocalyptic Discourse in the Gospel of Mark." Pages 11–44 in *The Intertexture of Apocalyptic Discourse in the New Testament.* Edited by Duane F. Watson. Atlanta: Society of Biblical Literature, 2002.

Robinson, John A. T. *The Body: A Study in Pauline Theology.* London: SCM, 1952.

Roetzel, Calvin J. "The Judgment Form in Paul's Letters." *Journal of Biblical Literature* 88 (1969): 305–312.

Roskam, Hendrika Nicoline. *The Purpose of the Gospel of Mark in Its Historical and Social Context.* Supplements to Novum Testamentum, 114; Leiden: Brill, 2004.

Rosner, Brian S. "'Οὐχὶ μᾶλλον ἐπενθήσατε': Corporate Responsibility in 1 Corinthians 5." *New Testament Studies* 38 (1992): 470–473.

Rosner, Brian S. *Paul, Scripture and Ethics: A Study of 1 Corinthians 5–7.* Arbeiten zur Geschichte des antiken Judentums und des Urchristentums 22. Leiden: Brill, 1994.

Rowland, Christopher, and Judith Kovacs, *Revelation: The Apocalypse of Jesus Christ.* Blackwell Bible Commentaries; Oxford: Blackwell Publishing, 2004.

Runesson, Anna. "Kontextuell exegetik i en postkolonial värld: Bibeltolkning i dagens Indien," Pages 122–149 in Anders Runesson, Torbjörn Sjöholm, and Institutet för kontextuell teologi, eds. *Varför ser ni mot himlen? Utmaningar från den kontextuella teologin.* Stockholm: Verbum; Institutet för kontextuell teologi i Sverige IKT, 2006.

Runesson, Anna. "Legion heter jag, för vi är många." Pages 475–481 in Mitternacht and Runesson, *Jesus och de första kristna.*

Runesson, Anna. *Exegesis in the Making: The Theoretical location and Contribution of Postcolonial New Testament Studies.* Unpublished licentiate thesis. Lund: Lund University, 2007.

Russell, D. S. *The Method and Message of Jewish Apocalyptic 200 BC – AD 100.* Old Testament Library. London: SCM, 1964.

Sacchi, Paulo. "The 2005 Camaldoli Seminar on the Parables of Enoch: Summary and Prospects for Future Research." Pages 499–512 in Boccaccini, *Enoch and the Messiah Son of Man.*

Said, Edward W. *Orientalism.* London: Penguin Books, [1978] 2003.

Said, Edward W. *Culture and Imperialism.* London: Chatto & Windus, 1993.

Said, Edward W., Anne Beezer, and Peter Osborne. "Efter Orientalism: Edward Said intervjuad av Anne Beezer och Peter Osborne." Pages 257–267 in Catharina Eriksson, Maria Eriksson Baaz, and Håkan Thörn, eds. *Globaliseringens kulturer: Den postko-*

loniala paradoxen, rasismen och det mångkulturella samhället. Nora: Nya Doxa, 1999.

Saldarini, Anthony J. "Delegitimation of Leaders in Matthew 23," *Catholic Biblical Quarterly* 54 (1992): 659–680.

Saldarini, Anthony J. "Pharisees." *Anchor Bible Dictionary*, vol. 5 (1992): 289–303.

Saldarini, Anthony J. *Matthew's Jewish-Christian Community.* Chicago Studies in the History of Judaism. Chicago and London: University of Chicago Press, 1994.

Samuel, Simon. "The Beginning of Mark: A Colonial/Postcolonial Conundrum", *Biblical Interpretation* 10 (2002): 405–419.

Samuel, Simon. *A Postcolonial Reading of Mark's Story of Jesus.* Library of New Testament Studies 340; London: T&T Clark, 2007.

Sanders, E. P. *Paul and Palestinian Judaism: A Comparison of Patterns of Religion.* London and Minneapolis: SCM and Fortress Press, 1977.

Sanders, E. P. *Judaism: Practice and Belief 63 BCE – 66 CE.* London: SCM, 1992.

Sanders, E. P. *The Historical Figure of Jesus.* London: Penguin, 1993.

Sandnes, Karl Olav. *Paul – One of the Prophets? A Contribution to the Apostle's Self-Understanding.* Wissenschaftliche Untersuchungen zum Neuen Testament 2. Reihe 43. Tübingen: Mohr Siebeck, 1991.

Sandnes, Karl Olav. "Whence and Whither: A Narrative Perspective on Birth *Anōthen* (John 3, 3–8)." *Biblica* 86 (2005): 153–173.

Satlow, Michael L. "Rhetoric and Assumptions: Romans and Rabbis on Sex." Pages 135–144 in *Jews in a Graeco-Roman World.* Edited by Martin Goodman. Oxford: Clarendon, 1998.

Schank, R. C. and T. R. Berman, "The Persuasive Role of Stories in Knowledge and Action." Pages 287–313 in *Narrative Impact: Social and Cognitive Foundations.* Edited by J. J. Strange *et al.* Mahwah, N.J.: Lawrence Erlbaum, 2002.

Schiffman, Lawrence H. "Purity and Perfection: Exclusion from the Council of the Community in the *Serekh Ha-'Edah.*" Pages 373–389 in *Biblical Archaeology Today: Proceedings of the International Congress on Biblical Archaeology, Jerusalem, April 1984.* Edited by J. Amitai. Jerusalem: Israel Exploration Society, 1985.

Schmithals, Walter. *Paul and the Gnostics.* Translated by J. Steely. Nashville: Abingdon, 1972.

Schmithals, Walter. "Judaisten in Galatien?" *Zeitschrift für die neutestamentliche Wissenschaft* 74 (1983): 27–58.

Schnackenburg, Rudolf. *The Gospel according to St John: Volume 2.* Translated by C. Hastings, F. McDonagh, D. Smith, and R. Foley. London: Burns & Oates, 1980.

Schneider, Johannes. *Das Evangelium nach Johannes.* Theologischer Handkommentar zum Neuen Testament. Sonderbd.; Berlin: Evangelische Verlagsanstalt, 1976.

Schottroff, Luise. *The Parables of Jesus.* Translated by L. M. Maloney. Minneapolis: Fortress Press, 2006.

Schröter, Jens. "The Son of Man as Representative of God's Kingdom: On the Interpretation of Jesus in Mark and Q." Pages 34–68 in *Jesus, Mark and Q: The Teachings of Jesus and Its Earliest Records.* Edited by M. Labahn and A. Schmidt. Journal for the Study of New Testament: Supplement Series 214. Sheffield: Academic Press, 2001.

Schüssler Fiorenza, Elisabeth. *The Book of Revelation: Justice and Judgment.* Philadelphia: Fortress Press, 1985.

Schüssler Fiorenza, Elisabeth. *In Memory of Her: A Feminist Theological Reconstruction of Christian Origins.* New York: Crossroad, 1994.

Schüssler Fiorenza, Elisabeth. *Rhetoric and Ethic: The Politics of Biblical Studies.* Minneapolis: Augsburg Fortress Press, 1999.

Schweizer, Eduard. *Der Brief an die Kolosser*. Evangelisch-katholischer Kommentar zum Neuen Testament. Zürich: Benziger, 1976.

Seaman, Kristen. "Personifications of the Iliad and Odyssey in Hellenistic and Roman art." Pages 173–189 in Stafford and Herrin, *Personification*.

Segovia, Fernando F. and Mary Ann Tolbert. *Reading from this Place. Vol 1 and 2*. Minneapolis: Fortress Press, 1995.

Segovia, Fernando F. "Mapping the Postcolonial Optic in Biblical Criticism: Meaning and Scope." Pages 23–78 in Stephen D. Moore and Fernando F. Segovia, eds. *Postcolonial Biblical Criticism: Interdisciplinary Intersections*. The Bible and postcolonialism; Edinburgh: T&T Clark, 2005.

Segovia, Fernando F. "Biblical Criticism and Postcolonial Studies: Toward a Postcolonial Optic." Pages 33–44 in Sugirtharajah, *Postcolonial Biblical Reader*.

Sharpe, J. L. *Prolegomena to the Establishment of the Critical Text of the Greek Apocalypse of Moses*. Diss. Duke University, 1969; unpublished.

Shemesh, Aharon. "Expulsion and Exclusion in the Community Rule and the Damascus Document." *Dead Sea Discoveries* 9 (2002): 44–74.

Sherif, M. *Group Conflict and Cooperation: Their Social Psychology*. London: Routledge, 1966.

Shore, B. *Culture in Mind: Cognition, Culture, and the Problem of Meaning*. New York: Oxford Univ. Press, 1996.

Sinnott, Alice M. *The Personification of Wisdom*. Society for Old Testament Studies Monograph Series; Aldershot: Ashgate, 2005.

Skinner, Marilyn B. *Sexuality in Greek and Roman Culture*. Malden, Mass.: Blackwell, 2005.

Smith, Dennis E. "Narrative Beginnings in Ancient Literature and Theory." *Semeia* 52 (1990): 1–9.

South, James T. "A Critique of the 'Curse/Death' Interpretation of 1 Corinthians 5.1–8." *New Testament Studies* 39 (1993): 539–561.

Spencer, F. Scott. *Acts*. (Readings: A New Biblical Commentary). Sheffield: Sheffield Academic Press, 1997.

Sperber, D. *Explaining Culture: A Naturalistic Approach*. Cambridge: Blackwell, 1996.

Spivak, Gayatri Chakravorty. "Subaltern Studies: Deconstructing Historiography." Pages 203–235 in Donna Landry and Gerald M. MacLean, eds. *The Spivak Reader: Selected Works of Gayatri Chakravorty Spivak*. New York: Routledge, 1985.

Spivak, Gayatri Chakravorty. "Can the Subaltern Speak?" Pages 271–313 in Cary Nelson and Lawrence Grossberg, eds. *Marxism and the Interpretation of Culture*. Communications and Culture; Houndmills: Macmillan Education, 1988.

Spivak, Gayatri Chakravorty. "Poststructuralism, Marginality, Post-coloniality and Value." Pages 219–244 in Peter Collier and Helga Geyer-Ryan, eds. *Literary Theory Today*. Cambridge: Polity, 1990.

Stafford, Emma. *Worshipping Virtues: Personification and the Divine in Ancient Greece*. London: Duckworth, 2000.

Stafford, Emma and Judith Herrin, eds. *Personification in the Greek World: From Antiquity to Byzantium*. CHS KCL Studies 7. Aldershot: Ashgate, 2005.

Standhartinger, Angela. *Das Frauenbild im Judentum der hellenistischen Zeit. Ein Beitrag anhand von 'Joseph und Aseneth'*. Arbeiten zur Geschichte des Antiken Judentums und des Urchristentums 26, Leiden: Brill, 1995.

Standhartinger, Angela. "Joseph und Aseneth. Vollkommenen Braut oder himmlische Prophetin." Pages 459–464 in *Kompendium Feministische Bibelauslegung*. 2. ed.

Edited by Luise Schottroff and Marie-Theres Wacker, Gütersloh: Chr. Kaiser /Gütersloher Verlagshaus, 1999.

Stark, R. *The Rise of Christianity: A Sociologist Reconsiders History*. Princeton, N.J.: Princeton Univ. Press, 1996.

Stegemann, Wolfgang, Bruce J. Malina, and Gerd Theissen. *The Social Setting of Jesus and the Gospels*. Minneapolis: Fortress Press, 2002.

Stenström, Hanna. *The Book of Revelation: A Vision of the Ultimate Liberation or the Ultimate Backlash? A Study of 20ᵗʰ Century Interpretations of Rev 14:1–5, with Special Emphasis on Feminist Exegesis*. Ph.D. diss. Uppsala University, 1999.

Stenström, Hanna. "New Voices in Biblical Exegesis: New Views on the Formation of the Church." Pages 72–90 in *The Formation of the Early Church*. Edited by Jostein Ådna. Tübingen: Mohr Siebeck, 2005.

Stenström, Hanna. "Feminists in Search for a Usable Future: Feminist Reception of the Book of Revelation." Forthcoming in *The Way the World Ends? The Apocalypse of John in Culture and Ideology*. Edited by William John Lyons and Jorunn Økland. The Bible in the Modern World 18. Sheffield: Sheffield Phoenix Press, 2008.

Stichele, Caroline Vander. "Just a Whore. The Annihilation of Babylon according to Revelation 17:16." *lectio.difficilior* 1 (2000). No pages. Cited 17 November 2007. Online http://www.lectio.unibe.ch.

Stichele, Caroline Vander, and Todd Penner, eds. *Her Master's Tools? Feminist and Postcolonial Engagements of Historical-Critical Discourse*. Edited by Sharon H. Ringe and Benjamin D. Sommer. Global Perspectives on Biblical Scholarship 9. Atlanta: Society of Biblical Literature, 2005.

Stowers, Stanley. *A Rereading of Romans: Justice, Jews, and Gentiles*. New Haven: Yale University Press, 1994.

Stratton, Beverly J. "Ideology." Pages 120–127 in *Handbook of Postmodern Biblical Interpretation*. Edited by Andrew Keith Malcolm Adam. St. Louis: Chalice Press, 2000.

Strauss, C. and N. Quinn. *A Cognitive Theory of Cultural Meaning*. Publications of the Society for Psychological Anthropology, 9. Cambridge: Cambridge University Press, 1997.

Strelan, Rick. *Paul, Artemis and the Jews in Ephesos*. Beihefte zur Zeitschrift für die neutestamentliche Wissenschaft und die Kunde der älteren Kirche 80. Berlin & New York: Walter de Gruyter, 1996.

Sugirtharajah, R. S. "A Postcolonial Exploration of Collusion and Construction in Biblical Interpretation." Pages 91–116 in *The Postcolonial Bible*. Edited by R. S. Sugirtharajah. Sheffield: Sheffield Academic Press, 1998.

Sugirtharajah, R. S. *Postcolonial Criticism and Biblical Interpretation*. Oxford: Oxford University Press, 2002.

Sugirtharajah, R. S. *Postcolonial Reconfigurations: An Alternative Way of Reading the Bible and Doing Theology*. St. Louis, Missouri: Chalice Press, 2003.

Sugirtharajah, R. S. *The Bible and Empire: Postcolonial Explorations*. Cambridge: Cambridge University Press, 2005.

Sugirtharajah, R. S. ed. *The Postcolonial Biblical Reader*. Oxford: Blackwell Publishing, 2006.

Sumney, Jerry L. *"Servants of Satan", "False Brothers" and Other Opponents of Paul*. Journal for the Study of the New Testament: Supplement Series188, Sheffield : Sheffield Academic, 1999.

Suter, David W. "Enoch in Sheol: Updating the Dating of the Book of Parables." Pages 415–443 in Boccaccini, *Enoch and the Messiah Son of Man*.

Svartvik, Jesper. *Bibeltolkningens bakgator: Synen på judar, slavar och homosexuella i historia och nutid.* Stockholm: Verbum, 2006.

Tajfel, Henri and John Turner. "An Integrative Theory of Intergroup Conflict." Pages 33–47 in *The Social Psychology of Intergroup Relations.* Edited by W. G. Austin and S. Worchel. Monterey, California: Brooks/Cole Publishing Company, 1979.

Tajfel, Henri. "Interindividual Behaviour and Intergroup Behaviour." Pages 27–60 in *Differentiation between Social Groups: Studies in the Social Psychology of Intergroup Relations.* Edited by H. Tajfel. European Monographs in Social Psychology 14. London: Academic Press, 1978.

Tajfel, Henri. *Differentiation between Social Groups: Studies in the Social Psychology of Intergroup Relations.* London: Academic Press, 1978.

Tajfel, Henri. *Human Groups and Social Categories: Studies in Social Psychology.* Cambridge: Cambridge University Press, 1981.

Tannehill, Robert C. *The Narrative Unity of Luke-Acts: A Literary Interpretation.* 2 vols. Vol. 2. Minneapolis: Fortress Press, 1990.

Taylor, J. R. *Linguistic Categorization.* Oxford Textbooks in Linguistics. Oxford: Oxford University Press, 2003.

Testamentum XII Patriarchum. Pseudepigrapha Veteris Testamenti Graece 1. Edited by M. de Jonge. Leiden: Brill, 1964.

Thagard, P. and C. Shelley. "Emotional Analogies and Analogical Inference." Pages 335–362 in *The Analogical Mind: Perspectives from Cognitive Science.* Edited by D. Gentner *et al.* Cambridge: MIT Press, 2001.

Theisohn, Johannes. *Der auserwählte Richter: Untersuchungen zum traditionsgeschichtlichem Ort der Menschensohngestalt der Bilderreden des äthiopischen Henoch.* Göttingen: Vandenhoeck & Ruprecht, 1975.

Theissen, Gerd. *Sociology of Early Palestinian Christianity.* Translated by J. Bowden. Philadelphia: Fortress Press, 1978.

Theissen, G. *The Social Setting of Pauline Christianity: Essays on Corinth.* Philadelphia: Fortress Press, 1982.

Theissen, Gerd. *Die Jesusbewegung: Sozialgeschichte einer Revolution der Werte.* Gütersloh: Gütersloher Verlagshaus, 2004.

Thiselton, Anthony C. *The First Epistle to the Corinthians.* New International Greek Testament Commentary. Grand Rapids: Eerdmans, 2000.

Thisted, Kirsten. "The Power to Represent: Intertextuality and Discourse in Smilla's Sense of Snow." Pages 311–342 in *Narrating the Arctic: A Cultural History of Nordic Scientific Practices.* Edited by M. Bravo and S. Sörlin. Canton: Science History Publications, 2001.

Thisted, Kirsten. "Danske Grønlandsfiktioner. Om billedet af Grønland i dansk litteratur." *Kosmorama* 232, *Film fra Nord* (2003): 32–67.

Thomson, J. E. H. "Apocalyptic Literature." Print ed.: James Orr, ed. *International Standard Bible Encyclopaedia,* 5 vols. Chicago: The Howard-Severance Company, 1915. No pages. Cited 2 May 2008. http://www.studylight.org/enc/isb/view.cgi?number=T604.

Thurén, Lauri. *The Rhetorical Strategy of 1 Peter, with Special Regard to Ambiguous Expressions.* Åbo: Åbo Academy Press, 1990.

Thurén, Lauri. "Hey Jude! – Asking for the Original Situation and Message of a Catholic Epistle," *New Testament Studies* 43 (1997): 451–465.

Thurén, Lauri. "Was Paul Angry? Derhetorizing Galatians." Pages 302–320 in *The Rhetorical Interpretation of Scripture: Essays from the 1996 Malibu Conference.*

Journal for the Study of the New Testament: Supplement Series 180. Edited by D. Stamps and S. Porter. Sheffield: Sheffield Academic, 1999.

Thurén, Lauri. *Derhetorizing Paul: A Dynamic Perspective on Pauline Theology and the Law.* Wissenschaftliche Untersuchungen zum Neuen Testament 124. Tübingen: Mohr, 2000.

Thurén, Lauri. *"EGO MALLON* – Paul's View of Himself." Pages 197–216 in *A Bouquet of Wisdom.* Edited by K.-J. Illman *et al.* Åbo Akademi University, 2000.

Thurén, Lauri. "'By Means of Hyperbole' (1 Cor 12.31b)." Pages 97–113 in *Paul and Pathos.* Edited by Th. Olbricht and J. Sumney. Society of Biblical Literature Symposium Series 16. Atlanta: SBL, 2001.

Thurén, Lauri. "Motivation as the Core of Paraenesis – Remarks on Peter and Paul as Persuaders." Pages 353–371 in *Early Christian Paraenesis in Context.* Edited by J. Starr and T. Engberg-Pedersen. Beihefte zur Zeitschrift für die neutestamentliche Wissenschaft 125. Berlin: de Gruyter, 2004.

Thurén, Lauri. "Paul Had No Antagonists." Pages 268–288 in *Lux Humana, Lux Aeterna – Essays on Biblical and Related Themes.* FS Lars Aejmelaeus. Edited by A. Mustakallio. Finnish Exegetical Society, Helsinki; Vandenhoeck & Ruprecht, Göttingen 2005.

Thyen, Hartwig. *Das Johannesevangelium.* Handbuch zum neuen Testament 6; Tübingen: Mohr Siebeck, 2005.

Tilborg, Sjef van. *The Jewish Leaders in Matthew.* Leiden: Brill, 1972.

Tiller, Patrick. "The Sociological Context of the Dream Visions of Daniel and 1 Enoch." Pages 23–26 in *Enoch and Qumran Origins: New Light on a Forgotten Connection.* Edited by G. Boccaccini. Grand Rapids: Eerdmans, 2005.

Tottie, H. W. "De kristnas förpligtelser i fråga om missionsarbetet ibland hedningarne (2 Mos. 17:8–13)." Pages 61–69 in *Missions-Tidning, under inseende af Svenska Kyrkans Missions-Styrelse,* 10/3 1885).

Towner, Philip H. *1–2 Timothy & Titus.* IVP. Edited by Grant R. Osborne. Downers Grove: InterVarsity 1994.

Trebilco, Paul. "Asia." Pages 291–363 in *The Book of Acts in Its Graeco-Roman Setting.* Edited by David W. J. Gill and Conrad Gempf. Vol. 2 of *The Book of Acts in Its First Century Setting,* ed. Bruce W. Winter; Grand Rapids: Eerdmans, 1993.

Tromp, Johannes, *The Life of Adam and Eve in Greek: A Critical Edition by Johannes Tromp.* Pseudepigrapha Veteris Testamenti Graece 6; Leiden: Brill, 2005.

Tuckett, Christopher M. "On the Stratification of Q." *Semeia* 55 (1991): 213–222.

Tuckett, Christopher M. *Christology and the New Testament: Jesus and His Earliest Followers.* Edinburgh: Edinburgh University Press, 2001.

Tuckett, Christopher M. "The Son of Man and Daniel 7: Q and Jesus." Pages 371–394 in Lindemann, *The Sayings Source Q and the Historical Jesus.*

Turner, John C., M. A. Hogg, P. J. Oakes, S. D. Reicher and M. S. Wetherell. *Rediscovering the Social Group: A Self-Categorization Theory.* Oxford: Blackwell, 1987.

Turner, John C. "Self and Collective: Cognition and Social Context." *Personality and Social Psychology Bulletin* 20 (1994): 454–463.

Turner, John. C. "Some Current Issues in Research on Social Identity and Self-Categorization Theories." Pages 6–34 in *Social Identity: Context, Commitment, Content.* Edited by N. Ellemers, R. Spears and B. Doosje. Oxford: Blackwell, 1999.

Turner, John C. and Katherine J. Reynolds. "The Social Identity Perspective in Intergroup Relations: Theories, Themes, and Controversies." Pages 133–152 in *Blackwell Handbook of Social Psychology: Intergroup Processes.* Edited by R. Brown and S. Gaertner. Oxford: Blackwell, 2001.

Turner, John C. "Explaining the Nature of Power: A Three-Process Theory." *European Journal of Social Psychology* 35 (2005): 1–22.

Turner, M. and G. Fauconnier, "Conceptual Integration and Formal Expression." *Metaphor and Symbolic Activity* 10 (1995): 183–203.

Tyson, Joseph B. "Paul's Opponents in Galatia." *Novum Testamentum* 10 (1968): 241–254.

Udoh , F. E. Review of J. A. Glancy, *Slavery in Early Christianity, Review of Biblical Literature. No pages.* Accessed 7.2. 2007. http://www.bookreviews.org/.

Vanderkam, J. C. "Righteous One, Messiah, Chosen One, and Son of Man in *1 Enoch* 37–71." Pages 169–191 in *The Messiah: Developments in Earliest Judaism and Christianity*. Edited by J. H. Charlesworth. Minneapolis: Fortress Press, 1992.

Verdoner, M. "Cultural Negotiations in the Psychomachia of Prudentius." Pages 227–243 in *Beyond Reception: Mutual Influences between Antique Religion, Judaism and Early Christianity*. Edited by D. Brakke, A. C. Jacobsen, J. Ulrich. Frankfurt a. M.: P. Lang, 2006.

Vescio, T. K. *et al.* "Percieving and Responding to Multiple Categorizable Individuals: Cognitive Processes and Affective Intergroup Bias." Pages 111–140 in *Social Identity and Social Cognition*. Edited by D. Abrams and M. A. Hogg. Oxford: Blackwell, 1999.

Vollenweider, Samuel. "Der Menschgewordene als Ebenbild Gottes. Zum frühchristlichen Verständnis der Imago Dei." Pages 53–70 in Samuel Vollenweider, *Horizonte neutestamentlicher Christologie: Studien zu Paulus und zur frühchristlichen Theologie*. Wissenschaftliche Untersuchungen zum Neuen Testament 144. Tübingen: Mohr Siebeck, 2002.

Vorster, Johannes. "The Context of the Letter to the Romans: A Critique on the Present State of Research." *Neotestamentica* 28 (1994): 127–145.

Votaw, Clyde Weber. "Review of Ezra P. Gould, A Critical and Exegetical Commentary on the Gospel according to St. Mark," *The Biblical World* 8 (1896): 66–70.

Vouga, Francois. "Der Galaterbrief: Kein Brief an die Galater? Essay über den literarischen Character des letzten grossen Paulusbriefes." Pages 243–258 in *Schrift und Tradition*. Edited by K. Backhaus and F. Untergaßmair. Wien: Schöningh, 1996.

Wachholder, Ben Zion, and Martin G. Abegg. *A Preliminary Edition of the Unpublished Dead Sea Scrolls: The Hebrew and Aramaic Texts from Cave Four.* 4 vols. Washington: Biblical Archaeology Society, 1991–96.

Waetjen, Herman C. *A Reordering of Power: A Sociopolitical Reading of Mark's Gospel.* Minneapolis: Fortress Press, 1989.

Walck, Leslie W. *The Son of Man in Matthew and the 'Similitudes of Enoch'.* Ann Arbor: UMI Dissertation Services, 1999 (not seen).

Walck, Leslie W. "The Son of Man in the Parables of Enoch and the Gospels." Pages 299–337 in Boccaccini, *Enoch and the Messiah Son of Man.*

Walters, Jonathan. "Invading the Roman Body: Manliness and Impenetrability in Roman Thought." Pages 29–43 in *Roman Sexualities*. Edited by Judith P. Hallett and Marilyn B. Skinner. Princeton: Princeton University Press, 1997.

Warner, Marina. *Monuments and Maidens: The Allegory of the Female Form.* London: Weidenfeld and Nicholson, 1985.

Wedderburn, A. J. M. "Adam in Paul's Letter to the Romans." Pages 413–430 in *Papers on Paul and Other New Testament Writers*. Edited by E. A. Livingstone; Journal for the Study of the New Testament: Supplement Series 3; Sheffield: Sheffield Academic Press, 1980.

Wegenast, Klaus. *Das Verständnis der Tradition bei Paulus und in den Deuteropaulinen.* Neukirchen: Neukirchener, 1962.

Wellhausen, Julius. *The Pharisees and the Sadducees: An Examination of Internal Jewish History.* Translated by M. E. Biddle. Mercer Library of Biblical Studies. Macon Georgia, Mercer University Press, 2001. Translation of *Die Pharisäer und die Sadducäer: Eine Untersuchung zur inneren Geschichte.* 3rd ed. Göttingen: Vandenhoeck & Ruprecht, 1967.

Werline, Rodney Alan. *Penitential Prayer in Second Temple Judaism: The Development of a Religious Institution.* Society of Biblical Literature Early Judaism and Its Literature 13. Atlanta: Scholars Press, 1998.

Whitman, Jon. *Allegory: The Dynamics of an Ancient and Medieval Technique.* Oxford: Clarendon Press, 1987

Williams, Craig A. *Roman Homosexuality: Ideologies of Masculinity in Classical Antiquity.* New York: Oxford University Press, 1999.

Winkler, John J. *The Constraints of Desire: The Anthropology of Sex and Gender in Ancient Greece.* New York: Routledge, 1990.

Winninge, Mikael. *Sinners and the Righteous: A Comparative Study of the Psalms of Solomon and Paul's Letters*, Coniectanea Biblica New Testament Series 26; Stockholm: Almqvist & Wiksell International, 1995.

Winther Jörgensen, Marianne and Louise Phillips. *Diskursanalys som teori och metod.* Lund: Studentlitteratur, 2000 [Danish original 1999].

Wolde, Ellen van. "Trendy Intertextuality?" Pages 43–49 in *Intertextuality in Biblical Writings: Essays in Honour of Bas van Iersel.* Edited by Sipke Draisma; Kampen: Kok, 1989.

Worchel, Stephen, Jonathan Iuzzini, Dawna Coutant and Manuela Ivaldi. "A Multidimensional Model of Identity: Relating Individual and Group Identities to Intergroup Behaviour." Pages 15–32 in *Social Identity Processes: Trends in Theory and Research.* Edited by D. Capozza and R. Brown. London: SAGE, 2000.

Wordelman, Amy L. "Cultural Divides and Dual Realities: A Greco-Roman Context for Acts 14." Pages 205–232 in *Contextualizing Acts: Lukan Narrative and Greco-Roman Discourse.* Edited by T. Penner and C. Vander Stichele. Atlanta, Georgia: Society of Biblical Literature, 2003.

Wright, Benjamin G. "Wisdom and Women at Qumran." *Dead Sea Discoveries* 11 (2004): 240–261.

Wright, N. Tom. *The Climax of the Covenant: Christ and the Law in Pauline Theology.* Edinburgh: T&T Clark, 1991.

Wright, Rosemary Muir. "The Great Whore in the Illustrated Apocalypse Cycles." *Journal of Medieval History* 23 (1997): 191–210.

Wyer, R. S. and T. K. Srull, *Handbook of Social Cognition.* Hillsdale, NJ: Lawrence Erlbaum, 1984.

Young, Steve. "Being a Man: The Pursuit of Manliness in *The Shepherd of Hermas.*" *Journal of Early Christian Studies* 2 (1994): 237–255.

Zanker, Paul. *The Power of Images in the Age of Augustus.* Translated by Alan Shapiro. Jerome Lectures 16. Ann Arbor: University of Michigan Press, 1988.

Zimmermann, Johannes. *Messianische Texte aus Qumran: Königliche, priesterliche und prophetische Messiasvorstellungen in den Schriftfunden von Qumran.* Wissenschaftliche Untersuchungen zum Neuen Testament 2. Reihe 104. Tübingen: Mohr Siebeck, 1998.

Zuesse, Evan M. "Ritual." Pages 405–422 in vol. 12 of *The Encyclopedia of Religion*. Edited by Mircea Eliade. 16 vols. New York: Macmillan, 1987.

Index of Ancient Sources

E. Ancient Christian Writings

Index of Modern Authors

Index of Subjects and Terms

Wissenschaftliche Untersuchungen zum Neuen Testament

Alphabetical Index of the First and Second Series

Bieringer, Reimund: see *Koester, Craig.*

Bittner, Wolfgang J.: Jesu Zeichen im Johannesevangelium. 1987. *Vol. II/26.*

Bjerkelund, Carl J.: Tauta Egeneto. 1987. *Vol. 40.*

Blackburn, Barry Lee: Theios Aner and the Markan Miracle Traditions. 1991. *Vol. II/40.*

Blanton IV, Thomas R.: Constructing a New Covenant. 2007. *Vol. II/233.*

Bock, Darrell L.: Blasphemy and Exaltation in Judaism and the Final Examination of Jesus. 1998. *Vol. II/106.*

Bockmuehl, Markus N.A.: Revelation and Mystery in Ancient Judaism and Pauline Christianity. 1990. *Vol. II/36.*

Bøe, Sverre: Gog and Magog. 2001. *Vol. II/135.*

Böhlig, Alexander: Gnosis und Synkretismus. Vol. 1 1989. *Vol. 47* – Vol. 2 1989. *Vol. 48.*

Böhm, Martina: Samarien und die Samaritai bei Lukas. 1999. *Vol. II/111.*

Böttrich, Christfried: Weltweisheit – Menschheitsethik – Urkult. 1992. *Vol. II/50.*

– */ Herzer, Jens* (Ed.): Josephus und das Neue Testament. 2007. *Vol. 209.*

Bolyki, János: Jesu Tischgemeinschaften. 1997. *Vol. II/96.*

Bosman, Philip: Conscience in Philo and Paul. 2003. *Vol. II/166.*

Bovon, François: Studies in Early Christianity. 2003. *Vol. 161.*

Brändl, Martin: Der Agon bei Paulus. 2006. *Vol. II/222.*

Breytenbach, Cilliers: see *Frey, Jörg.*

Brocke, Christoph vom: Thessaloniki – Stadt des Kassander und Gemeinde des Paulus. 2001. *Vol. II/125.*

Brunson, Andrew: Psalm 118 in the Gospel of John. 2003. *Vol. II/158.*

Büchli, Jörg: Der Poimandres – ein paganisiertes Evangelium. 1987. *Vol. II/27.*

Bühner, Jan A.: Der Gesandte und sein Weg im 4. Evangelium. 1977. *Vol. II/2.*

Burchard, Christoph: Untersuchungen zu Joseph und Aseneth. 1965. *Vol. 8.*

– Studien zur Theologie, Sprache und Umwelt des Neuen Testaments. Ed. by D. Sänger. 1998. *Vol. 107.*

Burnett, Richard: Karl Barth's Theological Exegesis. 2001. *Vol. II/145.*

Byron, John: Slavery Metaphors in Early Judaism and Pauline Christianity. 2003. *Vol. II/162.*

Byrskog, Samuel: Story as History – History as Story. 2000. *Vol. 123.*

Cancik, Hubert (Ed.): Markus-Philologie. 1984. *Vol. 33.*

Capes, David B.: Old Testament Yaweh Texts in Paul's Christology. 1992. *Vol. II/47.*

Caragounis, Chrys C.: The Development of Greek and the New Testament. 2004. *Vol. 167.*

– The Son of Man. 1986. *Vol. 38.*

– see *Fridrichsen, Anton.*

Carleton Paget, James: The Epistle of Barnabas. 1994. *Vol. II/64.*

Carson, D.A., O'Brien, Peter T. and *Mark Seifrid* (Ed.): Justification and Variegated Nomism.
Vol. 1: The Complexities of Second Temple Judaism. 2001. *Vol. II/140.*
Vol. 2: The Paradoxes of Paul. 2004. *Vol. II/181.*

Chae, Young Sam: Jesus as the Eschatological Davidic Shepherd. 2006. *Vol. II/216.*

Chester, Andrew: Messiah and Exaltation. 2007. *Vol. 207.*

Chibici-Revneanu, Nicole: Die Herrlichkeit des Verherrlichten. 2007. *Vol. II/231.*

Ciampa, Roy E.: The Presence and Function of Scripture in Galatians 1 and 2. 1998. *Vol. II/102.*

Classen, Carl Joachim: Rhetorical Criticsm of the New Testament. 2000. *Vol. 128.*

Colpe, Carsten: Iranier – Aramäer – Hebräer – Hellenen. 2003. *Vol. 154.*

Crump, David: Jesus the Intercessor. 1992. *Vol. II/49.*

Dahl, Nils Alstrup: Studies in Ephesians. 2000. *Vol. 131.*

Daise, Michael A.: Feasts in John. 2007. *Vol. II/229.*

Deines, Roland: Die Gerechtigkeit der Tora im Reich des Messias. 2004. *Vol. 177.*

– Jüdische Steingefäße und pharisäische Frömmigkeit. 1993. *Vol. II/52.*

– Die Pharisäer. 1997. *Vol. 101.*

Deines, Roland and *Karl-Wilhelm Niebuhr* (Ed.): Philo und das Neue Testament. 2004. *Vol. 172.*

Dennis, John A.: Jesus' Death and the Gathering of True Israel. 2006. *Vol. 217.*

Dettwiler, Andreas and *Jean Zumstein* (Ed.): Kreuzestheologie im Neuen Testament. 2002. *Vol. 151.*

Dickson, John P.: Mission-Commitment in Ancient Judaism and in the Pauline Communities. 2003. *Vol. II/159.*

Dietzfelbinger, Christian: Der Abschied des Kommenden. 1997. *Vol. 95.*

Dimitrov, Ivan Z., James D.G. Dunn, Ulrich Luz and *Karl-Wilhelm Niebuhr* (Ed.): Das Alte Testament als christliche Bibel in orthodoxer und westlicher Sicht. 2004. *Vol. 174.*

Dobbeler, Axel von: Glaube als Teilhabe. 1987. *Vol. II/22.*

Dryden, J. de Waal: Theology and Ethics in 1 Peter. 2006. *Vol. II/209.*

Du Toit, David S.: Theios Anthropos. 1997. *Vol. II/91.*

Dübbers, Michael: Christologie und Existenz im Kolosserbrief. 2005. *Vol. II/191.*

Dunn, James D.G.: The New Perspective on Paul. 2005. *Vol. 185.*

Dunn , James D.G. (Ed.): Jews and Christians. 1992. *Vol. 66.*

– Paul and the Mosaic Law. 1996. *Vol. 89.*

– see *Dimitrov, Ivan Z.*

–, *Hans Klein, Ulrich Luz* and *Vasile Mihoc* (Ed.): Auslegung der Bibel in orthodoxer und westlicher Perspektive. 2000. *Vol. 130.*

Ebel, Eva: Die Attraktivität früher christlicher Gemeinden. 2004. *Vol. II/178.*

Ebertz, Michael N.: Das Charisma des Gekreuzigten. 1987. *Vol. 45.*

Eckstein, Hans-Joachim: Der Begriff Syneidesis bei Paulus. 1983. *Vol. II/10.*

– Verheißung und Gesetz. 1996. *Vol. 86.*

Ego, Beate: Im Himmel wie auf Erden. 1989. *Vol. II/34.*

Ego, Beate, Armin Lange and *Peter Pilhofer* (Ed.): Gemeinde ohne Tempel – Community without Temple. 1999. *Vol. 118.*

– and *Helmut Merkel* (Ed.): Religiöses Lernen in der biblischen, frühjüdischen und frühchristlichen Überlieferung. 2005. *Vol. 180.*

Eisen, Ute E.: see *Paulsen, Henning.*

Elledge, C.D.: Life after Death in Early Judaism. 2006. *Vol. II/208.*

Ellis, E. Earle: Prophecy and Hermeneutic in Early Christianity. 1978. *Vol. 18.*

– The Old Testament in Early Christianity. 1991. *Vol. 54.*

Endo, Masanobu: Creation and Christology. 2002. *Vol. 149.*

Ennulat, Andreas: Die 'Minor Agreements'. 1994. *Vol. II/62.*

Ensor, Peter W.: Jesus and His 'Works'. 1996. *Vol. II/85.*

Eskola, Timo: Messiah and the Throne. 2001. *Vol. II/142.*

– Theodicy and Predestination in Pauline Soteriology. 1998. *Vol. II/100.*

Fatehi, Mehrdad: The Spirit's Relation to the Risen Lord in Paul. 2000. *Vol. II/128.*

Feldmeier, Reinhard: Die Krisis des Gottessohnes. 1987. *Vol. II/21.*

– Die Christen als Fremde. 1992. *Vol. 64.*

Feldmeier, Reinhard and *Ulrich Heckel* (Ed.): Die Heiden. 1994. *Vol. 70.*

Fletcher-Louis, Crispin H.T.: Luke-Acts: Angels, Christology and Soteriology. 1997. *Vol. II/94.*

Förster, Niclas: Marcus Magus. 1999. *Vol. 114.*

Forbes, Christopher Brian: Prophecy and Inspired Speech in Early Christianity and its Hellenistic Environment. 1995. *Vol. II/75.*

Fornberg, Tord: see *Fridrichsen, Anton.*

Fossum, Jarl E.: The Name of God and the Angel of the Lord. 1985. *Vol. 36.*

Foster, Paul: Community, Law and Mission in Matthew's Gospel. *Vol. II/177.*

Fotopoulos, John: Food Offered to Idols in Roman Corinth. 2003. *Vol. II/151.*

Frenschkowski, Marco: Offenbarung und Epiphanie. Vol. 1 1995. *Vol. II/79* – Vol. 2 1997. *Vol. II/80.*

Frey, Jörg: Eugen Drewermann und die biblische Exegese. 1995. *Vol. II/71.*

– Die johanneische Eschatologie. Vol. I. 1997. *Vol. 96.* – Vol. II. 1998. *Vol. 110.* – Vol. III. 2000. *Vol. 117.*

Frey, Jörg and *Cilliers Breytenbach* (Ed.): Aufgabe und Durchführung einer Theologie des Neuen Testaments. 2007. *Vol. 205.*

– and *Udo Schnelle (Ed.):* Kontexte des Johannesevangeliums. 2004. *Vol. 175.*

– and *Jens Schröter* (Ed.): Deutungen des Todes Jesu im Neuen Testament. 2005. *Vol. 181.*

–, *Jan G. van der Watt,* and *Ruben Zimmermann* (Ed.): Imagery in the Gospel of John. 2006. *Vol. 200.*

Freyne, Sean: Galilee and Gospel. 2000. *Vol. 125.*

Fridrichsen, Anton: Exegetical Writings. Edited by C.C. Caragounis and T. Fornberg. 1994. *Vol. 76.*

Gäbel, Georg: Die Kulttheologie des Hebräerbriefes. 2006. *Vol. II/212.*

Gäckle, Volker: Die Starken und die Schwachen in Korinth und in Rom. 2005. *Vol. 200.*

Garlington, Don B.: 'The Obedience of Faith'. 1991. *Vol. II/38.*

– Faith, Obedience, and Perseverance. 1994. *Vol. 79.*

Garnet, Paul: Salvation and Atonement in the Qumran Scrolls. 1977. *Vol. II/3.*

Gemünden, Petra von (Ed.): see *Weissenrieder, Annette.*

Gese, Michael: Das Vermächtnis des Apostels. 1997. *Vol. II/99.*

Gheorghita, Radu: The Role of the Septuagint in Hebrews. 2003. *Vol. II/160.*

Gordley, Matthew E.: The Colossian Hymn in Context. 2007. *Vol. II/228.*

Gräbe, Petrus J.: The Power of God in Paul's Letters. 2000. *Vol. II/123.*

Gräßer, Erich: Der Alte Bund im Neuen. 1985. *Vol. 35.*

– Forschungen zur Apostelgeschichte. 2001. *Vol. 137.*

Grappe, Christian (Ed.): Le Repas de Dieu / Das Mahl Gottes.2004. *Vol. 169.*

Green, Joel B.: The Death of Jesus. 1988. *Vol. II/33.*

Gregg, Brian Han: The Historical Jesus and the Final Judgment Sayings in Q. 2005. *Vol. II/207.*

Gregory, Andrew: The Reception of Luke and Acts in the Period before Irenaeus. 2003. *Vol. II/169.*

Grindheim, Sigurd: The Crux of Election. 2005. *Vol. II/202.*

Gundry, Robert H.: The Old is Better. 2005. *Vol. 178.*

Gundry Volf, Judith M.: Paul and Perseverance. 1990. *Vol. II/37.*

Häußer, Detlef: Christusbekenntnis und Jesusüberlieferung bei Paulus. 2006. *Vol. 210.*

Hafemann, Scott J.: Suffering and the Spirit. 1986. *Vol. II/19.*

– Paul, Moses, and the History of Israel. 1995. *Vol. 81.*

Hahn, Ferdinand: Studien zum Neuen Testament.
Vol. I: Grundsatzfragen, Jesusforschung, Evangelien. 2006. *Vol. 191.*
Vol. II: Bekenntnisbildung und Theologie in urchristlicher Zeit. 2006. *Vol. 192.*

Hahn, Johannes (Ed.): Zerstörungen des Jerusalemer Tempels. 2002. *Vol. 147.*

Hamid-Khani, Saeed: Relevation and Concealment of Christ. 2000. *Vol. II/120.*

Hannah, Darrel D.: Michael and Christ. 1999. *Vol. II/109.*

Hardin, Justin K.: Galatians and the Imperial Cult? 2007. *Vol. II /237.*

Harrison; James R.: Paul's Language of Grace in Its Graeco-Roman Context. 2003. *Vol. II/172.*

Hartman, Lars: Text-Centered New Testament Studies. Ed. von D. Hellholm. 1997. *Vol. 102.*

Hartog, Paul: Polycarp and the New Testament. 2001. *Vol. II/134.*

Heckel, Theo K.: Der Innere Mensch. 1993. *Vol. II/53.*

– Vom Evangelium des Markus zum viergestaltigen Evangelium. 1999. *Vol. 120.*

Heckel, Ulrich: Kraft in Schwachheit. 1993. *Vol. II/56.*

– Der Segen im Neuen Testament. 2002. *Vol. 150.*

– see *Feldmeier, Reinhard.*

– see *Hengel, Martin.*

Heiligenthal, Roman: Werke als Zeichen. 1983. *Vol. II/9.*

Heliso, Desta: Pistis and the Righteous One. 2007. *Vol. II/235.*

Hellholm, D.: see *Hartman, Lars.*

Hemer, Colin J.: The Book of Acts in the Setting of Hellenistic History. 1989. *Vol. 49.*

Hengel, Martin: Judentum und Hellenismus. 1969, ³1988. *Vol. 10.*

– Die johanneische Frage. 1993. *Vol. 67.*

– Judaica et Hellenistica. Kleine Schriften I. 1996. *Vol. 90.*

– Judaica, Hellenistica et Christiana. Kleine Schriften II. 1999. *Vol. 109.*

– Paulus und Jakobus. Kleine Schriften III. 2002. *Vol. 141.*

– Studien zur Christologie. Kleine Schriften IV. 2006. *Vol. 201.*

– and *Anna Maria Schwemer:* Paulus zwischen Damaskus und Antiochien. 1998. *Vol. 108.*

– Der messianische Anspruch Jesu und die Anfänge der Christologie. 2001. *Vol. 138.*

Hengel, Martin and *Ulrich Heckel* (Ed.): Paulus und das antike Judentum. 1991. *Vol. 58.*

– and *Hermut Löhr* (Ed.): Schriftauslegung im antiken Judentum und im Urchristentum. 1994. *Vol. 73.*

– and *Anna Maria Schwemer* (Ed.): Königsherrschaft Gottes und himmlischer Kult. 1991. *Vol. 55.*

– Die Septuaginta. 1994. *Vol. 72.*

–, *Siegfried Mittmann* and *Anna Maria Schwemer* (Ed.): La Cité de Dieu / Die Stadt Gottes. 2000. *Vol. 129.*

Hentschel, Anni: Diakonia im Neuen Testament. 2007. *Vol. 226.*

Hernández Jr., Juan: Scribal Habits and Theological Influence in the Apocalypse. 2006. *Vol. II/218.*

Herrenbrück, Fritz: Jesus und die Zöllner. 1990. *Vol. II/41.*

Herzer, Jens: Paulus oder Petrus? 1998. *Vol. 103.*

– see *Böttrich, Christfried.*

Hill, Charles E.: From the Lost Teaching of Polycarp. 2005. *Vol. 186.*

Hoegen-Rohls, Christina: Der nachösterliche Johannes. 1996. *Vol. II/84.*

Hoffmann, Matthias Reinhard: The Destroyer and the Lamb. 2005. *Vol. II/203.*

Hofius, Otfried: Katapausis. 1970. *Vol. 11.*

– Der Vorhang vor dem Thron Gottes. 1972. *Vol. 14.*

– Der Christushymnus Philipper 2,6–11. 1976, ²1991. *Vol. 17.*

– Paulusstudien. 1989, ²1994. *Vol. 51.*

– Neutestamentliche Studien. 2000. *Vol. 132.*

– Paulusstudien II. 2002. *Vol. 143.*

– Exegetische Studien. 2008. *Vol. 223.*

– and *Hans-Christian Kammler:* Johannesstudien. 1996. *Vol. 88.*

Holmberg, Bengt (Ed.): Exploring Early Christian Identity. 2008. *Vol. 226.*

– and *Mikael Winninge* (Ed.): Identity Formation in the New Testament. 2008. *Vol. 227.*

Holtz, Traugott: Geschichte und Theologie des Urchristentums. 1991. *Vol. 57.*

Hommel, Hildebrecht: Sebasmata.

Vol. 1 1983. *Vol. 31.*
Vol. 2 1984. *Vol. 32.*
Horbury, William: Herodian Judaism and New Testament Study. 2006. *Vol. 193.*
Horst, Pieter W. van der: Jews and Christians in Their Graeco-Roman Context. 2006. *Vol. 196.*
Hvalvik, Reidar: The Struggle for Scripture and Covenant. 1996. *Vol. II/82.*
Jauhiainen, Marko: The Use of Zechariah in Revelation. 2005. *Vol. II/199.*
Jensen, Morten H.: Herod Antipas in Galilee. 2006. *Vol. II/215.*
Johns, Loren L.: The Lamb Christology of the Apocalypse of John. 2003. *Vol. II/167.*
Jossa, Giorgio: Jews or Christians? 2006. *Vol. 202.*
Joubert, Stephan: Paul as Benefactor. 2000. *Vol. II/124.*
Judge, E. A.: The First Christians in the Roman World. 2008. *Vol. 229.*
Jungbauer, Harry: „Ehre Vater und Mutter". 2002. *Vol. II/146.*
Kähler, Christoph: Jesu Gleichnisse als Poesie und Therapie. 1995. *Vol. 78.*
Kamlah, Ehrhard: Die Form der katalogischen Paränese im Neuen Testament. 1964. *Vol. 7.*
Kammler, Hans-Christian: Christologie und Eschatologie. 2000. *Vol. 126.*
– Kreuz und Weisheit. 2003. *Vol. 159.*
– see *Hofius, Otfried.*
Karakolis, Christos: see *Alexeev, Anatoly A.*
Karrer, Martin und *Wolfgang Kraus* (Ed.): Die Septuaginta – Texte, Kontexte, Lebenswelten. 2008. *Vol. 219.*
Kelhoffer, James A.: The Diet of John the Baptist. 2005. *Vol. 176.*
– Miracle and Mission. 1999. *Vol. II/112.*
Kelley, Nicole: Knowledge and Religious Authority in the Pseudo-Clementines. 2006. *Vol. II/213.*
Kieffer, René and *Jan Bergman* (Ed.): La Main de Dieu / Die Hand Gottes. 1997. *Vol. 94.*
Kierspel, Lars: The Jews and the World in the Fourth Gospel. 2006. *Vol. 220.*
Kim, Seyoon: The Origin of Paul's Gospel. 1981, ²1984. *Vol. II/4.*
– Paul and the New Perspective. 2002. *Vol. 140.*
– "The 'Son of Man'" as the Son of God. 1983. *Vol. 30.*
Klauck, Hans-Josef: Religion und Gesellschaft im frühen Christentum. 2003. *Vol. 152.*
Klein, Hans: see *Dunn, James D.G.*
Kleinknecht, Karl Th.: Der leidende Gerechtfertigte. 1984, ²1988. *Vol. II/13.*
Klinghardt, Matthias: Gesetz und Volk Gottes. 1988. *Vol. II/32.*
Kloppenborg, John S.: The Tenants in the Vineyard. 2006. *Vol. 195.*

Koch, Michael: Drachenkampf und Sonnenfrau. 2004. *Vol. II/184.*
Koch, Stefan: Rechtliche Regelung von Konflikten im frühen Christentum. 2004. *Vol. II/174.*
Köhler, Wolf-Dietrich: Rezeption des Matthäusevangeliums in der Zeit vor Irenäus. 1987. *Vol. II/24.*
Köhn, Andreas: Der Neutestamentler Ernst Lohmeyer. 2004. *Vol. II/180.*
Koester, Craig and *Reimund Bieringer* (Ed.): The Resurrection of Jesus in the Gospel of John. 2008. *Vol. 222.*
Konradt, Matthias: Israel, Kirche und die Völker im Matthäusevangelium. 2007. *Vol. 215.*
Kooten, George H. van: Cosmic Christology in Paul and the Pauline School. 2003. *Vol. II/171.*
Korn, Manfred: Die Geschichte Jesu in veränderter Zeit. 1993. *Vol. II/51.*
Koskenniemi, Erkki: Apollonios von Tyana in der neutestamentlichen Exegese. 1994. *Vol. II/61.*
– The Old Testament Miracle-Workers in Early Judaism. 2005. *Vol. II/206.*
Kraus, Thomas J.: Sprache, Stil und historischer Ort des zweiten Petrusbriefes. 2001. *Vol. II/136.*
Kraus, Wolfgang: Das Volk Gottes. 1996. *Vol. 85.*
– see *Karrer, Martin.*
– see *Walter, Nikolaus.*
– and *Karl-Wilhelm Niebuhr* (Ed.): Frühjudentum und Neues Testament im Horizont Biblischer Theologie. 2003. *Vol. 162.*
Kreplin, Matthias: Das Selbstverständnis Jesu. 2001. *Vol. II/141.*
Kuhn, Karl G.: Achtzehngebet und Vaterunser und der Reim. 1950. *Vol. 1.*
Kvalbein, Hans: see *Ådna, Jostein.*
Kwon, Yon-Gyong: Eschatology in Galatians. 2004. *Vol. II/183.*
Laansma, Jon: I Will Give You Rest. 1997. *Vol. II/98.*
Labahn, Michael: Offenbarung in Zeichen und Wort. 2000. *Vol. II/117.*
Lambers-Petry, Doris: see *Tomson, Peter J.*
Lange, Armin: see *Ego, Beate.*
Lampe, Peter: Die stadtrömischen Christen in den ersten beiden Jahrhunderten. 1987, ²1989. *Vol. II/18.*
Landmesser, Christof: Wahrheit als Grundbegriff neutestamentlicher Wissenschaft. 1999. *Vol. 113.*
– Jüngerberufung und Zuwendung zu Gott. 2000. *Vol. 133.*
Lau, Andrew: Manifest in Flesh. 1996. *Vol. II/86.*
Lawrence, Louise: An Ethnography of the Gospel of Matthew. 2003. *Vol. II/165.*

Lee, Aquila H.I.: From Messiah to Preexistent Son. 2005. *Vol. II/192.*

Lee, Pilchan: The New Jerusalem in the Book of Relevation. 2000. *Vol. II/129.*

Lichtenberger, Hermann: Das Ich Adams und das Ich der Menschheit. 2004. *Vol. 164.*

– see *Avemarie, Friedrich.*

Lierman, John: The New Testament Moses. 2004. *Vol. II/173.*

– (Ed.): Challenging Perspectives on the Gospel of John. 2006. *Vol. II/219.*

Lieu, Samuel N.C.: Manichaeism in the Later Roman Empire and Medieval China. ²1992. *Vol. 63.*

Lindgård, Fredrik: Paul's Line of Thought in 2 Corinthians 4:16–5:10. 2004. *Vol. II/189.*

Loader, William R.G.: Jesus' Attitude Towards the Law. 1997. *Vol. II/97.*

Löhr, Gebhard: Verherrlichung Gottes durch Philosophie. 1997. *Vol. 97.*

Löhr, Hermut: Studien zum frühchristlichen und frühjüdischen Gebet. 2003. *Vol. 160.*

– see *Hengel, Martin.*

Löhr, Winrich Alfried: Basilides und seine Schule. 1995. *Vol. 83.*

Luomanen, Petri: Entering the Kingdom of Heaven. 1998. *Vol. II/101.*

Luz, Ulrich: see *Alexeev, Anatoly A.*

–: see *Dunn, James D.G.*

Mackay, Ian D.: John's Raltionship with Mark. 2004. *Vol. II/182.*

Mackie, Scott D.: Eschatology and Exhortation in the Epistle to the Hebrews. 2006. *Vol. II/223.*

Maier, Gerhard: Mensch und freier Wille. 1971. *Vol. 12.*

– Die Johannesoffenbarung und die Kirche. 1981. *Vol. 25.*

Markschies, Christoph: Valentinus Gnosticus? 1992. *Vol. 65.*

Marshall, Peter: Enmity in Corinth: Social Conventions in Paul's Relations with the Corinthians. 1987. *Vol. II/23.*

Martin, Dale B.: see *Zangenberg, Jürgen.*

Mayer, Annemarie: Sprache der Einheit im Epheserbrief und in der Ökumene. 2002. *Vol. II/150.*

Mayordomo, Moisés: Argumentiert Paulus logisch? 2005. *Vol. 188.*

McDonough, Sean M.: YHWH at Patmos: Rev. 1:4 in its Hellenistic and Early Jewish Setting. 1999. *Vol. II/107.*

McDowell, Markus: Prayers of Jewish Women. 2006. *Vol. II/211.*

McGlynn, Moyna: Divine Judgement and Divine Benevolence in the Book of Wisdom. 2001. *Vol. II/139.*

Meade, David G.: Pseudonymity and Canon. 1986. *Vol. 39.*

Meadors, Edward P.: Jesus the Messianic Herald of Salvation. 1995. *Vol. II/72.*

Meißner, Stefan: Die Heimholung des Ketzers. 1996. *Vol. II/87.*

Mell, Ulrich: Die „anderen" Winzer. 1994. *Vol. 77.*

– see *Sänger, Dieter.*

Mengel, Berthold: Studien zum Philipperbrief. 1982. *Vol. II/8.*

Merkel, Helmut: Die Widersprüche zwischen den Evangelien. 1971. *Vol. 13.*

– see *Ego, Beate.*

Merklein, Helmut: Studien zu Jesus und Paulus. Vol. 1 1987. *Vol. 43.* – Vol. 2 1998. *Vol. 105.*

Metzdorf, Christina: Die Tempelaktion Jesu. 2003. *Vol. II/168.*

Metzler, Karin: Der griechische Begriff des Verzeihens. 1991. *Vol. II/44.*

Metzner, Rainer: Die Rezeption des Matthäusevangeliums im 1. Petrusbrief. 1995. *Vol. II/74.*

– Das Verständnis der Sünde im Johannesevangelium. 2000. *Vol. 122.*

Mihoc, Vasile: see *Dunn, James D.G..*

Mineshige, Kiyoshi: Besitzverzicht und Almosen bei Lukas. 2003. *Vol. II/163.*

Mittmann, Siegfried: see *Hengel, Martin.*

Mittmann-Richert, Ulrike: Magnifikat und Benediktus. 1996. *Vol. II/90.*

Miura, Yuzuru: David in Luke-Acts. 2007. *Vol. II/232.*

Mournet, Terence C.: Oral Tradition and Literary Dependency. 2005. *Vol. II/195.*

Mußner, Franz: Jesus von Nazareth im Umfeld Israels und der Urkirche. Ed. von M. Theobald. 1998. *Vol. 111.*

Mutschler, Bernhard: Das Corpus Johanneum bei Irenäus von Lyon. 2005. *Vol. 189.*

Nguyen, V. Henry T.: Christian Identity in Corinth. 2008. *Vol. II/243.*

Niebuhr, Karl-Wilhelm: Gesetz und Paränese. 1987. *Vol. II/28.*

– Heidenapostel aus Israel. 1992. *Vol. 62.*

– see *Deines, Roland*

– see *Dimitrov, Ivan Z.*

– see *Kraus, Wolfgang*

Nielsen, Anders E.: "Until it is Fullfilled". 2000. *Vol. II/126.*

Nissen, Andreas: Gott und der Nächste im antiken Judentum. 1974. *Vol. 15.*

Noack, Christian: Gottesbewußtsein. 2000. *Vol. II/116.*

Noormann, Rolf: Irenäus als Paulusinterpret. 1994. *Vol. II/66.*

Novakovic, Lidija: Messiah, the Healer of the Sick. 2003. *Vol. II/170.*

Obermann, Andreas: Die christologische Erfüllung der Schrift im Johannesevangelium. 1996. *Vol. II/83.*

Öhler, Markus: Barnabas. 2003. *Vol. 156.*

– see *Becker, Michael.*
Okure, Teresa: The Johannine Approach to Mission. 1988. *Vol. II/31.*
Onuki, Takashi: Heil und Erlösung. 2004. *Vol. 165.*
Oropeza, B. J.: Paul and Apostasy. 2000. *Vol. II/115.*
Ostmeyer, Karl-Heinrich: Kommunikation mit Gott und Christus. 2006. *Vol. 197.*
– Taufe und Typos. 2000. *Vol. II/118.*
Paulsen, Henning. Studien zur Literatur und Geschichte des frühen Christentums. Ed. von Ute E. Eisen. 1997. *Vol. 99.*
Pao, David W.: Acts and the Isaianic New Exodus. 2000. *Vol. II/130.*
Park, Eung Chun: The Mission Discourse in Matthew's Interpretation. 1995. *Vol. II/81.*
Park, Joseph S.: Conceptions of Afterlife in Jewish Insriptions. 2000. *Vol. II/121.*
Pate, C. Marvin: The Reverse of the Curse. 2000. *Vol. II/114.*
Pearce, Sarah J.K.: The Land of the Body. 2007. *Vol. 208.*
Peres, Imre: Griechische Grabinschriften und neutestamentliche Eschatologie. 2003. *Vol. 157.*
Philip, Finny: The Origins of Pauline Pneumatology. 2005. *Vol. II/194.*
Philonenko, Marc (Ed.): Le Trône de Dieu. 1993. *Vol. 69.*
Pilhofer, Peter: Presbyteron Kreitton. 1990. *Vol. II/39.*
– Philippi. Vol. 1 1995. *Vol. 87.* – Vol. 2 2000. *Vol. 119.*
– Die frühen Christen und ihre Welt. 2002. *Vol. 145.*
– see *Becker, Eve-Marie.*
– see *Ego, Beate.*
Pitre, Brant: Jesus, the Tribulation, and the End of the Exile. 2005. *Vol. II/204.*
Plümacher, Eckhard: Geschichte und Geschichten. 2004. *Vol. 170.*
Pöhlmann, Wolfgang: Der Verlorene Sohn und das Haus. 1993. *Vol. 68.*
Pokorný, Petr and *Josef B. Souček:* Bibelauslegung als Theologie. 1997. *Vol. 100.*
– and *Jan Roskovec* (Ed.): Philosophical Hermeneutics and Biblical Exegesis. 2002. *Vol. 153.*
Popkes, Enno Edzard: Das Menschenbild des Thomasevangeliums. 2007. *Vol. 206.*
– Die Theologie der Liebe Gottes in den johanneischen Schriften. 2005. *Vol. II/197.*
Porter, Stanley E.: The Paul of Acts. 1999. *Vol. 115.*
Prieur, Alexander: Die Verkündigung der Gottesherrschaft. 1996. *Vol. II/89.*
Probst, Hermann: Paulus und der Brief. 1991. *Vol. II/45.*

Räisänen, Heikki: Paul and the Law. 1983, ²1987. *Vol. 29.*
Rehkopf, Friedrich: Die lukanische Sonderquelle. 1959. *Vol. 5.*
Rein, Matthias: Die Heilung des Blindgeborenen (Joh 9). 1995. *Vol. II/73.*
Reinmuth, Eckart: Pseudo-Philo und Lukas. 1994. *Vol. 74.*
Reiser, Marius: Bibelkritik und Auslegung der Heiligen Schrift. 2007. *Vol. 217.*
Syntax und Stil des Markusevangeliums. 1984. *Vol. II/11.*
Rhodes, James N.: The Epistle of Barnabas and the Deuteronomic Tradition. 2004. *Vol. II/188.*
Richards, E. Randolph: The Secretary in the Letters of Paul. 1991. *Vol. II/42.*
Riesner, Rainer: Jesus als Lehrer. 1981, ³1988. *Vol. II/7.*
– Die Frühzeit des Apostels Paulus. 1994. *Vol. 71.*
Rissi, Mathias: Die Theologie des Hebräerbriefs. 1987. *Vol. 41.*
Roskovec, Jan: see *Pokorný, Petr.*
Röhser, Günter: Metaphorik und Personifikation der Sünde. 1987. *Vol. II/25.*
Rose, Christian: Theologie als Erzählung im Markusevangelium. 2007. *Vol. II/236.*
– Die Wolke der Zeugen. 1994. *Vol. II/60.*
Rothschild, Clare K.: Baptist Traditions and Q. 2005. *Vol. 190.*
– Luke Acts and the Rhetoric of History. 2004. *Vol. II/175.*
Rüegger, Hans-Ulrich: Verstehen, was Markus erzählt. 2002. *Vol. II/155.*
Rüger, Hans Peter: Die Weisheitsschrift aus der Kairoer Geniza. 1991. *Vol. 53.*
Sänger, Dieter: Antikes Judentum und die Mysterien. 1980. *Vol. II/5.*
– Die Verkündigung des Gekreuzigten und Israel. 1994. *Vol. 75.*
– see *Burchard, Christoph*
– and *Ulrich Mell* (Hrsg.): Paulus und Johannes. 2006. *Vol. 198.*
Salier, Willis Hedley: The Rhetorical Impact of the Semeia in the Gospel of John. 2004. *Vol. II/186.*
Salzmann, Jorg Christian: Lehren und Ermahnen. 1994. *Vol. II/59.*
Sandnes, Karl Olav: Paul – One of the Prophets? 1991. *Vol. II/43.*
Sato, Migaku: Q und Prophetie. 1988. *Vol. II/29.*
Schäfer, Ruth: Paulus bis zum Apostelkonzil. 2004. *Vol. II/179.*
Schaper, Joachim: Eschatology in the Greek Psalter. 1995. *Vol. II/76.*
Schimanowski, Gottfried: Die himmlische Liturgie in der Apokalypse des Johannes. 2002. *Vol. II/154.*
– Weisheit und Messias. 1985. *Vol. II/17.*

Schlichting, Günter: Ein jüdisches Leben Jesu. 1982. *Vol. 24.*

Schließer, Benjamin: Abraham's Faith in Romans 4. 2007. *Vol. II/224.*

Schnabel, Eckhard J.: Law and Wisdom from Ben Sira to Paul. 1985. *Vol. II/16.*

Schnelle, Udo: see *Frey, Jörg.*

Schröter, Jens: Von Jesus zum Neuen Testament. 2007. *Vol. 204.*

– see *Frey, Jörg.*

Schutter, William L.: Hermeneutic and Composition in I Peter. 1989. *Vol. II/30.*

Schwartz, Daniel R.: Studies in the Jewish Background of Christianity. 1992. *Vol. 60.*

Schwemer, Anna Maria: see *Hengel, Martin*

Scott, Ian W.: Implicit Epistemology in the Letters of Paul. 2005. *Vol. II/205.*

Scott, James M.: Adoption as Sons of God. 1992. *Vol. II/48.*

– Paul and the Nations. 1995. *Vol. 84.*

Shum, Shiu-Lun: Paul's Use of Isaiah in Romans. 2002. *Vol. II/156.*

Siegert, Folker: Drei hellenistisch-jüdische Predigten. Teil I 1980. *Vol. 20* – Teil II 1992. *Vol. 61.*

– Nag-Hammadi-Register. 1982. *Vol. 26.*

– Argumentation bei Paulus. 1985. *Vol. 34.*

– Philon von Alexandrien. 1988. *Vol. 46.*

Simon, Marcel: Le christianisme antique et son contexte religieux I/II. 1981. *Vol. 23.*

Smit, Peter-Ben: Fellowship and Food in the Kingdom. 2008. *Vol. II/234.*

Snodgrass, Klyne: The Parable of the Wicked Tenants. 1983. *Vol. 27.*

Söding, Thomas: Das Wort vom Kreuz. 1997. *Vol. 93.*

– see *Thüsing, Wilhelm.*

Sommer, Urs: Die Passionsgeschichte des Markusevangeliums. 1993. *Vol. II/58.*

Sorensen, Eric: Possession and Exorcism in the New Testament and Early Christianity. 2002. *Vol. II/157.*

Souček, Josef B.: see *Pokorný, Petr.*

Southall, David J.: Rediscovering Righteousness in Romans. 2008. *Vol. 240.*

Spangenberg, Volker: Herrlichkeit des Neuen Bundes. 1993. *Vol. II/55.*

Spanje, T.E. van: Inconsistency in Paul? 1999. *Vol. II/110.*

Speyer, Wolfgang: Frühes Christentum im antiken Strahlungsfeld. Vol. I: 1989. *Vol. 50.*

– Vol. II: 1999. *Vol. 116.*

– Vol. III: 2007. *Vol. 213.*

Sprinkle, Preston: Law and Life. 2008. *Vol. II/241.*

Stadelmann, Helge: Ben Sira als Schriftgelehrter. 1980. *Vol. II/6.*

Stenschke, Christoph W.: Luke's Portrait of Gentiles Prior to Their Coming to Faith. *Vol. II/108.*

Sterck-Degueldre, Jean-Pierre: Eine Frau namens Lydia. 2004. *Vol. II/176.*

Stettler, Christian: Der Kolosserhymnus. 2000. *Vol. II/131.*

Stettler, Hanna: Die Christologie der Pastoralbriefe. 1998. *Vol. II/105.*

Stökl Ben Ezra, Daniel: The Impact of Yom Kippur on Early Christianity. 2003. *Vol. 163.*

Strobel, August: Die Stunde der Wahrheit. 1980. *Vol. 21.*

Stroumsa, Guy G.: Barbarian Philosophy. 1999. *Vol. 112.*

Stuckenbruck, Loren T.: Angel Veneration and Christology. 1995. *Vol. II/70.*

– , *Stephen C. Barton* and *Benjamin G. Wold* (Ed.): Memory in the Bible and Antiquity. 2007. *Vol. 212.*

Stuhlmacher, Peter (Ed.): Das Evangelium und die Evangelien. 1983. *Vol. 28.*

– Biblische Theologie und Evangelium. 2002. *Vol. 146.*

Sung, Chong-Hyon: Vergebung der Sünden. 1993. *Vol. II/57.*

Tajra, Harry W.: The Trial of St. Paul. 1989. *Vol. II/35.*

– The Martyrdom of St.Paul. 1994. *Vol. II/67.*

Theißen, Gerd: Studien zur Soziologie des Urchristentums. 1979, ³1989. *Vol. 19.*

Theobald, Michael: Studien zum Römerbrief. 2001. *Vol. 136.*

Theobald, Michael: see *Mußner, Franz.*

Thornton, Claus-Jürgen: Der Zeuge des Zeugen. 1991. *Vol. 56.*

Thüsing, Wilhelm: Studien zur neutestamentlichen Theologie. Ed. von Thomas Söding. 1995. *Vol. 82.*

Thurén, Lauri: Derhethorizing Paul. 2000. *Vol. 124.*

Thyen, Hartwig: Studien zum Corpus Iohanneum. 2007. *Vol. 214.*

Tibbs, Clint: Religious Experience of the Pneuma. 2007. *Vol. II/230.*

Tolmie, D. Francois: Persuading the Galatians. 2005. *Vol. II/190.*

Tomson, Peter J. and *Doris Lambers-Petry* (Ed.): The Image of the Judaeo-Christians in Ancient Jewish and Christian Literature. 2003. *Vol. 158.*

Trebilco, Paul: The Early Christians in Ephesus from Paul to Ignatius. 2004. *Vol. 166.*

Treloar, Geoffrey R.: Lightfoot the Historian. 1998. *Vol. II/103.*

Tsuji, Manabu: Glaube zwischen Vollkommenheit und Verweltlichung. 1997. *Vol. II/93.*

Twelftree, Graham H.: Jesus the Exorcist. 1993. *Vol. II/54.*

Ulrichs, Karl Friedrich: Christusglaube. 2007. *Vol. II/227.*

Urban, Christina: Das Menschenbild nach dem Johannesevangelium. 2001. *Vol. II/137.*

Vahrenhorst, Martin: Kultische Sprache in den Paulusbriefen. 2008. *Vol. 230.*

Vegge, Ivar: 2 Corinthians – a Letter about Reconciliation. 2008. *Vol. II/239.*

Visotzky, Burton L.: Fathers of the World. 1995. *Vol. 80.*

Vollenweider, Samuel: Horizonte neutestamentlicher Christologie. 2002. *Vol. 144.*

Vos, Johan S.: Die Kunst der Argumentation bei Paulus. 2002. *Vol. 149.*

Wagener, Ulrike: Die Ordnung des „Hauses Gottes". 1994. *Vol. II/65.*

Wahlen, Clinton: Jesus and the Impurity of Spirits in the Synoptic Gospels. 2004. *Vol. II/185.*

Walker, Donald D.: Paul's Offer of Leniency (2 Cor 10:1). 2002. *Vol. II/152.*

Walter, Nikolaus: Praeparatio Evangelica. Ed. von Wolfgang Kraus und Florian Wilk. 1997. *Vol. 98.*

Wander, Bernd: Gottesfürchtige und Sympathisanten. 1998. *Vol. 104.*

Waters, Guy: The End of Deuteronomy in the Epistles of Paul. 2006. *Vol. 221.*

Watt, Jan G. van der: see *Frey, Jörg*

Watts, Rikki: Isaiah's New Exodus and Mark. 1997. *Vol. II/88.*

Wedderburn, A.J.M.: Baptism and Resurrection. 1987. *Vol. 44.*

Wegner, Uwe: Der Hauptmann von Kafarnaum. 1985. *Vol. II/14.*

Weissenrieder, Annette: Images of Illness in the Gospel of Luke. 2003. *Vol. II/164.*

–, *Friederike Wendt* and *Petra von Gemünden* (Ed.): Picturing the New Testament. 2005. *Vol. II/193.*

Welck, Christian: Erzählte ‚Zeichen'. 1994. *Vol. II/69.*

Wendt, Friederike (Ed.): see *Weissenrieder, Annette.*

Wiarda, Timothy: Peter in the Gospels. 2000. *Vol. II/127.*

Wifstrand, Albert: Epochs and Styles. 2005. *Vol. 179.*

Wilk, Florian: see *Walter, Nikolaus.*

Williams, Catrin H.: I am He. 2000. *Vol. II/113.*

Wilson, Todd A.: The Curse of the Law and the Crisis in Galatia. 2007. *Vol. II/225.*

Wilson, Walter T.: Love without Pretense. 1991. *Vol. II/46.*

Winninge, Mikael: see *Holmberg, Bengt.*

Wischmeyer, Oda: Von Ben Sira zu Paulus. 2004. *Vol. 173.*

Wisdom, Jeffrey: Blessing for the Nations and the Curse of the Law. 2001. *Vol. II/133.*

Wold, Benjamin G.: Women, Men, and Angels. 2005. *Vol. II/2001.*

– see *Stuckenbruck, Loren T.*

Wright, Archie T.: The Origin of Evil Spirits. 2005. *Vol. II/198.*

Wucherpfennig, Ansgar: Heracleon Philologus. 2002. *Vol. 142.*

Yeung, Maureen: Faith in Jesus and Paul. 2002. *Vol. II/147.*

Zangenberg, Jürgen, Harold W. Attridge and *Dale B. Martin* (Ed.): Religion, Ethnicity and Identity in Ancient Galilee. 2007. *Vol. 210.*

Zimmermann, Alfred E.: Die urchristlichen Lehrer. 1984, ²1988. *Vol. II/12.*

Zimmermann, Johannes: Messianische Texte aus Qumran. 1998. *Vol. II/104.*

Zimmermann, Ruben: Christologie der Bilder im Johannesevangelium. 2004. *Vol. 171.*

– Geschlechtermetaphorik und Gottesverhältnis. 2001. *Vol. II/122.*

– see *Frey, Jörg*

Zumstein, Jean: see *Dettwiler, Andreas*

Zwiep, Arie W.: Judas and the Choice of Matthias. 2004. *Vol. II/187.*

For a complete catalogue please write to the publisher
Mohr Siebeck • P.O. Box 2030 • D–72010 Tübingen/Germany
Up-to-date information on the internet at www.mohr.de